T0268019

Corporate Coup looks at the attempted overthrow of the elected government of Venezuela, an intervention which, despite open backing by the United States, failed spectacularly.

In January of 2019, the Trump Administration recognized a little-known opposition lawmaker named Juan Guaidó as President of Venezuela. While Washington's history of coups in Latin America is well documented, this step was unprecedented: Never before had the United States offered legal recognition to a new government before an actual change in leadership had taken place.

Within months it became clear that the attempt at regime change had fallen flat: all Venezuelan territory, government ministries, and the country's military remained under the control of President Nicolás Maduro. While US officials, notably Trump's Venezuela Envoy Elliott Abrams, boasted that roughly fifty-four countries had followed Washington's lead in recognizing Guaidó's authority, the vast majority of United Nations member states rejected the attempted coup. Four years on, Venezuela's government is firmly in place and Guaidó is nowhere to be seen.

In this fast-paced story, investigative reporter Anya Parampil provides a narrative history of the Chavista revolution and offers character sketches of the figures who took over its leadership after Hugo Chávez's death in 2014. She shows how Guaidó's shadow regime consisted of individuals with deep connections to transnational corporations that sought to overturn the revolution and exploit Venezuela's resources. In particular, she uncovers their plot to steal Citgo Petroleum, the country's most valuable international asset. *Corporate Coup* exposes the hidden personalities and interests driving US policy on Venezuela, revealing that while the recognition of Guaidó failed at changing reality on the ground in Caracas, it succeeded in facilitating the unprecedented looting of the country's extensive foreign reserves.

This gripping story from Venezuela shines light on the grim, shadowy character of a US foreign policy that tramples on democratic norms around the globe. And it points to a dramatic consequence of such policy: the rise of a new, multipolar world heralding the end of US empire.

CORPORATE COUP

VENEZUELA AND THE END OF US EMPIRE

ANYA PARAMPIL

With a Foreword by Former Venezuelan
Foreign Minister Jorge Arreaza

OR Books
New York · London

© 2024 Anya Parampil

Published by OR Books, New York and London
Visit our website at www.orbooks.com

All rights information: rights@orbooks.com

All rights reserved. No part of this book may be reproduced or transmitted
in any form or by any means, electronic or mechanical, including photocopy,
recording, or any information storage retrieval system, without permission in
writing from the publisher, except brief passages for review purposes.

First printing 2024

Library of Congress Cataloging-in-Publication Data: A catalog record for this
book is available from the Library of Congress.
British Library Cataloging in Publication Data: A catalog record for this book is
available from the British Library.

Typeset by Lapiz Digital. Printed by BookMobile, USA, and CPI, UK.

paperback ISBN 978-1-68219-359-4 • ebook ISBN 978-1-68219-616-8

For Max and T, you make my dreams come true.

"If wars can be started by lies, peace can be started by truth."
— Julian Assange
(Free Julian Assange)

CONTENTS

FOREWORD

JORGE ARREAZA
Venezuelan Foreign Minister (2017–2021)

Nearly four decades before the Monroe Doctrine that defined Latin America and the Caribbean as Washington's "backyard" came into effect, US president Thomas Jefferson expressed concern that Spain would soon lose its South American colonies.

"My fear," wrote Jefferson, "is that they are too feeble to hold them till our population can be sufficiently advanced to gain it from them piece by piece."

This quote foreshadowed two subsequent centuries of attempted US domination of Venezuela, a period when Washington deployed all possible methods to maintain its control. The Bolivarian Revolution initiated by President Hugo Chávez in 1998—and continued under President Nicolás Maduro—represented a deliberate political action to reassert Venezuela's self-determination, overcome neo-colonialist dependency, and construct a profoundly democratic and participatory system of government. This model challenged Jefferson's vision, passed onto Monroe and successive US governments, that only understands Latin America and the Caribbean as the US's back—or now, front—yard.

The antagonism between two possible projects on the American continent emerged early on in its post-colonial history. One born out of the dominant elite in Washington, with its exceptionalism and manifest destiny to arbitrarily dominate our peoples; another represented by Simón Bolívar's effort to free the region's nations by consolidating their right to self-determination and political independence. The most recent aggression against Venezuela is but the latest chapter in this historic tension between the domination of the North and the liberty of the South on this immense continent.

Washington attacked my country's revolution from the very beginning, culminating with a brief military coup d'état in 2002. Since then, our people have overcome Washington's effort to sabotage our industries and economy, as well as open campaigns to finance violent opposition groups and so-called "non-governmental organizations" tasked with destabilizing our country and forcing regime change.

I was named foreign minister just days before US president Donald Trump issued a threat to militarily attack Venezuela in 2017, and a few weeks after his administration unveiled its first round of so-called "sanctions" against our economy, oil industry, and in consequence, our people. What I experienced while serving as Venezuela's foreign minister was a true war, carried out with hybrid attacks designed to pressure Venezuela politically, financially, militarily, diplomatically, and otherwise into accepting the "Washington Consensus."

This war, however, became clouded by a policy that claimed a little-known Venezuelan lawmaker, with the backing of the Trump administration, had the authority to appoint himself president of Venezuela. This decision represented a new style of coup d'état where Washington was not simply behind the action, but in front of it—and using all possible means to achieve it. It was Trump's National Security Advisor John Bolton himself who confessed that US oil companies were ready to come into Venezuela once Maduro left power, an open confession of the corporate interests that drove the White House's misguided strategy.

As part of its regime-change campaign, Washington organized coalitions of subordinate countries, such as the Lima Group, established for the sole purpose of isolating and attacking our government. Washington's obsession with Venezuela has taken hold of the elites in some of our neighboring countries, producing an outrageous circus of US subjects in the region. These subservient governments have granted renewed legitimacy to Monroeism despite their people's desire for independence and self-determination. This development is a complete shame and, ultimately, is destined for failure.

Through its subjugation of regional governments, the US turned the Organization of American States (OAS) into a main tool of its diplomatic aggression against Venezuela. Following the initiation of Washington's coup, the OAS took the extreme act of invoking the Rio Treaty, an outdated military agreement, to justify future aggression against my country. Such absurd posturing, combined with its decision to accept a representative of a coup government in contravention of its own charter, has rendered the OAS useless within the modern international system.

Washington's Venezuela coup policy has not only damaged the credibility of groups like the OAS. To legitimize its regime-change attempt, the US government has reduced itself to the absurd act of issuing official statements describing the government of President Maduro—the only effective government that has existed in Caracas since 2013—as Venezuela's "former government." When I was personally "sanctioned" in April 2019 while on an official visit to New York City, the Treasury Department described me as the "former" foreign minister of the Maduro regime—although the United Nations secretary general had just received me as the top diplomat representing Venezuela's government.

The sanctions issued against me were part of a new toolkit the US formed to overthrow a government that opted to write its own history rather than follow Washington's script. Never in two hundred years did tensions between our two countries rise as high as they did during the month of January 2019, when the US recognition of Guaidó led us to break all diplomatic ties with Washington. In the immediate aftermath, I participated in several meetings with US officials in New York during which Elliott Abrams, a veteran of the Iran-Contra fiasco who is also tied to the El Mozote massacre in El Salvador, spoke on behalf of the Trump administration. With a surreal Cold War mentality, he first approached my team to ask that we turn against our government and facilitate President Maduro's exit. A month later, when his miscalculations were more apparent and the US was attempting a forced incursion into my country's territory under the cover of a humanitarian aid shipment, Abrams took a more aggressive attitude. During a meeting in February, Abrams warned us that life in Venezuela would become unbearable, predicting that our electricity, fuel, and food would soon run out.

His premonition came true. In ensuing months, Venezuelans endured every possible obstacle, including gasoline shortages and power outages induced by US pressure. Years later, we found that despite having enough money in our foreign bank accounts to cover the cost of vaccinating our entire population, our access to these funds was illegally blocked because the US and the UK governments still recognized Guaidó's authority. This dilemma nearly made it impossible for our government to appropriately respond to the outbreak of Covid-19. Were it not for the early preventive measures taken by President Maduro and the solidarity of countries like Cuba, China, Russia, Turkey, or Iran, we may have faced a crisis on par with the dismal tragedies that our neighbors in Brazil and Colombia experienced.

The policy of aggression against Venezuela was so erratic and barbaric that Washington eventually went to the extreme length of dispatching mercenaries from a private security firm to kidnap President Maduro, an episode as dangerous as it was absurd. Taken together, the attacks against our government amount to what many would describe as "the perfect storm." Yet Washington's policy of maximum pressure was—and still is—destined for failure because it lacked one key element: it never truly considered what the people of Venezuela wanted. The Abrams, Boltons, and Pompeos of the world could never grasp that, beyond a small group of their extremist collaborators, Venezuelans across all ideological lines deeply reject threats of violence and interference in our sovereign affairs. Hailing from a country with a deep history of inequality and injustice, we Venezuelans will not be coerced into changing the social policy that has defined our country for the last twenty years—regardless of whatever ups, downs, and limitations come with it.

Throughout Washington's naked coup attempt, our government's diplomatic strategy was key to protecting our sovereignty. President Maduro now, like Chávez before him, is committed to the "Bolivarian Diplomacy of Peace," a doctrine which respects international law while promoting the consolidation of a multipolar and diverse world. Thanks to it, we managed to cross deserts and weather all storms that Western governments imposed upon us. Though a handful of foreign governments yielded to US pressure and accepted Guaidó's authority, over two-thirds of the world's nations have respected the will of the Venezuelan people and continue to recognize Maduro as the country's legitimate leader. These friends stood by our side at the United Nations and were particularly instrumental in blocking a US plot to remove our government's representative from the body. It turns out that diplomacy based on solidarity, mutual respect, and a defense of the principles enshrined in the UN charter is the best guarantee of peace and respect for one's own independence. Today, as my country strengthens its relationship with nations worldwide regardless of ideological boundaries, Washington and its friends remain in an increasingly isolated labyrinth.

Today, the US is stuck with its futile Venezuela coup project, a policy that it reluctantly embraces to please the whims of southern Florida. Yet as a multipolar world emerges in response to this moment of crisis, only governments that are willing to listen to their people and confront this decaying international order will survive. Just as we told Elliott Abrams during the UN Security Council session convened on February 26, 2019: Your coup d'état failed. Your brutal strategy of multidimensional aggression crashed against the dignity of a free Venezuelan people.

Still, Washington left many wounds on our populace. As confessed in the writings of Richard Nephew, former advisor to President Barack Obama on Iran sanctions and current Biden State Department official, unilateral US financial restrictions are intentionally designed to exact suffering upon the populations which they are imposed. In his book, *The Art of Sanctions: A View from the Field*, Nephew specifically described a massive retraction in Iran's economy as "a tremendous success" resulting from the policies he crafted. This same mentality applies to Washington's attacks against Venezuela's economy. The pain that the Venezuelan people endured in recent years have been the aches of a heroic resistance—the contractions of a historical birth that has consolidated our sovereignty with a certainty that we are not only on the right side of history, but the future as well.

In the pages you are about to read, Anya Parampil goes into the outrageous details of this *Corporate Coup* against my country—a regime change operation that was not only aimed at deposing President Maduro, but sought to punish *all* Venezuelans. It is a policy that seeks to exact irreversible damage to Venezuela's economy and make the possibility of an independent Venezuela a distant dream.

The author knows us well. In her thorough and detailed investigation, Parampil manages to depict not only the criminal strategy deployed against Venezuela, but also the truly heroic endeavors that the Venezuelan people and its revolutionary government have taken on to confront it. Parampil understands and presents to us what the Abramses of the world can never see: that people determined to be free will fight to overcome all obstacles thrown before them.

Throughout these years of intense struggle, Anya always stayed close to Venezuela. She is a courageous analyst who was never afraid to confront the most perverse characters driving the aggression against us. She was even one of the protagonists of a beautiful gesture from a group of US citizens that decided to protect the physical site of our embassy in Washington DC, a struggle that risked their lives and integrity. Anya has a great ability to identify and interview key actors, as well as a capacity that not all researchers and foreign policy analysts possess: the pure intuition characteristic of a woman who believes in liberation and respect for all peoples.

Anya's coverage of the Ministerial Meeting of the Non-Aligned Movement in Caracas was of great utility in understanding the new global order currently emerging before our eyes. It placed the brute pretensions of the US administration against the strength of a diverse and multipolar world that is united in its preservation of national sovereignty, territorial independence, and self-determination for all nations. As a result, it is not only US hybrid war policy that is destined to fail in its confrontation with Venezuela's Bolivarian Revolution. This publication is of immense value for understanding Venezuela's recent history and modern diplomacy, and it confirms a diagnosis of terminal disease gripping US empire.

PREFACE

WHY VENEZUELA?

"Why are you so interested in Venezuela?"

My answer to this question varied according to different stages in my life. When I was younger and intensely idealistic, my interest in Venezuela was driven by romantic fascination with a country that underwent a profound political transformation at the turn of the century, nationalized its raw materials, and invested its vast natural wealth into a domestic crusade against poverty with stunning success. As an opponent of US military misadventures in the Middle East, the fact that Venezuela's renewal occurred under the stewardship of a dynamic leader who once stood before the international community and declared that US President George W. Bush reeked of sulfur because he was the devil added significant appeal. My fascination piqued in January 2019, when an unprecedented regime change effort saw Washington appoint a virtually anonymous, objectively amateurish opposition politician as Venezuela's president, despite the fact that no physical transfer of government had actually occurred in Caracas.

By the time I completed the forthcoming manuscript in April 2023, my interest in Venezuela had expanded far beyond the allure of a single political project. It was informed not only by personal affection for Venezuelans of varying political stripes I've befriended over the years, but a realization that studying their country enabled me to fully comprehend the limitations of my *own* government's foreign policy in the twenty-first century. While getting to know Venezuela, I witnessed the miraculous conception of a multipolar world that without question represents the future of international relations on this planet. Or at least, what seemed like the future prior to the rapid evolution our world experienced during the roughly eighteen months it took me to complete this book. The current international campaign to ditch the US dollar as the world's reserve currency, break away from the Petrodollar system, and establish a global order free from US and European interference was foretold by tea leaves documented in the chapters ahead.

At the launch of Juan Guaidó's US-backed coup in January 2019, I was stuck in the right place at the perfect time to pursue a front-row seat for the high-stakes drama. The previous month, Russia's state-backed media outlet in Washington DC, RT America, terminated my contract after six years of employment (containing melodrama worthy of an entirely separate book altogether). As I recovered from the shock of losing my rigid, studio-centric job as a network television host, my partner, Max Blumenthal, decided to book us a flight to Caracas. The trip represented my first as an official member of the *Grayzone*, the independent news site Max founded in 2015. For us and our (also newly resettled) *Grayzone* colleague, Aaron Maté, the journalistic pursuit of Washington's outlandish coup in Venezuela was too hot to resist. For me, it evolved into a quest that was too riveting to quit.

Throughout the last four years, I've developed and maintained friendships with a diverse assemblage informing all sides of the US–Venezuela stand-off: US political figures, Venezuelan government officials, Venezuelan opposition sources, Western banking and oil insiders, fellow journalists, and international dignitaries representing several governments beyond Washington and Caracas. Combined with what at times appeared to be sheer acts of fate—see the story of Max's incredible score against the Center for Strategic and International Studies think tank in chapter seven, for example—these connections enabled me to produce a series of original, investigative reports that served as the basis for this book, exposing what I have come to understand as a *Corporate Coup* committed against Venezuela in 2019—and against the government in my own country long before then.

Before leaping into that narrative, there are a few issues I should clarify for readers. Off the bat, I must note that when digested within the context of US politics, partisan labels historically used to discuss Venezuela—and Latin America in general—do not provide a full picture of reality. For example, Venezuela is often maligned as proof of "socialism's failure" even though, as we will see, the private sector still operates the vast majority of its economy. Despite over two decades of "socialist" revolution, supermarkets, restaurants, hotels, shopping malls, and other privately run entities provide the backdrop of daily life in Venezuela to this day. This fact does not undermine Venezuela's claim to the "socialist" banner, which it carries with pride, but should help US readers understand that the word "socialism" carries specific meaning in the country. It should not conjure Cold War-informed visions of an economy entirely under the boot of the state. Rather, Caracas's vision of socialism is primarily based in the state's ownership of Venezuela's abundant natural riches, which include the largest crude oil reserves and untapped gold deposits in the world. Indeed, Venezuela easily ranks among the wealthiest countries on the planet. As noted in pages ahead, the Allied fight in World War II would have been impossible without Washington and London's monopoly on Venezuelan oil at the time, with Caracas-sourced crude accounting for 80 percent of UK oil imports by 1942. Are you starting to see why US and UK officials are so preoccupied with the country?

As we will learn, Venezuela's 1998 revolution and subsequent campaign to assert sovereign control of its natural wealth placed Caracas in direct confrontation with the foreign corporate interests that practically owned the country throughout previous decades. As a result, ever since the Bush II era, Washington's sole interest in Caracas has been regime change. This book confirms that efforts to smear Venezuela as a "communist" hellhole are not only inaccurate but designed to let its domestic oligarchy off the hook for enabling a devastating US-led siege of the country in pursuit of that goal. Regardless, I refer to Venezuela as a "socialist" state throughout this book because that is how its leadership and people characterize their national project.

Additionally, terms like "right-wing" and "left-wing," while increasingly insufficient to accurately mark our own domestic divides, represent specific characteristics in Latin America that do not always correspond with their assumed attributes in the US. The "right" and "left" camps in Latin America are divided straight down the line according to their relationship with imperial forces in the region: the "right" serving as the Washington Consensus's local enforcer via military juntas and neoliberal bureaucrats (some of whom we meet in forth-coming chapters), and the "left" that make up the social movements and governments that oppose US and European interference on the continent. Though this tension resulted in competing visions for eco-nomic policy (the right's neoliberal "Chicago Boys" program versus the left's "socialist" model that prioritizes sovereign control of resources), US readers should be aware that partisan divides in Venezuela do not carry the same social implications as in our own country. For exam-ple, Venezuela's revolutionary leader, Hugo Chávez, was deeply reli-gious, and even described his political vision as "very Christian." Furthermore, some may be surprised to learn that Venezuela's govern-ment has allowed for the formation of armed civilian militias, known as *colectivos*, that operate beyond the authority of the state as part of its grassroots defense strategy against foreign interference. As detailed in chapter fifteen, one such *colectivo* played a key role in repelling a covert US mercenary invasion of Venezuela in 2020. Though the basic "left" and "right" descriptors conceal such complexities, throughout this book I refer to Venezuela's political blocs according to their historic labels.

Finally, there is the big scary "E" word that appears in this book's subtitle. While the terms "empire" and "imperialism" have taken on a variety of (largely meaningless) understandings in the US lexicon, I operate according to the old school. My definition of empire is based on a simple litmus test: do the interests of capital (the financial and industrial sectors within a nation) dictate the policy of the state, or does the state dictate the policy of capital? If the former is true, you have fertile grounds for an empire.

According to this criterion, the only empire that exists in our world today is that which operates out of the power centers of the US and Western Europe—what some regard as the historic "West"—and its regional satellites across the globe. The modern imperial network, through which transnational corporations and banking institutions based in the US and Western Europe exercise unrivaled control of the global financial system and natural resource market, has reigned supreme since the end of World War II. It is maintained via a world order constructed through the process of the war, embodied by the North Atlantic Treaty Organization (NATO) military alliance and remnants of Bretton Woods such as the International Monetary Fund (IMF), the World Bank, their subsidiaries and regional equivalents, and plenary sessions like the World Economic Forum in Davos, the secretive Bilderberg conference, and the Trilateral Commission. In popular terms, this globalized postwar order is what we understand as "neoliberalism."

The "liberal" model of global development established via Bretton Woods and enforced through NATO has enabled Western powers to maintain their imperial status to this day, despite the end of conventional colonialism. Though Venezuela gained independence from Spain over a century prior to the outbreak of WWII, forthcoming chapters reveal that US and European interests commanded authority of the country's natural wealth and domestic policies until the dawn of the twenty-first century. As we will learn, Venezuela's postwar neoliberal government eventually enacted a series of IMF-prescribed reforms that produced staggering rates of inequality and popular turmoil. These conditions fueled Chávez's democratic ascent in 1998 based on the promise of a political and economic revolution that broke with the Washington Consensus. As we will see, the "officials" who filled the ranks of Venezuela's US-backed coup regime in 2019 were mere leftovers from Caracas's neoliberal era; local imperial collaborators who sought to submit their country under the reign of foreign capital once again.

As a patriot within the army who understood that his country was not free as long as the US and Europe owned its land and government, Chávez organized a clandestine group dedicated to reviving the vision of Venezuela's anti-colonial hero, Simón Bolívar, within military ranks. After leading a failed coup in 1992, he realized Venezuela's route to revolution ran not through its military, but the hearts and minds of its people. Upon his release from prison in 1994, Chávez spent four years traversing the entirety of his country and convening town halls with average Venezuelans to discover what they *actually wanted*. This deliberate conference with the public formed the campaign platform that ferried Chávez to popular electoral victory in 1998, and onto the Bolivarian Revolution that awaited Venezuela just around the bend.

As he broke the chains binding Venezuela to neoliberal enslavement, Chávez did not seek war with his powerful neighbor to the north.

Rather, he simply asked us to recall our own destiny as an imperfect nation defined, above all, by a belief in the duty of man to throw off those governments which subject them to absolute despotism. This is why, in my view, Chávez's most consequential legacy is not the enduring strength of *Chavismo* within Venezuela's borders, but his campaign to resurrect America's revolutionary spirit at the dawn of the twenty-first century. In death, he joins the chorus of those who declared our shared continent the land where man on earth secured his God-given rights to life, liberty, and the pursuit of happiness.

PROJECT FOR THE NEW AMERICAN CENTURY

Upon walking through the front doors of Venezuela's Foreign Ministry, or *Cancillería*, in Caracas, one is greeted by a peculiar art installation which, at first glance, appears to be a large, fractured, black-trimmed window with a tail stretching behind it. As you gaze past the structure to see what is labeled the *Sala de Salvador Allende*, or "Salvador Allende Room," located in the Cancillería lobby, the towering sculpture's full image becomes clear. It is an artistic rendering of former Chilean president Salvador Allende's glasses, left shattered on the floor of his office on September 11, 1973, after US-backed military forces stormed the Presidential Palace in Santiago and overthrew his government. Allende died from gunshot wounds, later ruled to be the result of suicide, amid the putsch.[1]

I first encountered the sculpture in February 2019, during what became the first of three extended reporting trips I made to Venezuela over the next two years. Days before my arrival, a little-known opposition lawmaker named Juan Guaidó had stood in the center of Caracas's John Paul II Square and declared himself president of Venezuela, announcing a direct challenge to the authority of President Nicolás Maduro—and sparking an international political crisis that lingers to this day.

Up until that point, the entirety of Guaidó's burgeoning career had been defined by his ascent within foreign-funded civic organizations in Venezuela. As we will learn, after studying at George Washington

---

1 "Chile Court Confirms Salvador Allende Committed Suicide," BBC, September 12, 2012.

University in Washington DC, he joined the ranks of Voluntad Popular, a US-backed opposition party born from foreign-sponsored student protests that rocked Venezuela throughout 2007. By 2016, Guaidó was representing his native *Estado La Guaira* in the country's national legislature at the tender age of thirty-two.

When he announced his self-declared presidency less than three years later, however, Caracas-based pollster Hinterlaces found that a whopping 81 percent of Venezuelans had no idea who Guaidó was.[2] Even so, the novice politician managed to woo officials in Washington. According to the *Wall Street Journal*, his confidence was inspired by a conversation with none other than US vice president Mike Pence, who placed a call to Caracas on the eve of Guaidó's makeshift swearing-in ceremony to "set in motion a plan that had been developed in secret over the preceding several weeks, accompanied by talks between US officials, allies, lawmakers and key Venezuelan opposition figures."[3] The scheme marked an unprecedented twist in US foreign policy: Washington had declared its regime change mission in Caracas "accomplished" before a physical transition in government had actually taken place—and it never would. Today, Guaidó's name is primarily evoked as a punchline, synonymous with the most infamous US-backed coup that wasn't.

To myself and my colleagues, the Venezuela dilemma presented a fascinating reporting opportunity—a chance to cover one of the Trump administration's most consequential foreign policy blunders while getting a firsthand look at Chavismo, a political movement that permanently altered the course of history on our shared American continent. Each time I touched down at Simón Bolívar International Airport in Venezuela's Estado La Guaira, it was evident the country was experiencing extraordinary times. The facility is cavernous and seemingly equipped to route a normal number of flights per day, but was usually empty aside from other passengers disembarking from my gate. I often

2   "Hinterlaces: 81% De Los Venezolanos Desconoce a Guaidó Como Líder Político," VTV, January 20, 2019, https://www.vtv.gob.ve/hinterlaces-81-venezolanos-desconoce-a-guaido-como-lider-politico/.

3   Jessica Donati and Vivian Salama, "Pence Pledged U.S. Backing Before Venezuela Opposition Leader's Move," *Wall Street Journal*, January 25, 2019.

imagined the ghosts of decades past cluttering the airport's vacant halls: suit-clad men and women rushing to board flights destined for Miami, Zurich, or Madrid at the height of Venezuela's neoliberal era. Since 2016, however, major airlines such as Aeromexico,[4] Lufthansa,[5] and Delta have halted flights to Venezuela,[6] citing its increasingly strained economic situation and hurdles to transferring foreign currency out of the country.

During the forty-minute ride from Venezuela's seaside airport to its capital, the bright blue hue of nigh Caribbean waters blurs into tropical greenery as the highway twists through serene coastal mountains before giving way to the unmistakable combustion of city life. Descending into the explosive metropolis, Caracas first spills out from either side with rainbow-speckled *barrios* that tumble down the edge of its surrounding hills. Suddenly, the colorful commotion of the neighborhoods is replaced by the frenetic industrial energy of downtown—a whistling mix of modern skyscrapers and brutalist government buildings sprouting amid archaic compounds adorned with delicate arches and wraparound balconies reminiscent of imperial Spain. The intractable pulse of the city center is only reined in by the Cordillera de la Costa Central mountain chain, magnificent emerald slopes that encase Caracas's roiling urban heart.

On my first ride into Caracas, I observed a bustling Latin American landscape pulsing with all the normal signs of daily life. According to Western media, however, the Venezuela I had entered was a hellish netherworld. Headlines such as "Pets on the Menu as Venezuelans Starve"[7] and "How Venezuela Became a "Warzone"[8] created the

4   Reuters Staff, "Grupo Aeromexico Suspends Venezuela Operations, Cites Economy," Reuters, June 23, 2016.

5   Reuters Staff, "Lufthansa Suspends Caracas Flights as Venezuelan Economy Struggles," Reuters, May 28, 2016.

6   Anatoly Kurmanaev, "U.S. Suspends Passenger and Cargo Flights to Venezuela," *New York Times*, May 15, 2019.

7   Yesman Utrera, "Pets on the Menu as Venezuelans Starve," *Daily Beast*, November 4, 2017.

8   Adam Weinstein, "How Venezuela Became a 'Warzone,'" *Gawker*, February 20, 2014.

impression that travelers should expect to encounter a virtual zombie flick playing out in its streets. The Obama administration's March 2015 decision to issue an executive order classifying the country as an "unusual and extraordinary threat" to the national security of the United States underscored the message that Venezuela was a place to fear.[9] Yet the more time I spent in the country, the more I came to understand the true nature of its struggle. Indeed, Venezuelans and their government *have* been thrust into a war—just not the one portrayed in the West's global media apparatus.

"Today, we proudly proclaim for all to hear: the Monroe Doctrine is alive and well," White House national security advisor John Bolton triumphantly declared before a group of Cuban Bay of Pigs veterans in April 2019, roughly three months after the US's recognition of Guaidó.[10] Days later, Ambassador Samuel Moncada, Venezuela's representative before the United Nations in New York, expressed to me his conviction that Bolton's Monroeist views were based in a two-hundred-year-old ideology that "in the twenty-first century is clearly racist, illegal, and against" the UN Charter and founding principles, enshrined to guarantee the territorial sovereignty, political independence, and self-determination of all nations.[11]

Unfortunately for the US and Venezuelan populations alike, Bolton's words represented not only the view of Trump's administration, but an unelected bureaucracy that has dominated Washington across decades of superficial changes in leadership. Indeed, one could draw a direct line between Washington's contemporary Venezuela policy and the CIA-backed putsch that ousted Chile's Allende, Latin America's first democratically elected socialist president, in 1973—an act of terror that colored a continent-wide campaign of US-sponsored counterinsurgency and lethal political repression. The statue of Allende's splintered spectacles on the floor of Venezuela's Foreign Ministry today are

9   "Fact Sheet: Venezuela Executive Order," National Archives and Records Administration, March 9, 2015.

10   "Ambassador Bolton Remarks to the Bay of Pigs Veterans Association – Brigade 2506.," United States Embassy in Cuba, April 17, 2019.

11   Anya Parampil, "Venezuela UN Ambassador: US Gov. 'Psychologically Manipulating' Public to Support 'Colonial War,'" *The Grayzone*, April 29, 2019.

a reminder of the threat that all independent governments in the region continue to face as Monroe's ghost wanders the halls of Washington, haunting its permanent guard with deranged visions of colonial conquest conjured in the cradled infancy of US empire.

This reality weighs heavily on the shoulders of Venezuela's current government officials, many of whom bear the legacy of underground movements that once resisted their own country's US-backed junta. In the decades preceding its 1998 revolution, Venezuela was ravaged by the same dark forces that reigned across Chile and the rest of the South American continent throughout the twentieth century: military dictatorship, a dirty war against leftist guerillas, and pro-market shock therapy prescribed to benefit a tiny domestic ruling class that placed the boundless wealth beneath its soil—including the largest oil and gold deposits in the world—under the command of foreign interests.

It's no surprise then that when a charismatic Venezuelan paratrooper stormed the country's political scene and declared war on its domestic oligarchy, the public was ripe for more than your average nationalist revival. Following decades of colonial and neoliberal subjugation, Venezuela's sole path to sovereignty was political revolution.

At around midnight on February 4, 1992, gunfire erupted near Venezuela's Presidential Palace in Caracas. Forces loyal to President Carlos Andrés Pérez were beating back an uprising within military ranks in the capital, while simultaneous revolts flared up in the cities of Valencia, Maracaibo, and Maracay. Using a tank to breach the palace door, rebels managed to kill three of the president's bodyguards and eventually force Pérez, who had just returned from an economic conference in Switzerland, to seek refuge in the studios of Venevisión, a private television station. After hours of battle, which saw Pérez's troops resort to using F-16 fighter jets to squash the mutiny in Valencia, the insurgents surrendered. At least 101 people, including 42 civilians, were killed in the fighting. By midday on February 5, authorities had arrested 133 military officers and 953 enlisted soldiers for participating in the failed coup.[12]

12   Associated Press, "Venezuela Crushes Army Coup Attempt," *New York Times*, February 5, 1992.

Among those detained was Lieutenant Colonel Hugo Rafael Chávez Frías, a paratrooper from humble beginnings in Venezuela's rural plains who had been organizing rebel patriots within army ranks since 1982, when he founded the Revolutionary Bolivarian Movement-200 (MBR-200). Described by Venezuela's current government as "an organization led by young military men that was born to fight against the neoliberal system,"[13] MBR-200 saw themselves as continuing the legacy of Latin America's liberator, Simón Bolívar. Such a vision is reflected in the group's founding pledge "not to rest an arm or relax the soul" until the chains binding their people were shattered. Bolívar famously uttered the same words to his mentor and tutor, Samuel Robinson, in 1805— just five years before the start of Venezuela's War of Independence.

To understand Chávez's political development, it is necessary to grasp Venezuela's historic evolution. For readers in the United States, the story of revolutionaries on the American continent declaring sovereignty from European kings is familiar lore; where we had the British, Venezuelans had the Spanish. In fact, as current government officials in Caracas are wont to recall, decades before Venezuelan military leader Francisco de Miranda fought alongside Bolívar to lead South American patriots to victory against the Spanish Crown, he laid siege to King George's troops in Pensacola, Florida, during the American Revolutionary War in the north. Venezuela's own fight for independence officially began in 1810, two years after a tiny French emperor set his sights on Madrid and shattered Spain's grip on the Americas. Bolívar, a Venezuelan-born military leader inspired by Enlightenment principles and North American revolutionaries including George Washington and Thomas Jefferson, eventually led the local charge against Spain and its Royalist forces in the South American region. In 1819, he established Gran Colombia, a state that spanned territories throughout modern-day Guyana, Venezuela, Colombia, Ecuador, Peru, Bolivia, and Panama.

13   Ailyn Chávez, "Movimiento Bolivariano Revolucionario 200, Organización Que Nació Para ...," Ministerio del Poder Popular de Economía y Finanzas, July 24, 2021.

The United States government, then led by James Monroe, recognized Gran Colombia's independence on June 19, 1822.[14] Yet Monroe's acceptance of Gran Colombia was not informed by brotherly sentiment for a nation which, like his own, had successfully bucked the bondage of European colonialism and gained independence. Instead, Monroe saw an opportunity to grow the imperial reach of his own country. In 1823, the US president first articulated his infamous "Monroe Doctrine," a policy that on its surface merely rejected European interference on the American continent.[15] Today, it is widely understood that Monroe's doctrine was not a repudiation of imperialism on principle, however, but the blueprint for a policy that historically defined South and Central America, as well as the Caribbean, as Washington's "backyard." In Monroe's view, it was the United States—not the newly formed independent republics in Central and South America—that was destined to inherit Spain's control of the region.

Fortunately for its neighbor to the north, Gran Colombia would never live up to its potential as a regional powerhouse. Almost as soon as it won independence from Spain, Bolívar's government became entangled with regional separatists seeking autonomy from his federal state. Tensions reached a head in 1828, when diplomatic disputes between Gran Colombia and its neighbor, Peru, sparked war. That conflict, combined with intensifying separatist revolts throughout Gran Colombia, eventually led to the disintegration of Bolívar's project.

In April 1830, Latin America's liberator resigned as president of Gran Colombia and embarked on a journey to exile that he would never complete. Bolívar died on December 17, 1830, as he awaited a ship to carry him from modern day Colombia to Europe. Though history books officially attributed his sudden demise at just forty-seven years of age to tuberculosis, others, including Chávez, have claimed Bolívar was poisoned. In 2010, an infectious disease expert at Johns Hopkins University conducted a review of Bolívar's medical records

14   Charles H. Bowman, "The Activities of Manuel Torres as Purchasing Agent, 1820-1821," *Hispanic American Historical Review* (Duke University Press, May 1, 1968).

15   "Monroe Doctrine, 1823," United States Department of State Office of the Historian, accessed April 4, 2023.

and concluded that he likely died after ingesting arsenic, insisting his poisoning was the accidental result of outdated medical treatments that saw doctors administer the toxic chemical to patients as a common painkiller.[16]

At the time of Bolívar's death, Venezuela and Ecuador had already declared independence from Gran Colombia, which officially dissolved in 1831. In the decades following Gran Colombia's disintegration, Venezuela fell under military dictatorship and was generally governed by strongmen who maintained friendly relations with the United States. It was not until 1922, when geologists working for the Royal Dutch Shell company uncovered the extreme depths of Venezuela's crude reserves, that the mad dash for control of the country that continues to this day truly began. By 1929, Venezuela was the world's second largest oil producer, rivaled only by the United States. Average Venezuelans were not the primary beneficiaries of this newfound wealth and status, however, due to the fact that three foreign companies—Shell, US Standard Oil, and US Gulf Oil—owned 98 percent of their domestic oil market.[17]

Venezuela's strategic importance to the US and Europe was underscored as Washington prepared to enter the Second World War. At the time, Washington's primary ally, London, was entirely reliant on oil imports to fuel its military, with Caracas providing roughly 40 percent of its supply as of 1939.[18] Faced with the prospect that domestic US oil reserves were insufficient to sustain Washington's own foray into the war, the Allies looked to Venezuela to fill the gap. By the time US troops touched down on the British Isles in January 1942, Caracas was supplying an astounding *80 percent* of London's crude imports from its strategic location just south of the transatlantic conflict (Seddon 2014). Simply put, Venezuelan oil fueled the Allied victory in WWII.

---

16   "What Killed Bolivar?" *Johns Hopkins Magazine*, September 10, 2010.

17   "Venezuela: The Rise and Fall of a Petrostate," Council on Foreign Relations, March 10, 2023.

18   Mark Seddon, "British and US Intervention in the Venezuelan Oil Industry: A Case Study of Anglo-Us Relations, 1941-1948" (PhD thesis, University of Sheffield, 2014).

Washington and London's plunder of Venezuelan oil was jeopard-
ized in 1945, when several years of popular discontent with the ruling
junta in Caracas led to a coup that installed self-styled democrat and
founder of the center left Acción Democrática party, Rómulo Ernesto
Betancourt Bello, as the country's interim president. During his brief
time in office, Betancourt enacted a series of political reforms, including
universal suffrage, that earned his legacy as the "Father of Venezuelan
Democracy." Betancourt's agenda, which focused on nationalizing
Venezuela's oil reserves and initiating Caracas's membership in the
Organization of Petroleum Exporting Countries[19]—therefore upend-
ing British and US control of the country—was overturned before it
could take shape. In 1948, less than one year after Venezuela held its first
ever participatory election, the country's military carried out a second
coup—this time ousting Betancourt's democratically elected successor.

After squashing Venezuela's flirtation with democracy, the coup of
1948 gave way to the rule of Marcos Pérez Jiménez, an army officer
who led the country from 1950 until 1958. Unlike his predecessors in
Acción Democrática, Pérez Jiménez welcomed foreign investment in
Venezuela's oil sector, particularly from the United States. As offshore
interests deepened their hold on the country, Pérez Jiménez waged a
violent campaign to suppress the aspirations of his domestic population. Though he is credited with overseeing a dramatic investment in
Venezuela's public infrastructure, the Pérez Jiménez era was ultimately
defined by his decision to ban political opposition (including the Acción
Democrática party), deploy secret police to torture and imprison union
leaders, and shutdown the country's national university as part of a war
on the left.

Upon his death in 2001, the *Guardian* characterized Pérez Jiménez's
rule as one in which "censorship, political persecution, torture and
assassination were blended with authoritarian efficiency and a flourishing public works programme."[20] Meanwhile, the *New York Times*
asserted that Pérez Jiménez "was feared and hated inside his country,"

19   "Venezuelan Profiles and Personalities," Brown University Library, accessed
April 4, 2023.
20   "Obituary: General Marcos Pérez Jiménez," *Guardian*, September 20, 2001.

describing the leader as "the prototype of the Latin American military despot."[21]

"His virulent anti-Communism and his tolerant attitude toward foreign oil companies, however, gained him the backing of the United States," the *Times* went on, noting that President Dwight D. Eisenhower even awarded Pérez Jiménez a Legion of Merit in 1954. Perhaps intoxicated by such recognition, Pérez Jiménez ultimately violated his relationship with Washington when he grew "the temerity to begin developing a national industrial base, rather than simply absorbing US capital at high rates of interest" (the *Guardian*, 2001). Pérez Jiménez's reign came to an end in 1958, when protests against his rule spurred yet another military mutiny in Caracas that forced his exile in the Dominican Republic.

The developments of 1958 inaugurated a new age in Venezuelan politics that marked the formal end of military rule and the establishment of a seemingly democratic state. Representing the final chapter in Venezuela's pre-Chávez history, the years following Pérez Jiménez's ouster were defined by the Pacto Puntofijo, a 1958 agreement between the country's three major political parties to hold democratic elections and mutually respect the outcome. On its face, the Pacto Puntofijo ended Venezuela's era of foreign-backed dictatorship. In practice, the Puntofijo period merely consolidated the same foreign and corporate interests that had backed Pérez Jiménez behind the guise of a multi-party, democratic state.

Throughout the forty years following Puntofijo's 1958 inauguration, Acción Democrática (AD) and El Comité de Organización Política Electoral Independiente (COPEI), Venezuela's Social Christian Party, fell into a dynamic that mirrors the modern day two-party financial duopoly in the United States. While AD and COPEI differed on small matters and in name, neither party dared to venture from the Washington Consensus program while rotating control of Venezuela's presidency. Beholden to global financial interests and neoliberal institutions such as the International Monetary Fund, the Puntofijo parties delivered Venezuelans little more than the same tired policies of dictatorships past. Throughout the '60s

21   Larry Rohter, "Marcos Pérez Jiménez, 87, Venezuela Ruler," *New York Times*, September 22, 2001.

and '70s, both parties worked to suppress the rise of Marxist guerillas in Venezuela, overseeing a dirty war that left an estimated 5,000 dead and 3,000 disappeared.[22] Among those killed was Jorge Antonio Rodríguez, a student militant whom intelligence services captured in 1976 and subsequently tortured to death.[23] His son, Jorge, and daughter, Delcy, both currently serve as high-level officials in the administration of Venezuelan president Nicolás Maduro.

As documented in forthcoming chapters, AD and COPEI's combined subservience to the neoliberal order eventually gave way to unprecedented political upheaval, a social crisis that set the stage for Chávez's democratic election in 1998.

Average Venezuelans were first introduced to Hugo Chávez at around midday on February 4, 1992, when he appeared on their television sets to take credit for leading the military uprising that had failed to depose President Carlos Andrés Pérez as they slept.

"Comrades, regrettably, for now, the objectives that we set were not achieved in the capital," the young lieutenant colonel announced, calling on his troops to surrender and avoid more bloodshed. "It is time to reflect. New situations will arise, and the country must move decisively toward a better destiny."[24]

Chávez's appeal, known as his "Por Ahora" (For Now) address, was hardly one minute long—yet its mark on Venezuelan history was eternal. Unlike most military leaders in his position, Chávez was quite deliberately—albeit subtly—refusing to accept defeat. With the simple phrase *"por ahora,"* he instead suggested his followers would one day rise again.

Though Chávez and his collaborators were jailed for their participation in the coup, the events of February 4, 1992, ultimately spread

22   Diego Sequera, "TAREK WILLIAM SAAB: 'EL MAYOR DESAFÍO ES LA REINVENCIÓN CONSTANTE,'" *Misión Verdad*, March 11, 2023.

23   Ailyn Chávez, "A 45 Años Del Asesinato Del Mártir Revolucionario Jorge Rodríguez, Su Ejemplo De Lucha Prevalece En La Patria," Ministerio del Poder Popular de Economía y Finanzas, July 25, 2021.

24   "'Por Ahora': 30 Años De La Rendición Que Catapultó a Chávez Tras UN Golpe Fallido," France 24, February 3, 2022.

his revolutionary vision far beyond the ranks of Venezuela's military—and inspired a public campaign for his freedom. In an effort to unify the country, Pérez's successor, Rafael Caldera, released Chávez and his cohorts from prison in March 1994. As Chávez predicted, a new political situation did eventually rise in Venezuela, and it carried him all the way to the presidency.

Throughout the four years following his release from prison, Chávez traveled the depths of his nation and met with average citizens to learn precisely what they wanted from their government. In 1998, he used that experience to shape the platform of a populist presidential campaign. Running on the promise to convene a national constituent assembly and rewrite Venezuela's constitution according to the public's desire, Chávez won in a landslide victory on December 6, 1998. The following July, Venezuelans elected representatives to serve in the constituent assembly, which officially got to work in August. Venezuelans approved their new constitution on December 15, 1999—less than one year after Chávez's swearing-in ceremony—formally establishing the Bolivarian Republic of Venezuela by an overwhelming 42-point margin.[25]

The 1999 constitution and subsequent laws passed under Chávez revolutionized Venezuelan society by defining social security, health care, education, and housing as fundamental rights guaranteed by the state. To fund such massive social investment, the constitution banned private monopolies and, most importantly, asserted that all natural resources "that exist within the territory of the nation, beneath the territorial sea bed, within the exclusive economic zone and on the continental shelf, are the property of the Republic, are of public domain, and therefore inalienable and not transferable."[26] In other words, Venezuela nationalized its vast natural wealth, including its oil reserves—the largest in the world[27]—and vowed to invest those riches in its people.

25   Serge F. Kovaleski, "Venezuelan Vote Gives President New Powers," *Washington Post*, December 16, 1999.

26   "Venezuela (Bolivarian Republic of) 1999 (Rev. 2009)," Constitute Project, accessed April 4, 2023.

27   Robert Rapier, "Inside Venezuela's Contradictory Oil Industry," *Forbes*, February 22, 2023.

Venezuela's achievements under Chávez's leadership are extensively documented.[28] As a result of its 1999 constitution, Venezuela doubled investment in government programs and raised social spending to 22.8 percent of its GDP by 2011. In turn, the country saw a 20 percent drop in poverty and a 50 percent reduction in extreme poverty during that same period. When Chávez was elected in 1998, roughly 700,000 students were enrolled in higher education. By 2011, that number had soared to over 2,000,000. These are just a few examples of Venezuela's transformation under Chavismo, a political project that Chávez himself would eventually brand as "Twenty-First-Century Socialism." As Venezuela thrived, however, the health of its leader deteriorated.

On June 10, 2011, Chávez traveled to Havana, Cuba, to undergo emergency surgery on his pelvis. At the end of the month, he emerged to speak before the public and reveal his cancer diagnosis, declaring: "I neglected my health, and I was reluctant to have medical check-ups. It was a fundamental mistake for a revolutionary."[29]

Chávez died shortly before 4:30 p.m. Venezuelan time on March 5, 2013, at age fifty-eight. Immediately, US and European media fell into a predictable chorus about Venezuela's "uncertain future" in the years ahead.

"Mr. Chávez's departure from a country he dominated for 14 years casts into doubt the future of his socialist revolution," reported the *New York Times*. It went on: "His death is sure to bring vast uncertainty as the nation tries to find its way without its central figure."[30]

Venezuela's former colonizers in Madrid echoed New York's tune. "Pain and uncertainty in Venezuela after the death of Chávez," blared a headline in *El País*, the most widely read Spanish-language newspaper in the world.[31]

---

28   Jake Johnson and Sara Kozameh, "Venezuelan Economic and Social Performance under Hugo Chávez, in Graphs," Center for Economic and Policy Research, March 7, 2013.

29   Tom Phillips, "Hugo Chávez Tells of Cancer Diagnosis," *Guardian*, June 30, 2011.

30   William Neuman, "Chávez Dies, Leaving Sharp Divisions in Venezuela," *New York Times*, March 5, 2013.

31   Ewald Scharfenberg, "Duelo e Incertidumbre En Venezuela Tras La Muerte De Chávez," *El País*, March 5, 2013.

Up until the death of its namesake, Chavismo was virtually undefeated at the ballot box. For fourteen years, Venezuela's opposition
failed to win a presidential election or gain a significant majority in
the country's legislature. Would Venezuela's revolutionary project die
alongside its steward? Many hoped as much. In Washington, Florida
senator Marco Rubio, a highly partisan Cuban American, openly fanta-
sized that Venezuela's "uncertain" future would result in its break with
Chavismo, asserting Chávez's death presented the country with "an
opportunity to turn the page on one of the darkest periods in its history
and embark on a new, albeit difficult, path to restore the rule of law,
democratic principles, security and free enterprise system."[32]

The Obama administration struck a more balanced tone while
expressing similar optimism that regime change was on Venezuela's horizon. "As Venezuela begins a new chapter in its history, the United States
remains committed to policies that promote democratic principles, the
rule of law, and respect for human rights," the White House declared.[33]

The question of whether Venezuela continued down its revolutionary path would be decided rather abruptly. According to Article 233 of
the country's 1999 constitution, in the event of the president's death,
"a new election by universal suffrage and direct ballot shall be held
within 30 consecutive days" (Constitute Project 2023). Within a week
of Chávez's March 5 passing, Venezuela's electoral commission scheduled a presidential election for April 14.

Presented with their first opportunity to overturn Chavismo
without Chávez, Venezuela's opposition looked to Henrique Capriles
Radonski of the US-backed Primero Justicia party. The son of a successful businessman responsible for bringing Kraft Foods to Venezuela
in the 1950s, Capriles had co-founded Primero Justicia alongside fellow
scion of Caracas aristocracy Leopoldo López in the year 2000. Just one
year later, the US State Department–funded International Republican
Institute poured at least $340,000 into Primero Justicia's coffers as
part of an initiative to train party members, molding them into a

32   "Rubio Comments on Venezuela's Future," United States Senator for
Florida, Marco Rubio, March 6, 2013.

33   "Statement of President Obama on the Death of Venezuelan President
Hugo Chavez," National Archives and Records Administration, March 5, 2013.

professional class of Chavismo opponents.[34] Representing Primero Justicia on behalf of a coalition of opposition parties known as the Mesa de la Unidad Democrática (MUD), Capriles ran against an ailing Chávez in October 2012 and lost by 900,000 votes.[35]

In his chance at electoral redemption, Capriles faced a man who had risen from union leader to national assembly member to foreign minister to Chávez's trusted vice president: Nicolás Maduro Moros. After announcing his relapse with cancer in December 2012, Chávez made a televised address in which he urged the country to support Maduro in the event his health took a turn for the worse.

"Choose Maduro as president of the Republic," he pleaded. "I am asking you this with all my heart."[36]

The same media apparatus that pushed a narrative of Venezuela's "uncertain future" following Chávez's death adopted a uniformly imperious refrain in its coverage of Maduro. US and European media reports on Venezuela's 2013 election almost universally reduced Maduro's character to that of "Chávez's hand-picked successor," while sowing doubt that someone who had launched their career as a public transportation worker could ever possibly navigate the ship of state.

"Maduro's journey is a strange one. He's risen from being a lowly bus driver to a powerful union leader, to eventually being Chávez's Vice President," read a piece in the *Atlantic* (Simpson 2013). "Yes, a former bus driver may be Venezuela's new President," the neoliberal standard bearer emphasized, underlining its classist disdain for Maduro. Meanwhile, a dispatch in the US government-backed National Public Radio conspicuously glossed over Maduro's decade-long career as civil servant, identifying him as simply a "former bus driver and Chávez confidant."[37] Maduro's work as a federal lawmaker and as Venezuela's

---

34   Eva Golinger, *The Chavez Code: Cracking U.S. Intervention in Venezuela* (Northampton, MA: Olive Branch Press, 2006), p. 39.

35   "Venezuela Presidential Election 2012: Everything You Need To Know in One Post," ABC, October 7, 2012.

36   Conner Simpson, "Hugo Chavez's Successor Is More or Less Decided," *The Atlantic*, March 5, 2013.

37   Juan Forero, "Even in Death, Chavez Dominates Venezuelan Election," NPR, April 13, 2013.

foreign minister—as well as the fact that *any* leader's vice president was *by definition* their close confidant and "hand-picked successor"—was evidently lost on the foreign press.

If the media had demonstrated an iota of intellectual curiosity about Chavismo's new leader (or bothered to treat Maduro with a modicum of respect), they would have discovered that he was a revolutionary in his own right. Born to a politically active father, Nicolás Maduro García, who was forced into exile after organizing a failed general strike against Venezuela's military junta in 1952 as a union leader,[38] Maduro was a militant student activist well before Chávez became a household name. At age twenty-four, he enrolled in a year-long political course at the Escuela Nacional de Cuadros Julio Antonio Mella in Havana, described by the Colombian outlet *El Tiempo* as "a political training center run by the Union of Young Communists" in Cuba.[39] Rather than pursue traditional higher education, a March 2013 profile of Maduro in Mexico's *La Jornada* newspaper asserted that "participation in social movements was his university."[40] After gaining employment as a bus driver for the Caracas Metro in 1991, Maduro rapidly rose in the ranks of union leadership due to the fact that he was "driven, friendly, committed to workers interests, and charismatic" (Hernández 2013).

It was in his capacity as a union leader that Maduro first met Hugo Chávez. While imprisoned for his coup attempt, Chávez convened a meeting with labor leaders, including Maduro, in December 1993 (Hernández 2013). Following the encounter, Maduro became a top advocate for Chávez's release and was eventually elected to the 1999 National Constituent Assembly following Chavismo's electoral ascent.

In this context, the fact that Chávez entrusted his entire political legacy to Maduro was unsurprising—even if foreign media only saw the latter as a "lowly bus driver." Just over a month after Chávez's death, Venezuelans heeded their revolutionary leader's call and elected

38   "El Papá De Nicolás Maduro Se Hizo Bachiller En Colombia," *El Heraldo*, March 30, 2013.

39   Valentina Oropeza, "El 'Delfín' Que Conducirá La Revolución Bolivariana," *El Tiempo*, April 15, 2013.

40   Luis Hernández Navarro, "Nicolás Maduro, El Conductor," *La Jornada*, March 19, 2013.

Maduro to the presidency. On April 14, 2013, Venezuela's National Electoral Council declared Maduro's victory over Capriles by a narrow margin of 234,935 votes.[41] Though Capriles initially refused to accept the results and leveled charges of fraud, he ultimately produced no evidence to back his claims.[42] Even so, Maduro struck a conciliatory tone toward Capriles and other members of Venezuela's opposition during his April 19 inaugural address, announcing his intention "to extend a hand" and "build an inclusive nation for everybody."[43]

While surely a Herculean duty, Maduro's rush to win a breakneck election within weeks of Chávez's death proved to be the easiest task placed before him. As soon as Maduro entered Miraflores Palace, the US and its allies unleashed an unprecedented assault on his ability to govern. It arrived in the form of a hybrid regime change war: stifling economic sanctions, covert destabilization tactics, and violent foreign-backed riots designed to overthrow the elected government in Caracas once and for all.

Eight months following Maduro's April 2013 victory, Chavismo swept regional elections and dealt its opposition yet another blow. Within days of the December vote, Maduro summoned newly elected opposition governors and mayors for a meeting at the presidential palace. The December 19 session, which lasted for nearly five hours, was branded as Venezuela's government and opposition "opening the door to dialogue" in a bid to foster national unity. According to the BBC, the summit "became a political debate" and even served as "a platform for local opposition leaders to accuse, denounce and make demands before the government."[44]

41   Chris Carlson, "Maduro Wins Venezuelan Presidential Election with 50.66 Percent of the Vote [Updated]," *Venezuelanalysis*, April 15, 2013.

42   Chris Carlson, "Capriles Falsifies Evidence in Order to Claim Fraud in Venezuela's Elections," *Venezuelanalysis*, April 17, 2013.

43   "Nicolas Maduro Sworn in as New Venezuelan President." BBC, April 19, 2013.

44   Daniel Pardo, "Maduro y Oposición En Venezuela Abren Una Puerta Al Diálogo," BBC, December 19, 2013.

"We are not weak for being here, nor did we come to listen to orders," Henri Falcón, a Maduro opponent and popular governor from Estado Lara, proclaimed upon arriving to the talks.

Falcón's words were directed at US-backed elements within Venezuela's opposition that considered engagement with Maduro not only unacceptable, but tantamount to treason. Indeed, the fact that such an unprecedented gathering had taken place amid Maduro's calls for political inclusivity directly undermined the extremist bloc's quest to overthrow Chavismo bar none. An internal fight for the future of Venezuela's opposition was underway, but it would not resolve through politics. It would be settled in the street.

The battle formally erupted in the early days of 2014, roughly a month after Maduro's summit with the opposition. As students returned to school following the holiday break, masked hooligans rushed the University of the Andes (ULA) campus in Estado Mérida and set up roadblocks on a nearby thruway, paralyzing traffic and obstructing access to the main regional hospital. Journalist Ryan Mallett-Outtrim described the ensuing mayhem:

> The students have no visible demands, and they have no mass support. Instead of holding a protest with a point, their action consists entirely of piling petrol-soaked timber and tires on a main road outside [ULA] and setting them ablaze . . . These kids just seem to wander around with rocks or bits of sharp shrapnel in their hands, intimidating pedestrians outside the university gates.[45]

Mallett-Outtrim noted the protests kicked off just weeks after a leaked document revealed that Washington, through the United States Agency for International Development (USAID), was actively backing a plot "to create crisis situations in the streets" of Venezuela with the aim of facilitating "the intervention of the United States and NATO forces" in the country.[46]

45   Ryan Mallett-Outtrim, "Inside Venezuela's 'Repressive' Regime," DISSENT! Sans Frontières, January 14, 2014.

46   Eva Gollinger, "Documento Evidencia Un Plan De Desestabilización Contra Venezuela," Actualidad RT, November 5, 2013.

Billed as a "Strategic Plan for Venezuela," the document was prepared by a DC-based consulting firm and several Colombian foundations, including one led by the country's former president, Alvaro Uribe—a fanatical opponent of Chavismo and any remotely progressive political movement—in the immediate aftermath of Chávez's death. Drafted during a June 2013 meeting of Venezuelan opposition figures and USAID's then director for Latin America, Mark Feierstein, in Colombia, the plan aimed to inspire an uprising in Venezuela's military by sparking anarchy in the streets, specifying that "whenever possible, violence should cause deaths or injuries." The document also stated the conspirators' intent to "amplify" images of the artificially aroused chaos in foreign media in order "to manage international public opinion."

As soon as violence broke out at ULA in the early weeks of 2014, the Venezuelan opposition figures charged with directing the depraved US-backed scheme sprang into action. On January 23, a flamboyantly right-wing opposition lawmaker named María Corina Machado— who reportedly attended the USAID summit in Colombia (Golinger 2013)—officially launched the "Salida" (Exit) protest campaign alongside Leopoldo López, co-founder of Capriles's US-funded Primero Justicia party. With middle-class students acting as their shock troops, López and Machado aimed to sabotage the budding dialogue between Venezuela's government and its moderate opposition, isolate Maduro, and ultimately force his exit from the political scene.

Machado articulated her strategy for regime change without filter, declaring "we must create chaos in the streets" until Maduro is ousted.[47] That "chaos" took the form of guarimba riots, Venezuelan slang for the massive street barricades erected by students in Mérida, that promptly erupted across the country. Throughout the early weeks of 2014, guarimberos vandalized universities, government buildings, and residences; ransacked public transportation hubs; barricaded major highways; and assailed shipping trucks transporting gas and

47   Lauren Carasik, "Opinion: Obama Continues Bush's Policies in Venezuela," Al Jazeera America, April 8, 2014.

food.[48] As *La Salida* spread, roving mobs assaulted *Chavistas* in the streets, hung effigies of government officials in public, and carried out physical attacks against Cuban doctors providing healthcare in underserved communities.

López and Machado's commanding roles in La Salida were not mere products of fate. Both figures represented political "movements" that a foreign power—the United States—had aggressively trained and financed for the sole purpose of overthrowing the Venezuelan state. By 2014, López was leading Voluntad Popular, a party he founded in 2009 that, as detailed in chapters four and nine, the US State Department intentionally cultivated as a pro-Washington alternative to Chavismo. Meanwhile, a US diplomatic cable published via WikiLeaks revealed that as of 2004, Washington was similarly funding Machado's organization, Súmate (Join Us), via USAID.[49] According to the February 2004 communique, US officials invested in Súmate because they considered it to be "a highly effective and well-organized opposition group." In 2005, US president George W. Bush even hosted Machado for a friendly meeting and photo-op in the White House Oval Office.[50] By the time La Salida kicked off in 2014, López and Machado were in direct competition for the gilded throne of Venezuela's hardline, US-backed opposition.

López's moment of glory arrived on February 12, when he delivered an impassioned speech directing his followers to march to the office of Venezuela's attorney general minutes before the mob was captured on video attempting to burn the building to the ground.[51] The event—and the entire Salida campaign—represented a genuinely violent, foreign-backed insurrection that made the January 6 US Capitol Riot, an eternal source of trauma for Beltway liberals, look like a Macy's Thanksgiving

48   Ryan Mallett-Outtrim and Tamara Pearson, "Venezuelan Guarimbas: 11 Things the Media Didn't Tell You," *Venezuelanalysis*, February 16, 2015.

49   "CHAVEZ ACCUSES USG OF FUNDING 'COUPMONGERS,'" Cablegate, WikiLeaks, accessed April 5, 2023.

50   "President George W. Bush Welcomes Maria Corina Machado," National Archives and Records Administration, May 31, 2005.

51   "The Case of Leopoldo Lopez," Global Freedom of Expression, accessed August 15, 2023.

Day Parade.[52] Venezuela's government swiftly issued an arrest warrant for López and detained him on February 18.

The Salida rampage continued for roughly three months following López's arrest, leaving behind billions of dollars in property damage, at least three dead, and hundreds more wounded (Mallett-Outtrim and Pearson 2015). Though the prolonged terror campaign failed to topple Maduro, it succeeded in polarizing the public, thus sidelining moderate opposition figures like Falcón in favor of Machado and López's US-backed extremist faction. Granted de facto martyrdom through his arrest, López successfully overtook Machado in the race to displace Capriles as that bloc's leader.

Despite ultimately receiving a fourteen-year prison sentence over his role in the Salida riots, López continued to command Venezuela's radical opposition from behind bars, adopting a strategy *El País* described as "preferring options beyond electoral ones to evict" Maduro's government.[53] Tensions between López's faction and Venezuela's government reached a fever pitch in December 2015, after the opposition MUD coalition won a two-thirds majority in the country's National Assembly. When results in the southern Estado Amazonas were called into question, López exploited the opening to plunge Venezuela deeper into political crisis.

Within days of the December 6, 2015, legislative election, an audio tape surfaced online in which a woman, purportedly a regional Amazonas official named Victoria Franchi, boasted about having paid people to vote.[54] Pending an investigation into the recording, Venezuela's Supreme Court temporarily barred all four Amazonas candidates—including one belonging to the Chavista coalition—from

52   Considering their decision to lock up a vegan shaman for entering the US Congress with assistance from Capitol Police, one can only imagine how elite Washington would react if foreign-funded political figures directed a months-long campaign of violent attacks on public infrastructure, official government residences, and domestic supply chains for necessities like food and gas.

53   Ewald Scharfenberg, "La Oposición Venezolana Convoca Una Gran Marcha Contra La Violencia," *El País*, February 16, 2014.

54   Lucas Koerner, "Maduro Calls for Investigation of Blank Votes as Video Shows Opposition Mayor Handing out Cash," *Venezuelanalysis*, December 17, 2015.

entering office. Rather than comply with the investigation, however, the opposition-controlled legislature flouted the court and inaugurated the compromised lawmakers on January 6, 2016. The Supreme Court reacted to the flagrant disregard for its authority days later, ruling that "decisions taken by the National Assembly while these citizens are incorporated will be absolutely null," effectively declaring Venezuela's legislature defunct until it removed the Amazonas representatives.[55]

Despite the high court's declaration, opposition lawmakers wasted no time wielding their newfound power to launch a concerted attack on Chavismo. In one of their first acts, they removed all portraits of Bolívar and Chávez from National Assembly chambers. Next, they hastily passed a slew of laws that would have effectively nullified over fifteen years' worth of Chavismo's social gains, including bills to privatize Venezuela's public housing projects,[56] overturn agrarian reform policies,[57] and release violent guarimberos—including López—from prison.[58] While it's unclear how the lawmakers intended to implement their policies without cooperation from other government branches, the opposition-controlled legislature continued to convene and pass measures without interference, revealing their neoliberal agenda to the public if achieving little else.

Conflict between Venezuela's legislature and judiciary reached a breaking point in March 2017, when the Supreme Court ruled that Maduro could make decisions regarding the management of Venezuela's state-run entities—particularly its oil company—without the National Assembly's stamp of approval. Justices announced the court itself would temporarily replace the legislature's authority on matters of public industry, reaffirming its position that as long as lawmakers failed to comply with an investigation into the Amazonas vote, they were acting in contempt of the law. The decision received widespread

55   Rachael Boothroyd Rojas, "Venezuelan Supreme Court: 'National Assembly Is Void,'" *Venezuelanalysis*, January 12, 2016.

56   Lucas Koerner, "Venezuelan Supreme Court Blocks Housing Privatization Law," *Venezuelanalysis*, May 9, 2016.

57   Lucas Koerner, "Venezuelan National Assembly to Investigate Expropriated Land, Communes Threatened," *Venezuelanalysis*, January 28, 2016.

58   "Venezuela's National Assembly Passes Amnesty Bill," BBC, March 30, 2016.

attention in international media, which highlighted the development to paint Maduro as a rogue dictator consolidating his personal authority.

"Venezuela Muzzles Legislature, Moving Closer to One-Man Rule," declared the *New York Times*.[59] Meanwhile, outlets including NPR and CNN accused Venezuela of "dissolving" the National Assembly, while Reuters sent out a wire reading: "Venezuela's Maduro decried as 'dictator' after Congress annulled."[60]

As the independent outlet *Venezuelanalysis* pointed out at the time, Western coverage willfully ignored the fact that the National Assembly could "rectify the situation by removing the lawmakers accused of electoral fraud, and continuing to legislate" at any moment.[61] What's more, though many news outlets characterized Venezuela's Supreme Court as a mere extension of Maduro, the country's top judges were not directly appointed by the president. Instead, Supreme Court justices were selected by a committee of lawmakers and legal experts—a process that was designed, in theory, to avoid the politicization of the judicial branch seen in countries like the United States. As foreign media howled about Maduro's dictatorial takeover, opposition lawmakers carried on meeting and legislating, even moving to unilaterally reprivatize Venezuela's oil sector without incident.[62]

With a legislature acting in open contempt of the judicial branch to directly overturn the agenda of the country's elected president, by spring 2017 Venezuela faced an extraordinary political impasse. Though Maduro was not constitutionally up for reelection until the following year, López seized on the turmoil to call for a fresh round of street protests—this time with the explicit goal of forcing an early presidential vote.

59   Patricia Torres and Nicholas Casey, "Venezuela Muzzles Legislature, Moving Closer to One-Man Rule," *New York Times*, March 30, 2017.

60   Diego Oré and Andrew Cawthorne, "Venezuela's Maduro Decried as 'Dictator' after Congress Annulled," Reuters, March 30, 2017.

61   Rachel Boothroyd Rojas and Ryan Mallett-Outtrim, "Has Maduro Really Dissolved the National Assembly in Venezuela?" *Venezuelanalysis*, March 31, 2017.

62   Paul Dobson, "Venezuela's Defunct National Assembly Attempts to Privatise Oil Industry," *Venezuelanalysis*, July 12, 2018.

"Let's organize a huge consultation in which the people can vote and decide if they want presidential elections in 2017," López proposed in a January prison dispatch, directing his supporters to engage in an "electoral rebellion."[63] Within weeks, his loyal guarimberos were back in the streets.

Throughout the spring and summer of 2017, rioters paralyzed daily life in Venezuela once again. As in previous years, guarimberos blockaded major highways, set fire to government food distribution centers, vandalized public infrastructure, and physically assaulted Chavistas in public. Though the guarimbas eventually died down, the events of 2017 marked a turning point in Venezuela's political crisis. From that point on, López's US-backed faction of the opposition totally withdrew from the country's sovereign democratic process, launching a boycott of all subsequent elections. Meanwhile, the nonstop cycle of externally imposed civil unrest inspired Maduro's government to launch formal negotiations with Venezuela's moderate opposition, represented by the MUD coalition, in the Dominican Republic.

Following months of deliberations brokered by Dominican officials, reports emerged in early 2018 that Venezuela's government and the MUD were prepared to sign a breakthrough "framework for democratic coexistence."[64] Yet when time to sign the Santo Domingo agreement arrived on February 6, MUD officials suddenly walked out of the talks and accused Maduro's representatives of altering the deal's final text. MUD's claims were undermined by Dominican mediators, who insisted the document's language had been "worked on by both parties" (Boothroyd Rojas 2018). Maduro's government promptly charged Washington with sabotaging the negotiations, asserting US officials lobbied for MUD's withdrawal as part of their effort to delegitimize Venezuela's upcoming presidential vote, which was slated for May 20.

Indeed, the US-backed opposition's decision to boycott the 2018 election accomplished little more than ostensibly prove Washington's

---

63   Rachel Boothroyd-Rojas, "Guarimba Victims Pursue New Charges Against Leopoldo Lopez as Opposition Marches," Venezuelanlysis, February 20, 2017.

64   Rachel Boothroyd Rojas, "Venezuelan Opposition Abandons Talks in Dominican Republic, Dismisses Deal with Gov't," *Venezuelanalysis*, February 8, 2018.

narrative that Venezuela was a one-party dictatorship. If Maduro was the only candidate on the ballot, optics would demonstrate that he was unwilling to face opponents at the polls. Unfortunately for Washington, however, not all opposition leaders were willing to forfeit their right to participate in the vote. When Henri Falcón, the governor of Estado Lara and de facto leader of Venezuela's moderate opposition, tossed his hat in the electoral ring, Washington swiftly threatened him with sanctions.[65] The sheer presence of a prominent opposition figure like Falcón—a vocal critic of US interference in his country's internal affairs—was so threatening to Washington that it was apparently prepared to undermine even those candidates *opposed* to Maduro. Despite Washington's subversion campaign—including a State Department denunciation of the vote published months before it even took place[66]—the election went ahead on May 20, 2018. Maduro emerged triumphant with roughly 68 percent of votes cast, while his closest challenger, Falcón, won about 21 percent. A third candidate, Evangelical pastor Javier Bertucci, secured the remaining 10 percent of votes. With three candidates on the ballot and a Maduro victory, Washington's delegitimization strategy had officially fallen flat.

"Today's so-called 'election' in Venezuela is an insult to democracy," an incensed US ambassador to the United Nations, Nikki Haley, declared on Twitter hours before polls had even closed. "It's time for Maduro to go."[67]

Though the European Union (EU) and Organization of American States (OAS) had previously declined invitations from the Caracas government to observe and verify the vote, both groups joined US officials in rebuffing its results. In a May 21 statement titled "The Day after the Farce," OAS secretary general Luis Almagro declared his organization would follow Washington's lead and reject Maduro's reelection, vowing

---

65   Mark Weisbrot, "Behind the Scenes in Venezuela," *U.S. News*, March 3, 2018.

66   Department of State (@StateDep), Twitter post, February 8, 2018, https://twitter.com/StateDept/status/961699730710564865.

67   U.S. Mission to the UN (@USUN), Twitter post, May 20, 2018, https://twitter.com/USUN/status/998304169982349313.

to "continue struggling for the end of the Venezuelan dictatorship."[68] That same day, US president Donald Trump signed an executive order imposing a fresh round of sanctions on Caracas, describing Maduro's reelection as a "sham."[69] Though a vast majority of the world's governments, including those in Russia, China, and India, accepted Maduro's triumph, US officials refused to admit defeat. In fact, Washington was already actively colluding with members of Venezuela's extremist opposition to overturn his mandate.

By refusing to accept Maduro's 2018 victory, the US, Europe, the Venezuelan opposition they sponsored, and the OAS set the stage for Washington's January 2019 recognition of Juan Guaidó, a virtually unknown opposition lawmaker, as Venezuela's president. As we will see, the fantasy of Guaidó's presidency promptly gave way to an unprecedented campaign of financial, diplomatic, covert, and information warfare directed at the Venezuelan state. Enabled by the US and Europe's outsized command of the global financial system, the characters behind Guaidó's coup regime would eventually execute an extraordinary heist of Venezuela's internationally stored wealth on behalf of their foreign corporate and government backers. Following two decades of failed attempts to overthrow Chavismo, Washington's frustrated regime change effort culminated with a hybrid *Corporate Coup*.

"Today, January 23, 2019, I swear to formally assume the powers of the national executive as president in charge of Venezuela," Guaidó declared, unveiling his self-declared mandate.[70]

Though the thirty-five-year-old lawmaker exercised no control over Venezuela's military, government ministries, borders, nor any other state institution, he projected an unusual air of confidence.

"We know this is not about just one person," the rookie politician proclaimed. "We know this will have consequences."

68   "Message from OAS Secretary General on Elections in Venezuela," The Organization of American States, May 21, 2018.

69   Julie Hirschfeld Davis, "U.S. Places New Sanctions on Venezuela Day After Election," *New York Times*, May 21, 2018.

70   Ana Vanessa Herrero, "After U.S. Backs Juan Guaidó as Venezuela's Leader, Maduro Cuts Ties," *New York Times*, January 23, 2019.

ONE

THE MEDIEVAL SIEGE

When he endeavored to fill the void left by Hugo Chávez's premature death, Nicolás Maduro signed up for a life in the shadow of Venezuela's most iconic leader, popularly regarded as one of the most charismatic international dignitaries of his time. Many of Chavismo's foreign sympathizers have since become prone to observing that "Maduro is not Chávez," insinuating the former is more authoritarian, less committed to revolutionary ideals, and less equipped to manage Venezuelan affairs than his predecessor, who was widely admired by Western progressives and even embraced by liberal celebrities. Such assertions, however, overlook material circumstances that each leader faced, particularly the foreign-directed hybrid war imposed on Maduro the very moment he set foot in Miraflores Palace.

As we have seen, Venezuela's US-backed opposition waged an open revolt against Maduro's presidency from its outset. Though Chávez weathered his own US-directed coup and periodic street protests (detailed in chapters four and nine), he was not subject to the same level of sustained, turbulent insurgency that his successor endured. In addition to the foreign-sponsored chaos and resulting political deadlock that defined the early years of his presidency, Maduro was forced to confront global economic shifts and sophisticated tactics of financial warfare that Chávez never lived to see.

Within a year of his inauguration, Maduro was met with an abrupt oil crash that saw international prices drop by 40 percent in just six months.[1] The precipitous plunge came on the immediate heels of US

---

1   Robert J. Samuelson, "Key Facts about the Great Oil Crash of 2014," *Washington Post*, December 3, 2014.

secretary of state John Kerry's June 2014 trip to Saudi Arabia, during which he lobbied Riyadh to boost crude production and collapse
the global market through the basic laws of supply and demand.[2] The
request came as part of the Obama administration's strategy to force
Iran, another top oil producer, into entering the Joint Comprehensive
Plan of Action (JCPOA) and comply with limits on its domestic
nuclear program. While weakening Tehran, which ultimately signed
the JCPOA, or Iran Deal, the following year, the 2014 slump had the
added effect of debilitating other oil-producing states the West sought
to weaken—including governments in Iraq, Russia, and Venezuela.

Aside from a brief blip amid the global recession in 2008, oil prices
steadily surged throughout the Chávez era,[3] enabling his government
to carry out aggressive social investment. By prompting a substantial
reduction in Venezuela's oil earnings and, therefore, government revenue in Caracas, the 2014 crash represented Maduro's first major obstacle
to sustaining Chavismo. As international crude prices plummeted, the
Obama White House launched a complementary assault aimed directly
at the financial coffers of Maduro's government. In December 2014,
Obama signed the first set of unilateral US sanctions on Venezuela,
officially kicking off a campaign of economic terror against Caracas
that has yet to cease. Dubbed the "Venezuela Defense of Human
Rights and Civil Society Act," the financial restrictions were billed
as punishment for Maduro's crackdown on the US-sponsored Salida
riots earlier that year.[4] Three months later, Obama issued an executive
order classifying Venezuela as an "unusual and extraordinary threat
to the national security" of the United States ("Fact Sheet: Venezuela
Executive Order" 2015), an absurd policy that the administration

2   Lesley Wroughton, "Kerry, Saudi King Discuss Oil Supply, U.S. Official Says,"
Reuters, June 27, 2014.

3   "Crude Oil Prices - 70 Year Historical Chart," Macrotrends, accessed April 4,
2023.

4   Alexandre Lamy, "President Obama Signs Venezuela Defense of Human
Rights and Civil Society Act of 2014 and Ukraine Freedom Support Act of
2014," Sanctions & Export Controls Update (Baker McKenzie, December 19,
2014).

never justified, and which predictably drove Venezuela's economy into a tailspin.

Obama's March 2015 announcement sent international financial institutions a message to steer clear of Venezuela or risk facing Washington's wrath, raising the implied risk of exchange with any bank account linked to the country virtually overnight. The national security declaration thus precipitated a massive reduction in the Venezuelan private sector's access to international credit lines, spurring an 80 percent drop in imports to the country between 2013 and 2019.[5] Stratfor, a private US intelligence contractor, illustrated the depths of the crisis by comparing two satellite images of Venezuela's main import hub, Puerto Cabello, captured over the course of just three years. In a 2015 assessment posted on its website, Stratfor juxtaposed a February 2012 photograph of the port that depicted thousands of shipping containers cluttering its harbor with an image of the same area taken in June 2015. In the second photo, Puerto Cabello was virtually empty.[6]

"Oil revenue accounted for nearly 95 percent of Venezuelan exports by value, so the country was among the hardest hit by the fall of the price of oil," Stratfor reported, adding that Venezuela's "government simply has much less money to import goods."

Stratfor failed to mention the Obama White House's sanctions blitzkrieg on Caracas, instead blaming Venezuela's hardship on Chavismo's "unwillingness" to reform. The firm went on to accurately predict that the import crunch would result in major wins for the anti-Chavista coalition in legislative elections slated for December 2015. Indeed, by then the external assault on Venezuela's import capacity had given way to a nationwide shortage of basic goods. The country's local oligarchy—which still controlled roughly 62 percent of its domestic commodity market despite Chavismo's rise[7]—happily exacerbated the crisis by

5   Mark Weisbrot, "Trump's Other 'National Emergency': Sanctions That Kill Venezuelans," *The Nation*, February 28, 2019.

6   "Bringing Venezuela's Economic Crisis Into Focus," Stratfor, August 27, 2015.

7   "Producto Interno Bruto (See: 'Producto Interno Bruto Por Sector Institucional (Base 1997), Precios Constantes,'" Banco Central de Venezuela, accessed April 4, 2023.

hoarding products linked to their supply chains.[8] In time, supply shortages drove the formation of a lucrative black market for fuel and other goods, sparking an infamous spike in the country's rate of inflation (Venezuela's import and inflation imbroglio is further explored in chapters two and three).

By the time Donald Trump assumed the US presidency in January 2017, the neoconservative ideologues that would take hold of his administration were likely salivating at the prospect of inheriting Washington's war on Caracas.

Though candidate Trump vowed to disentangle the US from decades of disastrous regime change wars, the American continent proved a consequential blind spot for the president. Hostage to sectarian Cuban and Venezuelan emigres in south Florida—a key electoral prize for any US presidential candidate—Trump eventually enabled Washington's most notorious jingoists to commandeer his approach to Latin America and the Caribbean. In April 2018, he shocked many of his supporters by appointing notorious neocon and Yosemite Sam cosplayer John Bolton to lead his National Security Council. Five months later, Bolton selected Latin America hawk Mauricio Claver-Carone, a Cuban American, to head the council's division for the Western Hemisphere.[9] Within a matter of weeks, Trump's Latin America policy had been hijacked by the very Beltway "swamp creatures" upon which he'd previously declared war. Rather than put "America First," they would soon convince him to make one of the most significant foreign policy blunders of his presidency.

Throughout his first year in the White House, Trump steadily ratcheted up the economic war his predecessor initiated against Venezuela. In August 2017, he signed an executive order that officially banned transactions related to the issuance of new debt to Venezuela's government in US markets, further restraining Maduro's access to foreign

8   Cory Fischer-Hoffman, "Venezuelan Officials Seize Warehouse with Enormous Cache of Hoarded Items as Opposition Calls for Strike," *Venezuelanalysis*, January 14, 2015.

9   John Bolton, *The Room Where It Happened* (New York, NY: Simon & Schuster, 2020), 250.

credit lines.[10] By March 2018—three years following the initiation of Obama's financial assault on Caracas—the international credit rating company, Moody's, had downgraded Venezuela to a "C" classification— its lowest possible grade.[11]

A direct result of US sanctions on Maduro's government, the Moody's decision delivered Venezuela's tortured economy a decisive blow. According to Caracas's ambassador to the United Nations, Samuel Moncada, the Moody's downgrade made it "so that everything going to Venezuela has three or four times the insurance premium" of shipments to other nations.[12] As a result, he explained, "ships don't want to go [to Venezuela], and companies don't want to deal with us." Yet the fact that Moody's awarded war-torn countries like Iraq and the Democratic Republic of Congo higher scores than Venezuela— enabling Baghdad and Kinshasa to access greater lines of international credit—exposed its politicized nature. Though Venezuela was technically at peace, Moody's action effectively imposed a "wartime" economy on the country, indefinitely limiting its ability to freely participate in the international financial market.[13] To US officials overseeing the controlled demolition of Venezuela's economy, however, Caracas's financial woes were merely the product of Chavismo.

10   Stephen M. McNabb and Kim Caine, "US Imposes New Economic Sanctions against Venezuela," Norton Rose Fulbright, August 30, 2017.

11   Reuters Staff, "Moody's Downgrades Venezuela Rating by Two Notches," Reuters, March 9, 2018.

12   "The Struggle Against Sanctions: The Case of Venezuela," The People's Forum NYC, June 25, 2019.

13   I experienced the baffling effects of this de facto "wartime" economy firsthand in May 2018, while working as a correspondent for RT America. Back then, I was told I could not cover Venezuela's presidential election because the insurance package required for a trip to Caracas was too expensive. I was puzzled by this reasoning, considering RT had previously sent me to Israel-Palestine and South Korea without encountering such exorbitant fees. During my trip to Israel-Palestine in February 2017, Tel Aviv was engaged in the routine bombing of its neighbor, Syria, rousing concerns it could ignite a regional war. When I visited Seoul later that year, North Korea was launching regular missile tests, sparking fears it would goad the US into direct military confrontation. Somehow, RT's insurance provider considered Venezuela as a more dangerous destination than either of those hot international conflict zones.

"Not long ago, Venezuela was one of the richest countries on Earth," Trump lamented during his September 2018 address before the seventy-third UN General Assembly meeting in New York, unrolling yet another round of sanctions on Caracas. "Today, socialism has bankrupted the oil-rich nation and driven its people into abject poverty."[14]

The White House's interventionist posture toward Latin America was further articulated in a landmark address Bolton delivered that November. Speaking at Miami Dade University, Bolton vowed Trump's administration would "no longer appease dictators and despots near our shores in this hemisphere," taking aim at what he characterized as a "Troika of Tyranny" that dominated the region: Cuba, Nicaragua, and Venezuela.[15]

Crafted in part as a rebuke to Obama's normalization efforts with Cuba, Bolton's address put governments in Havana, Managua, and Caracas on notice that their overthrow was a top priority for Trump's administration. Indeed, Bolton's "Troika of Tyranny" declaration represented far more than an alliterative smear campaign devised to tarnish the reputations of Washington's regional foes. Rather, it echoed the belligerent—and widely reviled—foreign policy that President George W. Bush inaugurated during his 2002 State of the Union address, when he classified the governments of Iraq, Iran, and North Korea as an "axis of evil, arming to threaten the peace of the world."[16] Widely regarded as a regime change wish list, Bush's Axis of Evil speech served as the formal declaration of Washington's "War on Terror," a fatal endeavor that spurred catastrophic NATO-led military campaigns in Afghanistan, Iraq, Libya, Syria, and the surrounding region.

The reverberation of "Axis of Evil" beyond Bush's original hit list was no accident. Months after the president's address, a senior State Department official delivered a talk entitled "Beyond the Axis of Evil," during which he added governments in Syria, Libya, and Cuba

14   Politico Staff, "Full Text: Trump's 2018 UN Speech Transcript," *Politico*, September 25, 2018.

15   David A Wemer, "John Bolton Takes Latin American 'Troika of Tyranny' to Task," *New Atlanticist*, November 1, 2018.

16   "President Delivers State of the Union Address," National Archives and Records Administration, January 29, 2002.

to the regime change docket. Speaking at the conservative Heritage Foundation think tank in Washington DC, the official tasked with expanding the Axis of Evil target list was none other than John Bolton.[17] Nearly twenty years later, Bolton would bring his regime change fantasies, knack for corny sloganeering, and distinctively walrus-like 'stache to the Trump White House—a turn of events that culminated with Washington's recognition of Guaidó just two months following his Troika of Tyranny tirade.

The neocon takeover of US Latin America policy was solidified in the immediate aftermath of Guaidó's January 2019 "swearing in" ceremony, when Trump tapped bona fide beast of the Beltway bog Elliott Abrams as his "special envoy" to Caracas. Described by Bolton as an "old friend" (Bolton 2020, 273), Abrams was best known for his lead role in the Iran-Contra Affair of the early 1980s, when he directed Washington's dirty war against leftist guerillas in Central America as a senior State Department official.[18] In 1991, Abrams pleaded guilty to withholding information about US material support for Nicaraguan paramilitary groups—a direct violation of Washington's official ban on such aid—from Congress, though President George H. W. Bush pardoned him the following year. Abrams would go on to serve on Bush Jr.'s national security team and orchestrate a failed military coup against Chávez in April 2002 (see chapter 9), just weeks following the US president's Axis of Evil address.

Alongside Bolton's resurgence, Abrams's 2019 resurrection marked a fateful reproach to Trump's pledge to "drain the swamp"—rather than drive a stake in the heart of the establishment zombies most responsible for ill-fated wars of the past, his White House had impulsively absorbed the most noxious detritus circulating throughout Washington's septic imperial core. Following Guaidó's ascent, these devious characters ratcheted up Washington's assault on Venezuela to heights previously imperceptible to not only Caracas, but also their own colleagues in Trump's administration. On January 28, 2019, Trump

17 John Bolton, "Beyond the Axis of Evil: Additional Threats from Weapons of Mass Destruction," The Heritage Foundation, May 6, 2002.

18 Julian Borger, "US Diplomat Convicted over Iran-Contra Appointed Special Envoy for Venezuela," *Guardian*, January 26, 2019.

signed a blanket ban on the sale of Venezuelan crude in US markets, a ploy designed to further restrict Maduro's access to vital revenue[19] (and one that previewed President Joseph Biden's subsequent embargo of Russian oil levied in 2022). The Treasury intensified its stranglehold on Venezuela's oil sector throughout the preceding months, even issuing so-called "secondary sanctions" against non-US entities that maintained commercial relationships with Maduro's government.[20] As far as The Swamp™ were concerned, not even sovereign borders were barriers to Washington's reign of financial terror; the US Treasury's jurisdiction permeated all corners of the planet.

Bolton took credit for personally crafting Washington's tyrannical Venezuela sanctions regime in his 2020 memoir, *The Room Where It Happened*, complaining that even Trump Treasury secretary and Goldman Sachs executive Steve Mnuchin expressed concern the measures would blowback against US interests. According to Bolton, Mnuchin believed the extreme policy would not only hinder US commercial activity abroad, but also prompt a surge in international oil prices that would inadvertently hurt US consumers (Bolton 2020, 367).

"Treasury treated every new sanction decision as if we were prosecuting criminal cases in court," Bolton bemoaned (Bolton 2020, 271).

"But that's not how sanctions should work," the veteran US official continued in his inadvertent confession, adding: "They're about using America's massive economic power to advance our national interests."

Like nearly all his professional ventures, the success of Bolton's crusade on Caracas would be measured in death and destruction. By 2020, Venezuela was in the midst of the largest economic contraction in modern Latin American history, reporting a 75 percent drop in gross domestic product from its recorded peak just eight years prior.[21] The downturn drove a pronounced fall in the purchasing power of ordinary Venezuelans, leading to a 72 percent decline in their living standards

19   Edward Wong and Nicholas Casey, "U.S. Targets Venezuela With Tough Oil Sanctions During Crisis of Power," *New York Times*, January 28, 2019.

20   Scott Smith, "Trump Sanctions Targeting Venezuela's Maduro Lead to Mexico," Yahoo! Finance, June 18, 2020.

21   Francisco Rodríguez, "Sanctions, Economic Statecraft, and Venezuela's Crisis," Sanctions and Security, January 2022.

over that same period. At last, Washington's medieval siege of its southern neighbor was complete.

In a political age of protracted polarity and performative partisan theater, Francisco Rodríguez is perhaps the most moderate Venezuelan one could encounter. Though he hailed from a prominent family (his father, Gumersindo, was a popular Acción Democrática lawmaker and government minister under President Carlos Andrés Pérez), Rodríguez did not enter politics himself until 2000. That year, the Harvard-educated economist returned to Caracas to lead Venezuela's equivalent of the Congressional Budget Office. Selected as a "Consensus" pick tasked with mediating between the freshly inaugurated Chavista government and its political opposition, Rodríguez's discreet disposition eventually placed him in direct conflict with ideologues on both sides of the aisle—including a young lawmaker named Nicolás Maduro.

In his soon to be published memoir, *Scorched Earth: The Political Economy of Venezuela's Collapse*, Rodríguez recalled that one of his most intense conflicts with Chavismo came in the form of a spat with Maduro, then head of the National Assembly's Social Development Commission, over the former's unfavorable review of proposed social security legislation. The economist's critical nature eventually inspired a successful Chavista-led campaign to remove him from office in March 2004. Though Rodríguez legally protested the controversial move, Venezuela's Supreme Court ultimately upheld the National Assembly vote for his dismissal.

Following his ouster, Rodríguez moved stateside and established himself as one of Chavismo's most prominent detractors while animating coveted posts in academia and on Wall Street, including as a Latin America analyst for Bank of America Merrill Lynch in New York. In 2018, he advised anti-Chavista presidential candidate Henri Falcón in his failed bid to unseat Maduro. To this day, neither Falcón nor Rodríguez have recognized the vote's outcome. Yet while other US-based opposition figures featured in this book, including Harvard professor and Guaidó advisor Ricardo Hausmann, used their influence to agitate for increased economic warfare—and even military action—against their homeland, Rodríguez remained true to his analytical, balanced character. Rather than fan the flames of hybrid war, Rodríguez employed his academic chops to produce a series of reports thoroughly documenting, detailing, and exposing the gruesome legacy of Washington's Venezuela policy.

Rodríguez published one such review, an exhaustive study outlining the impact of US sanctions on Venezuela's economy, in January 2022. Through in-depth data production and analysis, he determined that Washington's sanctions were the decisive factor behind a rapid collapse in Venezuelan oil production between the years 2016 and 2021—a development that in turn drove the country's unprecedented economic contraction.

In the chart below, Rodríguez traced four significant drops in Venezuelan oil production between the years 2008 and 2021, illustrating that three of the downturns directly corresponded with a new US sanction on Caracas. In Rodríguez's words, the time series data represented a statistical "smoking gun" implicating the US in Venezuela's economic meltdown.

"Yes, the economy was being poorly managed," Rodríguez told me shortly after publishing the data, emphasizing his critical view of Maduro's fiscal policy. "But its oil sector was not collapsing and

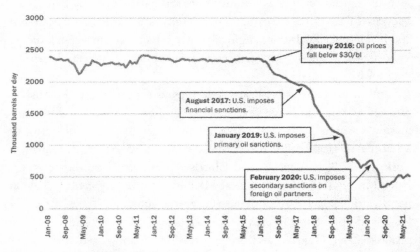

Sources: Own calculations, OPEC Secondary Sources.

Figure 1 (Rodríguez January 2022)

nobody—no macroeconomic analyst, no oil sector analyst—predicted something remotely resembling the type of collapse that we saw."[22]

The economist went on: "Sanctions were, essentially, a surgical strike directed at Venezuela's oil sector."

By suffocating Caracas's oil sector earnings, access to international credit, and import capacity, US sanctions not only deprived Maduro's government of the cash required to sustain Chavismo, but plunged Venezuela into a nationwide humanitarian emergency. In April 2019, the DC-based Center for Economic and Policy Research (CEPR) think tank published a bracing paper that concluded US sanctions amounted to the "collective punishment" of the Venezuelan population. According to co-authors Jeffrey Sachs and Mark Weisbrot, US sanctions drove a 31 percent increase in Venezuelan mortality rates recorded between the years 2017 and 2018 alone.[23]

CEPR's findings were bolstered by international legal scholar Alfred de Zayas, the first UN rapporteur to visit Venezuela in over two decades. Following a reporting trip to the country in 2017, de Zayas published a scathing review of US policy toward Venezuela that determined Washington's sanctions were "comparable with medieval sieges of towns with the intention of forcing them to surrender."[24]

"Twenty-first-century sanctions attempt to bring not just a town, but sovereign countries to their knees," the lawyer declared in his 2018 report. According to de Zayas, this modern-day siege warfare was "accompanied by the manipulation of public opinion through 'fake news,' aggressive public relations and a pseudo-human rights rhetoric" that ultimately reinforced Washington's regime change narrative the world over.

22   Anya Parampil, "'Smoking Gun' Analysis Finds US Sanctions Produce 'War Time' Economy in Venezuela," *The Grayzone*, January 14, 2022.

23   Mark Weisbrot and Jeffrey Sachs, "Economic Sanctions as Collective Punishment: The Case of Venezuela," Center for Economic and Policy Research, April 2019.

24   Alfred de Zayas, "Report of the Independent Expert on the Promotion of a Democratic and Equitable International Order on His Mission to the Bolivarian Republic of Venezuela and Ecuador" United Nations Digital Library, August 3, 2018.

Indeed, foreign media typically painted Maduro as a comically inept autocrat lolling about Caracas, blithely indifferent to the suffering of his people. Conveniently, the press's played-out projection of a Venezuelan despot feasting on the remains of a vanquished petrostate accompanied their conscious erasure of Washington's years-long financial assault on Caracas. By the time Guaidó arrived on the world stage, the very media apparatus that once eagerly sold the Western public a war in Iraq was spinning the trite tale of a rogue communist regime lurking just beyond Florida's southern coast.

Unceremoniously transformed from populist revolutionary to de facto wartime president, by 2019 Maduro stood toe to toe with the veritable architects of Washington's most criminal foreign exploits. To survive, he would have to craft his own signature defense against US hybrid war.

TWO

ALEX SAAB'S STORY

The tiny island nation of Cape Verde produced one of the African continent's most preeminent revolutionary figures, Amílcar Cabral. Until his 1973 assassination, Cabral led West Africa's fight for sovereignty from Portugal, a prolonged guerilla campaign that achieved the independence of Guinea-Bissau and Cape Verde just months following his murder. A skilled military strategist and cunning political theorist, Cabral stands among the giants of the twentieth century's anti-colonial resistance. In fact, Chávez would credit Cabral with inspiring his own effort to free Venezuela from foreign subjugation at the dawn of the second millenium.[1]

Each January 20, on the anniversary of Cabral's death, Cape Verdeans observe National Heroes Day, an official commemoration of those who died in the battle for independence. Unfortunately for those heroes, contemporary Cape Verdean officials have nakedly disgraced their patriotic sacrifice. In June 2020, they willfully converted Amílcar Cabral International Airport into the site of an unprecedented US-directed kidnapping scheme—betraying their anti-colonial history in a humiliating display of imperial servitude.

Washington's extrajudicial abduction in Cape Verde targeted a Colombian-born Venezuelan official who had by then established his own legacy in the global struggle against Western hegemony: Alex Nain Saab Morán.

---

1 "Intervención Del Comandante Presidente Hugo Chávez Durante Encuentro Con Partidos Aliados Por El Sí a La Enmienda Constitucional," Todo Chávez, January 15, 2009.

Long before Trump's maximum pressure campaign against Venezuela began, it was clear President Maduro had been dealt a much trickier hand than his predecessor. In 2016, steep inflation and unpredictable supply chains wrought by US sanctions forced Maduro to completely overhaul Venezuela's economy. On January 19, he inaugurated the National Council for a Productive Economy, a roundtable of forty-five businessmen, government officials (including opposition figures), union leaders, and representatives from communes tasked with revamping domestic production capacity. The following month, he established a National Productive Corporation to oversee management of "state, communal, and mixed firms."[2] To complement the reforms, Maduro initiated a crackdown on what he described as "a cancer" of corruption in state industries. By mid-February, his government had arrested and charged over fifty federal bureaucrats, including three high-level officials overseeing food production, for participating in fraud schemes.[3]

The most significant aspect of Maduro's 2016 economic offensive would prove to be his dramatic expansion of Venezuela's Comités Locales de Abastecimiento y Producción (Local Committees for Supply and Production), or CLAP program. Launched amid a national sanctions-fueled shortage of basic commodities, CLAP aimed to insulate Venezuelans from external assaults on their government's import capacity—and would become Maduro's single most effective intervention against US financial war.

CLAP aimed to remedy Venezuela's import crisis by delivering regular shipments of government-subsidized pantry staples and household products to millions of families nationwide. Neighborhoods were directed to form CLAP committees that would essentially serve as a middleman between their locality and the central government by assessing the needs of their community and coordinating with Caracas to procure and distribute supplies accordingly.

At its core, CLAP represented a direct lifeline from Venezuela's government to its sanctions-ravaged populace; a path to circumvent erratic

2   Lucas Koerner, "Venezuelan's Maduro Creates Socialist Enterprise System to Kickstart Production," *Venezuelanalysis*, February 24, 2016.

3   Lucas Koerner, "Venezuela Arrests 55 State Food Employees in Anti-Corruption Raid," *Venezuelanalysis*, February 17, 2016.

supply chains controlled by its domestic oligarchy and ensure average citizens did not starve amid Washington's economic war. Venezuelan economist and outspoken Maduro critic Francisco Rodríguez conducted an in-depth assessment of CLAP in 2021 and determined the program "was associated with a more than doubling of the households with access to food assistance." As a result, he concluded that without CLAP's intervention, "Venezuela's food crisis would almost certainly have been much worse."[4]

The US government's maniacal obsession with CLAP further underscored its success. In February 2019, Trump Venezuela envoy Elliott Abrams took the floor of the UN Security Council to rail against the initiative, declaring "Maduro has continued to politicize aid, via the CLAP program," to provide "benefits to his supporters."[5] When the Treasury Department hit CLAP with sanctions that June, Secretary of State Mike Pompeo lauded his colleagues for targeting Venezuela's "oil-for-food scheme" while paradoxically claiming that Caracas "had no intent of providing food to the people."[6] Venezuela's vice president, Delcy Rodríguez, promptly thanked Pompeo for his honest confession of US financial terror, asserting his statement proved Washington's "illicit sanctions are [designed] to prevent the arrival of food in Venezuela."[7] Others in Washington routinely denounced CLAP as a form of "social control," arguing Maduro's government used the program to arouse artificial support.[8]

Indeed, though wealthy members of the anti-Chavista opposition were less likely to seek its benefits, claims of rampant political discrimination within CLAP did not square with reality. By the time I arrived in Venezuela in February 2019, roughly six million households

4   Francisco Rodríguez, "The Economic Determinants of Venezuela's Hunger Crisis," June 23, 2022.

5   "Remarks at a UN Security Council Briefing on Venezuela," United States Mission to the United Nations, February 26, 2019.

6   Mike Pompeo, (@secpompeo), Twitter post, June 18, 2020, https://twitter.com/SecPompeo/status/1273712766340259841?s=20.

7   Delcy Rodríguez, (@drodriven2), Twitter post, June 18, 2020, https://twitter.com/drodriven2/status/1273730550151421957?s=20.

8   Diálogo Américas, "Social Control: Maduro's CLAP," January 24, 2020.

were receiving CLAP boxes every month. I witnessed the fruits of the program myself while staying with friends in Cumbres de Curumo, a bastion of opposition support in Caracas. One shipment my hosts received contained pasta, dry beans, and cooking oil from Turkey. During a subsequent visit in December 2020, the house buzzed with excited anticipation of the slow-roasted pernil that CLAP distributed for the Christmas holiday. Teri Mattson, a US peace activist who lived in Venezuela for several months around the time of my February 2019 visit, described a similar experience.

"My neighborhood was predominantly opposition," Mattson recalled. "Those people got food just as we in the Chavista household got food. The food was distributed through the Community Council, and the Community Council was majority opposition."

Rodríguez's academic review of CLAP confirmed that Mattson's experience—and my own—was not anecdotal. Synthesizing data from twenty-seven separate surveys conducted by Venezuelan pollster Datanalisis, Rodríguez calculated that nearly 70 percent of self-identified opposition respondents received CLAP benefits between the years 2016 and 2021 (Rodríguez June 2022).

While satiating sanctioned bellies, the CLAP initiative scored a key rhetorical point against the tale of a wicked Venezuelan dictator happily starving his own people.[9] If Washington's narrative were true, why would Maduro's government send millions of Venezuelan households a bounty of basic supplies on a monthly basis, virtually free of charge? In July 2019, an increasingly frustrated US Treasury lobbed sanctions against ten individuals and thirteen international corporations responsible for CLAP's triumph.

"They use food as a form of social control, to reward political supporters and punish opponents, all the while pocketing hundreds of millions of dollars through a number of fraudulent schemes," Treasury secretary Steve Mnuchin declared while announcing the measures.[10]

---

9   Siobhán O'Grady, "The U.S. Says Maduro Is Blocking Aid to Starving People. The Venezuelan Says His People Aren't Beggars." *Washington Post*, February 19, 2019.

10   "Treasury Disrupts Corruption Network Stealing from Venezuela's Food Distribution Program, CLAP," United States Department of the Treasury, July 25, 2019.

In time, Washington's mission to overthrow Venezuela's government would place the Colombian businessman most responsible for CLAP's success in the direct crosshairs of hybrid war.

In conjunction with its crusade against hunger, Maduro's government continued a Chávez-initiated campaign against homelessness in Venezuela. Since the 2011 launch of La Gran Misión Vivienda Venezuela (the Great Venezuelan Housing Mission), or GMVV, the Venezuelan state has provided over four million free or subsidized homes to low-income families.[11] While a portion of the properties were built following GMVV's initiation, others were procured through the federal expropriation of existing constructs like Fuerte Tiuna, a military base in southwest Caracas that Chávez partially converted into public housing. I visited Fuerte Tiuna in February 2019 and observed an oasis of urban security within a city previously defined by abject poverty and petty crime. It was through its effort to construct new social housing developments, however, that Maduro's government first encountered Alex Nain Saab Morán, a Colombian businessman who would ultimately sacrifice a life of wealth and privilege in defense of Venezuela's sanctioned public.

Saab was born to Lebanese immigrant parents in Barranquilla, Colombia, on December 21, 1971. The son of a successful industrialist in Colombia's textile sector, Saab launched his first business venture when he was just eighteen years old. As his compatriots scoffed at the revolutionary fervor engulfing their Venezuelan neighbor at the turn of the century, Saab eagerly looked across the border to cut deals. By 2004, his export company, Shantex S.A., relied on the Venezuelan market to supply roughly 82 percent of its earnings.[12]

Saab cemented his relationship with Chavismo in 2011, when he won a contract to provide building materials for Venezuela's public housing mission. Five years later, he signed a deal to procure goods for ten million CLAP boxes, marking his formal foray into Venezuela's

11   "Venezuelan Government Has Built 4.2 Million Homes So Far," Telesur, October 28, 2022.

12   "Los Países a Los Que Llegó La Plata Del Alex Saab," *El Espectador*, October 23, 2018.

fight against US hybrid war. In April 2018, Saab's successful effort to sustain CLAP inspired Venezuela's government to appoint him a special envoy of its Foreign Ministry, an act that granted the businessman official diplomatic status.[13]

Saab's work for CLAP was, for obvious reasons, shrouded in secrecy. Considering the entire program was designed to subvert unilateral US sanctions, the supply lines and deals Saab brokered were naturally subject to sabotage—especially as the Trump administration began issuing "secondary sanctions" against foreign entities conducting business with Caracas. The Treasury Department's 2019 attack on CLAP was primarily focused on Saab, asserting he operated "a vast corruption network" that enabled Venezuela's government to illegally profit from food imports and distribution (United States Department of the Treasury 2019).

The charges stemmed from a 2017 report by the pro-opposition Venezuelan news site Armando that purported to reveal a scheme through which Saab overcharged Venezuela's government for services related to CLAP so that he and others could pocket the surplus and profit immensely.[14] On its surface, the exposé appeared damning. Yet further analysis of the allegations—and reality of US financial war— placed Saab in a more sympathetic light.

Armando presented its fraud case against Saab by contrasting figures listed on his CLAP invoices with the market price of those same goods in other countries, concluding he overcharged the Caracas government for his own benefit. Yet without proper context, such comparisons were grossly misleading. By 2017, Washington's sanctions and decision to classify Venezuela as a "national security threat" had sufficiently raised the cost of doing business with Maduro's government in both figurative and literal terms. Francisco Rodríguez, the economist and Maduro critic, therefore argued that "the fact

13   "Defensa Presenta Cartas De Misión Aceptadas Por Irán En Inicio De Audiencia Probatoria De Alex Saab," *Fuser News*, December 12, 2022.

14   Armando.info (@ArmandoInfo), "Dos Apoderados Manejan a Group Gran Limited En México. Uno De Ellos Sería Hijo De Álvaro Pulido Vargas," Twitter post, September 3, 2017, https://twitter.com/ArmandoInfo/status/916800313377427457?s=20.

any firm providing goods or services to the Venezuelan government runs the risk of being accused of materially assisting" a sanctioned government—and thus risks incurring US sanctions itself—"implies that the prices of these goods and services will include a large risk premium that could well explain the difference with international prices" (Rodríguez June 2022). According to Rodríguez, the price discrepancies in Saab's invoices were therefore explained by "many factors and cannot in and of themselves be taken as evidence of corruption—particularly if they [happened] at the same time at which the risks of doing business with the Venezuelan government [were] increasing sharply." The economist highlighted Washington's decision to sanction two Mexican companies for establishing an oil-for-food agreement with Caracas as evidence that state and private entities alike faced major financial risks if they engaged with Venezuela's government.

A second allegation consistently lobbed at Saab was that he managed Venezuela's relationships with allies in Turkey and Iran, overseeing what is often characterized as an "illicit" network through which he traded Venezuelan gold for food and other goods. An April 2019 article in *Bloomberg*, for example, cited US investigators alleging that "Venezuela's gold and food trade with Turkey has evolved into a multilayered scheme built on a foundation of criminality," and placed Saab "at the center" of the conspiracy.[15] Though the US periodically threatened to punish Turkey for its economic relationship with Venezuela, Washington has so far resisted the urge to officially sanction its NATO ally.[16] Regardless, it is clear that both Turkey and Iran provided lifesaving assistance to Venezuela as its government resisted Washington's economic siege.

Turkish exports to Venezuela have increased dramatically since the onset of US sanctions on Caracas, reaching a monthly height of just under $30 million in March 2020 alone (before 2018, that figure rarely

15   Michael Smith and Monte Reel, "Venezuela's Trade Scheme With Turkey Is Enriching a Mysterious Maduro Crony," *Bloomberg Businessweek*, April 25, 2019.

16   Reuters Staff, "U.S. Will Act If Turkish Trade Violates Venezuela Sanctions, Official Says," Reuters, January 31, 2019.

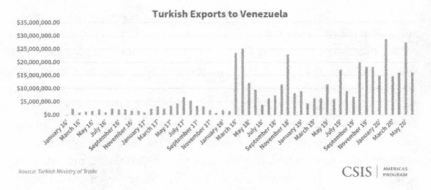

Source: Turkish Ministry of Trade

exceeded $5 million).[17] The surge began in March 2018, shortly after Saab became involved with Venezuelan trade negotiations.

Food products including wheat flour and chocolate make up the majority of Turkish exports to Venezuela. In 2021, pasta alone accounted for 40 percent of Turkish shipments to the country.[18] That same year, Turkey ranked as the second most common destination for Venezuelan exports, rivaled only by China. Venezuelan exports to Turkey consisted almost entirely of raw materials, with scrap iron accounting for just shy of 80 percent.

I have observed the results of the fortified Caracas-Ankara relationship firsthand. While staying with friends in Venezuela, I have seen Turkish products, including pasta, arrive as part of their monthly CLAP shipments. In fact, when I first visited Caracas in February 2019, posters welcoming Turkish president Recep Tayyip Erdoğan were still peeling from public street posts. Erdoğan had toured the Venezuelan capital just two months prior, marking the first time in history that a Turkish leader traveled to Venezuela for an official state visit.

"Political problems cannot be resolved by punishing an entire nation," Erdoğan said, articulating his contempt for US sanctions

17   Moises Rendon and Claudia Fernandez, "The Fabulous Five: How Foreign Actors Prop up the Maduro Regime in Venezuela" (See: "Turkish Exports to Venezuela"), Center for Strategic and International Studies, October 19, 2020.

18   "Turkey (Tur) and Venezuela (VEN) Trade," The Observatory of Economic Complexity, accessed April 6, 2023.

on Venezuela while standing shoulder to shoulder with Maduro in Caracas. "We do not approve of these measures that ignore the rules of global trade."[19]

Yet perhaps no alliance has proven more consequential for Venezuela than its blossoming partnership with Iran, a top target of US hybrid war ever since its 1979 Islamic Revolution. Chávez prioritized friendship with Iran from the outset of his presidency, signing roughly three hundred deals with Tehran, including the establishment of a joint-development fund, between 2001 and 2013 (Rendon and Fernandez 2020). Since Saab entered the picture, he has been credited with (or accused of, depending on who you ask) stimulating ties between Caracas and Tehran to unprecedented heights—an act that would eventually rescue Venezuela from the depths of a nationwide fuel crisis brought about by US economic war.

To fully grasp Venezuela's fuel crisis of 2020—and Saab's role in ending it—the fundamentals of oil production are instructive. While there are several ways to evaluate crude, it is primarily categorized according to weight: light, medium, or heavy. Light crude is the easiest to refine and therefore yields the highest percentage of fuel. Heavy crude, on the other hand, is thick and very difficult to pump (as one energy industry insider explained to me, "think of it as molten rubber"). Venezuela has *by far* the largest crude reserves in the world, with the US Geological Survey estimating that somewhere between 380 to 652 billion barrels flow beneath its territory.[20] Meanwhile Saudi Arabia, the country with the second largest reserves, sits atop a comparatively meager 87 billion barrels of oil and natural gas.[21]

Most of Venezuela's reserve consists of heavy crude. To become the gasoline and diesel required for fuel, Venezuelan oil must pass through an exhaustive extraction and refining process during which it is mixed

19   Corina Pons, "Turkey's Erdogan Slams Venezuela Sanctions, Maduro Defends Gold Exports," Reuters, December 3, 2018.

20   "An Estimate of Recoverable Heavy Oil Resources of the Orinoco Oil Belt, Venezuela," United States Geological Survey, accessed April 6, 2023.

21   "Does the Bakken Formation Contain More Oil than Saudi Arabia?" United States Geological Survey, accessed April 6, 2023.

with so-called "inputs," such as lighter crude and chemicals, that dilute it into a usable substance. Venezuela's capacity to implement that process was severely hampered in 2017, when Washington applied sanctions that severed Caracas from US financial markets (McNabb and Caine 2017), therefore blocking its access to foreign suppliers of the inputs needed to refine its crude. Within weeks of the measures' introduction, Venezuela experienced a steep decline in domestic oil production (Rodríguez January 2022).

Washington compounded attacks on Venezuela's petroleum sector amid its January 2019 push to install Guaidó as president, when the Trump administration banned the country's state oil company, PdVSA, from exporting crude to the US or conducting business with US entities (Wong and Casey 2019). Those measures, combined with Washington's repeated vow to administer secondary sanctions against third-party governments and entities willing to work with Caracas, led to yet another dramatic plunge in Venezuelan oil production, officially sparking a nationwide fuel shortage (Rodríguez January 2022).

Throughout 2019 and 2020, Venezuela was plagued with seemingly endless lines at gas stations. The resulting foreign media headlines perfectly served Washington's intent in administering the sanctions, deriding a socialist government endowed with the world's largest oil reserves for failing to provide fuel to its own citizens. According to the mainstream narrative, Maduro's mismanagement and socialist policies were to blame for the shortage—the rest was commentary.

As the crisis deepened and gas queues lengthened, Maduro dispatched a team of negotiators, including Saab, to an ally seven thousand miles away that had decades of experience struggling against US sanctions on its oil sector. Iran quickly agreed to a deal that exchanged Venezuelan gold for the light crude and other chemical inputs Caracas needed to revive domestic production capacity. When five Iranian oil tankers set out for the Venezuelan coast in early 2020, Washington transformed the Caribbean Sea into a theater for hybrid wargames.

"We're deploying additional navy destroyers, combat ships, aircraft and helicopters, coast guard cutters and air force surveillance aircraft, doubling our capabilities in the region," President Trump announced in April,[22] weeks before the Iranian ships were scheduled to dock. As the tankers entered Venezuela's territorial waters, however, the looming US naval patrol proved to be a futile bluff. On May 25, Venezuelan naval ships and fighter jets safely escorted the first Iranian tanker to its reception at Puerto Cabello in Estado Maracaibo.

"On behalf of all of us, we say to Iran from the Caribbean Sea: thank you for your solidarity and courage," Venezuelan oil minister Tareck El-Aissami proudly declared upon welcoming the ship and embracing its captain. "We are not anyone's colony, and we never will be. We are rebellious, Caribbean people, full of glory and virtue."[23]

Iran's intervention marked the dramatic end of Venezuela's fuel crisis, enabling Caracas to double domestic oil production in the year 2021.[24] Yet just as the Tehran-Caracas partnership succeeded in alleviating the suffering of ordinary Venezuelans, so it placed a target on the back of the men who'd fostered it. El-Aissami, an eternal object of obsession for US media thanks to his Syrian-Lebanese heritage (which the press routinely capitalized on to brand him a secret agent of Hezbollah), earned a spot on Washington's de facto hit list as a result of the shipments. Mere weeks before the Iranian tankers docked at Puerto Cabello, the US State Department placed a $10 million bounty on El-Aissami's head, which it justified with allegations of narcotrafficking.[25]

Yet no man bore the brunt of Washington's frustrated hybrid war quite like Saab. As he set out for Tehran in the immediate aftermath of Venezuela's triumph at Puerto Cabello, US officials initiated a depraved plan to hinder his diplomatic effort to feed and fuel Venezuela once and for all.

---

22   "US Sends Warships to Caribbean to Stop Illegal Drugs," BBC, April 2, 2020.

23   Gianfranco Ruggiero, "El Aissami: 'El Buque Fortune Se Convirtió En Símbolo De Hermandad Entre Irán y Venezuela,'" *El Co-Operante*, May 25, 2020.

24   Mardo Soghom, "Venezuela Boosting Oil Exports With Iranian Light Crude Supplies," *Iran International*, May 23, 2022.

25   "Tareck Zaidan El Aissami Maddah- New Target," United States Department of State, March 26, 2020.

On June 12, 2020, Maduro dispatched Saab on an official mission to Iran, where he tasked the diplomat with procuring medicine, food, and other humanitarian supplies for Venezuela's sanctioned population. En route to Tehran, Saab's jet made a brief service stop on the Cape Verdean Island of Sal, a routine excursion that did not require him to exit the plane or pass through immigration. Yet as Saab's aircraft refueled on the tarmac of Amílcar Cabral International Airport, Cape Verdean authorities suddenly demanded that he disembark from the jet and purchase a visa—despite the fact he did not plan to enter the country. When Saab complied with the bizarre request, local police promptly placed him under arrest—an extraordinary act that disregarded his diplomatic status, immunity, and by extension, international law.

To justify their action, authorities in Praia claimed to have detained Saab in compliance with an Interpol Red Notice seeking his arrest. Yet while Interpol did eventually post a Red Notice for Saab, it did not issue the communique until June 13—one day following the diplomat's detention in Cape Verde.

"They were simply trying to work out the answer after the arrest," Femi Falana, a member of Saab's legal team, told me in June 2021. "They went looking for the Red Notice to justify [it]."[26]

Interpol's former director of legal affairs, Dutch lawyer Rutsel Martha, reinforced Falana's view, asserting the agency "breached" official protocol "in Mr. Saab's case."[27] Speaking to Nigerian media in January 2021, Martha offered his own explanation for discrepancies in the timing of Saab's arrest, alleging US authorities only submitted a formal Interpol request for his detention *after* they learned the diplomat planned to refuel in Cape Verde. Martha pointed to the fact that local authorities took multiple unnecessary steps designed to delay Saab's departure from Sal—including forcing him to obtain a visa—as evidence that Washington had ordered Praia to stall his takeoff until Interpol issued the Red Notice.

26   Anya Parampil, "US Kidnaps Venezuelan Diplomat: the Case of Alex Saab," *The Grayzone*, June 4, 2021.

27   Samson Adenekan, "Ex-INTERPOL Director Faults Arrest of Venezuelan Diplomat in Cape Verde," *Premium Times*, January 30, 2021.

"Without doubt, at the time they arrested him there was no Red Notice from Interpol, nor arrest warrant from Cape Verde—this makes his arrest arbitrary and illegal," the ex-Interpol chief argued, noting the agency's Red Notice protocol is "not instantaneous," and would have even required Washington to notify Saab that it planned to pursue his detention.

"Cape Verde was acting on the orders of the United States government," Femi Falana, Saab's lawyer, informed me with confidence.

Felana's claims were further backed by media reports that a private jet owned by US government contractor Presidential Aviation idled at Amílcar Cabral International Airport for days following Saab's detention.[28] According to tracking data, the plane was on standby for a chartered flight to Miami, Florida—where a sealed indictment on money laundering charges secretly awaited Saab.[29]

Assertions that Washington orchestrated the diplomat's extrajudicial kidnapping were ultimately confirmed by Trump's own secretary of state. In his 2023 memoir, *Never Give an Inch*, Mike Pompeo wrote that Trump's Venezuela Envoy and Iran-Contra crook Elliott Abrams first briefed him on the plot days before it went into effect. According to Pompeo, Abrams informed him that "some clever Drug Enforcement Agency folks had a chance to nab" Saab "while he was on a mission to arrange a swap of Venezuelan gold for Iranian oil."[30] Upon learning the diplomat's jet would stop in Sal to refuel, Pompeo said he "called Attorney General Bill Barr and arranged for our ambassador in Cape Verde and the Department of Justice to file the paperwork for Saab's extradition to the United States."

Pompeo continued his unrestrained admission of guilt with pompous imperial pride: "Suffice it to say that no other nation has the global reach to interrupt an Iranian-Venezuelan plot in real time and convince a small island nation to hold a wanted man."

28   Joshua Goodman, "Venezuela Demands Release of Businessman Connected to Maduro," Associated Press, June 15, 2020.

29   "Colombian Businessman Charged with Money Laundering Extradited to the United States from Cabo Verde," United States Department of Justice (Southern District of Florida, October 19, 2021).

30   Mike Pompeo, *Never Give an Inch: Fighting for the America I Love* (New York, NY: Broadside Books, 2023).

Yet even as Pompeo and his collaborators succeeded in extralegally apprehending Saab, the diplomat's journey to Florida was not guaranteed. Before the US could put Saab on trial in Miami, it would have to physically transfer him to Florida—a task complicated by the fact that no formal extradition treaty existed between Washington and Praia.

"Unless Cape Verde is a banana republic, it cannot allow the United State government to order the detention of an envoy who was on a humanitarian mission," Falana asserted during our June 2021 interview, underscoring his client's claim to diplomatic immunity.

For the neoconservative ideologues commandeering Trump's Latin America policy, however, ducking and dodging the law was a preferred pastime.

Four months following Saab's June 2020 arrest, a US naval cruiser called the USS *San Jacinto* set out from the Chesapeake Bay of Norfolk, Virginia, on a 3,500-mile transatlantic quest. The 567-foot warship and its 393-strong crew were destined for the coast of Africa's western-most archipelago, Cape Verde.

Though no formal war had been declared upon Praia, hawks embedded within Trump's administration had dispatched the *San Jacinto* in a bid to pressure Cape Verde into extraditing Saab. Their belligerent ploy was exposed in a December 2020 *New York Times* report detailing how "hard-liners at the Justice and State Departments," particularly Abrams, had pushed for the ship's deployment out of fear "the United States would lose an unusual opportunity to punish Mr. Maduro" if Saab's detention lingered on.[31] Abrams and his cronies claimed that without a strong US naval presence in West African waters, Iranian or Venezuelan Special Forces units would venture to invade Cape Verde and break Saab out of prison.

According to then US defense secretary Mark Esper, the paranoiac allegation was just one of several unsubstantiated rumors that Abrams circulated about the diplomat. In his 2022 memoir, *A Sacred Oath,* Esper

---

31   Eric Schmitt and Julie Turkewitz, "Navy Warship's Secret Mission Off West Africa Aims to Help Punish Venezuela," *New York Times*, December 22, 2020.

detailed a slew of wild theories that Abrams and his colleagues floated regarding Saab:

> Maduro persuaded President Putin and Russian special forces to spring Saab from jail; Russian mercenaries in Libya were going to travel hundreds of miles in small boats to either rescue or kill Saab; Venezuelan intelligence was chartering a special plane to fly to Cape Verde to repatriate Saab; and Iranian Revolutionary Guard troops were preparing similar rescue missions.[32]

Just as their weapons of mass destruction had nearly two decades prior, the Axis of Evil's commando squads failed to materialize, and the *San Jacinto* ultimately returned to Norfolk in time for the Christmas holiday. By then, US taxpayers had financed the warship's deployment to the tune of $52,000 a day—a total of roughly $1.5 million for its month-long mission to nowhere.

"It seemed that somebody was watching too many *Mission: Impossible* movies," Esper joked, referring to one of the US officials (perhaps Abrams?) who concocted the hysterical drama. "I never saw intelligence that backed any of it up."

Weeks before the *San Jacinto*'s journey, the US sent another vessel, a coast guard cutter called the *Bear*, to Cape Verde, establishing an armed presence in its waters under the guise of countering illegal fishing.[33] On top of military pressure, Washington attempted to effectively bribe Cape Verde into extraditing Saab. Following the diplomat's detention, US officials rolled out a conveniently timed $100 million direct investment initiative in the Cape Verdean economy alongside plans to spend $300 million renovating its Praia embassy.[34] Meanwhile, Saab's lawyers accused Cape Verdean authorities of routinely blocking them

32   Mark T. Esper, *Sacred Oath: Memoirs of a Secretary of Defense during Extraordinary Times* (New York, NY: HarperCollins, 2023), 328.

33   "U.S. Coast Guard Cutter Bear Underway," Defense Visual Information Distribution Center, October 28, 2020.

34   "US to Inject $100m into Cape Verdean Economy; Begins Construction of New Embassy," *Business and Financial Times Online*, July 6, 2021.

from meeting with their client while subjecting him to dehumanizing, torturous conditions. On top of obstructing his legal counsel, local authorities denied Saab access to his personal medical team despite the fact he was a recovering cancer patient.

"He is being kept substantially incommunicado," Falana told me in June 2021 (Parampil June 2021). That same month, CNN published a handwritten interview with Saab that offered a portrait of his persecution in Praia's hands.

"I've been physically and psychologically tortured, I've been denied the specialized medical attention that I need. I was kept in a cell with only an hour of daylight a day," Saab wrote, denouncing the US case against him as a "political action" that lacked proof or legal justification.[35] Indeed, earlier that year prosecutors in Geneva concluded an investigation into Saab's Swiss bank accounts and determined there was "no further evidence" to pursue a money laundering case against the diplomat.

"The public prosecutor's office will move to discontinue these criminal proceedings," Swiss authorities announced on March 26, dealing a major blow to Washington's persecution of Saab.[36]

In December 2020, a regional court for the Economic Community of West African States (ECOWAS), of which Cape Verde is a member, demanded that its government transfer Saab to house arrest[37]—an order which Praia complied with the following month. Weeks later, the ECOWAS court formally ordered Cape Verde to release Saab based on the fact that the Interpol Red Notice seeking his detention had only been issued *after* his arrest.[38] The court further demanded Praia "discontinue all proceedings and processes aimed at extraditing Saab to the US," and even instructed its government to pay the diplomat $200,000

35   Vasco Cotovio and Isa Soares, "Alleged Financier for Venezuelan President Nicolas Maduro Says He Fears Being Extradited to the US," CNN, June 18, 2021.

36   "Switzerland Not To Investigate Venezuelan Diplomatic Envoy," Telesur English, March 26, 2021.

37   Reuters Staff, "Court Grants House Arrest to Maduro Envoy Jailed in Cape Verde, Lawyers Say," Reuters, December 4, 2020.

38   Reuters Staff, "West African Court Orders Release of Maduro Envoy in Cape Verde," Reuters, March 15, 2021.

in damages. Praia ignored the decision. Instead, on March 16, 2021—mere hours after the ECOWAS ruling—Cape Verde's Supreme Court formally approved Saab's extradition to the United States.

Praia did not officially ship the diplomat to Miami until October 16. At around 4:52 p.m. local time, a Gulfstream owned by the US Justice Department took off from Cape Verde for an unlisted, northwestern-bound destination.[39] Hours later, Cape Verde's national radio station confirmed that its government had indeed extradited Saab to the US,[40] where federal prosecutors promptly unsealed a money laundering indictment against him. The diplomat's first Miami court appearance was set for October 18.

The timing of Saab's extradition exposed yet another layer of Cape Verde's neocolonial subservience. Within hours of his October 16 extradition, Cape Verde's ruling Movement for Democracy Party suffered an overwhelming defeat in national elections, losing to the African Party for the Independence of Cape Verde (PAICV) by a nearly 10-point margin.[41] The triumph of PAICV—the inheritor of anti-colonial leader Amílcar Cabral's political legacy—spelled disaster for US efforts to extradite Saab. It was impossible to imagine a scenario in which PAICV's candidate, José Maria Neves, complied with Washington's extradition request. Though we may never know what pressure the US unleashed on Praia in its final push to obtain Saab, it is clear Washington fast-tracked his extradition in anticipation of the Cape Verdean left's electoral victory.

Fit for the catwalks of Milan or the cover of *Vogue*, it is unlikely that Italian model Camilla Fabri Saab ever expected to be the face of an international campaign to free an abducted diplomat, yet that is precisely what she has become. On October 18, 2021, she emerged into the Caracas sunlight and delivered an emotional statement about the

---

39   Joshua Goodman, (@APjoshgoodman), Twitter post, October 16, 2021, https://twitter.com/APjoshgoodman/status/1449459796151840776.

40   Mayela Armas and Deisy Buitrago, "Venezuelan Government Suspends Negotiations with Opposition," Reuters, October 17, 2021.

41   Julio Rodrigues, "Opposition Candidate Neves Wins Cape Verde Election," Reuters, October 18, 2021.

plight of her husband, Alex, who appeared in US court for the first time that same day.

"We will always be a united family, we are very close to each other," Fabri Saab declared as she addressed a crowd of supporters and media gathered in the Venezuelan capital.[42]

"Now that he has been kidnapped, we feel kidnapped as well," she continued between sobs. "But like him, we will continue this struggle."

I spoke with Fabri Saab in December 2021.

"I am doing this interview for Alex," she told me.[43]

"All the interviews and all the demonstrations, that is for Alex," she continued. "I want the world to know the truth. Alex is innocent, and he was only trying to bring medicine and food to the Venezuelan people."

Fabri Saab went on to recount how Alex maintained regular contact with her throughout his internment in Cape Verde by smuggling letters in and out of prison. She also described the difficulties she faced while raising her two daughters—the youngest of which was only five months old when Alex was kidnapped—without their father.

"She doesn't even know her father," Fabri Saab lamented. "My other daughter, Maryam Rose—she is in love with her father. She's four and a half years old now, and she always asks me for [him]," she added, explaining the situation was too complex for either girl to comprehend.

Fabri Saab twice attempted to visit Alex with their daughters during his detention in Cape Verde, but authorities in Praia denied their request on both occasions and eventually declared her "persona non grata." While cutting him off from his wife and children, Saab's captors deprived him of the ability to grieve the death of his mother and father. Fabri Saab informed me that when her husband's parents passed away within nine days of each other in April 2021, Cape Verdean authorities denied him permission to attend their funerals.

In addition to psychological torment, Fabri Saab was keenly aware of the physical torture her husband endured in Cape Verde. She recalled

---

42   MV English, (@MV_Eng), Twitter post, October 18, 2021, https://twitter.com/MV_Eng/status/1450226433264078850.

43   Anya Parampil, "Alex Saab: Wife of Kidnapped Diplomat Describes His Torture & Illegal Arrest," *The Grayzone*, December 7, 2021.

that the first letter she received from her husband was dated five days after his arrest. In the note, Saab explained that he spent the first three days of his detention in a subterranean jail cell, where authorities placed a bag over his head, denied him food and water, and interrogated him. Guards eventually transferred Saab to a cell that lacked a mattress, pillow, or bathroom. Though his new quarters offered a small window to the outside world, Saab's captors covered it with a black panel.

Cape Verdean authorities ultimately moved Saab to solitary confinement after claiming he was cutting himself with pens—an allegation of self-harm that his wife firmly rejected. According to Fabri Saab, authorities crafted the accusation as justification for their decision to confiscate her husband's writing utensils, an act that effectively severed Alex's communication with his legal counsel and family. Fabri Saab said the move backfired, however, when other prisoners in the jail "saw the injustice" and formed an effort to pass their own pens to the diplomat through a small opening in his cell.

"In solidarity, every prisoner threw one pen every time they passed [Alex's cell]," Fabri Saab divulged, adding that the detainees would shout the Portuguese word for pen, *caneta*, while carrying out the act. Alex told Camilla that the longer he resisted his captors' demand that he sign off on his voluntary extradition to the US, the more violent they became.

Saab's prosecution—and persecution—was designed to achieve a far more ambitious goal than one man's personal torment. Though the US government's case against the diplomat concerned allegations that he laundered funds related to the construction of Venezuela's public housing mission, Saab's advocates maintained the charges were simply a pretext for his extradition. Once the diplomat was in Miami, US authorities would focus on their actual target: the nascent international network forming in opposition to Washington's global financial war.

Even by their own admission, US authorities were far less interested in pursuing their money laundering case against Saab than they were in pressuring him to defect from Venezuela's government and disclose the clandestine avenues through which Caracas evaded Washington's sanctions. A confession of the true motive behind Saab's detention and torture was printed in the December 2020 *Times* report on the USS *San*

Jacinto's deployment to Cape Verde. Buried in the piece, the *Times* conceded that Saab's captivity "stripped Mr. Maduro of an important ally and a major financial fixer at a time when fewer countries are willing or able to come to Venezuela's aid" (Schmitt and Turkewitz 2020).

"If Mr. Saab cooperates with American officials," the *Times* posited, "he could help untangle Mr. Maduro's economic web of support and assist the authorities in bringing charges against other allies of the Venezuelan government."

An October 2021 explanation of the diplomat's case in *Forbes* similarly admitted that "for the US, Saab is the key that unlocks the Venezuelan monetary mystery—that is, how a country facing sanctions from the US, the UK and the European Union—is still able to export things like gold and oil."[44] The article described Saab as "the only man who can actually explain how the country survives today," before noting that "when he arrives in US custody, [he] will become a serious information asset for the US in understanding just how the country does business."

Defense Secretary Esper and Secretary of State Pompeo confirmed Washington's desire to flip Saab in their respective memoirs. Both men explained their interest in Venezuela was largely driven by frustration with Caracas's fruitful alliance with designated US enemy states, with Esper asserting that "allowing countries like Russia, China, and Iran to gain strength . . . in the Western Hemisphere was of great concern" (Esper 2022, 296). Pompeo took a more openly ideological position, writing without a hint of irony that when it came to Venezuela, "in the Spirit of the Monroe Doctrine, we shouldn't allow China, Russia, and Iran to interfere in the system of sovereign nations" (Pompeo 2023, 346–347). Neither man appeared to consider the fact that it was Washington's own misguided economic war that had driven Caracas into the arms of Moscow, Beijing, and Tehran to begin with.

To Esper and Pompeo, Saab was the linchpin of these "illicit" relationships. His detention, therefore, was part of Washington's overall strategy to besiege Venezuela and its powerful friends. While boasting of his hand in the diplomat's kidnapping, Pompeo remarked: "We may never know how much oil we kept away from Maduro—it depends on

---

44   David Dawkins, "Moneyman for Venezuela-Accused of Looting Billions-Nears Extradition to the U.S.," *Forbes*, October 1, 2021.

what Saab, who is now in jail in the United States on money-laundering charges, chooses to share with us" (Pompeo 2023, 351).

Esper echoed Pompeo's hope the diplomat would cooperate with US authorities and divulge Venezuela's methods for evading sanctions, writing "Saab was a very important player, and access to him could really help explain how Maduro and his regime worked" (Esper 2022, 327).

"It was important to get custody of him," the former Raytheon executive continued, adding, "This could provide a real road map for the US government to unravel the Venezuelan government's illicit schemes and bring them to justice."

What the *Times*, *Forbes*, Pompeo, and Esper failed to understand, however, was that their allegations of Saab's "illicit schemes" were informed through the prism of US law.

While Saab may have overseen bank transfers between Caracas and Tehran, for example, that violated US sanctions in theory, in reality the US Treasury's jurisdiction did not include agreements and transactions established between foreign (and therefore, sovereign) governments. What's more, over a year of torment and isolation in Cape Verde failed to move Saab to sell out Caracas—a reality that appeared unchanged following his arrival in Miami, much to the chagrin of Pompeo and Esper.

"What bothers the United States the most about him, my husband, is that he will never, ever surrender," Fabri Saab announced during the press conference following her husband's extradition.

"*Never*," she emphasized before a crowd of cheering Venezuelans.

Acting as de-facto guerilla units resisting a modern medieval siege, Venezuela's CLAP committees would have been powerless against the force of US hybrid war if not for the sacrifice of Alex Saab. This fact, combined with Saab's successful drive to neutralize US attacks on Venezuela's oil sector, transformed the businessman turned diplomat into a lieutenant general in the global fight against Western financial tyranny. Though international law seldom hindered Washington's imperial exploits in the past, US officials had yet to make the exceptional decision to kidnap and torture a foreign dignitary before their treatment of Saab. The only comparable case is perhaps that of WikiLeaks founder Julian Assange, an Australian citizen whom British authorities extralegally abducted from Ecuador's London embassy in 2019 under orders from the United States. As with Saab, Washington sought Assange's extradition over a sealed indictment that US prosecutors unveiled *after* his arrest. Ultimately, the cases of Saab and Assange demonstrate Washington's conviction that its legal jurisdiction knows no Earthly boundary.

Judge Robert Scola of the US District Court of Southern Florida dismissed all seven money laundering charges filed against Saab in November 2021, leaving him to face a single count of *conspiracy* to commit money laundering. The following December, I attended an evidentiary hearing in Saab's Miami trial. Over the course of two days, Saab's defense team implored Judge Scola to honor their client's diplomatic status and throw out the case altogether. To support Saab's claim to diplomatic immunity, his lawyers disclosed that he was carrying official Venezuelan government documents, including a letter personally addressed from President Maduro to Iran's Supreme Leader, Ayatollah Ali Khamenei, at the time of his detention. Photographs of the envelopes and dramatic testimony from Saab's Cape Verdean attorney, Florian Mandl, revealed that an anonymous hand—Cape Verdean or otherwise—had opened the sealed diplomatic communiques following his arrest.

Maduro's letter to Ayatollah Khamenei was a heartfelt expression of gratitude for Iran's assistance in recuperating his country's sanctioned oil sector.

"I am writing to you in the name of God, the Merciful, on behalf of the people of Venezuela and the Government that honors me preside, to thank you from the deepest soul of this Earth, for the support you have bravely and resolutely given to Venezuela, upholding international law and laying bare empires made of paper," Maduro wrote.[45]

Judge Scola denied Saab's request for diplomatic immunity on December 23, 2022. The US released Saab and returned him to Venezuela as part of a prisoner swap in December 2023.

45   Anya Parampil, "US Trial of Venezuela's Alex Saab Exposes Diplomatic Espionage," *The Grayzone*, December 12, 2022.

THREE

THE "SEXY TRICKS" OF INFORMATION WAR

As far as Anglos are concerned, Mexican American news anchor Jorge Ramos is the most popular TV personality in Spanish language media. He is the face of Univision, a multinational corporate network that consistently ranks as the most-watched Spanish language channel in the United States. Within days of Washington's recognition of Guaidó, Venezuelan president Nicolás Maduro attempted to reach Univision's vast audience by welcoming Ramos to Caracas—a media strategy that was virtually guaranteed to result in superfluous melodrama.

Around the time of Ramos's February 2019 visit with Maduro, Washington announced its intent to force a convoy of "humanitarian aid" into Venezuela and began assembling a military presence on its border with Colombia to oversee the delivery.[1] Venezuelan officials—and many average citizens—viewed the shipment, which was scheduled for February 23, as an attempted invasion of their country. They noted that because neither the United Nations nor the International Red Cross were managing the operation, the aid would ultimately have to be rammed across Venezuela's border by the US military. Fears the cargo contained more than charity were underscored by the fact that Elliott Abrams—a man who previously weaponized "humanitarian aid" deliveries to covertly ship arms to paramilitary groups in Nicaragua[2]—was actively crafting US policy toward Venezuela at the time.

1   Reuters Staff, "Venezuela's Guaido Says Humanitarian Aid Will Arrive on Feb 23," Reuters, February 12, 2019.

2   AP, Special to the *New York Times*, "Abrams Denies Wrongdoing In Shipping Arms to Contras," *New York Times*, August 17, 1987.

In anticipation of the US military threat, Venezuela's government set up a makeshift blockade consisting of an oil tanker and shipping containers along the Tienditas bridge that ran across its border with Colombia. Though the bridge had never been open to public traffic,[3] the resulting visual fueled Washington's narrative that Maduro was not only starving his own people, but so indifferent to their suffering that he would even deny them foreign charity. The stunt's success was entirely reliant on the press' willingness to accept that version of events without question—and Washington found no greater collaborator than Univision's leading man.

Like many in corporate US media, Ramos made his name in television via a relentless drive to place himself at the center of The Story. His most notable exhibition in showmanship came in 2015, when he courted the attention of establishment liberals by confronting then candidate Trump at a press conference in Dubuque, Iowa. Though Trump opened the junket by calling on a different reporter, Ramos immediately leapt from his seat and began barking out questions on immigration policy.

"Sit down, you weren't called. Go back to Univision," Trump demanded, attempting to proceed with the presser.[4]

When Ramos refused to yield the floor, Trump bodyguard Keith Schiller escorted the spotlight-hungry reporter out of the room. Though Ramos was eventually allowed to return and ask questions, his grandstanding and subsequent ejection transformed him into an instant hero of the anti-Trump Beltway Resistance™. Corporate media outlets played his exchange with the candidate on loop, heralding Ramos as a crusading journalist standing up to Trump on behalf of voiceless migrants. Yet while the urge to challenge Trump's comments about Mexican immigrants (whom he characterized as criminals, drug dealers, and rapists)[5] may have been understandable, the truth is that no reporter, no matter

3   Intercepted, "NEOLIBERALISM OR DEATH: THE U.S. ECONOMIC WAR AGAINST VENEZUELA," *The Intercept*, February 13, 2019.

4   Joy Y Yang, "Donald Trump Says Anchor Jorge Ramos Was 'Totally, Absolutely Out of Line'," NBC News, August 25, 2021.

5   "'Drug Dealers, Criminals, Rapists': What Trump Thinks of Mexicans," BBC, August 31, 2016.

how prominent, is entitled to ask questions at a press conference. Any workaday journalist who has sat through hours of interminable questions and long-winded answers is well aware they could never get away with the flamboyant behavior Ramos displayed in Dubuque.

That reality did not stop Ramos's Anglo colleagues from inundating him with praise and admiration. Canadian government broadcaster CBC, for example, produced a thirteen-minute profile of the Univision host titled "Why Jorge Ramos Took on Trump." During the report, Ramos admitted that his crew had conspired to stage the confrontation with Trump before they even boarded the plane to Iowa.

"Television does not happen, television is produced," Ramos explained. "It's created."[6]

The confession offered a window into Ramos's bizarre view of his function as a "journalist." Most reporters operate with an awareness that their duty is not to *produce* the news, but digest and report it. Ramos, however, apparently imagined himself as the star of his own personal telenovela in which he "created" the news and performed it for viewers—a role he took far beyond US borders.

Ramos's theatrical style was on full display when he traveled to Venezuela's Miraflores Palace for a sit-down interview with President Maduro. Long before any footage of the exchange was published, reports emerged that local authorities had "detained" Ramos as the conversation concluded. The news anchor eventually surfaced on social media to claim that Venezuelan police had indeed sequestered his team, held them for two hours, confiscated their equipment, and seized their cell phones. In a video posted from his Caracas hotel, Ramos explained the incident occurred after he whipped out an iPad and offered to show Maduro footage of hungry Venezuelan children scouring dumpsters for food.

"He just couldn't stand it, he didn't want to continue the interview," the white-haired, delicate-featured newsman recalled.[7] Less than twenty-four hours later, Ramos and his crew left Venezuela.

6   "Why Jorge Ramos Took on Trump," *CBS News: The National*, October 18, 2016.

7   "Jorge Ramos Explains What Happened during the Interview with Maduro and in His Detention," Univision Noticias, February 26, 2019.

As corporate media and international freedom of the press organizations rallied to denounce Venezuela's government for its handling of Ramos,[8] Caracas released limited information about the imbroglio. Communications Minister Jorge Rodríguez, the government's de facto spokesman, promptly denounced the episode as a "montage" choreographed by the State Department. In a February 25 tweet, Rodríguez noted that "hundreds of journalists have passed through Miraflores and received decent treatment."[9]

"We don't lend ourselves to cheap shows," he added.

Indeed, Maduro sat down for hostile interviews with Western networks including the BBC,[10] ABC,[11] and Euronews[12] within days of Ramos's trip to Venezuela. Though each of those interviews were subsequently published, Ramos expressed doubt that his conversation with Maduro would ever see the light of day.

"At this point we don't have a cellphone or the interview, I think we'll never have that interview," he bemoaned. "They don't want the world to see what we did."

But the world *would* eventually see what they did. Just over three months following Ramos's trip to Caracas, Univision announced that it would air the interview between its lead anchor and Venezuela's embattled president. According to the network, it secured a copy of the ostensibly disappeared tape thanks to "news sources in Venezuela" who "got their hands on the video" and "smuggled" it out of the country.[13] Univision's account sounded more like a played out TV script than a plausible explanation for the tape's sudden appearance, but no

8   Carlos Garcia Rawlins, "Univision Team Deported from Venezuela after Maduro Interview," Reuters, February 26, 2019.

9   Jorge Rodríguez, Twitter post, February 25, 2019, https://x.com/jorgerpsuv/status/1100210145592774658?s=20.

10   Orla Guerin, "Venezuela President Nicolás Maduro Interview: Full Transcript," February 12, 2019.

11   Tom Llamas, "Venezuelan President Nicolas Maduro's Defiant Interview with Tom Llamas: TRANSCRIPT," ABC News, February 27, 2019.

12   Anelise Borges, "Maduro Declares Challenge to His Leadership 'over' as He Attacks EU," Euronews, March 13, 2019.

13   Veronica Villafañe, "Univision Recovers And Will Air Confiscated Jorge Ramos Interview With Nicolás Maduro," *Forbes*, May 30, 2019.

one bothered to question Ramos. Instead, outlets from the Associated Press[14] to the *Daily Mail*[15] printed virtual commercials for "La Entrevista Censurada," pumping up a broadcast that would feature "Ramos providing context to what transpired during and following the exchange in pre-recorded special segments" (Villafañe 2019).

The "censured" interview aired at 7:00 p.m. on Sunday, June 2. It opened with a shot of President Maduro and Ramos seated face to face in ornate, gold chairs situated within the gardens of Venezuela's presidential palace. A cascading water fountain splashed behind them, generating a constant, serene gurgle. Ramos opened the interview with an insult.

"You know you are not the legitimate president. So, what should I call you?"[16]

Maduro briefly referenced a pocket-sized edition of Venezuela's constitution, which he held to his shoulder, before launching his response.

"I only have one name: Nicolás. Nicolás Maduro Moros. I am a worker. A simple man. I am popular. I was voted and reelected into office. So, it is up to you what to call me. But I have welcomed you here at Miraflores Presidential Palace," he calmly replied as Ramos leapt to interrupt him.

The Univision host's antagonistic tone had been established. Ramos proceeded to direct one loaded question or charged statement after another at Maduro, loudly speaking over the president's words and cutting off his attempts to reply.

"I am just a journalist," Ramos insisted with an air of self-importance as their exchange heated up.

"You are not a journalist Jorge, you know this," Maduro shot back, branding Ramos a "right-wing opponent of the revolution."

---

14   Jorge Rueda, "Univision Says It Recovered Contentious Maduro Interview," *Associated Press*, May 30, 2019.

15   Adry Torres and The Associated Press, "'You Are Going to Swallow Your Provocations with a Coca-Cola': Univision Recovers the Footage of Its Tense Interview with Venezuelan President Nicolás Maduro That Was Cut Short and Led to the Detention and Deportation of Journalist Jorge Ramos," *Daily Mail*, May 30, 2019.

16   Jorge Ramos, "Complete Interview of Jorge Ramos to Nicolás Maduro," *Univision Noticias*, June 2, 2019.

Venezuela's president went on to explain that he agreed to sit down with Ramos knowing the interview would be contentious because he wanted to "speak to the many Venezuelans who live in the United States."

Yet Maduro was hardly allowed to speak or even finish a thought, as his interviewer peppered him with relentless declarations, including "Your revolution has failed terribly." At one point, Ramos tried to hand Maduro a list of four hundred Venezuelan "political prisoners," many of them violent *guarimberos*, in a ploy to embarrass the president with a prepared political prop.

"Take your trash, Jorge Ramos," Maduro declared, rejecting the papers. "You will swallow your provocation with Coca-Cola," he added, equating Ramos's performance with a corporate US formula.

"People are eating from the trash, I saw it," Ramos pressed Maduro near the conclusion of their discussion.

"I saw it in New York, I saw it in Miami," Maduro retorted.

After subjecting himself to just over fifteen minutes' worth of Ramos's sensationalistic antics, Maduro ended the discussion.

"This interview doesn't make any sense for me or for you," he posited as Ramos announced his wish to show the president a video of a man picking through trash in central Caracas. "I think it's best to end it."

Maduro thanked Ramos for his time and walked off camera as the Univision anchor held up his iPad and continued blabbing at an invisible subject. With that, Ramos's "entrevista censurada" came to an end.

Video of the exchange contradicted Ramos's claim that Maduro had canceled their discussion after being presented with a video of hungry children. Instead, it captured the president of a sovereign nation growing increasingly agitated with his interviewer's constant interruptions and disrespectful behavior until he simply gave up on the conversation. By the time the interview aired, however, Ramos had already fulfilled his duty to "create" news. As was often the case, the controversy generated by Ramos's histrionics proved far more significant than the actual content of his "report."

Washington's hype campaign for its February 23 invasion of Venezuela under the guise of a humanitarian aid mission transcended Univision's studios. Leading the festival of interventionist cheerleading was CNN correspondent Nick Valencia, who filed a February 17 dispatch from an airport tarmac in Cúcuta, Colombia, as US military aircraft described simply as "aid planes" taxied behind him.[17] From his post mere miles from the border, Valencia reported the planes contained goods such as "rice, beans," and other household products that could not be found in Venezuela—an assertion easily debunked by anyone who bothered to actually visit the country.

My colleagues and I watched Valencia's report from our Caracas apartment with bemusement. By then, we had perused several local grocery stores and confirmed for ourselves that the products he listed were readily available for purchase. It seemed the images of empty supermarket shelves churned out at the height of Venezuela's supply shortage were by then a relic of the past. Instead, the question for Venezuelans we met was not whether they could find certain goods, but whether they could afford them. At the time, the buying power of average Venezuelans was severely hampered by a skyrocketing hyper-inflation rate that soared to an all-time high of 165,400 percent in February 2019.[18]

Venezuela's absurdly high inflation rate was the deliberate prod-uct of neoliberal design. Throughout modern history, Venezuela's vast oil wealth had allowed it to function as a "petrostate"—a reality long predating its 1998 revolution. This meant the country largely failed to develop domestic production capabilities beyond its oil sector and was therefore overwhelmingly reliant on imports to secure basic goods like toilet paper and baby formula.[19] Throughout its neoliberal period, the US and Europe happily enabled Caracas's import dependence in exchange for dominion of its oil fields. As Venezuela reasserted sovereign authority over its land, however, those vital foreign supply chains withered.

17   Nick Valencia, "U.S. Aid Blocked by President Maduro," CNN, February 17, 2019.

18   Steve Hanke, "Venezuela's Hyperinflation, 29 Months and Counting," Jewish Policy Center, 2019.

19   William Neuman and Patricia Torres, "Venezuela's Economy Suffers as Import Schemes Siphon Billions," New York Times, May 5, 2015.

As detailed in chapter one, by 2015 US sanctions had drastically limited Venezuela's import capacity, spurred a nationwide scarcity crisis, and plunged the country into the most dramatic economic contraction in Latin America's recorded history (Rodríguez, January 2022). As products became unavailable, a robust black market for basic goods cropped up beyond the government's reach, driving up inflation through the rudimentary laws of supply and demand.

Throughout the import crunch, foreign media broadcast images of Venezuela's barren supermarket shelves and winding breadlines as an indictment of the country's "socialist" system.[20] Such reports typically failed to mention, however, that Venezuela's private sector—not its government—controlled the majority of its domestic commodity market throughout the crisis, with non-state entities accounting for an average of 61 percent of GDP between the years 2009 and 2018.[21] Sensationalist media reports also overlooked the fact that Venezuela's inflation rate was not a mere side-effect of US sanctions, but their intended result. As Agathe Demarais, global forecasting director for the *Economist*'s Intelligence Unit, confessed during a February 2023 interview with the Carnegie Endowment think tank: "Sanctions that tend to work best are the ones that impose hardship on the population of targeted countries."[22]

"We want the population of targeted countries to tell their governments that they want them to change course," Demarais explained. "So, one tool to do that is to fuel inflation in targeted countries by essentially making access to, for instance, resources more difficult."

Demarais continued: "We need to recognize that this is a policy dilemma. On the one hand, we don't want people in sanctioned countries to suffer. But on the other hand, that's the most effective way for the US to gain concessions."

20   Chris McGonigal and Jesselyn Cook, "Photos Of Empty Grocery Shelves Show Dire Situation In Venezuela," *Huffington Post*, January 10, 2018.

21   "Producto Interno Bruto (See: 'Producto Interno Bruto Por Sector Institucional (Base 1997), Precios Constantes,'" Banco Central de Venezuela, accessed April 4, 2023.

22   "Backfire: The Global Ripple Effects of U.S. Sanctions," Carnegie Endowment, February 28, 2023.

Demarais's blatant admission that US sanctions were explicitly designed to drive supply shortages and fuel inflation was exemplified in the case of Venezuela. By the end of 2018, the opposition-controlled National Assembly claimed that prices for basic goods in the country were doubling every nineteen days,[23] subjecting Venezuelans to a financial rollercoaster that kept a stranglehold on their local economy even as products returned to the shelves. Even if Venezuelan supermarkets were well stocked, the price for a liter of milk, for example, could cost up to one quarter to a third of the local monthly wage.[24]

By the time of my February 2019 arrival in Caracas, Venezuela's economy had fallen so far that the daily exchange rate between the US dollar and local *bolívar* was set not by any state or genuine market force—but by Twitter. Each morning, a US-based news site called DolarToday sent out a tweet dictating the bolívar's worth. Whether we were cashing out at a restaurant, paying for groceries, or picking up snacks from a street merchant, vendors calculated our check based on DolarToday's arbitrary exchange rate—they would quite literally take out their phones, show us a tweet, and tabulate the bill before our eyes. Caracas made several attempts to block DolarToday's reach inside Venezuela to no avail, and even filed a case in US courts formally accusing its operators of cyberterrorism.[25]

DolarToday's stunning ability to drive up Venezuela's inflation rate from beyond the country's borders eventually led the *Wall Street Journal* to brand it "the enemy Maduro fears most."[26] According to the *Journal*, a Venezuelan émigré named Gustavo Díaz ran the enterprise while moonlighting as a Home Depot employee in central Alabama—adding yet another mysterious layer to the case of Venezuela's unusual bout of inflation.

23   The Visual Journalism team, "Venezuela: All You Need to Know about the Crisis in Nine Charts," BBC, February 4, 2019.

24   Seana Davis, Emmanuelle Saliba, and Alex Morgan, "Venezuela: 1 Litre of Milk Could Cost a Third of Your Wage," Euronews, July 26, 2019.

25   Andrew Cawthorne, "Venezuela Sues Black Market Currency Website in United States," Reuters, October 23, 2015.

26   Anatoly Kurmanaev, "DolarToday, El Enemigo Más Temido De Nicolás Maduro," *Wall Street Journal*, November 20, 2016.

According to economists Jeffrey Sachs and Mark Weisbrot, US sanctions not only contributed to Venezuela's soaring inflation rate, but also prevented Maduro's government from redressing the crisis. They noted that in the seven hyperinflationary periods recorded in Latin America since World War II, governments successfully remedied the situation through simple policy fixes. Thanks to government intervention, the median length of these hyperinflationary periods was roughly four months (Weisbrot and Sachs 2019).

Venezuela, on the other hand, was bogged by hyperinflation for four *years*—twelve times longer than the regional median. According to Weisbrot and Sachs, this phenomenon was the result of US sanctions that cut Venezuela off from international financial markets, an act that impeded Caracas's ability to implement policies historically deployed against hyperinflation, which is typically driven by a population's unwillingness to hold their domestic currency if it is expected to rapidly lose value. They pointed to the example of Bolivia, which in 1985 was able to rid itself of hyperinflation within ten days by pegging its currency to the US dollar. Because La Paz maintained a fixed dollar exchange rate, Bolivians gained confidence in their domestic currency and hyperinflation came to a rapid end. In modern Venezuela, however, US financial restrictions blocked its government from accessing the dollars needed to execute a similar policy.

Such considerations of history and economy were of little importance to the international press, particularly as they greased the wheels of Washington's February 23 Venezuela "aid" invasion. According to the regime change media mill, Maduro's rejection of the US military presence on his border was rooted in pure despotic spite.

"Humanitarian Aid Arrives for Venezuela—But Maduro Blocks It," complained NPR.[27]

"Maduro Rejects Humanitarian Aid," read a headline on Deutsche Welle.[28]

27   Lauren Wamsley, "Humanitarian Aid Arrives For Venezuela — But Maduro Blocks It," NPR, February 8, 2019.

28   "Maduro Rejects Humanitarian Aid," Deutsche Welle, February 8, 2019.

"Maduro's Government Rejects Humanitarian Aid, Announces Shipment of Food to Colombia," grumbled CNN en Español.[29]

Indeed, Venezuela's government did unroll an initiative to deliver 20,000 boxes of food to the impoverished Colombian border town of Cúcuta in the lead-up to February 23—a clear effort to highlight Washington's hypocritical lack of concern for those suffering under the pro-US government in Bogotá. To the charge that he was ignoring the plight of his populace by refusing to accept US "aid," however, Maduro retorted that if Washington truly cared about ordinary Venezuelans, all it had to do was lift its sanctions regime. As one Venezuelan official once remarked to me, "if we are so bad at managing our economy, then why do they have to sanction us so severely?"

While the US government and its corporate media proxies demonized Maduro, Caracas summoned the popular power of Chavismo to flaunt their rejection of Washington's regime change scheme. Throughout February 2019, Venezuela's government invited the myriad of social movements and working-class supporters that had thrust it into power to defend their nation in the streets. As February 23 approached, thousands of Venezuelans poured into the Caracas city center to sign an open letter to the US public that explicitly denounced foreign intervention in their country's internal affairs—a direct rebuke to Guaidó and the looming "aid" operation.

"We are here because we elected a president, not Guaidó," a stout woman with short, graying hair remarked to me. *"Con votos!"* she exclaimed, widening her eyes and raising her arm to emphasize that she and her fellow countrymen had voted to reelect Maduro less than a year before the launch of Guaidó's coup.[30]

I walked up and down the seemingly endless line of people waiting to sign the letter in Caracas's Plaza Bolívar all afternoon, repeating a simple question: "What is your message to the US public?"

29   Caitlin Hu and Bianca Britton, "El Gobierno De Maduro Rechaza La Ayuda Humanitaria y Anuncia Envío De Alimentos a Colombia," CNN En Español, February 19, 2019.
30   Anya Parampil, "Venezuelans' Message to the US: Hands off Our Country," *The Grayzone*, February 11, 2019.

"Tell Trump: 'Don't come here!'" a petite elderly woman proclaimed, waving her finger defiantly. "Don't come here, Trump! We don't want him. None of these animals!" she insisted, an apparent reference to the likes of Pompeo and Bolton.

A man with tan, leathery skin and frosty hair echoed her sentiments, telling me: "I am here supporting my country, I am not going to let any of that trash come here. Our country is sovereign."

Many of the people I spoke with genuinely feared that Washington would soon escalate military aggression against their country.

"I am signing for peace," a bespectacled young man explained timidly. "Because I don't want any intervention."

"We are going to sign this so that they cannot come here," a toothless man with a baseball cap said of himself and his companion, who added: "We don't want war."

I followed up my initial inquiry with the question that would obviously plague future international viewers: Had anyone paid or coerced them to participate in this action? Every person I spoke with answered in the negative. But what about the humanitarian crisis in Venezuela? According to these Venezuelans, US sanctions were to blame.

"We are here of our own free will, for the legacy of our eternal commander, Hugo Rafael Chávez Frías. We will keep this revolution going, and no empire is going to take it away," the short-haired woman assured me.

"We are here so that they lift the blockade! Let us live calmly and happily, because we are a people of peace, and the riches that we have belong to us, not the empire," asserted another.

I was surprised by the political awareness permeating the crowd. Though I understood Western media exaggerated the crisis in Venezuela and ignored the role US sanctions played in fomenting it, the pain felt on the ground in the country was impossible to deny. The fact that so many Venezuelans blamed US policy—not their own government—for their hardship demonstrated to me that sanctions were unlikely to foment Maduro's ouster. If anything, sanctions actually obscured factors that foreign media blamed for the country's strained economic situation, such as corruption and mismanagement, in the eyes of the Venezuelan public.

What struck me most about the massive congregation I encountered in Plaza Bolívar, however, was the fact it did not exist in foreign media. The faces of the Venezuelans I met did not appear on CNN or the BBC; their pleas for peace never printed in the *New York Times* or Reuters. As a result, think tankers and officials in Washington were left to craft Venezuela policy based on their own self-fulfilling propaganda loop rather than a genuine view from the country's streets.

"Tell the news that we don't need anything," a female shopper instructed my colleague, Max Blumenthal, as we arrived at a government-subsidized market. "What we want is for the US to lift the blockade it has put on us here in Venezuela!"[31]

Max and I visited the market, run by CLAP, days after CNN's Nick Valencia flew into the region aboard a US military plane and filed his sensationalized dispatch from the Colombian border. Nestled between a major highway and the metro tracks of Macarao parish just outside Caracas, the bazaar resembled a typical farmers market. There, I watched dozens of shoppers bustle between canopied stands to inspect government-subsidized items including bread; fresh fruit and vegetables; canned sardines from Venezuela's Caribbean Island chain and breathtaking national park, Los Roques; and even a knock-off brand of toothpaste called "Colgane." Any Venezuelan, regardless of political affiliation, was free to drop in and peruse the ample piles of locally sourced goods.

For Abrams, Bolton, Mnuchin, and others in Washington, this CLAP market not only diminished the desired impact of their economic blockade, but undermined the narrative that Venezuelans were in desperate need of Western intervention. The testimonies I collected at the market, in Plaza Bolívar, and beyond confirmed to me that a broad swath of the Venezuelan public rejected Washington's push to overthrow their government and force humanitarian "aid" on them. Consequently, the foreign press rendered them invisible.

Other than myself and my colleagues in alternative media, there were virtually no international reporters at the "pro-government" events we attended, including the CLAP market and letter signing

31   Max Blumenthal, "The Real Humanitarian Aid: Inside Venezuela's State-Subsidized Communal Markets," *The Grayzone*, February 24, 2019.

event. That was not because major outlets like the *New York Times*, CNN, and Reuters did not dedicate personnel and considerable resources to Venezuela—Caracas was often crawling with Western correspondents. It just so happened that aside from a notable few, such as AP's Joshua Goodman,[32] most foreign reporters happened to function as impressively disciplined stenographers for US officials and little else.

As Max and I waited to attend a Maduro press conference at Miraflores Palace in December 2020, a Caracas-based reporter for Reuters approached us to offer up some awkward chitchat. A self-described DC native clad in an ensemble complete with khaki pants and a matching vest adorned with useless flappy pockets, he appeared to have walked straight out of central casting for a gringo correspondent in Latin America. In between gulps of coffee, he boasted that Venezuelan officials habitually complained about his refusal to cover US sanctions targeting their country. When I asked how he could overlook such a significant contributor to Venezuela's economic crisis, the reporter was indignant.

"It's hard to know where the impact of sanctions ends and where the corruption begins," he grumbled, pivoting to a hackneyed anecdote about government officials handing out heaping sacks of cash to their cronies.

This correspondent, like most, had no interest in investigating the impact of US sanctions on Venezuela's economy, instead focusing his adversarial energy on the miscreancy of a socialist government placed under virtual siege by its powerful northern neighbor. By rendering the economic war nonexistent, he had found his voice—and paycheck—in Washington's information battle.

Anatoly Kurmanaev, a Latin America-focused reporter with a résumé spanning the *New York Times, Bloomberg,* and the *Wall Street Journal,* articulated the mercenary-like mentality of Western correspondents covering Venezuela with inhibition in a stunningly frank interview with left-wing media critic Alan MacLeod.[33] Over the

---

32 Joshua Goodman, "AP Breaks Global News with Unprecedented Maduro Interview," Associated Press, February 22, 2019.

33 Alan MacLeod, "'Sexy Tricks': How 'Mercenary' Journalists Demonize Venezuela, in Their Own Words," *The Grayzone,* December 9, 2019.

years, Kurmanaev churned out a steady stream of dispatches painting Venezuela as an impoverished hellscape overrun by gangs[34] and an incompetent tyrant.[35] Yet according to Kurmanaev's own words, his reports were not an honest reflection of life in Venezuela, but the preferred narrative of his corporate paymasters.

"Every journalist has an audience he caters for," Kurmanaev, who worked for *Bloomberg* at the time, divulged. "In my case, it's the financial community."

To Kurmanaev, the lives of ordinary Venezuelans were simply bait he deployed to "hook" readers into learning about socialism's failures on behalf of *Bloomberg*'s backers in the global financial industry.

"A couple of times from my experience you try to use, I wouldn't call them 'cheap tricks,' but yeah, kind of 'sexy tricks,'" Kurmanaev remarked with commendable candor.

According to Kurmanaev, he employed one such "sexy trick" to generate a sensational *Bloomberg* headline that claimed a pack of condoms in Venezuela cost a whopping $755.[36] In the ninth paragraph of Kurmanaev's report, he conceded that condoms on Venezuela's black market were in fact selling for about $25, roughly the same price as in the United States. Even so, he tabulated the astounding "$755" figure by digging up a listing for condoms on an online auction site and calculating its price based on Venezuela's official dollar exchange rate. In other words, no one in Venezuela was *actually* paying $755 for a pack of condoms—the number merely reflected the price of a cherry-picked listing according to Venezuela's absurd rate of inflation.

What's more, though Kurmanaev blamed the inflated price on Venezuela's scarcity crisis, he claimed the phenomenon was purely the result of a collapse in global oil prices and dearth of US dollars in the country. His version of events not only ignored Washington's hand in fomenting that oil crash (Wroughten 2014), but papered over the role

---

34   Isayen Herrera and Anatoly Kurmanaev, "Bouncy Castles and Grenades: Gangs Erode Maduro's Grip on Caracas," *New York Times*, May 30, 2021.

35   Anatoly Kurmanaev, "Venezuela's Leader Trades Old Guard for Slick Technocrats to Keep Power," *New York Times*, March 2, 2022.

36   Anatoly Kurmanaev and Andrew Rosati, "The $755 Condom Pack Is the Latest Indignity in Venezuela," *Bloomberg*, February 4, 2015.

US sanctions played in propelling Venezuela's scarcity crisis and blocking Caracas's access to dollars. Kurmanaev has adopted a more holistic
approach to his work since leaving *Bloomberg* for the *New York Times*,
publishing a landmark report dismantling conventional narratives surrounding an OAS-enabled coup carried out against Bolivia's elected
government in October 2019.[37]

"You are a mercenary in a sense," Kurmanaev told MacLeod,
describing the job of mainstream reporters. "You're there to provide
information to a particular client that they find important and it's not
good or bad, it's just the way it is."

Though his interview with Maduro did not air for several months,
Ramos's hyperbolic tale of repression and near-captivity in Miraflores set
the tone for international media as Venezuela braced for Washington's
February 23 "aid" delivery: the vicious dictator in Caracas was not only
ungrateful for Elliott Abrams's charity, but had deported a foreign
journalist for the crime of asking tough questions.

With a bit of luck, my colleagues and I soon learned just
how closely officials in Washington had watched—or, perhaps,
advised—Ramos's performance.

When Max boarded his departure flight from Caracas on February
26, he noticed Ramos lounging in the front row of first class. Upon
their arrival in Miami, a swarm of reporters greeted the Univision
host and his crew at the airport gate. As Ramos chronicled his kerfuf-
fle in Caracas for his corporate colleagues, Max forced his attention.
Did Ramos also plan to confront US officials about their sanctions
policy or threats to militarily invade Venezuela, Max asked? Would
Ramos challenge Marco Rubio, the Cuban American senator from
Florida, over his call for the US military to murder Maduro in the
streets of Caracas?[38]

37   Anatoly Kurmanaev and María Silvia Trigo, "A Bitter Election. Accusations
of Fraud. And Now Second Thoughts." *New York Times,* June 7, 2020.

38   Colin Kalmbacher, "Rubio Posts Graphic Image of Gaddafi's Murder
in Apparent Threat to Maduro. Twitter Says It Didn't Violate Their Terms of
Service," *Law and Crime*, March 2, 2019.

"What I can tell you is that many people here in the United States are supporting what we're doing," Ramos blithely boasted to Max's camera. "Marco Rubio, Vice President Pence, and many others were supporting what we were doing over there."[39]

What precisely Univision's lead broadcaster meant by those words remains open to interpretation.

39   Max Blumenthal, (@MaxBlumenthal), Twitter post, February 26, 2019, https://twitter.com/MaxBlumenthal/status/1100485398353113088?s=20& t=qSsRoFN_WY3JoPgOT7cJ9w.

FOUR

JUAN GUAIDÓ, IMPERIAL INCUBATOR BABY

Throughout February 2019, international media were completely captivated by the made-for-TV drama playing out on the Colombia-Venezuela border. In the Colombian town of Cúcuta, a caravan of tractor trailers packed with cardboard boxes displaying USAID's logo readied for a provocative incursion into Venezuelan territory. On the other side of the perimeter, Venezuela's government constructed physical blockades and deployed national guard troops to secure their country's frontier. Meanwhile, on February 12, on a boulevard in eastern Caracas's affluent Chacao district, a crowd of Venezuelans who yearned for a US invasion of their country gathered to cheer on the Cúcuta convoy. They comprised a sea of white.

White is the US-backed opposition's unifying color in Venezuela. Whenever they hold rallies, attendees sport white t-shirts, white visors, and yes, are typically much fairer in appearance than the mostly black, brown, and *mestizo* Venezuelans I met at pro-government demonstrations. Racial divides in Venezuela are far more pronounced along class lines than in the United States, with wealthier, pro-opposition supporters almost universally tracing their family lineage back to Spain and Italy. The men in Chacao appeared to have wandered off the country club and into the city streets, clad in ironed polo shirts and trousers; the women modeled salon-treated hair and powdered faces that melted in the Caracas heat.

Max filed a video report from the scene. As we filmed an introduction, a sturdy man wearing a Ralph Lauren button-down took up position behind Max, carefully listening to every word of his stand-up while waving a massive Venezuelan flag.

"We are in a lot of need," the man's wife, a sandy-blonde-haired woman who looked to be in her mid-fifties, told Max when we turned to them for an interview.[1]

"Are you hungry?" Max asked.

"Yes." She answered.

"What would you eat?"

"Well, anything that I have in my house," she replied without thought. Realizing her plea for humanitarian intervention was losing legitimacy, she quickly added: "But I have to work all day long, and then go out to find something to buy!"

"And the prices are too high?" Max helped her along.

"Very high, very high," she fretted. "A bunch of kale costs 6,000 bolívares ($2)!"

It felt as though we were victims of a prank. One by one, lipsticked women in designer sunglasses spun their yarns of agony. It was clear they were accustomed to foreign reporters believing anything they said.

"We don't have medicine, we don't have food, we don't have anything!" a heavyset woman with a coiffed gray bob complained. Another implored us to look at the size of her pants, explaining that she had shed close to twenty pounds in just two years.

Yes, Venezuela's economy had been ravaged. Yes, Venezuelans were struggling to purchase food and going hungry. Yes, the country was unable to import basic supplies and medicine. But if there was starvation in Venezuela, this crowd was not afflicted by it. These were not the country's poor. Most revealing of all, these people openly begged Washington to intensify its siege of their nation.

One man held a hundred-bolívar bill in front of our camera and griped about inflation before announcing that he not only supported US sanctions on his country but believed they were too "weak." The woman who claimed her pants no longer fit wished to skip the tired foreplay of financial wargames altogether, informing us that Venezuela's National Assembly had "the right to authorize a foreign military mission" in her country. In other words, according to Venezuela's radical opposition, Washington's hybrid assault had exacted insufficient adversity on their

---

1   Max Blumenthal, "Venezuela's Opposition Pleads for US Intervention - Max Blumenthal Reports from Caracas March," *The Grayzone*, February 15, 2019.

compatriots—only direct military intervention funded by the US tax-payer could truly "liberate" them.

The possibility that their fantasy of endless war and kale salad would soon be reality in Venezuela seemed more likely by the rally's conclusion. When Guaidó addressed the crowd from the main stage—framed with banners reading *Ayuda Humanitaria*—he revealed that he would travel to Colombia and participate in the US military effort to cross into Venezuela on February 23. Considering Caracas had placed Guaidó under an international travel ban at the start of his coup attempt, the announcement added yet another level of provocation to the tense standoff.

"This humanitarian aid is getting in no matter what," Guaidó vowed before climbing onto the back of a motorcycle and riding away through throngs of opposition supporters.

Was this what it felt like to be president? Guaidó was enjoying a meteoric political rise. In a matter of days, he had transformed from an anonymous lawmaker into the "President of Venezuela" in the eyes of Washington and its allies in foreign capitals and the international media. Just a few weeks prior, many in Venezuela's opposition had been shocked when Voluntad Popular (VP) opted to bypass more senior party leaders and appoint Guaidó president of Venezuela's National Assembly. As was often the case for the Washington-backed party, US officials—not Venezuelan opposition apparatchiks—were behind the surprise decision.

"In the weeks prior to switching our recognition, about half of the parties in the National Assembly didn't recognize Guaidó as the country's legitimate leader," US secretary of state Mike Pompeo explained in his memoir. "Thankfully, our capable diplomat, Ambassador James Story, worked magic to help line them up behind Guaidó, and we made our decision" (Pompeo 2023, 348).

As Venezuelan journalist Diego Sequera told the *Grayzone* at the time, the US preferred Guaidó over more recognizable opposition figures because he had "common mestizo features like most Venezuelans do and seems more like a man of the people."[2] Indeed, unlike his col-

2   Max Blumenthal, "The Making of Juan Guaidó: How the US Regime Change Laboratory Created Venezuela's Coup Leader," *The Grayzone*, January 29, 2019.

leagues, who largely hailed from oligarchic families with European lineage, Guaidó had emerged from the middle class: his father was an airline pilot, his mother a schoolteacher (and, for what it's worth, he bore an odd resemblance to Barack Obama).

Beyond the prisms of race and class, however, Guaidó shared important characteristics with his opposition cohorts. Like virtually all Voluntad Popular's leading officials, "President Guaidó" was a carefully crafted product of the universities, non-governmental organizations, and covert intelligence networks that form elite Washington's laboratory for the global ruling class.

Back in 2007, Guaidó was concluding his university studies and Chavismo had established itself as a political juggernaut in Venezuela and the surrounding region. Progressive governments allied with Chávez had cropped up in Bolivia, Argentina, and beyond as Venezuela's economy boomed. After almost ten years of revolution, Chavismo appeared unstoppable.

That summer, Chávez introduced a ballot referendum to enshrine his vision of "Twenty-First-Century Socialism" in Venezuela's constitution and scheduled a vote for December 2. The initiative proposed reforms including a reduction in the work week from forty-four to thirty-six hours, the abolition of presidential term limits, and an official declaration that Venezuela was a "socialist" nation[3]—an ambitious endeavor that voters ultimately rejected.[4]

The opposition's rare triumph over Chavismo had not been delivered by an existing party or prominent political detractor, but by a group of previously unknown student activists. Known as "Generation 2007," the students first tested their organizing skills in March of that year, when they launched nationwide campus protests against the government's failure to renew a broadcast license for Radio Caracas Televisión,[5]

3　Alan Woods, "Venezuela: The Referendum Defeat - What Does It Mean?" *Venezuelanalysis*, December 4, 2007.

4　Chris Kraul, "Venezuelan Voters Reject Bid by Chavez to Extend Powers," *LA Times*, December 3, 2007.

5　Brian Ellsworth, "Venezuelans March against Closure of TV Station," Reuters, May 26, 2007.

a corporate network that had actively supported the US-backed military coup which temporarily removed Chávez from power in 2002 (chapter nine). While those demonstrations ultimately died down, they reignited in the weeks leading up to Venezuela's December 2 constitutional referendum. This time, however, the students took their campaign off campus and directly to the streets.[6]

Throughout November, the students transformed university grounds into bases of anti-government fervor. The situation escalated after masked gunmen opened fire on a student gathering on November 8.[7] Though no one was killed, the incident contributed to a sense of popular turmoil surrounding the vote.

"Some here say they feel that the situation is as tense as in 2002,"[8] journalist Fred Fuentes reported that week, referring to the US-directed military coup that rocked Venezuela five years prior.

Weeks later, on November 28, opposition rioters shot and killed a Chavista in the city of Valencia during street protests billed as a "march of no return."[9] Four days later, voters rejected Chávez's ballot initiative by a narrow 2 percent margin.

Having delivered Chavismo's first defeat at the ballot box since its inception nearly a decade prior, the students behind the anarchic street demos were credited with reviving Venezuela's feeble political opposition. Yet while "Generation 2007" appeared to be a spontaneous revolt, the US government had been quietly molding Venezuela's student population into the anchor of its anti-Chavista operation for years.

In February 2012, the international media group WikiLeaks began publishing "The Global Intelligence Files," a cache of over five million

6   James Orr, "Venezuelans March against Chávez Reforms," *Guardian*, November 30, 2007.

7   Simon Romero, "Gunmen Attack Opponents of Chávez's Bid to Extend Power," *New York Times*, November 8, 2007.

8   Fred Fuentes, "Dramatic Escalation in Campaign against Constitutional Reform," *Venezuelanalysis*, November 5, 2007.

9   Kiraz Janicke, "Venezuelan Opposition Protesters Shoot Chavez Supporter," *Venezuelanalysis*, November 28, 2007.

internal emails from an Austin-based firm called Stratfor. Marketing itself as a "shadow CIA" to its bevy of corporate and government clients—including Bank of America, Dow Chemical, and Lockheed Martin—Stratfor specialized in intelligence gathering and global risk assessment. While much of the initial reporting on the leaks concerned revelations that the Department of Homeland Security had contracted Stratfor to spy on the Occupy Wall Street demonstrations that swept the US following the 2008 financial crash,[10] the WikiLeaks archive has since provided journalists with an infinite bounty of primary source material exposing the inner workings of Washington's global intelligence apparatus.

Among the files' most significant contributions to the public record was the window they offered into the Center for Applied Nonviolent Action and Strategies, or CANVAS, organization. A self-described "network of international trainers and consultants with expertise in building and running successful non-violent movements,"[11] CANVAS was at the forefront of several international regime change operations launched throughout the early 2000s. A 2007 Stratfor report touted the group's success in fomenting the so-called "color revolutions" that befell a number of Eastern European and Central Asian states during that period, namely those in Georgia, Kyrgyzstan, Uzbekistan, Azerbaijan, Ukraine, and Belarus.[12] Though their campaigns did not always achieve regime change, Stratfor declared that CANVAS's "ability to mobilize and unite disparate factions" of a target country's opposition "are among the best on the planet."

Though CANVAS billed itself as a non-governmental organization (NGO), the Stratfor leaks revealed the group relied heavily on funding from the US State Department and USAID ("Information on CANVAS" 2013). According to Stratfor, CANVAS's top "allies" were the Freedom House organization and Albert Einstein Institution, two US-funded entities that effectively served as a money wash for

10   Allison Kilkenny, "Leaked Documents: Homeland Security Monitoring Occupy Wall Street," *In These Times*, February 29, 2012.

11   "Who We Are," Canvas, accessed March 8, 2023.

12   "Information on CANVAS," The Global Intelligence Files, WikiLeaks, February 13, 2013.

State Department and USAID-supplied cash.[13] CANVAS's reliance on grants from US-backed organizations like Freedom House—rather than direct support from the US government itself—enabled it to claim nominal NGO status while maintaining financial dependence on Washington.

Considering CANVAS's "pro-democracy campaigns" universally targeted designated enemies of the US government, such dependence was no surprise. Yet the group's own history provided additional evidence that it functioned as a mere extension of US regime change ops. CANVAS was the official outgrowth of Otpor ("Resistance"), a student group that directed mass street protests against Serbian president Slobodan Milošević and eventually forced his ouster in October 2000.

Within weeks of his removal, the *New York Times* published a blockbuster report titled "Who Really Brought Down Milošević?" that extensively documented how US-funded organizations, specifically the National Endowment for Democracy (NED) and International Republican Institute (IRI), poured millions of dollars into the effort to topple Serbia's president.

"Otpor was certainly the largest recipient," a former NED official divulged to the *Times*, explaining his group spent nearly $3 million on the campaign to overthrow Milošević between 1998 and 2000.[14] Formed in 1983, NED represented a Reagan-era initiative to outsource covert US regime change ops beyond the traditional—and increasingly controversial—confines of Washington's official intelligence networks. As NED co-founder Allen Weinstein once famously confessed to the *Washington Post*, "A lot of what we do today was done covertly twenty-five years ago by the CIA."[15]

In the aftermath of Milošević's overthrow, Otpor faded into the background of Serbian politics and eventually incorporated itself into a

13   Tom Barry, "The New Politics of Political Aid in Venezuela," *Militarist Monitor*, July 17, 2007.

14   Roger Cohen, "Who Really Brought Down Milosevic?" *New York Times*, November 26, 2000.

15   "The National Endowment for Democracy Responds to Our Burma Nuclear Story — And Our Response," ProPublica, November 24, 2010.

marginal national party. Its former student leaders, however, were destined for horizons far beyond Serbia.

"After they toppled Milosevic, the kids who ran OTPOR grew up, got suits and designed CANVAS," Stratfor analyst Marko Papic remarked in a February 2010 email, characterizing the organization as an "'export-a-revolution' group that sowed the seeds for a NUMBER of color revolutions."[16]

"They are still hooked into US funding and basically go around the world trying to topple dictators and autocratic governments (ones that US does not like)," Papic continued.

Indeed, after applying their Serbia blueprint to stimulate color revolutions in Eastern Europe and Central Asia, Otpor's founders, Srđa Popović and Slobodan Đinović, formally established CANVAS in 2005—officially taking their model for disguising clandestine, US-backed protest campaigns as organic, popular revolts to the international level. As CANVAS's executive director, Popović was tasked with overseeing the organization's training programs from the Philippines to Belarus, Iran, and beyond. A 2013 investigation by Occupy Wall Street's media offshoot revealed just how seriously Popović took his job as an international agent of regime change. By 2007, the CANVAS chief had successfully leveraged his international connections into a stint with private intelligence.

Based on a review of the Stratfor leaks, journalists Carl Gibson and Steve Horn explained that "Popović passed information" to the intelligence firm "about on-the-ground activist events in countries around the world."[17] The report chronicled how, following a 2007 speaking engagement at Stratfor, Popović began providing its employees with "actionable intelligence" on CANVAS's global operations, even transmitting his private communications with foreign activists to the firm's analysts.

16   "Re: INSIGHT - VENEZUELA: CANVAS Analysis," The Global Intelligence Files, WikiLeaks, June 18, 2012.
17   Carl Gibson and Steve Horn, "EXPOSED: GLOBALLY RENOWNED ACTIVIST COLLABORATED WITH INTELLIGENCE FIRM STRATFOR," Occupy.com, December 2, 2012.

"Popović passed on the information to Stratfor without the consent of the activists and likely without the activists ever knowing that their emails were being shuttled to the private security firm," the journalists explained.

Stratfor was so grateful for Popović's cooperation that it eventually hired his would-be wife, Marija Stanisavljevic, for a part time gig.

"The CANVAS guy is a close friend/source," Stratfor's Vice President of Analysis stressed in a March 2010 email discussing Stanisavljevic's employment, noting Popović "recommended her" for a job while failing to disclose she was dating the CANVAS executive.[18] The following year, the lovebirds invited a handful of Stratfor employees to their Belgrade nuptials, a ceremony that Popović promised would be "followed by (serious) [*sic*] rock party."[19]

A significant portion of Popović's collaboration with Stratfor concerned covert US operations in Venezuela, a top interest of CANVAS ever since its 2005 foundation. On October 5 of that year—two days before the fifth anniversary of Milošević's ouster—CANVAS convened a conference in Serbia's capital to train the next generation of international, US-backed regime change operatives. Among the foreign activists who descended upon Belgrade for the color revolution crash course were five Venezuelan university students. The disclosure emerged in an October 2007 Stratfor assessment that confidently announced "another color revolution may be forming in Latin America."[20]

"Student movements are only at the beginning of what could be a years-long effort to trigger a revolution in Venezuela," Stratfor declared, crediting CANVAS with inciting the unrest. "When you see students at five Venezuelan universities hold simultaneous demonstrations, you will know that the training is over and the real work has begun," Stratfor informed its clients.

Within weeks of Stratfor's report, "Generation 2007" was born.

18   "Re: Question-Marija Stanisavljevic," The Global Intelligence Files, WikiLeaks, March 6, 2013.

19   "Re: and Now for Something Completely Official," The Global Intelligence Files, WikiLeaks, February 19, 2013.

20   Stratfor, "Venezuela: The Marigold Revolution?" October 5, 2007.

Having completed his undergraduate studies that year, Guaidó threw himself into the US-sponsored "Generation 2007" tumult. Two years later, he and his cohorts co-founded Leopoldo López's Voluntad Popular party, the opposition bloc at the forefront of violent guarimba riots that periodically swept Venezuela following Chávez's death. By January 2019, the grunts of "Generation 2007" had matured from youthful student activists into the leading representatives of Guaidó's US-backed coup regime. Within weeks of their ascent, CANVAS's work in Venezuela would become more relevant than ever before.

At around 5:00 p.m. on March 7, 2019, as millions of Venezuelans concluded their workday, commuter trains nationwide suddenly came to a halt. The red, yellow, and green hues of traffic lights faded to brown. Television screens went black, cellphones became useless bricks, and dining rooms plunged into darkness.

The blackout swept up the majority of Venezuelan territory, devouring schools, hospitals, and airports. Venezuelan officials eventually traced the outage to Guri Dam in Estado Bolívar, home to a hydroelectric plant that produced between 70 and 80 percent of the country's power.[21] According to Caracas, foreign actors had targeted the Simón Bolívar Hydroelectric plant—located in one of the largest reservoirs on earth—with a cybernetic attack.[22] Oddly, the debilitating blackout struck just hours after Florida senator Marco Rubio issued Caracas an ominous warning.

"Venezuela is going to enter a period of suffering no nation in our hemisphere has confronted in modern history," Rubio presaged before a Senate Foreign Relations Subcommittee hearing on Venezuela that featured Elliott Abrams and USAID administrator Mark Green as witnesses.[23] Within minutes of Venezuela's subsequent power outage, Rubio giddily reported the news on Twitter.

21 Lily Hay Newman, "Why It's So Hard to Restart Venezuela's Power Grid," *Wired*, March 12, 2019.

22 "Está En Vías de Consolidarse La Victoria Del Pueblo al Restituirse En Todo El País El Suministro Eléctrico," Ministerio del Poder Popular del Despacho de la Presidencia, March 12, 2019.

23 Michael Bowman, "US Lawmakers Warn Maduro Loyalists in Venezuela," Voice of America, March 7, 2019.

"18 of 23 states & the capital district are currently facing complete blackouts," the Senator tweeted. "Main airport also without power & backup generators have failed."[24]

The mysterious timing of Senator Rubio's depraved forecast of suffering in their country was not lost on Venezuelan leadership. In a televised address, government spokesperson Jorge Rodríguez charged Washington with conducting the attack on his country's electrical system, describing Rubio and Secretary of State Pompeo as "psychopaths" for overseeing the plot ("Está En Vías de Consolidarse" 2019). Rodríguez asserted that even his own government was unaware that backup generators had failed at the time of Rubio's March 7 tweet. How had the Florida senator secured accurate information about the outage before Venezuela's own government had fully investigated the incident?

The charge that Washington was capable of and willing to execute such a monumental act of industrial sabotage was not unreasonable. In fact, tech analyst Kalev Leetaru argued the allegation was "quite realistic."[25]

"Remote cyber operations rarely require a significant ground presence, making them the ideal deniable influence operation," Leetaru explained in a March 9 article for *Forbes*. "Given the US government's longstanding concern with Venezuela's government, it is likely that the US already maintains a deep presence within the country's national infrastructure grid, making it relatively straightforward to interfere with grid operations."

US officials eventually confessed their ability to conduct such large-scale industrial terrorism themselves. In June 2019, the *New York Times* reported Washington had increased remote cyberattacks on Russia's electrical grid "in a warning" to President Vladimir Putin. Based on conversations with an anonymous "senior intelligence" source, the *Times* declared Washington's "digital incursions" into Moscow's electrical

---

24   Marco Rubio, (@marcorubio), Twitter post, March 7, 2019, https://twitter.com/marcorubio/status/1103782022537977857?s=20.

25   Kalev Leetaru, "Could Venezuela's Power Outage Really Be A Cyber Attack?" *Forbes*, March 9, 2019.

infrastructure were "a demonstration of how the Trump administration is using new authorities to deploy cybertools more aggressively."[26]

Evidence of Washington's involvement in the Venezuela blackout was not limited to the realm of theoretical capability. At the *Grayzone*, Max dredged up a 2010 memo authored by none other than CANVAS founder Srđa Popović that explicitly described a potential outage at Guri Dam as a "watershed event" and unprecedented boon to Venezuela's anti-Chavista opposition. [27] The intelligence assessment, which Popović compiled for Stratfor, asserted that hypothetical blackouts in Venezuela "would likely have the impact of galvanizing public unrest in a way that no opposition group could ever hope to generate."[28] In the event his imagined catastrophe came to fruition, Popović advised Venezuela's opposition "to take advantage of the situation and spin it against [Chavismo] and towards their needs." Nine years later, Venezuela's CANVAS-trained shadow regime had their chance to heed Popović's call.

"Light comes with the end of usurpation," Guaidó tweeted within minutes of the March 2019 outage, oddly connecting the return of electricity in Venezuela with the fall of Maduro's government.[29]

"No food. No medicine. Now, no power. Next, no Maduro," Pompeo tweeted hours later, echoing Guaidó's politicization of the blackout.[30]

By the time Venezuela finally managed to recuperate its electrical capacity that April, however, Maduro remained firmly in place.

Though Washington denied official responsibility for Venezuela's blackout, Popović enthusiastically detailed his personal coordination

26   David E. Sanger and Nicole Perlroth, "U.S. Escalates Online Attacks on Russia's Power Grid," *New York Times*, June 15, 2019.

27   Max Blumenthal, "US Regime-Change Blueprint Proposed Venezuelan Electricity Blackouts as 'Watershed Event' for 'Galvanizing Public Unrest,'" *The Grayzone*, March 11, 2019.

28   "VZ Elections," The Global Intelligence Files, WikiLeaks, October 18, 2012.

29   Juan Guaidó, Twitter post, March 7, 2019.

30   Secretary Pompeo, (@jguaido), Twitter post, March 7, 2019, https://twitter.com/jguaido/status/1103798495587287040?s=20.

with the Caracas coup regime immediately following Guaidó's self-declared presidency.

"It is no secret that many representatives of the Venezuelan democratic movement are my friends, that we have known each other for years and have talked countless times about the political situation," Popović told Serbian media in February 2019, describing Guaidó as "a high-quality, young and educated man."[31]

Speaking to the *Balkan Times*, Popović added that he wished, in his words, "my friend Juan Guaidó" success in his bid to unseat Maduro.

Yet CANVAS was not the only US government initiative that took credit for molding Venezuela's coup regime. Speaking with academics Tim Gill and Rebecca Hanson, a US government contractor for USAID's Office of Transitional Initiatives (OTI) similarly boasted of having nurtured Guaidó and his "Generation 2007." The anonymous source divulged that leading up to the 2007 campus protests, "the US had a very daring movement and brought a lot of money to the students through OTI, and it grew a lot as a result."[32]

According to the contractor, the US government's "most successful time was during 2007, when the student movement developed."

"I'm proud. It's like you see your son and daughter grow up," the OTI contractor gushed, referring to "Generation 2007" and Voluntad Popular. "The potential leaders when/if there is a change of government, and we were the ones who showed them the first steps."

As far as the Trump administration and its allies were concerned, that change of government took place in January 2019, when they recognized Guaidó as Venezuela's leader. Finally, as international media printed promising profiles introducing the world to "Venezuela's new president," a generation of imperial incubator babies directly cultivated by Washington reached adulthood.

31   Maja Zivanovic, "Serbian Activist Denies 'Training' Venezuela's Guaido in Rebellion," *Balkan Insight*, February 13, 2019.

32   Tim Gill and Rebecca Hanson, "How Washington Funded the Counterrevolution in Venezuela," *The Nation*, February 8, 2019.

FIVE

BOLTON'S BLOWBACK; MONROE'S MISERY

To consume corporate media from within Venezuela following Guaidó's self-declared presidency was to experience life in a parallel reality. Though the US, Europe, and their Latin American allies had declared an end to Maduro's mandate, I found that support for Chavismo extended far beyond the CLAP markets and anti-war actions I attended in Venezuela's streets. Regardless of Washington or London's official position on the matter, not one government ministry fell to Venezuela's opposition in the wake of Guaidó's coup attempt. Venezuela's shadow government similarly failed to gain significant international legitimacy. In fact, as Western media painted the picture of an isolated and desperate Maduro, his government emerged at the forefront of a powerful bloc of nations that threatened to upend the international Washington Consensus for the first time in history.

This reality was especially evident when I visited Venezuela's Cancillería on February 15 for an interview with the country's foreign minister, Jorge Arreaza. When I arrived at the gray-paneled office building with my colleagues, we noticed the inside walls were plastered with images of several diplomats who had previously represented Venezuela abroad. These individuals, according to the Foreign Ministry cadres shepherding us through the halls, were among the minority group of officials who had defected from Venezuela's government and allied themselves with Guaidó following his coup launch. In the words of the Cancillería staff we met, these people were *traidores*.

While climbing the winding staircase that leads to the foreign minister's office on the top floor, I got a sense of the internationalist vision that drives Chavista foreign policy. The Cancillería not only displayed portraits of Venezuelan revolutionaries, but large photographs of internationalist figures like South Africa's Nelson Mandela, who visited Caracas in 1991 to give thanks for its opposition to apartheid on the African continent.[1]

Arreaza's diplomatic style was an expression of his government's internationalist politics. During official visits to New York, the Cambridge-educated dignitary always made a point of meeting with anti-war groups and communicating his perspective on Venezuela-US affairs to local activists. He was also known to request their insights into domestic US politics, recognizing the country was far more complex than government officials or corporate media would lead one to believe. Yet Arreaza's mark on Venezuelan diplomatic history transcended the American continent. In addition to overseeing direct negotiations with Trump officials, Arreaza led consequential delegations to Russia, China, and Europe in the aftermath of Guaidó's January 2019 ascent. In March of that year, he even embarked on a multicity, weeks-long tour of the African continent that culminated in a visit with Syrian president Bashar al-Assad in Damascus.

"So much experience, wisdom, and advice for resistance, victory, and peace," Arreaza tweeted[2] following the meeting with Assad, himself the target of a violent, years-long regime-change war waged by the West and its regional allies.

A former university professor, Arreaza first joined Venezuela's government under Hugo Chávez, whose daughter he married. He would go on to act as the family's de-facto spokesperson throughout the president's later years, delivering bedside updates to the press as Chávez's health declined. In 2013, Maduro selected Arreaza as his running mate in the whirlwind election convened following Chávez's death. Four years later, Arreaza moved into the foreign minister's office.

1   "1991: Nelson Mandela Visitó a Venezuela," *Con El Mazo Dando*, July 22, 2021.

2   Jorge Arreaza, (@jaarreaza), Twitter post, April 4, 2019, https://twitter.com/jaarreaza/status/1113831506781384704?s=20.

When I met Arreaza in Caracas, he had just returned from a week of talks with US officials in New York City. During his trip, the diplomat had also announced the formation of a team of countries at the United Nations dedicated to reasserting the principles enshrined in the organization's founding charter: territorial sovereignty, political independence, and self-determination.[3]

"It's really important, this group, because it's not about defending President Maduro or even Venezuela, this is about defending international law," Arreaza told me, adding, "It wasn't an initiative from Venezuela, this was a suggestion from our friends."[4]

Arreaza went on to relate that while in New York, he attended a fortieth anniversary celebration for Iran's Islamic Revolution hosted by Tehran's UN mission. Throughout the reception, several ambassadors in attendance expressed concern over the precedent Washington had set when it recognized a parallel government in Venezuela days prior.

"One of them said: 'If we let this happen to Venezuela, who's next?'" Arreaza recalled, describing the moment the dignitaries decided to form "The Group of Friends in Defense of the Charter of the United Nations."

"You cannot be a member of the United Nations and not respect the most basic principles of the United Nations," he continued, referring to unilateral US sanctions on his country.

Indeed, though the UN charter included a special mechanism for imposing punitive financial measures on member states, Washington has increasingly bypassed debate with the international community in recent years by issuing unilateral sanctions out of its own Treasury Department's Office of Foreign Asset Control (OFAC), or via executive order. On average, Trump issued more than twice as many unilateral sanctions per year than both of his predecessors,[5] suggesting Washington leaned more heavily on this form of hybrid economic war

3 "Venezuelan Foreign Minister Announces Group to Protect UN Charter's Principles," Telesur English, February 14, 2019.

4 Anya Parampil, "Venezuela's Foreign Minister on 'Failed' Coup and Building New Non-Aligned Movement," *The Grayzone*, February 19, 2019.

5 Gibson, Dunn & Crutcher, "2019 Year-End Sanctions Update" (Gibson, Dunn & Crutcher, January 23, 2020).

as it lost the ability to conduct traditional military campaigns like those waged in Iraq and Afghanistan. Many of the countries that launched the "Group of Friends" initiative alongside Venezuela—including Russia, China, Iran, and Syria—were also targets of these arbitrary sanctions, which they described as "unilateral coercive measures."

According to the *Atlantic*, however, the success of Washington's sanctions strategy was not a measure of international support for the policy, but "the centrality of the United States financial system in the global economy, and the dollar's status as the world's dominant reserve currency."[6] As a result, Washington's overreliance on sanctions has ultimately blown back against US interests abroad. Though the measures successfully exacted suffering on the populations of Venezuela and other foreign targets in the short term, the modern international landscape has adapted to US financial hostility. Rather than spark regime change, Washington's global economic war has forced sanctioned governments to find ways of doing business with each other despite US policy. With Russia and China leading the way, countries like Venezuela have moved to circumvent the Western financial system altogether and are increasingly dropping the US dollar when hashing out international trade deals (chapter twelve).[7]

"It is like the natural flow of a river, now we come together because it's the only way to survive. The US elite are attacking all of us," Arreaza explained. "We have to be together and stop this from happening."

Venezuela's long-standing relationship with Russia was of particular concern to Trump officials. In his memoir, secretary of state Mike Pompeo expressed his frustration that the "Russian and Venezuelan militaries have trained together, and Russia is the main source of the Venezuelan military's arms" (Pompeo 2023, 347). Yet as Venezuela's foreign minister explained to me, that reality was the direct outcome of Washington's 2006 decision to ban the sale of commercial arms to Caracas in futile protest of Chávez's leadership.[8]

6   Kathy Gilsinan, "A Boom Time for U.S. Sanctions," *The Atlantic*, May 3, 2019.
7   Eustance Huang, "A 'Growing Club' of 'Very Powerful Countries' Is Steering Away from Using the Dollar," CNBC, October 30, 2019.
8   Ewam MacAskill and Duncan Campbell, "Bush Bans Arms Sales to Chávez," *Guardian*, May 10, 2006.

"Our relationship with Russia is fair, it's transparent," Arreaza insisted. "All of our military equipment was originally from the States, but then they blocked everything. We had to defend ourselves, we had to protect our people, so we looked over to Russia."

Moscow is not the only friend Caracas gained in light of Washington's misguided Venezuela policy. As detailed in chapter two, Turkey and Iran have similarly emerged as reliable allies to Venezuela. Turkey, a NATO member, has become a top trading partner of Venezuela in recent years, with Turkish products such as pasta and flour regularly appearing in monthly CLAP deliveries.

Commercial ties between Venezuela and Iran have also reached new heights thanks to US sanctions on both countries. During a reporting trip to Caracas in December 2020, I visited a newly opened Iranian-owned supermarket, Megasis, and was amazed by the variety of Iranian delicacies that had found their way to the Venezuelan capital. Luxurious carpets, chocolate-covered dates stuffed with pistachios, and pickles soaked in the flavors of the Orient represented just a small sample of the Iranian products available at the Walmart–style superstore, which reserved roughly 32 percent of its shelving space for goods produced in Venezuela.[9] As of 2020, Megasis planned to open at least four more locations in the South American country.

Iran has also stepped up to breathe new life into Venezuela's oil sector, which experienced a sharp decline after US sanctions—crafted primarily by Trump national security advisor John Bolton—barred Caracas from purchasing the products and parts necessary to maintain crude production (chapters one and two). In May 2022, Tehran signed a €100 million (note: not dollar) contract to repair Venezuela's El Palito refinery[10] and was reportedly preparing to revamp the country's largest refining plant.[11] Later that year, an Iranian firm announced

9   Anya Parampil, "An Exclusive Look inside Iran's Supermarket in Venezuela," *The Grayzone*, December 30, 2020.

10   Reuters, "Iran Signs 110 Million Euro Contract to Repair Venezuelan Refinery," Reuters, May 13, 2022.

11   News Desk, "Iran Set to Repair Venezuela's Largest Oil Refinery Complex: Report," *The Cradle*, May 23, 2022.

plans to restore Venezuela's electrical capacity[12] while pursuing similar deals with sanctioned Troika of Tyranny governments in Cuba and Nicaragua.[13]

In other words, a policy overseen by rabid neocons including Bolton, Pompeo, and Elliott Abrams—who served as Trump's "special envoy" to *both* Venezuela and Iran—directly enabled Tehran to establish a previously inconceivable base of influence on the American continent. Their beloved Monroe Doctrine, it would seem, was impotent against the force of the twenty-first century.

On top of alliances with Moscow, Ankara, and Tehran, Caracas has forged beneficial relationships with New Delhi and Beijing. When Washington halted the sale of Venezuelan petrol in US markets in 2019, India, the world's third largest oil consumer, offset the loss by purchasing Caracas's crude through Russia's Rosneft company.[14] China has also aided Venezuela's economic development, boosting Caracas's export earnings through crude purchases[15] and providing it with nearly $60 billion worth of oil-backed loans between 2007 and 2018.[16]

According to Arreaza, his "Group of Friends" initiative at the UN reflected this nascent world order. Born as a response to decades of unchecked transatlantic supremacy, he described Caracas's new friendships as a part of a Non-Aligned Movement "reloaded" for the twenty-first century. Indeed, while neither Turkey nor India, both US allies, have officially joined the UN group, their independent relationships

12 "Iranian Firm Planning to Repair Power Plants in Venezuela," Press TV, November 22, 2022.

13 Latin America News, "Iran Negotiates with Cuba, Nicaragua and Venezuela to Build Power Plants," *Rio Times*, January 2, 2023.

14 Olga Yagova, Chen Aizhu, and Marianna Parraga, "Rosneft Becomes Top Venezuelan Oil Trader, Helping Offset U.S. Pressure," Reuters, August 22, 2019.

15 Marianna Parraga and Mircely Guanipa, "Venezuela's Oil Exports in Sept Boosted by Sales to China, Swaps with Iran," Reuters, October 4, 2022.

16 Matt Ferchen, "China, Venezuela, and the Illusion of Debt-Trap Diplomacy," Carnegie Endowment, August 16, 2018.

with Venezuela demonstrated that Caracas was not nearly as isolated as Western media claimed.

"Maduro Isolated as Latin American Nations Back Venezuela Opposition Leader," reported Reuters on January 23, 2019.[17]

"Venezuela's Maduro: How Long Can an Isolated Strongman Last?" wondered the *Washington Post* on February 5,[18] days before my meeting with Arreaza.

"I believe that the think tanks must be working twenty-four hours a day trying to understand what's happening in Venezuela, because nothing that they have planned happens as they would like it to," the foreign minister quipped.

When I asked if he noticed a difference in the Trump and Obama administrations' approach to diplomacy, Arreaza hinted that Washington's recognition of Guaidó had made his job easier.

"This administration is shameless," he answered, referring to Trump's team. "They took the mask off and say exactly what they want out loud."

The diplomat continued: "All the interests they have are clear: 'We want Venezuelan oil, we don't want an independent process and government in Venezuela, we hate socialism, and we have to destroy that government.' So in a way, it's better, because we know exactly what they want and can negotiate on a real basis."

The night before our interview, the Associated Press reported that during Arreaza's trip to New York, Abrams had personally threatened him with a US military invasion of Venezuela.[19] Did the foreign minister believe such a rabidly unpredictable administration would take the drastic step of declaring all-out war on his country?

"The threats of the US government happen every hour now," he shrugged. "It wasn't that threatening, no."

17   Reuters Staff, "Maduro Isolated as Latin American Nations Back Venezuela Opposition Leader," Reuters, January 23, 2019.

18   Adam Taylor, "Venezuela's Maduro: How Long Can an Isolated Strongman Last?" *Washington Post*, February 5, 2019.

19   Joshua Goodman and Ian Phillips, "AP Interview: Maduro Reveals Secret Meetings with US Envoy," Associated Press, February 15, 2019.

In the days following our discussion, Arreaza returned to the UN in New York to denounce the US military presence amassing on his country's border as Washington's declared "aid delivery" date approached.

"Tomorrow represents the last lashes of a prehistoric animal in extinction," Venezuela's foreign minister proclaimed on February 22, hours before the attempted US invasion of his country was slated to take place.

SIX

SEX, DRUGS, AND DISORDER ON THE BORDER

As Arreaza and his colleagues sounded the alarm over Washington's hostile military incursion into their sovereign territory, the US president was overwhelmingly focused on the domestic political front. On February 18, Trump traveled to Florida International University in Miami for a rally with local Venezuelan expats sporting bright red "Make America Great Again" hats. There, he promised his fans among the regime-change hungry diaspora that "a new day is coming in Latin America."[1]

"In Venezuela and across the Western Hemisphere, socialism is dying, and liberty, prosperity, and democracy are being reborn," the US president announced before a roaring crowd.

During the speech, which served as a de facto campaign address, Trump honored a figure who, while unfamiliar to most Americans, was notorious inside Venezuela. He was Óscar Pérez, a former Venezuelan law enforcement officer and failed B movie actor who had formed an anti-government terrorist organization, hijacked a police helicopter, and launched grenades at the country's Justice Ministry during guarimba riots in June 2017.[2] Venezuelan authorities killed Pérez six months later in a raid that left six of his collaborators and at least two police officers dead.[3]

---

1   America Reports, "Trump: A New Day Is Coming in Venezuela and Latin America," Fox News, February 18, 2019.

2   Girish Gupta and Brian Ellsworth, "Venezuela Movie Actor behind Helicopter Attack on Government Buildings," Reuters, June 28, 2017.

3   Brian Ellsworth and Eyanir, "Rogue Ex-Policeman, Six Others Die in Venezuela Forces Raid," Reuters, January 16, 2018.

"Oscar was an incredible man who will not have died in vain," Trump vowed after a short intervention by Pérez's mother. In typical Trumpian fashion, he then boasted of the US military presence assembling on Venezuela's border.

"Two days ago, the first US Air Force C-17—that's a big, beautiful plane—landed in Colombia loaded with crucial assistance," Trump beamed. "Unfortunately, Dictator Maduro has blocked this life-saving aid from entering the country. He would rather see his people starve than give them aid."

Shortly before noon on February 22—less than twenty-four hours before the US military planned to invade Venezuela—Virgin Group CEO Richard Branson strutted across a colossal concert stage constructed near the country's border in Cúcuta, Colombia. The self-styled rebel billionaire, who once peddled lucrative technology to address climate change while lobbying to privatize Britain's railways,[4] had apparently found a new hot cause to paper over his rapacious behavior.

"My friends, we must break the impasse and end the humanitarian crisis, people are dying in Venezuela," Branson informed the crowd of several hundred thousand people standing before him. They were gathered in Cúcuta to attend Venezuela Aid Live, a concert Branson organized and funded to, in his words, "help the country's suffering people."[5]

Behind his charitable air, Branson added a fresh front in the foreign aggression against Venezuela's people. What began as a potential face-off between the militaries of Venezuela and the United States was now a cultural confrontation as well, with outlets such as *Rolling Stone* and *Billboard*—which may have otherwise ignored the news—taking notice of the conflict thanks to Branson's spectacle. By doling out untold amounts of cash to build a flashy performance venue and ferry musicians to Colombia for the event, the billionaire had constructed a festival-like atmosphere for Washington's regional collaborators as they actively plotted to invade their Venezuelan neighbor. Several opposition

---

4   Stefan Bielik, "The Great Virgin Train Robbery," *Tribune*, April 19, 2020.

5   Richard Branson, (@richardbranson), Twitter post, February 25, 2019, https://twitter.com/richardbranson/status/1096401760476909568?s=20.

politicians from Venezuela, including Guaidó himself, attended the concert alongside heads of state from Colombia, Paraguay, and Chile. The secretary general of the Organization of American States, Luis Almagro, was also present.

Branson's Coachella for Washington's regional political instruments did not take shape without drawing critics. Days before the event was scheduled to take place, British rock legend and antiwar activist Roger Waters blasted his billionaire compatriot's posturing, charging that Branson's project had "nothing to do with democracy" and merely represented the tycoon's acceptance of Washington's war propaganda.

"I've just seen a video clip of Branson with his bleeding heart worn openly on his Virgin Airways t-shirt," Waters remarked in an online video statement,[6] mocking the CEO's professed concern for Venezuelan suffering. Waters went on to reference his "friends that are in Caracas right now," whose testimonies he said easily dispelled the myths about Venezuela that were circulating in Western media.

Indeed, Max and I maintained regular contact with Roger throughout our time in Venezuela. Max met the recording artist while participating in the 2014 Russell Tribunal on Palestine, a Brussels-based people's initiative to document Israeli war crimes in the Gaza Strip, where Roger had defined himself as the world's most prominent advocate for Palestinian liberation. By 2019, Roger had become even more outspoken about US-backed conflicts across the globe, particularly the hybrid wars Washington waged from Syria to Venezuela.[7]

"We just need to back off," Waters said of US and European citizens feigning interest in Venezuela. "Particularly Richard Branson."

Waters's remarks received widespread attention in international media, forcing outlets to acknowledge that one of the world's most influential musicians had articulated an alternative view of Venezuela's crisis. More critically, his words disrupted the public relations hype surrounding Branson's pageant in Cúcuta. Around the time that Waters published his statement, UK artist Peter Gabriel announced that he

6   "Pink Floyd's Roger Waters Says Richard Branson's Venezuela Concert Has 'Nothing to Do with Aid'," *Global News*, February 20, 2019.

7   Seth J Frantzman, "Roger Waters Slams Syria Intervention, Attacks 'White Helmets' as 'Fake'," *Jerusalem Post*, April 17, 2018.

would not headline the concert,[8] dealing Branson another blow. When the Virgin CEO finally appeared on his Potemkin stage, he stood before roughly 300,000 anti-Chavista Venezuelans and right-wing Colombians clad in their obligatory white hats and t-shirts.[9]

"If we can take people into space, why is it so difficult to get people out of poverty?" the bleach-blonde oligarch ruminated without a hint of irony as he kicked off the regime-change extravaganza. Throughout the proceeding concert, roughly thirty of Latin America's most adored artists, including Lele Pons and Maluma, performed their greatest hits—and took turns denouncing Venezuela's government from Branson's billionaire-supplied platform.

"Thanks to dear Colombia and the United States," vintage Venezuelan balladeer José Luis Rodríguez gushed when he took the stage. "Enough of left-wing dictatorships in Latin America!"

On the other side of the border, Venezuela's government organized a counter-concert that took place for three days and featured over one hundred artists, including a video statement from Waters. Roberto Messuti, president of Venezuela's House of Artists Foundation, told Colombian media the festival was dedicated to "peace and solidarity," charging artists on the Colombian side of the border with "lending themselves to the war game" out of fear of losing their US visas.[10] Ultimately, Branson's Cúcuta festival failed to excite cultural critics even as it succeeded in turning their attention to Venezuela.

"With regards to the musical production itself, Venezuela Aid Live left much to be desired," *Rolling Stone* said of the concert, adding, "the most crucial goal of all was well beyond the experience of the show

8　"Peter Gabriel Will Not Perform at Venezuela Aid Live!" Genesis News, February 19, 2019.

9　Roberto Cardona, "As It Happens: Venezuela Live Aid Kicks Off Amid Calls For Liberty, Richard Branson Comments," *Billboard*, February 22, 2019.

10　"El Listado De Los Artistas Del Concierto Chavista En La Frontera," Blu Radio, February 22, 2019.

itself. If Branson wanted to put the eyes of the world on the border, he succeeded."[11]

The most apropos summary of the day's events appeared in *Billboard Magazine*, which captured the clumsy absurdity of Branson's hoopla in just a few sentences: "At the end, Chilean president Sebastián Piñera, Colombian president Iván Duque Márquez and Paraguayan president Mario Abdo Benítez all took the stage with Branson," the magazine reported in its "as it happened" breakdown of the festival (Cardona 2019).

"Juan Guaidó, the Venezuelan opposition leader, was going to join them, but opted not to at the last minute due to security concerns," it continued, describing the concert's final scene: "Branson shouted, '*libertad!*' and the event concluded without incident."

In fact, the event concluded with Branson leading the crowd in an awkward rendition of John Lennon's anti-war ballad, "Imagine."

With Washington's militarized aid delivery looming, my colleagues and I were faced with a choice: travel to cover events from the Venezuelan side of the border in Estado Táchira or remain in Caracas to document how the day played out in the capital. Considering both sides of the border were already oversaturated with international correspondents, we decided to keep our eyes on Caracas.

As February 23 approached, we spent hours gaming out potential scenarios with the Venezuelan journalists we'd befriended since arriving in Caracas. Was the US truly prepared to launch an all-out war? Or was the whole affair on the border merely a carefully constructed media exhibition designed to terrorize Venezuela's population? If the latter were true, Washington's plan was working. On February 16, I sat in the parking lot of our apartment building with Érika Ortega Sanoja, RT en Español's Venezuela correspondent. She was crying.

"I saw from far away what happened to countries like Iraq, Libya, and Syria," she told me. "I am afraid something like that could now happen here in my home, in Venezuela."

11   "Venezuela Aid Live: A Music Event Spurs Confrontations at the Border," *Rolling Stone*, February 23, 2019.

Earlier that day Érika recounted how, at the height of guarimba terror in years past, she had been forced to obscure her identity when traveling throughout our east Caracas neighborhood. As a well-known Chavista journalist, she was a walking target for the violent opposition rioters who had temporarily seized control of Venezuela's streets and launched physical attacks against government supporters.

Would guarimbas soon break out again? Diego Sequera, a journalist with the investigative Venezuelan outlet Misión Verdad, didn't think so. A bohemian intellectual who was almost always puffing a cigarette below his pantos-style spectacles and driver's cap (and who was equipped with more US history and pop culture references than your average Millennial American), Diego would become our guide to Venezuela—and a brotherly figure to myself and Max.

In some ways, Diego explained, Guaidó's foreign-backed ascent had sucked all momentum out of the opposition's street strategy. As far as they were concerned, "regime change" had been achieved with Guaidó's swearing-in ceremony. What purpose would riots serve other than undermine the illusion that the novice politician was now at the helm of Venezuela's government?

Rather than ignite chaos in Venezuela's streets, the February 23 plot was designed to test the loyalty of the country's armed forces. By forcing Venezuelan troops to prepare for an invasion, Washington waged a psychological war against the military's rank and file with the aim of intimidating them into defection. Trump and his advisors did not hide this objective.

"To the Venezuelan military high command, now is the time to stand on the side of the Venezuelan people," White House national security advisor John Bolton tweeted on February 2. "It is your right and responsibility to defend the constitution and democracy for Venezuela!"[12]

Weeks later, during his February 18 rally in Miami, President Trump issued a formal ultimatum to Venezuelan troops.

"We seek a peaceful transition of power, but all options are on the table," he warned. "We believe that the Venezuelan military and its

12   John Bolton (@AmbJohnBolton), Twitter post, February 2, 2019, https:// twitter.com/AmbJohnBolton/status/1091769750068305921?s=20.

leadership have a vital role to play in this process," he went on, informing the armed forces that if they continued "to support Maduro" they would "find no safe harbor, no easy exit, and no way out."

"You will lose everything," the US president vowed.[13]

Among the journalists who traveled to the Venezuela-Colombia border for the events of February 23 was Nicole Kramm, a young Chilean photographer with the Russian-backed media outlet Redfish. In a video posted to the since-deleted Redfish Twitter account that morning, Kramm documented what began as a predictable scene for such a tense day: rows of Venezuelan soldiers guarded by yellow concrete barriers plastered with the Venezuelan flag and text reading "GUARDIA NACIONAL BOLIVARIANA." On the other side of the border, throngs of Colombians and Venezuelan migrants hurled taunts and trash at the Venezuelan troops.

Kramm was aiming her camera at the rowdy civilians on the Colombian side when they suddenly turned around and bolted away in fear. Shrieks broke out behind her. Viewers then heard a loud *bang* as the screen went black. Static. When the camera came back to life, it broadcast an eerie, ground-level view of the deserted concrete street. Eventually, Venezuelan military boots appeared in the frame as soldiers arrived to carry Kramm to safety.

Kramm had been struck by an armored military vehicle as three Venezuelan soldiers inside hastily sped across their country's border and into Colombia. They were among the handful of military personnel who heeded Trump and Bolton's call to defect from Venezuela's armed forces on February 23 under the threat of a US invasion.

"This was an attack on civilians," Kramm said following the accident. "I can't believe they are being treated as heroes. If I didn't run, and was fifteen centimeters closer, I would not be here to tell you this."[14]

As terrifying and potentially deadly as Kramm's experience was, the three soldiers responsible for injuring her represented a minority

13 Steve Holland, "Trump Urges Venezuelan Military to Abandon Maduro or 'Lose Everything,'" Reuters, February 18, 2019.

14 "'They Attacked Civilians, They Are Not Heroes': Journalist Recounts Trampling by Venezuela Defectors," RT, February 24, 2019.

within Venezuela's military. As February 23 progressed, it became clear that Washington's stunt was not going according to plan. Rather than surrender, Venezuela's armed forces stood with their government and reinforced their country's border as the US military fortified on the other side. If the US truly wanted to ram its military equipment and "aid" into Venezuela, it would have to declare war.

Back in Caracas, the drama unfolding on the border seemed far away. As foreign correspondents rotated in and out of live positions before the backdrop of US military trucks stationed on the Tienditas bridge, denouncing Venezuela's government for "refusing" to accept Washington's generous "assistance," Caracas remained secure.

In the capital, the task of assembling opposition support was left to María Corina Machado, the US-backed politician who had served as one of the most radical figures in Venezuela's opposition for over a decade, particularly during the 2014 Salida riots. On the afternoon of February 23, Machado rallied supporters outside of the Generalissimo Francisco de Miranda Air Base located blocks from our eastern Caracas apartment.

When Max and I arrived on the scene, we once again found ourselves in a wave of white fabric as the protest swarmed an overpass bordering the air base and shut down traffic. Older couples wandered around aimlessly in a picnic-like atmosphere while young, masked men on motorcycles waved Venezuelan flags and sped up and down the highway. The bleached blur momentarily swelled with excitement as Machado emerged on a makeshift stage to shout promises of a new Venezuela free of *corrupción*. The lack of a sound system—or even a megaphone—made it difficult to hear the entirety of her brief message. After only a few minutes, she climbed down from the platform to take selfies with the crowd.

I elbowed my way toward Machado, who appeared to be in a daze of ecstasy, and asked her why she had previously made calls for the US to invade her country.

"Watch how the fight for liberty continues," the glassy-eyed politician replied as aides whisked her away.

By mid-afternoon, Machado was gone. None of the troops inside Francisco de Miranda had defected to the opposition's cause and the crowd dispersed like a group of vanquished soccer hooligans, Venezuelan flags draped across their slouched shoulders. As we left, I noticed a couple dozen of them frantically encircling a female news reporter and her cameraman.

"*Viva Guaidó! Viva Guaidó!*" they chanted loudly as the reporter filed her dispatch, visibly stressed. I quickly realized the mob wasn't providing exciting background noise for her report—they were angrily trying to shut down her broadcast.

"*Fuera (Get out!)! Fuera! Fuera!*"

Their taunting intensified as several hecklers physically rushed her live shot, forcing the reporter to end her communique. The crowd cheered victoriously as the reporter, who worked for a private Spanish outlet, Telecinco, wrapped up her microphone and hung her head in defeat. I asked a man standing next to me why they wanted to sabotage her report.

"Because she tried to say that we represent a minority here in Venezuela!" he explained. And these were Washington's supposed democrats—the very people who complained Maduro's government censored critical media.

The excitement was over. Max and I began the short walk back to our apartment flanked by opposition fanatics filtering in and out of the Italian, Japanese, and vegan restaurants that cluttered Caracas's Chacao district. As we passed a Chinese joint, an older man in a white guayabera barreled past us and through the restaurant doors, bellowing into the dining hall: "Maduro!"

In unison, the diners replied: "*Coño e' tu madre!*"

They were repeating the vulgar rallying cry of Venezuela's opposition that literally translates to mean "cunt of your mother." In this context, it basically meant: "Maduro, you motherfucker."

"Maduro!" the man called again.

"*Coño e' tu madre!*" the diners roared in between bites of sugar-coated chicken and pork.

Even as they failed to win over the rank and file of Venezuela's military with their petite charm, Venezuela's bourgeoisie seized the moment to engage in some family-friendly political merrymaking.

In western Caracas, the capital's base of Chavismo support, the mood was surprisingly jubilant. Throughout the afternoon of February 23, tens of thousands of Venezuelans participated in a pro-government rally dubbed "The Bolivarian March of Dignity."

"Raise the Venezuelan flag!" President Maduro thundered from a large stage, surrounded by government ministers and prominent socialist party officials, before leading the crowd in singing Venezuela's national anthem, "Gloria Al Bravo Pueblo."[15]

"The people of Caracas swelled the streets to support peace, to support the union of the civil military, and to say to imperialism and to Donald Trump: 'Hands off Venezuela! Yankee go home!'" Maduro continued, standing before a podium decorated with a sign reading "Hands Off Venezuela."

A massive poster with the text "#TrumpHandsOffVenezuela" hung above him. Both slogans were printed in English, suggesting their message was directed at an audience beyond Venezuela's shores.

The atmosphere in western Caracas was celebratory. As far as these Venezuelans were concerned, their country had just stared the US military in its face and refused to surrender. As Venezuelans rejoiced in defense of their sovereignty, however, a fresh attack against their homeland brewed on the border.

At 2:12 in the afternoon on February 23, the private Colombian television station NTN24 posted an urgent message to Twitter.

Venezuelan national police "burn three aid trucks by launching tear gas canisters at the caravan," the dispatch read, featuring a video of correspondent Luis Gonzalo Pérez standing before a semi truck engulfed in orange and black brume.[16]

---

15   Luigino Bracci Roa, "Discurso Completo De Nicolás Maduro Ante Gran Marcha Este 23 Febrero 2019," February 23, 2019.

16   NTN24 Venezuela (@NTN24ve), Twitter post, February 23, 2019, https://twitter.com/NTN24ve/status/1099386437957574658?s=20.

"The humanitarian aid is being consumed by flames at this moment," Gonzalo exclaimed, pointing his camera toward billowing clouds of smoke.

A masked youth wearing sunglasses and brandishing a police shield jumped into the shot and shouted illegibly as Gonzalo continued down the bridge that connected Colombia to Venezuela. Every US aid truck in sight was aflame. Finally, Guaidó's coup regime operation and their US handlers had a narrative they could broadcast to the world.

Leading the propaganda blitz was Marco Rubio, the Florida senator born into Miami's notoriously reactionary Cuban expat community. A middle-aged career politician with boyish looks and cowlick-y hair, Rubio was once considered a rising Republican star—despite a questionable past. In 2011, the *Washington Post* revealed that Rubio had based his entire political coming-of-age story on a lie. Though he repeatedly spouted a clichéd south Florida tale of his parents' escape from Fidel Castro's socialist hellscape, immigration records demonstrated that the Rubios had in fact gained permanent US residency nearly three years *before* Cuba's 1959 revolution—meaning they had actually fled the regime of the country's US-backed military dictator, Fulgencio Batista.[17]

Aside from pathetic dishonesty, Rubio's character was tarnished by revelations that throughout the 1980s, his brother-in-law, Orlando Cicilia, directed a $75 million cocaine smuggling ring out of his home in West Kendall, Florida. Cicilia was convicted of drug trafficking and sentenced to thirty-five years in prison in 1989, but released early in the year 2000. In his 2013 memoir, Rubio—who by then had featured Cicilia at numerous campaign events—claimed that he was unaware of his brother-in-law's criminal activity and had been "stunned" by news of his arrest. Yet a 2016 investigation by the *Miami New Times* cast doubt on the senator's account, revealing that as a teenager, Rubio had actually lived in the home at the center of Cicilia's drug operation.

"For anyone to argue that teens or adults living at this time in Miami didn't know their family members were in the coke business is

17   Manuel Roig-Franzia, "Marco Rubio's Compelling Family Story Embellishes Facts, Documents Show," *Washington Post*, October 20, 2011.

total horseshit," a former Miami-Dade detective told the publication in response to Rubio's claims of ignorance.[18]

Though Rubio declined to comment on the story, it earned him the nickname "Narco Rubio" among Venezuelans, including government officials whom the senator repeatedly accused of trafficking drugs. The senator's most well-known moniker, however, was "Little Marco," an alias bestowed upon him by then candidate Trump during the 2016 Republican primary, when the future president publicly mocked Rubio's affinity for high-heeled boots—an apparent product of his dearth of height.[19]

Despite suffering routine public humiliations at the hands of Trump—who dealt a lethal blow to the senator's national political ambitions—Rubio would become a giddy servant of the president's aggressive Latin America policy. In February 2019, he traveled to Cúcuta to drum up support for the impending US invasion of Venezuela.

"The aid is going to get through," Rubio assured CNN on February 17. "I think ultimately the question is whether it gets through in a way that [Maduro is] cooperative with or in a way that he's not."[20]

As news that the aid was ablaze emerged, Rubio leapt to accuse Venezuela's government of sparking the fire.

"Maduro National Police set fire to an aid truck carrying food & medicine while people in #Venezuela starve," he tweeted, linking to video of the burning convoy. Secretary of State Pompeo repeated Rubio's narrative, similarly blaming the melee on "Maduro's thugs."

"What kind of a sick tyrant stops food from getting to hungry people? The images of burning trucks filled with aid are sickening," Pompeo tweeted.[21]

---

18   Tim Elfrink, "Marco Rubio's Ties to a Drug-Smuggling Brother-in-Law Were Closer Than Advertised," *Miami New Times*, October 26, 2016.

19   Rohan Nadkarni, "Marco Rubio May Never Live Down the Time He Wore Those Cool Chelsea Boots," *GQ*, January 22, 2016.

20   Jamie Ehrlich and Kate Sullivan, "Rubio Visits Venezuela-Colombia Border, Says Aid Will Get Through," CNN, February 17, 2019.

21   Mike Pompeo (@secpompeo), Twitter post, February 23, 2019, https://twitter.com/secpompeo/status/1099472381838585856.

My colleagues and I anxiously monitored developments on the border from our Caracas apartment. As it turned out, we did not need to be present on the border to dispel the media deception rapidly emerging out of Cúcuta. Max spent the evening of February 23 glued to his laptop, poring through images, witness testimonies, and video footage of the disorder on the border. Shortly after midnight, he surfaced with an article that documented how hooligans on the Colombian side of the frontier—resembling the masked youth who appeared in Gonzalo's report—had lit fire to the convoy, torching the aid in order to frame Maduro's government.[22] It was a classic false flag operation, albeit incredibly sloppy.

Max linked to multiple videos and photos chronicling the moments that young men, looking more like guarimberos than Venezuelan troops, tossed Molotov cocktails onto the dormant aid trucks.

"Even *Bloomberg News*, which has run a relentless stream of pro-opposition reports, published video showing guarimberos on the bridge making Molotov cocktails, which could easily set a truck cabin or its cargo alight," Max explained. Images posted by Telesur correspondent Madelein Garcia even captured one youth dousing the inflamed convoy with gasoline.[23]

Once again, Washington's official narrative had crashed against the hard rocks of reality. The *New York Times* published a recycled version of Max's report weeks later, confirming that "the opposition itself, not Mr. Maduro's men, [appeared] to have set the cargo alight."[24] The paper of record characterized the fire as accidental, however, and neglected to credit the *Grayzone* for our initial reporting. Regardless, these facts mattered little to US officials, who deployed images of the burning aid to agitate for further intervention in Venezuela.

22   Max Blumenthal, "Burning Aid: An Interventionist Deception on Colombia-Venezuela Bridge?" *The Grayzone*, February 24, 2019.

23   Madelein Garcia (@madeleintlSUR), Twitter post, February 23, 2019, https://twitter.com/madeleintlSUR/status/1099429021857861633?s=20.

24   Nicholas Casey, Christoph Koettl, and Deborah Acosta, "Footage Contradicts U.S. Claim That Nicolás Maduro Burned Aid Convoy," *New York Times*, March 10, 2019.

"The tyrant in Caracas danced as his henchmen murdered civilians and burned food and medicine," Vice President Mike Pence tweeted on February 25,[25] drawing a comparison between Maduro dancing with supporters in Venezuela's streets and the Roman Emperor Nero, who allegedly played his fiddle as Rome burned to the ground.

No one was more emotionally distraught by the events of February 23, however, than Marco Rubio. As the day came and went leaving nothing but smoldering aid on the Colombia-Venezuela border, the senator descended into an impassioned Twitter meltdown.

The outburst began shortly after 2:00 a.m. on February 24, when Rubio tweeted side-by-side photographs of the former head of Panama's military junta, Manuel Noriega. One image showed Noriega delivering a fiery speech; the other was his mugshot, taken within a Miami prison after the US invaded his country and ended his rule.[26] Several hours later, Rubio followed up with two photos of late Libyan leader Muammar Gaddafi: one depicting him proudly seated in a golden throne; the other taken shortly after NATO-backed mercenaries captured him and raped him with a bayonet, his face lifeless and bloodied.[27] Rubio ended the unhinged series of not-so-cryptic tweets with images of former Romanian head of state Nicolae Ceaușescu and his wife Elena's arrest, taken days before they were both executed.[28] Though none of the snapshots were accompanied with words, Rubio's message was clear: you're next, Maduro.

Amid his barrage of manic threats, Rubio found time to suggest that Venezuela's government was poisoning opposition figures in Cúcuta.

"Grave situation developing right now inside of #Colombia," he tweeted on the night of February 23. "@freddysuperlano a member of the National Assembly of #Venezuela was poisoned this morning at

25   Mike Pence (@VP45), Twitter post, February 25, 2019, https://twitter.com/VP45/status/1100168044863721472?lang=en.

26   Marco Rubio (@marcorubio), Twitter post, February 24, 2019, https://twitter.com/marcorubio/status/1099565854100992000?s=20.

27   Marco Rubio (@marcorubio), Twitter post, February 24, 2019, https://twitter.com/marcorubio/status/1099726515292508162?s=20.

28   Marco Rubio (@marcorubio), Twitter post, February 24, 2019, https://twitter.com/marcorubio/status/1099808766894190592?s=20.

breakfast inside of Colombia & is in serious condition at the hospital. His assistant Carlos Salinas has died from poisoning."[29]

Twitter immediately lit up with rumors that Maduro had targeted the men, but the drama would not play out the way Rubio hoped. It was later revealed that Superlano and Salinas—who were cousins—had been drugged and robbed by two prostitutes they met after attending Branson's Venezuela Aid Live concert.

"The Salinas cousins enjoyed Friday night in the company of two women, after picking them up at the Bolívar Shopping Center," reported Cúcuta-based media outlet *La Opinión*. The foursome stayed out all night before deciding "to go to a motel and continue the party while having drinks."[30]

At the motel, the women reportedly drugged the cousins and made off with their cash, cellphones, and rings. An autopsy confirmed that Salinas died after ingesting a combination of alcohol and benzodiazepine—a victim of his own corrupt and decadent lifestyle.[31] As it turned out, Superlano and Salinas were not the only members of Venezuela's opposition living large in Cúcuta—and the women who poisoned them were not alone in carrying out a massive heist.

Throughout months following Washington's border stunt, throngs of desperate Venezuelan military defectors and their families roamed the streets of Cúcuta like hopeless zombies. They had initially been "received as heroes" for defecting on February 23, but, as *El Colombiano* explained, had since "passed from the happiness of a new beginning to uncertainty; from holding high military ranks into anonymity, to living in fear, and with hunger."[32]

---

29   Marco Rubio (@marcorubio), Twitter post, February 23, 2019, https://twitter.com/marcorubio/status/1099512202799779841.

30   "Diputado Venezolano Grave y Su Primo Muerto Por Burundanga," *La Opinión*, February 23, 2019.

31   "Medicina Legal De Colombia Confirma Que Diputado Superlano y Su Primo Fueron Drogados," *El Tiempo Ve*, October 10, 2020.

32   "Un Hotel, La Vivienda De Los Militares De Guaidó," *El Colombiano*, April 24, 2019.

By April, some of the defectors were preparing to embark on a 364-mile march from Cúcuta to Colombia's capital, Bogotá, where they planned to apply for refugee status. Others resorted to joining local paramilitary groups and narco gangs to survive. The men complained to Colombian media that the UN refugee agency, Colombian government, and Guaidó coup regime had effectively abandoned them. As their presence in Cúcuta became increasingly impossible to ignore, Spanish-language media noted their plight "received little attention from Kevin Javier Rojas Peñaloza and Edith Rossana Barrera Castillo,"[33] the individuals Guaidó tapped to oversee defector's affairs in Colombia.

Rojas and Barrera's failure to carry out their duties went far beyond negligence. In June 2019, the Miami-based *PanAm Post* published an explosive story revealing the pair had in fact embezzled funding earmarked for the defectors. The investigation, authored by the site's passionately anti-Maduro editor in chief, Orlando Avendaño, explained that defecting soldiers had been lured across the border with promises of "stays in hotels, care for them and their families; medicines, food, hospital visits" and whatever else they needed.[34] But the assistance never materialized—and dozens of families were ultimately evicted from their hotels and dumped on Colombia's streets. According to the report, Rojas and Barrera had squandered tens of thousands of dollars appropriated for the soldiers on their own lavish lifestyles. Avendaño based his investigation on information from multiple sources, including Colombian intelligence, which he said caught wind of the fraud when "Barrera and Rojas began to lead lives that did not correspond with who they were."

"They gave me all the evidence," Avendaño wrote, including, "invoices that show excesses" and "expenses of more than 3,000,000 pesos ($800 USD) in Colombian hotels and nightclubs per night. About a thousand dollars for food and drinks. Clothing expenses in very

---

33   Sebastiana Barráez, "Grupos Delictivos Reclutan En Cúcuta a Militares Venezolanos Desertores: 'Lo Que Esconde La Oferta Final Es La Muerte,'" *Infobae*, April 18, 2019.

34   Orlando Avendaño, "Enviados De Guaidó Se Apropian De Fondos Para Ayuda Humanitaria En Colombia," *PanAm Post*, June 14, 2019.

pricey stores in Bogotá and Cúcuta. Vehicle rental reports and expensive hotel payments . . . A lot of money."

Rojas and Barrera kept the cash flowing by inflating the number of defectors under their care. Though they officially reported to be managing 1,450 people, Colombian intelligence independently determined there were only about 700 Venezuelan defectors in Cúcuta. According to itemized receipts, Rojas and Barrera ran expenses totaling roughly US$47,000. What's more, Avendaño alleged that 60 percent of the food donated by pro-Guaidó governments on February 23 had rotted on the border, stating his sources showed him photographs of the decaying aid.

Avendaño's investigation reverberated beyond the traditional realm of Guaidó critics. "Does 'humanitarian aid' also include alcohol and prostitutes?" ran a headline in the Catholic Spanish-language site Aleteia, a reference to the fraud revelations and saga of the Salinas cousins.[35] The news even prompted the fanatically anti-Chavista OAS secretary general, Luis Almagro, to call for an investigation into Rojas and Barrera, declaring: "There is no democratization possible under the darkness of corrupt acts."[36] Sensing growing political insecurity, Guaidó attempted to distance himself from the duo and ordered his "ambassador" in Bogotá to request that Colombian authorities formally investigate the allegations.[37] For its part, Venezuela's government announced a criminal inquiry into Guaidó's role in the scheme, claiming he personally directed the corrupt mafia.

The Rojas and Barrera scandal provided only a small window into the fraud of February 23, 2019. In April 2021, USAID published an internal audit that confirmed what Venezuela's government had claimed all along: the border stunt had been driven by entirely political—not humanitarian—objectives. The audit reported that

35   Carlos Zapata, "Venezuela: ¿'Ayuda Humanitaria' También Incluye Alcohol y Prostitutas?" Aleteia, June 17, 2019.

36   Luis Almagro (@Almagro_OEA2015), Twitter post, June 14, 2019, https://twitter.com/Almagro_OEA2015/status/1139658418573234179?s=20.

37   Karen Sánchez, "Representantes De Guaidó Solicitan a Fiscalía Colombiana Investigar Mal Uso De Fondos," Voice of America, June 18, 2019.

the State Department and White House National Security Council had overseen the shipment, directly inhibiting "USAID's ability to adhere to humanitarian principles and mitigate operational risks." Additionally, the report asserted the aid package had not been designed based on need-assessment, but as "a key tool to elevate support to the Venezuela Interim Government and increase pressure on the Maduro regime."[38] The Inspector General argued that US government resources may have fallen into corrupt hands, revealing that though USAID spent two million taxpayer dollars "to purchase and transport" the aid, it neglected to impose proper fraud controls on its distribution.

Meanwhile, the roughly $2.4 million raised from Branson's Cúcuta concert were funneled into the formation of a non-profit called the Aid Live Foundation, which claimed to be "promoting the integral development and well-being of Venezuelan children in vulnerable communities and Venezuelan migrants in Colombia"[39] at the time of this book's publication. Though the foundation's website boasted it has provided services to over 11,000 people, it is impossible to review an assessment of Aid Live's work beyond their own internal reports.

Cúcuta was abused. For several weeks in February 2019, US government officials like Marco Rubio converted the urban backwater into the staging ground for a media spectacle that risked sparking all-out war on the American continent. Venezuela's opposition treated the city as their personal playground, partying with local prostitutes and leaving hundreds of military defectors turned refugees desperately wandering its barrios. A publicity-obsessed British tycoon spent unknown sums of money building a mammoth concert venue on its grounds that was only used for one afternoon. By the end of it all, no charity dollars were truly accounted for and not one box of supplies ever made it to Venezuela.

Long after Branson returned to his routine as an international oligarch—taking solo trips to outer space, waterskiing with naked

38   "Enhanced Processes and Implementer Requirements Are Needed To Address Challenges and Fraud Risks in USAID's Venezuela Response," USAID Office of Inspector General, April 16, 2021.

39   "Our Mission," Aid Live Foundation, accessed March 11, 2023.

models, and enjoying Caribbean splash fights with Barack Obama— Cúcuta remained one of Colombia's poorest localities. Long after the ashes of charred humanitarian aid turned to dust and dirt, 52 percent of Colombians in the surrounding region remained mired in poverty,[40] virtually abandoned by their US-backed government, at the mercy of paramilitaries and narco-gangs patrolling their streets.

40   "Pobreza Monetaria y Pobreza Monetaria Extrema," Departamento Administrativo Nacional de Estadística, accessed April 11, 2023.

SEVEN

THE ORGANIZATION OF AMERICAN SATELLITE STATES

In the early morning hours of February 20, 2019, María Faría Faría made the most important statement of her diplomatic career. She did so on Twitter.

"In fulfillment of the diplomatic function assigned by President Juan Guaidó and recognized by the Costa Rican government, we assume control of the administrative headquarters of the Embassy of Venezuela in San José," Faría tweeted, attaching an image of herself shooting a Blue Steel gaze past the camera.[1] Behind her, staffers held up an uncomfortably lopsided Venezuelan flag.

Faría, whom Guaidó named as his "ambassador" to Costa Rica, had broken into Venezuela's diplomatic compound in San José under the early morning twilight. A senior Venezuelan official later told me that Faría gained access to the embassy by bribing the building's owner into handing over its keys.

Putting on her best impersonation of a diplomat, Faría looked proud of her feat in the image posted to Twitter. But as the day progressed, that feeling must have given way to humiliation. Within hours of the break-in, Costa Rica's Foreign Ministry declared the government in San José "deplored [her] unacceptable entry" into Venezuela's embassy and expressed its "strong rejection of the performance of the diplomatic representative María Faría."[2]

1   Maria Faría Faría (@MariaFariaVE), Twitter post, February 20, 2019, https://twitter.com/MariaFariaVE/status/1098192617295237120.

2   "Ministerio De Relaciones Exteriores Deplora Ingreso Inaceptable De Diplomáticos a Sede De La Embajada De Venezuela En Costa Rica," Ministerio de Relaciones Exteriores y Culto, February 20, 2019.

Having sufficiently outraged her host country through her unilateral takeover of Venezuela's embassy, Faría was forced to cancel a press conference scheduled for that afternoon, telling reporters she would instead spend time discussing her actions with Costa Rican foreign minister Manuel Ventura Robles.[3] It was only her first day of school, and Faría had already been summoned to the principal's office for a crash course in diplomatic law.

Though Costa Rica was among the handful of US-allied governments that officially recognized Guaidó as president of Venezuela, it had given representatives of Maduro's government an April 15 deadline for departure from the country[4]—meaning until that date, Maduro's diplomats legally represented Venezuela in San José. When those dignitaries arrived for work on the morning of Faría's break-in, a horde of violent Guaidó supporters physically blocked them from entering the embassy.[5] Two of the thugs photographed assaulting the diplomats were identified as the sons of Eduardo Manuitt, a former Chavista governor who fled corruption charges in Venezuela in 2009.[6]

The Manuitt boys were the perfect duo to play diplomatic bouncer for Faría, herself the child of a Venezuelan fugitive. Her father, Colonel Jesús Faría Rodríguez, fled Venezuela in 2006 after breaking out of the prison where he was serving a nine-year sentence for overseeing the Daktari Farm plot,[7] a foiled plan to assassinate then president Hugo Chávez by disguising Colombian paramilitary fighters as Venezuelan soldiers.[8]

---

3   Rita Valverde (@ritvv), Twitter post, February 20, 2019, https://twitter.com/ritvv/status/1098328982095835136?s=08.

4   "Costa Rica Demands Maduro-Accredited Diplomats Leave Country," *The Tico Times*, February 16, 2019.

5   Elyangelica González (@ElyangelicaNews), Twitter post, February 20, 2019, https://twitter.com/ElyangelicaNews/status/1098273951627833346?s=20.

6   Anya Parampil, "Meet Juan Guaido's First Ambassador, Fake Twitter Diplomat Slammed by Costa Rica for 'Unacceptable Entry,'" *The Grayzone*, February 21, 2019.

7   Natalie Obiko Pearson, "Leader of Strike to Oust Chavez Escapes," Associated Press, August 14, 2006.

8   Jeremy Lennard, "Colombian Paramilitaries Arrested in Venezuela," *Guardian*, May 24, 2004.

At the time of the elder Faría's prison-break, a since-deleted article in the Venezuelan outlet *El Nacional* reported that the retired colonel had three children, including a daughter who had recently "graduated as an accountant."[9] The younger Faría's education left her seemingly unprepared for her eventual diplomatic gig, as Costa Rica's government said her break-in at the embassy and subsequent tweet violated "elementary diplomatic norms of respect and trust in relations in the international community, and above all, in international law."

The episode provided the perfect metaphor for Guaidó's entire shadow regime, which was far more active on social media than within any real-world government building. With US assistance, however, that would soon change.

The hostile takeover of Venezuela's embassy in Costa Rica was the opening salvo in Washington's all-out diplomatic assault on Maduro's government. In the days following the Faría affair, US authorities escorted Guaidó officials as they seized three Venezuelan government offices, including the military attaché in DC and the New York City consulate.[10]

"This is an asset that belonged to Venezuelans," announced Carlos Vecchio, Guaidó's "ambassador" to the United States, shortly after removing a portrait of Maduro from the wall of Venezuela's military attaché and replacing it with a stern-looking photograph of his boss.[11]

Still, beyond Faría's fluke and a few US-assisted gains, Guaidó faced a crisis of legitimacy in the months following his self-declared presidency. By April, his project was losing momentum, a reality most clearly reflected by the United Nation's continued recognition of Maduro's government. Before taking Guaidó's putsch to Manhattan, however, the Trump administration would test its regime change stratagem on the UN's regional equivalent in the Americas.

---

9   David González, "Coronel Jesus Rodriguez 'Salio a Buscar La Libertad'," Venezuela Awareness, August 15, 2006.

10   "Guaido Loyalists Seize Diplomatic Properties in US," Deutsche Welle, March 19, 2019.

11   Camilo Montoya-Galvez and Christina Ruffini, "Venezuelan Opposition Seizes Diplomatic Offices in U.S.; Maduro Official Warns of 'Reciprocal' Action," CBS, March 18, 2019.

A former Honduran government minister once wondered aloud to me: What happened to Luis Almagro? What did the US government have on the Organization of American States' (OAS) secretary general that made him so eager to act as perhaps the most loyal servant of Washington the institution had ever known?

Having served as the foreign minister of Uruguay under center-left president José "Pepe" Mujica, Almagro received support from progressive regional governments during his initial bid to lead the OAS in 2015. After emerging victorious, however, Almagro abandoned any pretense of independence from the Washington Consensus and used his position as secretary general to issue stentorian denunciations of left-wing governments in the region—all while ignoring repression handed down by their US-allied counterparts.

Critics accused Almagro of providing the OAS with a progressive face as it advanced Washington's position on regional affairs. Yet those with knowledge of its inner workings take a more holistic view of the organization, noting its power does not lie in Almagro's office.

"Almagro has unfortunately put himself in the situation in which he gets blamed for a lot because he talks too much," Sir Ronald Sanders told me, referring to the secretary general's regular Twitter activity and provocative public statements. According to Ambassador Sanders, who has represented Antigua and Barbuda before the OAS since 2015, though the charge that Almagro dictated the organization's agenda "is a popular opinion, it simply isn't so."

"The OAS is its member states," the dignitary stressed, insisting OAS policy was not set by its secretary general but by the representatives of its thirty-four member states.

Such a comprehensive evaluation of the OAS's function did not let Washington off the hook for its effort to subjugate regional governments. The decidedly pro-US bend of Almagro's OAS directly coincided with several successful US-backed regime change campaigns in the region, anti-democratic efforts that experienced a renaissance during the tenure of President Barack Obama.

In years preceding Obama's rise, US foreign policy was largely focused on carrying out President George W. Bush's "War on Terror" in the Middle East—a distant obsession that created space for the rise of the so-called "Pink Tide," a collection of left-aligned governments that emerged throughout Latin America and the Caribbean around the turn of the century. Seemingly overnight, progressive leaders—many of them inspired by Venezuela's 1998 revolution—arrived at the helm of government in Argentina, Paraguay, Brazil, Bolivia, and beyond. With Chávez as their de facto lodestar, this united bloc of independent governments threatened to outweigh Washington's grip on the American continent for the first time in its history. During this period, Chávez even initiated a plan to establish a regional Latin American bank that US financial institutions could not control.[12]

While Obama attempted to draw down the US presence in the Middle East, he renewed Washington's focus on Latin America. Throughout his presidency, Washington effectively rolled back the Pink Tide through a series of hybrid coups that returned pro-US governments to power in regional capitals from Honduras[13] to Brazil.[14] As the dominoes of progressive change on the American continent fell one by one, Venezuela remained Washington's ultimate target.

Like many of Trump's high-level foreign service appointees, Carlos Trujillo was not a career diplomat. A commercial lawyer by training, Trujillo was first elected to Florida's State Senate when he was just twenty-seven years old, but his ambition transcended Tallahassee. The son of anti-Castro Cuban exiles, Trujillo quickly established himself as an ally of hardline Florida Republicans and was summoned to Washington in 2017, when President Trump appointed him to represent the US at the OAS. Baby-faced and eager to please, Trujillo emerged as one of Washington's most effective coup-mongers when he oversaw the campaign to install a representative of Guaidó's shadow regime at the

12   Rory Carroll, "Nobel Economist Endorses Chávez Regional Bank Plan," *Guardian*, October 11, 2007.

13   Sandra Cuffe, "Ten Years after Coup, Hondurans Flee amid Violence and Repression," Al Jazeera, June 28, 2019.

14   Alex Main, "A Blow to Brazilian Democracy: The Illegitimate Removal of Dilma Rousseff from Power," Center for Economic and Policy Research, January 17, 2017.

OAS, completely flouting the organization's rules and furthering his own career in the process.

Following his self-declared presidency, Guaidó appointed a seasoned right-wing lawyer named Gustavo Tarre to represent his coup regime before the OAS. Established in 1948, the OAS was partial to US policy by design, with Washington supplying between 50 and 60 percent of its annual budget.[15] The organization provided a theater for Washington's diplomatic attacks on regional adversaries throughout the Cold War, prompting Cuban leader Fidel Castro to brand it the "Yankee Ministry of Colonies" on the American continent.[16] Even so, OAS support for Guaidó was hampered by rules enshrined in its founding charter, which established two decision-making bodies tasked with codifying the organization's policy: the Permanent Council and General Assembly.[17]

The Permanent Council contained one representative from each member state and met in DC on a regular basis to debate and vote on OAS affairs. Yet its charter defined the General Assembly, a yearly summit of member states' foreign ministers, as its "supreme organ" tasked with dictating major policy decisions, including changes to its "structure and functions." This meant that according to OAS rules, the group could not alter its structure and accept Tarre as Venezuela's representative without the approval of its General Assembly, which was slated to convene in Colombia in June 2019.

For Trujillo, waiting to confirm Tarre at the General Assembly was not an option. Guaidó's star was not only fading with each passing day, but OAS rules stipulated that its General Assembly required support from two-thirds of its members to approve a resolution. Though Washington had successfully pressured a few dozen allies into recognizing its Caracas coup, the pro-Guaidó bloc still represented a regional minority in the Americas. Lacking the votes needed to rubber stamp Guaidó's authority in accordance with OAS rules, Trujillo instead

15   "Contributions to OAS Funds," Organization of American States, 2022.
16   Stella Krepp, "Cuba and the OAS: A Story of Dramatic Fallout and Reconciliation," Wilson Center, December 18, 2017.
17   "CHARTER OF THE ORGANIZATION OF AMERICAN STATES," Organization of American States, 1967.

launched a personal campaign to force Tarre's recognition through the organization on his own terms.

As soon as the US took over as chair of the OAS Permanent Council in April 2019, Trujillo convened a special session to debate a resolution that would install Tarre as Venezuela's representative before the body. I attended the April 9 session myself, aware that Trujillo's success was entirely dependent on his colleagues' willingness to flout the organization's basic rules—and purpose. According to its charter, the OAS had been established by member states "to promote their solidarity, to strengthen their collaboration, and to defend their sovereignty, their territorial integrity, and their independence." Accepting Tarre—the representative of an unelected US-backed coup regime—directly undermined that mission.

This reality was not lost on all member states. While arguing against the resolution to receive Tarre, Ambassador Sanders of Antigua and Barbuda asserted that "in international law and practice, such recognition is based on the test of who is in charge of the country, who administers its affairs, [and] who controls its borders." Because Guaidó controlled no government ministries and exercised no authority in Venezuela, Sanders argued that accepting his OAS representative was tantamount to ignoring "this essential test of international law."

Tarre's entry was further complicated by the fact that Venezuela's elected government had initiated the formal process of withdrawing from the OAS years before his nomination. Then foreign minister Delcy Rodríguez announced Venezuela's exit from the group in April 2017, citing the OAS's vocal support for the guarimba riots that had paralyzed her country since 2014.[18] While making the announcement, Rodríguez noted that the OAS withdrawal process took two years to finalize—meaning Venezuela's official exit happened to perfectly coincide with Washington's April 2019 attempt to install Tarre as the country's legitimate representative.

None of these concerns troubled the US and its allies, which pressed ahead with a vote on Tarre's recognition on April 9. By pushing Tarre's acceptance on the Permanent Council, a body that required

18   Reuters Staff, "Venezuela to Withdraw from OAS, Denounces Campaign by Washington," Reuters, April 26, 2017.

the approval of a *simple* majority of member states to pass resolutions, Trujillo hoped to sidestep the higher, two-thirds majority needed in a General Assembly vote. It was on that basis that a handful of OAS diplomats argued the Permanent Council's vote on Tarre's acceptance was illegitimate.

"The presentation of this resolution is part of a disturbing trend in which any simple majority of eighteen member states can impose their will on all other member states," cautioned Ambassador Sanders. Those fears were shared by his Guyanese counterpart, Riyad Insanally, who asserted a decision to recognize Tarre would "set a dangerous precedent and ultimately damage irreparably the institutional frame-work of the OAS." The rancorous debate, which took place in the OAS's ironically named "Liberator Simón Bolívar Room," reached its apex when Trujillo was forced to yield the floor to Venezuela's *actual* representative, Asbina Marin.

"I am the Venezuelan representative and there is no other, that is why I am seated here," Marin proclaimed from behind Venezuela's OAS placard. She then turned to face her US counterpart.

"You cannot appoint a head of my delegation," she informed Trujillo. "You, Mr. Chairman, do not have that power."

Unphased by Marin's intervention, Trujillo moved the meeting along without acknowledging her comments. Minutes later, a simple majority of present OAS Permanent Council representatives voted to accept Tarre by a margin of 19 to 6.[19] Six other countries—including Venezuela's ally, Nicaragua—abstained from the vote, while another, Belize, missed the session altogether.

"You have converted the OAS into an empty shell that has violated its own principles, and you're now proving that our decision to with-draw was the correct one. We are leaving the OAS and we will never come back," Marin declared, exiting OAS grounds with her head held high. Venezuela adhered to its original plan and formally left the organ-ization on April 27, 2019.

19   "Permanent Council Accepts Appointment of Designated Permanent Representative of Venezuela's National Assembly to the OAS," The Organization of American States, April 9, 2019.

Moments after the April 9 vote, Trujillo cheerfully mingled with friendly reporters and Guaidó delegates, including Tarre, in the OAS gallery. I approached the US representative and asked why he had rammed a vote on Tarre's acceptance through the Permanent Council rather than wait for the General Assembly.

"I am sure it will be revisited at the General Assembly," he replied with bumptious assurance.[20]

But what was the legal basis for the vote, I asked? What about the OAS charter? Trujillo suddenly reminded me of a hung-over frat boy asked to summarize the week's reading assignment during a Friday morning university lecture.

"Article, article, yeah, in the charter," he stuttered before offering a non sequitur, turning his back to me, and scurrying away.

Apparently, Trujillo did not expect to be quizzed on the rules and regulations governing the organization where he worked. And who could blame him? As Ambassador Sanders told me in 2022, Trujillo always "had his eye on becoming a deputy assistant secretary of state," but could only secure the post through "the route of becoming the US ambassador to the OAS." According to Sanders, Trujillo's "sole purpose was to deliver south Florida for Trump" by appealing to the region's extremist expat community.

Trump ultimately promoted the Florida Republican to assistant secretary of state for Western Hemispheric affairs in March 2020. Though Trump's subsequent electoral defeat stifled Trujillo's ascent, his work to legitimize Guaidó demonstrated his worth as a party asset. Despite—or perhaps thanks to—Trujillo's total lack of regard for diplomatic law, Trump's administration successfully converted the OAS into a blunt instrument of its Venezuela coup policy.

On a cool April evening following the OAS vote to accept Tarre, I met Max on a street corner in Washington DC's Shaw district. Though he was supposed to be preparing to deliver a talk on his book, *The*

---

20 Anya Parampil (@anyaparampil), Twitter post, April 10, 2019, https://twitter.com/anyaparampil/status/1115840724182994944?s=20.

Management of Savagery, he was entirely fixated on two rumpled papers in his hand.

The papers, emblazoned with the logo for the Center for Strategic and International Studies (CSIS) think tank, appeared to be a check-in list. Beneath the title "Assessing the Use of Military Force in Venezuela," they indexed the names of several State Department and USAID officials alongside those of Guaidó's DC-based representatives, including his "ambassador" to the US, Carlos Vecchio. Representatives from Brazil and Colombia's US embassies were also listed, as were heavy hitters including former head of US Southern Command, Kurt Tidd, and Roger Noriega, Washington's OAS representative under the administration of George W. Bush.

The documents Max held before us confirmed what many Venezuelans feared: US officials, their regional allies, and Guaidó's coup regime were actively gaming out scenarios for a military offensive against their country.

The following day, Max cold-called several people listed on the check-in sheet to question them about the event. While most played dumb, two attendees acknowledged their participation in the April 10 roundtable discussion, allowing Max to move ahead with an article revealing that the meeting had in fact taken place.[21]

Venezuela's UN ambassador, Samuel Moncada, swiftly condemned the event as a "sinister meeting" that "will remain marked by the disgraceful history of US wars."[22]

"CSIS, funded by the largest US oil companies, arms producers, and the US government itself, can only be what it is: an organ promoting US colonial wars," the diplomat added.[23]

Indeed, since its founding amid the Cold War, CSIS had established itself as one of Washington's premier pro-war think tanks. Originally

21   Max Blumenthal, "US Military Attack on Venezuela Mulled by Top Trump Advisors and Latin American Officials at Private DC Meeting," *The Grayzone,* April 13, 2019.

22   Samuel Moncada (@SMoncada), Twitter post, April 15, 2019, https:// twitter.com/SMoncada_VEN/status/1117643332975566848.

23   Samuel Moncada(@SMoncada), Twitter post, April 15, 2019, https://twitter. com/SMoncada_VEN/status/1117975927089242113.

founded as part of Georgetown University's international relations department,[24] CSIS evolved into the private project of US secretary of state Henry Kissinger upon his retirement from government in 1977.[25] Drawing on a seemingly endless stream of arms, banking, and oil industry–supplied funds,[26] CSIS provided a training camp for some of Washington's most influential policy makers, including US secretaries of state Madeline Albright and Anthony Blinken. While priming the minds of Washington's neoliberal diplomatic core, CSIS served as an incubator for US foreign collaborators abroad, including the man eventually tapped to represent Venezuela's US-backed coup government at the OAS: Gustavo Tarre.

Tarre's background highlighted the brazen nature of Trump's Venezuela coup. Having fled Venezuela in 2014 after he was implicated in an alleged plot to assassinate President Maduro,[27] by the time of his appointment to Guaidó's shadow regime Tarre had established himself as a leading voice of Venezuela's extremist opposition within DC's think tank network, working as an advisor to the Inter-American Dialogue before joining CSIS as a senior associate. Considering his history, I was not surprised to find Tarre's name listed among the individuals who gathered at CSIS to plot a US invasion of his homeland.

Following Max's exposé, I tracked Tarre and his staff down in the OAS halls to question them about their participation in the summit. My first encounter was with David Smolansky, a Tarre underling who earned his stripes as part of the US-backed "Generation 2007" movement (chapter four). When I reached for his doughy hand, Smolansky flashed a toothy grin.

"Why was your name on the CSIS list?" I asked with a smile of my own as our handshake broke. Suddenly, his friendly demeanor dropped.

---

24   "About CSIS," Center for Strategic and International Studies, accessed April 11, 2023.

25   "A Harvard-Henry Kissinger Détente?" *Harvard Magazine*, March 28, 2012.

26   "Corporations: Our Donors," Center for Strategic and International Studies, accessed April 11, 2023.

27   Z.C. Dutka, "Venezuelan Government Exposes Plot to Assassinate President Maduro, Opposition Rejects Charges," *Venezuelanalysis*, May 31, 2014.

"You know that because you were the one that published it," the bearded, towering Smolansky griped, attempting to place his hand over my camera.[28]

"I was there," he conceded. "I was invited to the meeting."

When asked to share what was discussed at the session, Smolansky accused me of supporting a Russian and Cuban invasion of Venezuela and stormed off. His boss, however, lingered behind.

"What does your government control in Venezuela?" I asked Tarre.

"The streets, *niña*!" the pudgy septuagenarian barked.[29] I told him that I had visited Venezuela two months prior and failed to find evidence that Guaidó controlled the streets. Tarre proceeded to remove his glasses and wave them in my face, explaining he was offering me "a gift" to improve my eyesight.

Based on Smolansky and Tarre's unrivaled charisma and grace, it was difficult for me to understand why their political camp was so unpopular in Venezuela.

Within twenty-four hours of Trujillo's victory at the OAS, the US sent its forces to a new theater of diplomatic war: the United Nations. Leading the blitzkrieg was Vice President Mike Pence, who appeared before the UN Security Council on April 10 with a simple mission: pressure members states into following the OAS's lead and officially recognize Guaidó's coup regime as Venezuela's legitimate government.

"This body should revoke the credentials of Venezuela's representative to the United Nations, recognize Interim President Juan Guaidó, and seat the representative of the free Venezuelan government in this body without delay," Pence instructed, stiffly turning to face Venezuela's UN ambassador, Samuel Moncada.[30]

"With all due respect, Mr. Ambassador, you shouldn't be here. You should return to Venezuela and tell Nicolás Maduro that his time is up.

28   Anya Parampil (@anyaparampil), Twitter post [VIDEO], April 23, 2019, https://twitter.com/anyaparampil/status/1120806261518471168?s=20.

29   Anya Parampil, "Venezuela Coup Regime's OAS Rep Likens Situation to Nazi Invasion of USSR," *The Grayzone*, April 24, 2019.

30   Margaret Besheer, "US Vice President Urges UN to Recognize Venezuela's Guaido," Voice of America, April 10, 2019.

It's time for him to go," Pence lectured. Moncada took breaks from looking at his phone to gaze at the US vice president directly, defiantly shaking his head in disbelief and outrage.

I traveled to New York City shortly after Pence's performance to discuss the escalating diplomatic row with Ambassador Moncada and follow up on my previous interview with Foreign Minister Jorge Arreaza, who was in town for meetings at the UN.

On the day of our scheduled interviews, the US Treasury hit Arreaza with personal financial sanctions, marking the first time in history that Washington targeted a sitting foreign minister with such penalties. Treasury secretary Steve Mnuchin made it clear the measures were designed to punish Arreaza for simply doing his job.

"Treasury will continue to target corrupt Maduro insiders, including those tasked with conducting diplomacy and carrying out justice on behalf of this illegitimate regime," he declared while announcing the sanctions.[31] Apparently, Washington viewed diplomacy as a criminal act.

When I met Venezuela's delegation in New York minutes following the Treasury's announcement, Arreaza was unbothered.

"It's supposed to mean that all my goods, assets, and bank accounts in the United States are frozen," the diplomat informed me, appearing bemused.[32]

"I have one bank account, in Caracas, in bolívares, our currency," he added with pride.

Arreaza explained that while he was not impacted by the sanctions financially, they could complicate his future travels to the United States. In conjunction with the economic measures, the US placed physical restrictions on Arreaza and his underlings—including Venezuela's full-time UN delegation—that limited their movement to a twenty-five-mile radius around the UN's Manhattan headquarters. In Arreaza's view, the measures were meant to send a message to other foreign officials not to challenge Washington as sharply as he did. Indeed,

31   "Treasury Sanctions Venezuelan Minister of Foreign Affairs," United States Department of the Treasury, April 26, 2019.

32   Anya Parampil, "Trump Admin. Behaves 'like Thugs in a Barrio': Interview with Venezuelan Foreign Minister Jorge Arreaza," *The Grayzone*, April 30, 2019.

Washington penalized the diplomat mere hours after he launched an official UN campaign to research and document the impact of unilateral US sanctions on Venezuela's population.[33]

"I knew they would react this way because they have a primitive instinct in this administration," he said of Trump's team. "They are like thugs, no? In a barrio."

To illustrate their mafia-like behavior, Arreaza informed me that US officials had previously attempted to bribe him and his colleagues into defecting from Venezuela's government. He claimed that Trump envoy Elliott Abrams and others had promised "money, visas to live in the United States, green cards, and places at universities for their children" if they turned their back on Maduro.

Following our interview, Arreaza grabbed his suitcase and hurried off to catch a flight to Caracas. A member of his staff later told me they spent the entire journey home worrying that US authorities would arrest them for violating Washington's sudden restriction on their movement. Having finalized their travel arrangements before the rules were imposed, the team had a layover in Atlanta, Georgia—far beyond their newly designated travel zone.

Ambassador Samuel Moncada exuded an entirely different energy than his superior. While Arreaza spoke in a soft, deliberate rhythm, Moncada communicated with flair and whimsical intensity. During our conversation in New York, Moncada described how Washington planned to repeat its OAS strategy at the UN and replace him with a representative of Guaidó's shadow regime (Parampil April 2019). As with the OAS, such a decision was technically required to clear the UN's annual General Assembly meeting with a two-thirds majority vote, and a solid plurality of member states rejected Guaidó's coup. Still, Moncada believed that the US would use its OAS precedent to call for a vote on his removal during an ordinary Security Council session and succeed in doing so by winning a *simple* majority of whichever member states happened to be present.

---

33   "US Sanctions 'Have Taken Thousands of Venezuelan Lives' Says Arreaza to UN," Telesur English, April 25, 2019.

"They are trying," Moncada stressed with dramatic intonation. "They even sent their own vice president to announce the action. And nobody does that kind of high-level presence just to do nothing."

I asked Moncada to recall the day Vice President Pence visited the Security Council and ordered his return to Venezuela.

"How dare you? How dare you, what gives you the right?" a visibly angered Moncada playacted as though Pence were sitting with us. "This is such an arrogant person full of hate . . . such a fake representation of what the American people really are."

According to Moncada, Pence's grandstanding had backfired.

"That's not diplomacy, that's bullying," Moncada reflected, demonstrating his faith in the UN system. "'Might is right' is not the kind of thinking that succeeds here."

The diplomat continued: "I thought, 'this can only act in our favor.' If he thought that he was doing harm to myself or the Venezuelan government, I think that he overdid it in such a way that we gathered sympathy from the rest of the world."

Moncada was not a career diplomat. For decades, he worked as a professor of history in pre-revolutionary Venezuela, only entering government when Chávez tapped him to serve as minister of higher education in 2004. From there, he went to work as Venezuela's ambassador to the United Kingdom before serving a brief stint as foreign minister in 2017. Moncada has worked in the United States since then, representing Venezuela before both the OAS and the UN.

Despite a decade of experience in the diplomatic field, my conversations with Moncada revealed that he will always be a historian at heart, often punctuating his analysis with archival anecdotes and analogies. Moncada displayed his professorial qualities throughout our interview, especially when discussing the secret CSIS meeting to plan for the invasion of Venezuela. He compared the gathering to the notorious Wannsee Conference of 1942, where Nazi and SS officials devised the Final Solution.

"Of course, it is not the same scale, but it has a similar feeling," the ambassador contended. "Forty people met in Washington to plan for the killing of hundreds of thousands of Venezuelans."

Moncada was particularly concerned that the OAS would escalate threats against his country following its acceptance of Tarre.

"They just picked someone from a Washington think tank, which is paid by weapons manufacturers and oil companies . . . and they put him there as the Venezuelan representative!" Moncada complained. "Believe me, what that man is going to do, is he is going to ask, sooner or later, for a military intervention in his own country."

Moncada's unease was not unfounded. In the months following our discussion, the OAS voted to invoke its Inter-American Treaty of Reciprocal Assistance (TIAR), a regional agreement similar to NATO's mutual defense pact, against Venezuela, declaring the country "a threat to the security of the region."[34] As Moncada predicted, Tarre voted in favor of applying the TIAR, also known as the Rio Treaty, to his own homeland.

Tarre did not hide his lust for war while participating in a subsequent CSIS panel discussion titled "Can the Rio Treaty Help Venezuela?" Seated next to Bush II's devotedly anti-Chavista ambassador to Caracas, William Brownfield, Tarre declared that "all the possibilities opened by the treaty must be on the table."[35] Conceding that most OAS governments would not support direct military intervention, Tarre instead advocated for the imposition of a no-fly zone in Venezuela, a policy that would require member states to use military force against any aircraft flying in or out of the country's airspace.

"In Syria, there has been the use of force to give food and medicine to people," Tarre insisted, "and I am personally open [to] this kind of solution."

It is hard to imagine how anyone could look at the decade-long US-backed dirty war in Syria—a violent and costly campaign that left hundreds of thousands of civilians and soldiers dead while creating more than six million refugees—and request that such a policy be applied to their own country. But that is precisely what Tarre did.

"Of course, that man doesn't have his family [in Venezuela]," Moncada said of Tarre, asserting he and his CSIS colleagues sought "to

34   Vakkas Doğantekin, "Venezuela Slams Regional Efforts to Invoke Rio Treaty," Anadolu Agency, December 9, 2019.

35   "Can the Rio Treaty Help Venezuela?" The Center for Strategic and International Studies, January 21, 2020.

spill US soldiers' blood and spill Venezuelan families' blood for their own business and profit."

Indeed, Tarre and CSIS's financial backers, including Chevron, Northrop Grumman, ExxonMobil, and Boeing, would get rich from a war in Venezuela that resulted in the re-privatization of its vast natural wealth. According to Moncada, never in its history had Venezuela faced the threat of such bloodshed.

"To dedicate your life to stopping that catastrophe is the worthiest effort ever," the ambassador explained.

For most dignitaries stationed at the UN in New York, the job is a glamorous gig that enables fruitful connections and future job opportunities in the international hub of the diplomatic champagne circuit. This was not the case for Moncada and his staff. Sanctions prevented Caracas from depositing their regular salaries in US bank accounts, forcing them to live off credit throughout the duration of their assignment in New York. For Venezuelans seeking to prevent a US invasion of their homeland, however, the financial sacrifice was worth it.

"Personally, my family lives in Venezuela, the only one outside is myself," Moncada said as he solemnly pondered the threat of armed conflict. "They would be the subject of all the killing and all the awful stuff that's going to happen if they work out any kind of war."

EIGHT

ONE TOUGH COOKIE

"As somebody who has helped plan coups d'état—not here, but you know, other places—it takes a lot of work."

John Bolton uttered these words during an interview with CNN's Jake Tapper in July 2022,[1] nearly three years following his departure from the Trump White House. When Tapper followed up with a request for details of the US official's apparently criminal past, Bolton replied: "Well, I wrote about Venezuela in [my memoir] and it turned out not to be successful."

For Venezuelans, Bolton's confession underscored his already transparent role in directing Washington's failed coup in Caracas—and the infamously incompetent military putsch that eventually came with it.

From the outset of Guaidó's self-declared presidency, Bolton acted as his most enthusiastic cheerleader inside the White House. Days after the Trump administration's January 2019 recognition of Guaidó, Bolton appeared on Fox Business to articulate the stakes of Washington's new Venezuela policy.

"It will make a big difference to the United States economically if we could have American oil companies invest in and produce the oil capabilities in Venezuela," the veteran US official declared.[2] In just a few words, Bolton shattered the myth that Washington's preoccupation with Venezuela was rooted in an abstract moral commitment to ideals like freedom and democracy.

---

1   "Watch: Tapper and Bolton Debate Trump's Ability to Plan a Coup | CNN Politics," CNN, July 13, 2022.

2   *Trish Regan: Primetime*, "John Bolton: I Don't Think Maduro Has the Military on His Side," Fox Business, January 25, 2019.

According to Bolton, Trump was always skeptical of Guaidó's ability to dislodge Maduro, whom the US president considered "too smart and too tough" to fall (Bolton 2020, 253). In his memoir, Bolton disclosed that Trump instead expressed a desire to meet with Maduro directly and "resolve our problems with Venezuela" on multiple occasions (Bolton 2020, 249). He further revealed that the president did not even want to issue the initial White House statement in support of Guaidó under his own name, only caving after Vice President Pence held a phone conversation with the unknown Venezuelan politician on the eve of his self-directed "swearing in" ceremony.

Bolton happened to be on hand for that discussion. He later recounted how "after the call, I leaned over Pence's desk to shake hands, saying, 'This is a historic moment'" (Bolton 2020, 256). Yet even months before Guaidó's unexpected rise, Bolton stood accused of meddling in Venezuela's internal affairs.

"It all points to John Bolton, who has a criminal mentality, a murderer's mentality," Maduro told Max during an August 2019 interview.[3] The Venezuelan president was referring to an assassination attempt that he had survived the previous year, months before Guaidó's ascent.

On the evening of August 4, 2018, Maduro was delivering an outdoor address to the ranks of Venezuela's national guard when a thunderous explosion erupted from the sky above him. Venezuela's president remained still but was visibly alarmed as bodyguards unfurled protective shields to defend him from the sudden blast. National guard troops scattered in the streets as though they had been ambushed.

As Maduro; his wife, Cilia Flores; Defense Minister Vladimir Padrino López; and the thousands of national guard troops present managed to escape without significant injury, authorities traced the fireworks-like combustion to a pair of bomb-strapped, manually operated drones recovered from the scene. While Venezuela's government promptly characterized the incident as a foreign-directed assassination

3   Max Blumenthal, "'John Bolton Tried to Assassinate Me': Interview with Venezuelan President Nicolás Maduro," *The Grayzone*, August 6, 2019.

attempt on Maduro,[4] others, including Bolton, hastily dismissed it as a false-flag operation.

"I can unequivocally say there is no US involvement in this at all," Bolton told *Fox News Sunday* within twenty-four hours of the attack, positing it had been "a pretext set up by the regime itself."[5]

Bolton's theory was discredited months later, when a group of Venezuelan military defectors claimed responsibility for the botched assassination and provided CNN with cell phone video documenting their preparation for the assault. The organizers claimed that after establishing a base of operations on a rural Colombian farm, they purchased retail drones online and spent weeks practicing how to fly them "high enough to avoid detection" before "swooping down at a steep angle to strike their target."[6] They ultimately failed to evade authorities in Caracas, who destroyed the drones midair after noticing their violation of Venezuelan airspace.

What precisely inspired the would-be assassins' confession to the press was unknown. In their public account, however, the conspirators made certain to emphasize that authorities in Bogotá and Washington were totally unaware of their plot. At the same time, they bizarrely admitted to meeting with "several US officials" on three occasions in the *aftermath* of the attack—once again, for reasons that remain unclear.

Venezuela's government, on the other hand, maintained that its own investigation into the assassination plot uncovered an evidence trail leading all the way to the White House.

Maduro agreed to speak with the *Grayzone* in August 2019, during our second visit to Venezuela. For the interview's venue, the president's office selected El Ávila National Park (*Waraira Repano* to the local indigenous population) located in the Cordillera de la Costa Central mountain chain resting between northern Caracas and the

---

4   "Venezuela President Maduro Survives 'Drone Assassination Attempt'," BBC, August 5, 2018.

5   Greg Re, "Bolton: 'No US Government Involvement' in Attempted Drone Assassination of Venezuelan President Maduro," Fox News, August 7, 2018.

6   Nick Patton Walsh et al., "Inside the August Plot to Kill Maduro with Drones," CNN, June 21, 2019.

Caribbean Sea. Curious as to why the president wished to meet amid the lofty slopes of a coastal mountain, we made the bumpy trek up El Ávila's winding dirt trail with excitement, happy to explore one of Venezuela's most treasured natural wonders. After a thirty-minute climb, we arrived at our final destination: a national guard outpost perched on the mountain's ledge. Beyond El Ávila's luscious verdure, the location featured a boundless view of Venezuela's buzzing capital in the distance—the perfect backdrop for an interview with the country's president.

While waiting for Maduro, Max and I mingled with a group of uniformed men patrolling the outpost, including the burly leader of a local colectivo who spoke at length about General Smedley Butler's 1935 exposé of corporate influence in the US military, *War Is a Racket*. Over a lunch of rice, yucca, and grilled chicken, he informed us the president was visiting El Ávila to address a graduation ceremony for the firefighting division of Venezuela's national park service. Soon enough, we heard Maduro's basso profundo thundering over the cheers of fired up cadets gathered nearby.

"They fight fires with drones!" Maduro quipped upon greeting us, a joking reference to the attempt on his life the previous summer. Our meeting took place on August 2, 2019—almost exactly one year to the date since the drone incident.

"I'm a man of faith. I believe in God very much," the president reflected on surviving the attack (Blumenthal, August 2019). "I believe there was an event that day; that God saved our lives."

In Maduro's view, his assassination would have plunged Venezuela into a "deeper phase" of "armed revolution" if successful, risking all-out civil war.

"They planned it to perfection, with so much evil, to assassinate us," he stressed, insisting the plot's Miami-based "intellectual authors" and "financiers" were part of "networks established by the White House."

"I can't accuse President Trump," Maduro said of his government's inquiry into the conspiracy.

"But I do have all the evidence to accuse and ask for a landmark investigation into John Bolton," Venezuela's president asserted. "He's a criminal. He failed."

Bolton would later cite Max's interview in his memoir, *The Room Where It Happened*, recounting that his "spirits were high" upon learning of Maduro's accusations against him (Bolton 2020, 263).

Bolton built up his cred as one of the world's most ruthless putschists in April 2019, roughly three months following the US recognition of Guaidó. By then, Trump had adopted the view that Guaidó was a "kid" who "nobody's ever heard of" and recognized that Maduro still maintained the support of, in his words, "all those good-looking generals" (Bolton 2020, 275–258). Bolton, on the other hand, bolstered Guaidó's estimate that 80 percent of Venezuela's military and 90 percent of its population secretly supported his US-backed shadow regime—an assessment that even the opposition's most loyal followers would have found laughable. On April 30, Bolton put his confidence to the test.

By Bolton's own account, that date represented a turning point for which Guaidó and his US backers had long prepared. He recalled starting the day with a 5:25 a.m. phone call with secretary of state and former CIA director Mike Pompeo. As the US officials debriefed, a contingent of Venezuelan opposition activists began shutting down sections of Caracas's main throughway, the Francisco Fajardo Highway. Then, for the first time since joining the White House one year prior, Bolton made the decision to rouse the president from his sleep to deliver important news: a military revolt was underway in Caracas.

"Wow," was reportedly the extent of Trump's reply, suggesting a blend of disinterest and mild discomfort (Bolton 2020, 281).

Twenty minutes after Bolton and Pompeo's conversation, Guaidó launched a Twitter livestream from his position in the middle of the highway, just outside Generalissimo Francisco de Miranda air base in eastern Caracas. The wannabe leader proceeded to call for a military uprising against Maduro, gawkishly waving his hands to emphasize his appeal for mass rebellion.

"We push forward, we are going to achieve freedom and democracy in Venezuela," he vowed at the end of his awkward plea.[7]

---

7   Juan Guaidó, Periscope Stream, April 30, 2019.

Sunlight had just begun its morning stretch over the sky-high ridges of El Ávila that border Caracas. Even so, it was clear that only a handful of military personnel—fewer than a dozen—flanked Guaidó as he spoke. Though his statement failed to demonstrate that a serious mutiny was underway, one of Guaidó's silhouetted accomplices was notable. Just over his left shoulder stood Leopoldo López, the sandy-haired star of Venezuela's US-backed opposition who was widely believed to be pulling the strings of Guaidó's shadow regime. As a key architect of the coup attempt underway, dubbed "Operation Freedom," López had successfully broken out of house arrest, where he was serving a fourteen-year sentence for his role directing the deadly guarimba riots of 2014.

As the drama in Caracas unfolded, nonchalant Venezuelan officials assured me that Guaidó's attempted insurrection was doomed. Indeed, by mid-afternoon Reuters reported that "an uneasy peace had returned" to the streets "and there was no indication that the opposition planned to take power through military force."[8] By nightfall, López and his family had reportedly taken refuge in Chile's local diplomatic residence (they eventually settled in Spain's Caracas embassy) and Guaidó was nowhere to be found.

Multiple accounts—including Bolton's—later revealed that Venezuelan defense minister Vladimir Padrino López had duped Leopoldo, Guaidó, and their US handlers into following through with their foolish scheme by providing it with "passive support."[9] Trump's inner circle remained convinced Padrino López was their man on the inside until the last minute, when he and his forces stood squarely beside Maduro.

Throughout the day of Guaidó's miscarried mutiny, credulous corporate media correspondents repeated assertions from US officials that Venezuela's government would soon collapse. Pompeo even

8   Vivian Sequera, Angus Berwick, and Luc Cohen, "Venezuela's Guaido Calls for Uprising but Military Loyal to Maduro for Now," Reuters, April 30, 2019.

9   Anthony Faiola, "How a Plot Filled with Intrigue and Betrayal Failed to Oust Venezuela's President," *Washington Post*, May 3, 2019.

told CNN that President Maduro was on the verge of fleeing to Havana, Cuba.[10]

"He had an airplane on the tarmac. He was ready to leave this morning as we understand it, and the Russians indicated he should stay," the US secretary of state insisted with total certainty.

Even as hours passed with no developments in Caracas, Bolton continued to publicly indulge his regime change fantasy.

"Your time is up. This is your last chance," the mustachioed militarist tweeted at Venezuelan military and intelligence officials, including Defense Minister Padrino López.[11]

"Accept Interim President Guaidó's amnesty, protect the Constitution, and remove Maduro, and we will take you off our sanctions list. Stay with Maduro, and go down with the ship," Bolton threatened, tacitly admitting sanctions were a tool of US blackmail.

Despite Guaidó's evident failure, US media neglected to scrutinize Bolton and Pompeo's narrative of imminent triumph in Caracas. CNN's Jake Tapper, an inveterate neocon who spent his days lamenting Obama's failure to overthrow Syria's government,[12] was particularly hot for their scheme. Though he often sought viewers' attention—or at least, that of the twenty-three-year-old Media Matters staffers paid to watch CNN full-time—with overblown anti-Trump tirades, painting the president as a Russian puppet who betrayed the grand traditions of American exceptionalism, Tapper was in complete lockstep with the White House when it came to Venezuela. For a smug broadcaster with a personality envious of drying paint, it seemed that trashing Trump while clamoring for endless regime change war was the perfect formula to advance his middling Beltway celebrity.

"CNN live in Venezuela as Maduro government mows down citizens in streets," Tapper tweeted on the afternoon of April 30, attaching a photo of Venezuelan soldiers firing their guns at a target beyond

10   Nicole Gaouette and Jennifer Hansler, "Pompeo Claims Russia Stopped Maduro Leaving Venezuela for Cuba," CNN, May 1, 2019.

11   John Bolton (@AmbJohnBolton), Twitter post, April 30, 2019, https://twitter.com/AmbJohnBolton/status/1123298012145516545?s=20.

12   The Lead, "That Time Tapper Asked Obama about Syria Inaction," CNN, September 2016.

the camera's view. There was just one problem: the soldiers Tapper described were donning the blue armbands that mutinying Venezuelan troops had adopted throughout the day, meaning they were in fact allied with Guaidó—not the Maduro government. Tapper deleted his tweet after enduring hours of sustained mockery.[13]

As Guaidó floundered before the world, Washington's sole victory on April 30 was in the theater of propaganda. Amid the blitz of fantastical coverage, I called on someone I knew would be willing to interrupt the media's regime change racket. Having met Tucker Carlson during one of the most consequential diplomatic meetings of Trump's presidency, I was confident the Fox host would be an ally in the fight against further intervention in Venezuela.

In the summer of 2018 I traveled to Helsinki, Finland, to cover the historic summit between US president Donald Trump and Russian president Vladimir Putin. Convened at the height of "Russiagate" hysteria, the Helsinki meeting represented a direct rebuke to US hawks and their media collaborators, both of which aimed to sabotage any improvement in US-Russia relations. At the time, I was working as a roving correspondent and news anchor for the US branch of Moscow's flagship state-funded media outlet, RT.

Though I obtained official White House press credentials as a correspondent for RT America—the outlet at the center of Putin's alleged conspiracy to influence the US public and electoral process in support of Trump—I was predictably alienated from the Beltway media mannequins assigned to the Helsinki junket. While waiting to clear security for the Trump-Putin presser in a hotel dining room overlooking the Baltic Sea, I listened as US network personalities agonized over the idea our president would even so much as *sit across* from his Russian counterpart. At one point, I overheard a reporter joke that Trump and Putin were having sex when their bilateral meeting ran late. Alas, chalking the delay up to vigorous negotiations regarding Europe's energy

---

13   "'Goebbels Would Be Proud': Twitter Users Expose Jake Tapper's Misleading Maduro Message," RT, May 1, 2019.

supply, war in Syria and Ukraine, or nuclear arms reduction would have been absurd!

The White House press corps' juvenile view of the world was on full display when the joint Trump-Putin news conference finally began, and I had a front row seat to the Cold War melodrama. The presser consisted of opening statements from each leader and four questions: two from the US side, represented by AP and Reuters; and two from the Russian camp, represented by Interfax and RT International.[14] Russian media were concerned with the material stakes of Washington-Moscow relations, with Interfax prompting Trump and Putin to discuss the future of Nord Stream 2, a pipeline designed to transport Russian natural gas to Germany. The pipeline, which was still under construction, was an object of obsession for Washington because it would allow Berlin to source its energy from Russia rather than the United States. Meanwhile, RT International asked whether the two leaders had discussed the war in Syria. As Putin wrapped his answer, a member of his entourage approached the podium with a soccer ball.

"President Trump just mentioned that we have successfully concluded the world football cup," Putin said, smiling as he referenced the international soccer tournament that Russia hosted that summer. "Speaking of football, actually, Mr. President, I will give this ball to you—and now the ball is in your court."

A handful of Russian journalists applauded as Putin handed the ball to Trump, who proceeded to thank his counterpart and state that he would pass the gift along to his son, Barron, before tossing it to Melania Trump, who was seated in the first row. The friendly gesture brought an air of optimism to the room and for a moment, it seemed as if a breakthrough between the US and Russia were truly possible. That hopeful spirit was squashed moments later, when AP reporter Jonathan Lemire took the floor to demand Trump address "high confidence" claims by US intelligence officials that Russia had interfered in the 2016 presidential election to secure his victory.

"Just now, President Putin denied having anything to do with the election interference in 2016. Every US intelligence agency has

14   "FULL Donald Trump, Vladimir Putin Press Conference," Global News, July 17, 2018.

concluded that Russia did," Lemire whined before demanding to know whom Trump believed.

"Would you now, with the whole world watching, tell President Putin—would you denounce what happened in 2016 and would you warn him to never do it again?" Lemire continued, goading the US president to treat his Russian counterpart like a naughty child.

Lemire's grandstanding mimicked the act his colleague from Reuters staged moments before, when he similarly pressed Trump to denounce Russia's government. Trump's refusal to accept their narrative of Russian interference in the 2016 election outraged Western media, which used the Helsinki summit to further cast the US president as a puppet of Moscow. Rather than analyze the substance of Putin's and Trump's statements, virtually all US and European coverage of the summit consisted of a variation of the following headlines:

- Trump sides with Russia against FBI at Helsinki summit (BBC)[15]
- Trump's Helsinki Bow To Putin Leaves World Wondering: Why? (NPR)[16]
- Donald Trump in Helsinki was terrifying. Cancel the Washington sequel. (USA Today)[17]

Not to be outdone in the realm of pro-war hysterics, CNN put an absurdly conspiratorial spin on the Russian president's attempt at football diplomacy, publishing a report that claimed "Putin gave Trump a soccer ball that may have a transmitter chip."[18]

The mainstream media's parrot jungle of Cold War hostility was only interrupted by the presence of Tucker Carlson, who traveled to Helsinki to conduct an interview with President Trump. Having long

15   "Trump Sides with Russia against FBI at Helsinki Summit," BBC, July 16, 2018.

16   Ron Elving, "Trump's Helsinki Bow To Putin Leaves World Wondering: Why?" NPR, July 17, 2018.

17   Aaron David Miller and Richard Sokolsky, "Donald Trump in Helsinki Was Terrifying. Cancel the Washington Sequel.," *USA Today*, July 24, 2018.

18   Clare Foran, "Putin Gave Trump a Soccer Ball That May Have a Transmitter Chip," CNN, July 26, 2018.

abandoned the signature bowtie and conventional policy views that once defined his career, by the time of the Helsinki reunion Tucker had emerged as the premier critic of Washington's foreign policy establishment in US media. Most importantly, Tucker exhibited a willingness to consider arguments regardless of their assumed political silos, a fact I discovered when he hosted Max to offer a "left-wing" critique of Russiagate in the months following Trump's election.[19]

While many in the media project strident public personas to shield their vanity and lack of real-world charm, the larger-than-life personality Tucker displayed on air was his genuine character. The concerned gaze, over-the-top laugh, and mischievous twinkle in his eye were not an act for the camera. And though he could provide an endless stream of fascinating life stories himself (such as the time he accompanied civil rights icon Al Sharpton and left-wing academic Cornel West to civil war–torn Liberia[20]), he was just as inquisitive in person as with guests on his show. When I met Tucker in Finland, I found that despite our seemingly polarized political allegiances, we agreed on quite a lot. Unlike the jumped-up lapdogs overrunning Helsinki, Tucker was comfortable enough in his rank to view Washington's elite with scorn—a consequential self-security he demonstrated during Trump's tenure.

Throughout Trump's presidency, Tucker solidified his place among the most influential media personalities in US history, with his primetime Fox program, *Tucker Carlson Tonight*, eventually earning the title of most-watched cable news show of all time.[21] Tucker set himself apart from other corporate news hosts, including those at Fox, as the most articulate—and humorous—voice of Trump's freshly awakened America First base. Each weeknight, Tucker spoke for millions of Americans who had borne the brunt of neoliberal policies such as NAFTA, deindustrialization, and the military's misadventures in the

19   "Dem: Why My Fellow Democrats Are Wrong on Russia," Fox News, July 17, 2017.

20   Tucker Carlson, "The League Of Extraordinary Gentlemen," *Esquire*, July 14, 2009.

21   Luke Lahut, "Tucker Carlson, the Most Popular Cable News Host in US History, Claims He Has No Idea What His Ratings Are: 'I Don't Know How to Read a Ratings Chart'," Yahoo! News, July 7, 2022.

Middle East. Personally burned by his own support for the Iraq War years prior, by 2019 Tucker had matured into a fervent anti-interventionist who regularly opened his show with lengthy monologues that systematically debunked his media colleagues' narrative du jour.

"Leaders on both sides of the aisle in Congress, in the media, in our intelligence services, and in virtually every overfunded think tank in Washington have suddenly aligned tonight on a single point of agreement: America must go to war in Syria immediately," he announced at the start of a broadcast on April 9, 2018, hours after US officials accused Syria's government of carrying out a chemical weapons attack in the city of Douma.[22]

"This ought to make you nervous. Universal bipartisan agreement on anything is usually the first sign that something deeply unwise is about to happen, if only because there's nobody left to ask skeptical questions. And we should be skeptical of this," Tucker told viewers, accusing US officials of crafting "propaganda designed to manipulate Americans."

While conducting routine examinations of pro-war disinformation, Tucker mercilessly grilled Washington's top policymakers before millions of disaffected Americans hungry for a reckoning with their elite.

"To hear you say 'we need to knock off the Assad regime and things will be better in Syria,' you sort of wonder like, well, maybe you should choose another profession? Selling insurance, painting houses, something you're good at?" Tucker slammed Max Boot, a fixture of Washington's neoconservative intelligentsia and member of the Council on Foreign Relations, during a memorable confrontation in July 2017.[23]

"Is there no sanction for being as wrong as you have?" Tucker continued to badger a visibly rattled Boot.

Yet perhaps no figures attracted Tucker's ire more than Trump officials who actively undermined the president's "America First" agenda. He held particular contempt for Bolton, whom he characterized as a "bureaucratic tapeworm."

---

22   Aidan McLaughlin, "Tucker Carlson Goes on Marathon Rant Questioning Whether Assad Is Behind Attack in Syria," Mediaite, April 9, 2018.
23   "Tucker vs Critic Who Calls Him Cheerleader for Russia," Fox News, July 12, 2017.

"Try as you might, you can't expel him," Tucker said of Trump's national security advisor during a June 2019 broadcast.[24] "He seems to live forever in the bowels of the federal agencies, periodically emerging to cause pain and suffering."

Tucker's attack on Bolton came days after Iran shot down a US drone that had violated its sovereign airspace. In the aftermath of Tehran's response to Washington's naked aggression, the *New York Times* revealed that Bolton and others in the White House had pressured Trump to bomb Iran—belligerent advice the president rejected thanks to Tucker's intervention.

"While national security advisers were urging a military strike against Iran, Mr. Carlson in recent days had told Mr. Trump that responding to Tehran's provocations with force was crazy," the *Times* reported, crediting Tucker with personally preventing war with Iran (and possibly World War III).[25]

Tucker's influence over Trump transcended their personal relationship. Without question, the most significant pair of eyeballs (among millions) fixed on Tucker's show throughout the Trump years belonged to the president himself. As Washington's dime store foreign policy "experts" leapt to rally support for Guaidó's coup on April 30, 2019, I reached out to Tucker with a request. As Guaidó summoned military defectors to the Caracas streets, an invitation to Fox's DC studio arrived in my inbox.

Tucker's broadcast on the night of April 30 was a fervent anti-war rampage perhaps unseen on cable news networks since 2003, when MSNBC host Phil Donahue's militant opposition to the Iraq invasion made him the network's highest rated host (and ultimately, led to his termination).

"Will the overthrow of Maduro make Venezuela a more stable and prosperous country? More to the point, would it be good for the United States?" Tucker asked his viewers. He then mocked Republican senator

24   "Tucker: US Came within Minutes of War with Iran," Fox News, June 21, 2019.

25   Peter Baker, Maggie Haberman, and Thomas Gibbons-Neff, "Urged to Launch an Attack, Trump Listened to the Skeptics Who Said It Would Be a Costly Mistake," *New York Times*, June 21, 2019.

Rick Scott for demanding the deployment of US troops to Venezuela during an interview with Fox earlier that day.[26]

"Before the bombers take off, let's just answer a few quick questions, starting with the most obvious: when was the last time we successfully meddled in the political life of another country? Has it ever worked? How are the democracies we set up in Iraq, in Libya, in Syria, and Afghanistan tonight? How would Venezuela be different? Please explain, and take your time," the host continued.

As I walked through Fox's offices and into the greenroom, a tall, barrel-chested man in a dark suit strode by and said hello. It was Douglas Macgregor, a retired US army colonel renowned in military ranks for his innovations in battlefield strategy—and resented in polite Washington society for his straightforward, realist approach to world affairs.

My friends among DC's marginalized circle of former military and intelligence professionals with anti-interventionist views hoped that Macgregor could one day replace the uber-militarist Bolton on Trump's National Security Council. Until then, as Trump remained captive to the neoconservative blob of Latin American expats, arms industry–funded think tanks, and the Pentagon Joint Chiefs, Macgregor was relegated to the Fox studio. And it was from there that the rock-ribbed Republican who had led US tanks into Iraq during the first Gulf War railed against further intervention in Venezuela.

"Over time, our history in Latin America is a disaster," Macgregor cautioned Tucker, making his case in a commanding baritone. "We will incur the hostility of the population; they'll want us ultimately to leave. And if [Guaidó] is viewed as a puppet, he is going to have trouble lasting."[27]

Tucker made sure to feature one pro-Guaidó voice on his show on the night of April 30, however. It was Republican congressman Mario Díaz-Balart, a stalwart of the Cuban American regime-change lobby

26   Tucker Carlson, "Tucker Carlson: A Few Quick Questions We Should Ask before the U.S. Decides to Meddle in Venezuela's Affairs," Fox News, May 1, 2019.

27   "Journalist: Fake News Media Are Lying about the Situation in Venezuela," Fox News, April 30, 2019.

in Miami, who used his time on air to conjure a cast of foreign evildo-
ers exploiting Venezuela as a base from which to threaten—and even
attack—the US homeland. It was a well-worn script the Cuban expat
community had deployed over the years while appealing in vain for a
US taxpayer–sponsored Bay of Pigs revenge.

"You have Hezbollah, you have Cuba, you have Iran, you have
Russia, you have China there," Díaz-Balart moaned, "so imagine if this
regime that now is receiving a lot of international pressure survives? Is
it, or is it not, potentially a green light, an open door for the Russians
and for the Chinese and for others, to increase their activity against our
national security interests, right here in our hemisphere?"

Tucker looked at Díaz-Balart with puzzlement. "Yeah, no? I mean,
it's kind of hard to see what you're talking about exactly." The host then
transitioned the conversation to the US border, implicitly addressing
his most important viewer: President Trump.

"So they have a small number of Russian advisers there, I'm supposed to think it's a threat because, why? No one really explains. Why
should I not be worried about eight million people leaving Venezuela?"
Tucker asked, referring to a 2018 Brookings report that estimated
eight million refugees would flee Venezuela in the event of increased
instability.[28]

By then, Díaz-Balart had run out of talking points and presumably
lost Tucker's audience of America Firsters. Fumbling for a reply, he
claimed the only way to prevent the flow of Venezuelan refugees to the
US border was "to do what we can to make sure that the regime is no
longer there."

"Or that the regime remains there, but there isn't a scene like this,"
Tucker retorted, pointing to images of Guaidó's botched revolt flashing
on screen. "I mean, that is kind of the message from Syria," he added.

Tucker's carefully staged anti-interventionist theater—capped by
the performance of Colonel Macgregor, who would go on to advise
Trump's Afghanistan withdrawal strategy (and be systematically

---

28   Dany Bahar and Douglas Barrios, "How Many More Migrants and Refugees
Can We Expect out of Venezuela?" Brookings, December 10, 2018.

sabotaged by the Joint Chiefs along the way[29])—suggested that support for Guaidó was limited to Miami and Washington's permanent war lobby, what the president and his supporters called "the deep state." Trump himself must have known that a significant portion of his base, from immigration hardliners to isolationist paleocons, could not support an escalation of force against Venezuela that would destabilize yet another region of the globe and fuel a fresh migration crisis—this time on their own border.

I planned to use my time on air to reinforce that message in a direct appeal to Trump. By the time I sat down across from Tucker, less than four minutes were left in the broadcast. As Tucker sought my opinion of the day's events, I felt my adrenaline surge.

"The fake news media are lying about the situation in Venezuela," I began, imagining I was addressing the president himself. "Let me put it for you this way: imagine if Hillary Clinton had refused to admit defeat after losing to President Trump in 2016, banded together a group of twenty-four US soldiers, and attempted to take the White House by force? I don't think that she would be walking freely on the streets the way Juan Guaidó is walking right now in Caracas."

I then addressed reports of a humanitarian crisis in Venezuela, noting the media never acknowledged the role US sanctions played in fomenting it. To illustrate my point, I cited a report that the Center for Economic and Policy Research think tank published days prior, which found that US sanctions contributed to thousands of excess deaths in Venezuela between the years 2017 and 2018 alone (Weisbrot and Sachs 2019).

"President Trump, if he truly cared about the Venezuelan people—and the American people, for that matter—he would end this disastrous policy," I said as rapidly as possible, sensing the ticking clock. "He would end the sanctions and he would look into John Bolton's eyes, into Elliott Abrams's eyes, and Mike Pompeo's eyes and say: 'You are fired. You are leading me down a disastrous path, another war for oil.'"

"You are passionate!" Tucker laughed. He was right. For me, speaking against the war on Venezuela was a defense of the people I had met

29   Gareth Porter, "How the US Military Subverted the Afghan Peace Agreement to Prolong an Unpopular War," *The Grayzone*, March 16, 2021.

in the country months before—several of whom I count among my dearest friends to this very day.

"I'm not sure I agree with everything you said, but I'm glad that you could say it here," Tucker announced as our segment wound to a close. "You were just there, and I don't think that you would be allowed to say that on any other show."

I agreed with Tucker's assessment before jamming in a final denunciation of Trump's team: "President Trump promised to drain the swamp, and he flooded his national security team with that exact swamp!"

"Well, I agree with that, actually," Tucker concluded.

With that, Tucker handed the Fox airways over to a visibly uncomfortable Sean Hannity, the bloviating GOP hack who literally wore his allegiance to Washington's establishment on his sleeve, donning a CIA and FBI lapel pin on his jacket every night. Hannity struggled to hold back his contempt and surprise as he labored through a few seconds of banter with Tucker. Yet the segment electrified millions of others.

By the next morning, our interview had been translated into Spanish and gone viral in Latin America, especially Venezuela, which broadcast the exchange on state television. Days later, Tucker informed me that our interview not only garnered top ratings (which predictably plummeted as *Hannity* kicked off) but had caught the attention of Trump himself.

According to Tucker, the president phoned him shortly after the events of April 30 to venerate the perspectives featured on his show that evening. Trump complained that if he actually listened to Bolton's advice, he would have already started "World Wars Three, Four, and Five," explaining he merely kept the rabid hawk on his shoulder to send a message to world leaders that "all options" were on the table.

Indeed, Trump brandished Bolton as his "big stick" in international negotiations, fashioning the neocon as a prop in his *Art of the Deal* diplomacy. In reality, however, Bolton outmaneuvered the president, exploiting his Swamp connections and control over the flow of information in the White House to sabotage virtually all of Trump's meaningful engagement efforts. In his memoir, Bolton boasted of undermining Trump's push to draw down the US military occupation of northeastern Syria as well as the president's attempts to détente with governments in Russia and North Korea.

Bolton paid particular attention to the Helsinki summit, even confessing his hope that "Trump would be irritated enough" by Putin's delayed arrival "that he would be tougher" on his Russian counterpart (Bolton 2020, 153) while exalting the US media's belligerent conduct at the leaders' joint press conference. He also described instructing Trump to reject further bilateral arms reduction agreements with Russia, along with his view that the US should withdraw from the Cold War-era Intermediate-Range Nuclear Forces (INF) Treaty. Trump heeded that advice and announced the US's unilateral withdrawal from the INF Treaty in February 2019,[30] marking a 180-degree turn from the promising and amicable posture he set with Putin in Helsinki just seven months prior.

While Bolton's treacherous behavior eventually led to his dismissal, it won him a veneer of respectability within the imperial cesspit of elite Washington—and a hero status among the liberal anti-Trump Resistance™ embodied by the likes of CNN's Jake Tapper. Without this rebrand, the crux of Bolton's legacy would have instead been his promotion of the catastrophic Iraq War and deranged Axis of Evil conspiracy.

Though Trump did not fire Bolton until September, the president's frustration with his national security advisor reached a breaking point following the events of April 30, 2019. Echoing Tucker's account of Trump's reaction to the Venezuela imbroglio, the *Washington Post* cited senior administration officials who claimed the president felt "misled" by Bolton and other advisors, whom he believed had "underestimated Maduro."[31]

"The president's dissatisfaction has crystallized around national security adviser John Bolton and what Trump has groused is an interventionist stance at odds with his view that the United States should stay out of foreign quagmires," the *Post* disclosed.

---

30   Julian Borger, "Donald Trump Confirms US Withdrawal from INF Nuclear Treaty," *Guardian*, February 1, 2019.

31   Anne Gearan, Josh Dawsey, and Seung Min Kim, "A Frustrated Trump Questions His Administration's Venezuela Strategy," *Washington Post*, May 8, 2019.

Bolton's coup policy had not only flopped, but boomeranged. As it became clear that Venezuela's military leadership had rejected his call to mutiny, a photograph of Guaidó standing in the middle of an empty highway with a stunned expression on his face and cell phone pressed against his ear circulated online.[32] Though who exactly was on the other line remains unknown, many on social media joked that Pompeo and Bolton were likely scolding their useless marionette for embarrassing them so badly.

Designed to convince Trump of Guaidó's strength, the botched revolt instead left the novice politician looking bug-eyed, unwanted, and alone. In the days following April 30, administration officials informed the media that Trump began referring to Maduro as a "tough cookie" in conversations around the White House (Gearan et al. 2019). Meanwhile, Bolton said the president had taken to describing Guaidó as the "Beto O'Rourke of Venezuela" (Bolton 2020, 277), accurately equating the US-backed coup leader with an uninspired Obama knock-off.

32   Jorge Martin, "Venezuela: Guaidó's Botched Coup – What Does It Mean and What's Next?" *Venezuelanalysis*, May 2, 2019.

NINE

CARLOS VECCHIO: FROM EXXON TO AMBASSADOR

On the afternoon of May 1, one day following Guaidó's flaccid military putsch in Caracas, an angular-faced, dark-haired Venezuelan opposition figure named Carlos Vecchio confidently marched down Thirtieth Street in Washington DC's upscale Georgetown district, prepared for a coup of his own.

As Guaidó's "ambassador" to Washington, Vecchio was on a mission to complete his shadow regime's takeover of Venezuelan government buildings in the US. Though US authorities had previously aided his seizure of Venezuela's DC military attaché and New York City consulate, the country's embassy in Washington represented Vecchio's ultimate prize. Situated on Georgetown's scenic Chesapeake and Ohio Canal, the diplomatic command and control center was officially vacated on April 21, when Washington kicked Maduro's US-based diplomats out of the country. At the time, Vecchio's ascent to the ambassador's office seemed inevitable. And it would have been—if not for a group of US peace activists who mounted an extraordinary defense of the compound.

The Venezuela Embassy Protection Collective (EPC) was born as a response to Vecchio's capture of Venezuelan diplomatic offices throughout the month of March 2019. Conceptualized by Medea Benjamin, cofounder of the anti-war organization CODEPINK, the EPC's strategy was guided by international diplomatic law that stipulated embassy property was "inviolable," and that "agents of the receiving State may not enter them, except with the consent of the head of the mission."[1] In other words, authorities in Washington could not enter Venezuela's US embassy without stated permission from Maduro's government in Caracas.

"We saw that the coup government was able to take over the military attaché building in Georgetown, and they were able to do that because it was pretty much empty already," Benjamin later told me, recalling her decision to approach Venezuela's UN mission in New York City with a creative pitch. "I said, 'this is terrible, we've gotta do something about it.' So, I put forward the idea: peace activists could start staying in the embassy and be a kind of protection."

When Benjamin tweeted an image of herself lounging on a couch within the embassy on the morning of March 20, she officially kicked off the slumber party of John Bolton's nightmares.

"Slept overnight at DC Venezuela embassy when we heard opposition might try to take it over," she announced alongside a photograph of herself wrapped in a cobalt-blue sleeping bag. "This is insane!!!"[2]

For the next eight weeks, anti-war activists from all corners of the US convened upon Washington to join Benjamin's defense of the embassy. In the early days, the EPC converted the four-story, Georgian-style edifice into a festival ground for the anti-war movement, working their jobs at embassy desks by day, hosting public teach-ins and concerts in its event halls by night. By simply maintaining a constant physical presence inside the building at the invitation of Venezuela's elected government, the EPC forced Washington's hand: would US authorities violate international law in order to enter a foreign embassy, arrest non-violent US citizens gathered inside, and turn the building over to an unelected coup regime?

The carnival-like atmosphere at the embassy came to an abrupt halt on April 30, the day of Guaidó's failed military revolt. In coordination with his coup regime's effort to ignite an insurrection in Caracas, Vecchio summoned their supporters among the US Venezuelan diaspora to Georgetown. Upon their arrival from the Washington-area suburbs

1   "Vienna Convention on Diplomatic Relations, 1961," United Nations Office of Legal Affairs, 1961.

2   Medea Benjamin (@medeabenjamin), Twitter post, May 20, 2019, https://twitter.com/medeabenjamin/status/1108344878700904449

and south Florida, this horde of petty-bourgeois hooligans promptly transformed the streets outside the embassy into an autonomous zone of fanatical chaos. Acting as storm troops for the US State Department, they pitched tents along the mission's perimeter and established a twenty-four-hour guard at each of its entry points. After setting up their encampment—an act US authorities would have never permitted on the grounds of any other foreign embassy—the mob proceeded to block food and other basic supplies from entering the building. Bouncing to the beat of trashy *reguetón*, which they blasted from Bluetooth speakers at all waking hours, Vecchio's infantrymen aimed to force the EPC's surrender through a violent guarimba-style intimidation campaign.

"The siege was an effort to terrorize us to leave," Kevin Zeese, a veteran US peace activist and lead EPC organizer, later reflected. "I think the government was very insecure about going into the embassy and violating international law. So, they were using this coup mob to frighten us."

When I entered the embassy on the afternoon of May 1, I had no idea that I would remain inside the building for the next ten days, hostage to an aggressive expat class that appeared to enjoy total immunity from the law. In plain view of Secret Service agents deployed to the property, Vecchio's gang of putschists spent roughly two weeks violently assailing any EPC supporter who got close to the building or attempted to deliver food to those of us inside.[3] To prevent us from sleeping, they banged pots and pans, blared airhorns, and trumpeted whistles from sunup to sundown—only taking respite from 10:00 p.m. to 7:00 a.m. after local residents lodged noise complaints against their cacophonous din. They smashed embassy windows and removed its garage door in at least two failed break-in attempts[4] and were even filmed physically blocking the postman's access to the compound[5]—a federal crime. Though international diplomatic law stipulated that it

3   Alex Rubinstein, "Violent, Bigoted Supporters of Juan Guaidó Attempt to Invade Venezuela's D.C. Embassy," *MintPress News*, May 1, 2019.

4   Wyatt Reed (@wyattreed13), Twitter post, May 1, 2019, https://twitter.com/wyattreed13/status/1123587231665487878?s=20.

5   Anya Parampil (@anyaparampil), Twitter post, May 5, 2019, https://twitter.com/anyaparampil/status/1125113467676045312?s=20.

was the responsibility of the Secret Service to prevent damage to the embassy, US agents never arrested any of the vandals responsible for carrying out the destruction, even when presented with cellphone[6] and security footage[7] documenting their delinquent conduct. After days of sustained harassment and intimidation failed to dislodge us, Vecchio and his allies in Washington successfully pressured DC's local utility company, Pepco, to cut the embassy's electricity.[8] By May 11, a mystery assailant had even severed the building's main waterline.

For those of us inside, the experience felt like a dream—especially as we became acquainted with hunger and the lightheadedness that accompanies it. We had no idea how long the confrontation would last, but were prepared to remain in the compound for weeks. EPC participant and licensed medical practitioner, Margaret Flowers, even calculated the minimum number of calories each of us required daily so we could make the most of our meager supplies. I ate one piece of bread with peanut butter in the morning and another at night. Sometimes I gave my second meal to David Paul, a retired nurse who traveled from San Francisco to defend the embassy (and eventually took on the role of overseeing security inside the complex). Aside from the hunger pains, however, life in the embassy was vibrant. In addition to the reassuring company of friends, the compound provided extremely livable quarters including a kitchen, showers, and plenty of offices to serve as temporary bedrooms. Its library contained hundreds—if not thousands—of books, enabling us to pass the time lost in Venezuelan history and literature.

Our goal was to remain inside the building until the US and Venezuela established a mutual protecting power agreement that would allow a third country to oversee operations at each government's respective embassy as they negotiated a long-term diplomatic solution. For a time, it seemed that deal was imminent—we were informed that

6   Alex Rubinstein (@RealAlexRubi), Twitter post, May 8, 2019, https://twitter.com/RealAlexRubi/status/1126029731260981248?s=20.

7   Samuel Moncada (@SMoncada), Twitter post, May 2, 2019, https://twitter.com/SMoncada_VEN/status/1123805417241554946?s=20.

8   Carlos Vecchio (@carlosvecchio), Twitter post, May 8, 2019, https://twitter.com/carlosvecchio/status/1126285926668414976?s=20.

Turkey had agreed to take over Venezuela's diplomatic offices in DC and that the US had entrusted its Caracas embassy to Switzerland. Two days after the water shutoff, however, the Secret Service posted a notice on the embassy's front door informing us that Gustavo Tarre, Guaidó's OAS envoy, had formally ordered us to vacate the building. By then only Kevin, Margaret, David, journalist Alex Rubinstein, and American University professor Adrienne Pine remained inside with me. Unwilling to risk arrest, Alex and I exited the building on the afternoon of May 13.

Less than thirty-six hours later, over two dozen federal US agents donning flack vests and night vision goggles—looking more prepared to raid the Bin Laden compound than a sovereign diplomatic office—beat down the embassy door with a battering ram[9] and arrested the four peace activists who remained inside.

Carlos Vecchio's first official act as Guaidó's representative in Washington DC was to beseech US officials to violate his country's sovereignty. Days before the arrest of the EPC final four, Vecchio's staff sent a dispatch to the State Department formally requesting that it "support" their effort "to take physical occupancy" of Venezuela's US diplomatic compound. In the April 26 letter, which I obtained, Vecchio even provided "his consent" for US agents to enter the building, temporarily "waived" its legal inviolability, and vowed not to pursue charges against any US agents who damaged embassy property while arresting the anti-war activists inside.[10] Vecchio's missive—which openly flaunted his obeisance to US authorities and absolute disregard for Venezuela's independence—offered a perfect distillation of the coup regime he represented. Just as Vecchio's takeover of Venezuela's DC embassy was only made possible by the US Secret Service, by May 2019 it was clear that Guaidó and his band of preppy putschists would only come to power in Caracas on the back of US tanks.

9 "Raw Footage: Police Raid Venezuelan Embassy in DC, Remove 'Embassy Protection Collective,'" *NEWS2SHARE*, May 16, 2019.

10 Anya Parampil (@anyaparampil), Twitter post, May 18, 2019, https://twitter.com/anyaparampil/status/1129795470488944640?s=20.

Though Guaidó served as the official face of Washington's coup policy in Venezuela, during my time embedded with the EPC I realized that lesser-known figures, such as Vecchio, were the plot's true power players. As I ventured to learn more about Guaidó's team— enlisting the help of my Caracas-based friend and colleague, Diego Sequera—I discovered that Vecchio's past unveiled the true character of Venezuela's US-backed opposition.

Throughout the struggle for the embassy, the clean-cut, unquestionably charming operative established himself as the leader of Venezuela's US-based expat community. Though he clearly enjoyed basking in his supporters' admiration, earnestly shaking their hands and posing for photographs as if mimicking a local city council candidate, Vecchio had not set out for a life in politics. Instead, he spent the early days of his career as a corporate tax lawyer rising in the ranks of Venezuela's oil industry, first providing legal counsel to Mobil before it merged with Exxon, then moving to the country's state oil company, Petróleos de Venezuela (PdVSA). Like other leading figures of the extremist opposition, Vecchio belonged to the replacement generation of pro-US Venezuelan elites that had watched their futures disappear following Chávez's 1998 revolution. Ever since, he and others among this scorned ruling class had colluded with Washington to reassert US corporate interests in Venezuela, an ill-fated effort that culminated with Guaidó's self-declared presidency in 2019.

Around the time of Chávez's inauguration in February 1999, Vecchio left Venezuela to pursue a Fulbright Scholarship in the United States. According to his 2018 memoir, US operatives plucked the young lawyer right out of Mobil's corporate office after he aced an interview with US embassy staff in Caracas.[11] Vecchio recalled that during his Fulbright audition, US officials were particularly keen to know what he would do "if he were Venezuela's finance minister?" So interested, in fact, that it was the only question they allowed him to answer in Spanish. Though Vecchio did not disclose the content of his reply, the State Department

11   Carlos Vecchio, *Libres: El Nacimiento De Una Nueva Venezuela* (Venezuela: Dahbar, 2018), 38-39.

apparently found it worthy of a full-ride scholarship to study English and tax law at Georgetown University.

Vecchio continued his journey through the US Ivy League circuit after graduating from Georgetown, pursuing a degree in public administration at the premier boot camp for neoliberal thought leaders both foreign and domestic: Harvard's Kennedy School of Government (HKS). At the time of this book's publication, the Kennedy School is home to notable officials including former US Treasury secretary and architect of President Bill Clinton's austerity policy, Larry Summers,[12] ex-Mexican president Felipe Calderón, and ex-Colombian president Juan Manuel Santos (both former leaders are HKS graduates themselves and led stridently pro-US governments while in office). Obama's UN ambassador, Samantha Power, also teaches at HKS, but is on leave at the time of publication while serving as President Joe Biden's Administrator for USAID, the State Department's soft power regime-change front. Meanwhile, Ricardo Hausmann, a pre-revolution Venezuelan official who served as a prominent member of Guaidó's coup regime (and is the subject of chapter ten), directs an entire center at HKS dedicated to mapping out international capitalist growth trends.

For budding bureaucrats aspiring to command influence in Washington or a US-aligned foreign capital, HKS is both a rite of passage en route to the halls of power and a comfortable place to land once their public gig is up. For Vecchio, it was the training ground for his eventual return to Venezuela, where he and his US government sponsors aimed to overthrow Chávez and restore Caracas's compliance with the pro-corporate Washington Consensus. He reflected that while at Harvard, he "learned a lot about the best political practices and how I could implement them in my country" (Vecchio 2018, 42).

As Vecchio drilled English grammar and the intricacies of tax law in the United States, his home country underwent profound political changes. In 1999, Venezuelans voted to approve a new constitution that redefined their system of government, drastically expanded social programs, and classified basic services such as housing, healthcare, and higher education as guaranteed rights. Yet before Chávez could escalate

---

12   Sam Mitchell, "Larry Summers Is Not Your Friend," *Jacobin*, July 2, 2020.

his transformation of Venezuela, he would have to win a fresh mandate under the country's updated constitution. When an election was set for November 2000, the United States and its allies in the Venezuelan oligarchy were presented with their first chance to stall the winds of revolution.

Leading the charge to undermine Venezuela's 2000 vote was a US-backed activist named Elías Santana, whom Vecchio met while studying at Harvard.[13] Santana had been pocketing paychecks from Washington since at least 1993, when his organization Queremos Elegir (We Want to Choose) partnered with the US government "to promote voter education programs" in Venezuela. That year, the State Department-funded International Foundation for Electoral Systems (IFES) declared that Queremos Elegir was a worthy recipient of US funding because it was "part of an agenda" that advocated "a greater role for the private sector in the solution of community and national problems."[14]

As Chávez gained popularity and overturned that pro-corporate agenda, Washington and Santana launched an active campaign to sabotage his leadership at every turn. In fact, during the 1998 presidential vote that saw Chávez's initial victory, a public survey circulated by Queremos Elegir openly thanked the US-backed Inter-American Development Bank for funding its production.[15] Santana ran a failed effort to halt Venezuela's National Constituent Assembly process the following year, then set his sights on subverting the November 2000 election. According to Latin America researcher Rickard Lalander, Santana and his Queremos Elegir colleagues "played important roles" opposing the vote and were even "called to the Supreme Court

13   Anya Parampil and Diego Sequera, "From Exxon to 'Ambassador': How Carlos Vecchio Became Venezuela's Top Coup Lobbyist," *The Grayzone*, June 18, 2019.

14   Esteban Caballero Carrizos, *Venezuela* (International Foundation for Electoral Systems, 1993).

15   Though IFES deleted their PDF of the survey after Sequera and I cited it in an exposé of Vecchio, a copy was archived on the internet's Wayback Machine; see: "SABÍAS QUE LOS VENEZOLANOS ELEGIREMOS," International Foundation for Electoral Systems, November 8, 1998.

as voices of Venezuelan civil society" to present arguments for its postponement.[16]

Like his previous US-backed endeavors, Santana's bid to impair Venezuela's revolutionary momentum proved futile. Chávez won nearly 60 percent of votes cast in November 2000, securing a six-year term under Venezuela's new constitution. He then endeavored to revamp the national education system, immediately issuing a presidential decree that expanded public schooling and established a joint venture with Cuba's government to fund sport and literacy programs for Venezuelan youth. For his political rivals, Chávez's open partnership with the socialist government in Havana was a red line. When Caracas erupted with protests denouncing the "Cubanization" of Venezuelan education in December 2000, the first sustained phase of civil revolt against Chávez's embryonic government had finally arrived. As with prior efforts to stop Chavismo in its tracks, Santana quickly materialized at the uprising's forefront.

Chávez "tried to mess with our schools and civil society and we will not accept it," he informed the Associated Press in January 2001, during a demonstration described as the "largest protest against President Hugo Chávez's government to date."[17]

Known as Movimiento 1.011, the street campaign heated up just as Vecchio's studies in the United States wound to a close. Near the end of his time at Harvard, the young lawyer accepted Santana's invitation to participate in a Movimiento 1.011 demonstration in Caracas that would forever change the course of his career. Having received his first taste of the US taxpayer–fueled gravy train driving opposition to Chávez's government, Vecchio writes that upon his return to Venezuela after graduation, "Elías was the first one I called" (Vecchio 2018, 48). Fresh off Harvard's campus, Vecchio thus began his ascent within the clandestine network of US-funded civil society groups hellbent on obstructing Chavismo by any means necessary. Their offensive reached a head in April 2002, when Chávez initiated a complete overhaul of the country's

16   Rickard O. Lalander, *Suicide of the Elephants? Venezuelan Decentralization between Partyarchy and Chavismo* (Helsinki: University of Helsinki, 2004).

17   "Thousands Protest against Chavez's Education Reforms in Venezuela," Associated Press, January 19, 2001.

state oil company, PdVSA, replacing its entire board and triggering a backlash that placed his entire future on the line.

The events of April 11, 2002, are well established in popular history: in response to the shakeup at PdVSA, Venezuela's business elite collaborated with rogue military forces to kidnap Chávez and detain him on an island prison. The oligarchy then drafted a document that temporarily installed Pedro Carmona, leader of Venezuela's equivalent of the Chamber of Commerce, as the head of a national "transitional government."[18] The document, known as the Carmona Decree, established a de facto dictatorship. It dissolved Venezuela's newly formed National Assembly and Supreme Court, suspended powers of local government officials, and voided the 1999 constitution.

For several hours, Western media celebrated Chávez's ouster with unbridled cheer. The *New York Times* even printed a glowing profile of Carmona within hours of the coup, legitimizing the putsch leader as Venezuela's "conciliator."[19]

"In one day, the man in charge in the presidential palace went from a strong-willed populist known for his rambling speeches to a mild-mannered businessman who chooses every word carefully," the paper raved. Separately, the *Times* ran an official staff op-ed rejoicing that "Venezuelan democracy is no longer threatened by a would-be dictator," since "the military intervened and handed power to a respected business leader."[20] Yes, thanks to an intervention by the country's US-aligned armed forces, Venezuelan democracy was no longer threatened by a president who had triumphed in not one, but two democratic elections convened over the course of just two years.

Regardless of the *Times*'s opinion on the matter, the Venezuelan public swiftly rejected the overthrow of their fledgling revolution. Throughout the country, masses of people poured onto the streets to

18   Dan Beeton, "The Venezuela Coup, 20 Years Later," Center for Economic and Policy Research, April 12, 2022

19   Juan Forero, "UPRISING IN VENEZUELA: MAN IN THE NEWS; Manager and Conciliator — Pedro Carmona Estanga," *New York Times*, April 13, 2002.

20   The Opinion Pages, "Hugo Chávez Departs," *New York Times*, April 13, 2002.

demand their president's freedom. As the popular mobilization swelled, pro-Chávez presidential guard troops waged a successful fight to retake the seat of power in Caracas. Just after midnight on April 13, a military helicopter returned Chávez to jubilant throngs of his supporters gathered outside the presidential palace. To Venezuela's overwhelmingly Catholic population, Chávez's miraculous comeback mirrored the Holy Resurrection commemorated during the *Semana Santa* holiday just weeks prior, giving way to the local dictum *"Cada 11 tiene su 13,"* or, "every (April) eleventh has its thirteenth."

The putsch had failed in less than forty-eight hours. Diplomatic sources at the OAS in Washington eventually charged US officials with directing the futile plot, revealing to the *Guardian*'s *Observer Worldview* that "Venezuelans plotting a coup, including Carmona himself" had personally visited the White House to coordinate its launch. Serving as "the crucial figure" overseeing the scheme from his post on Bush II's national security team was none other than Iran-Contra architect and would-be Trump Venezuela envoy Elliott Abrams.[21]

Though Vecchio was officially employed as a lawyer for the private oil industry at the time, he and Santana managed to leave their mark on the US-directed coup. Just three months prior to the short-lived putsch, in January 2002, the pair co-founded a Caracas-based "civil society" group called Ciudadanía Activa (Active Citizenry). When the oligarchy moved to oust Chávez that April, Ciudadania Activa wasted no time backing the de facto military junta that replaced him. As Venezuela's elected president languished in an offshore jail cell, one of Ciudadania Activa's co-founders, Rocío Guijarro, rushed to endorse the now infamous Carmona Decree, physically signing the document as an official representative of Venezuelan civil society.[22]

Though they achieved little more than their own embarrassment in the interim, in signing the Carmona Decree groups like Ciudadania Activa announced themselves as willing partners in future US destabilization plots. As the State Department set out to expand its Venezuela soft power operation in the coup's immediate aftermath,

21   Ed Vulliamy, "Venezuela Coup Linked to Bush Team," *Observer Worldview*, April 21, 2002.

22   Eva Golinger, "¿Quién Es Ciudadanía Activa?" Aporrea, August 27, 2010.

the list of Carmona Decree signatories provided a useful roster of local collaborators.

Where covert US-backed insurrections are concerned, USAID's Office of Transition Initiatives (OTI) is ubiquitous. Aptly named to describe its mission to foment "transitions" in independent foreign governments, USAID established its global OTI in 1994. According to USAID's website, the OTI "supports US foreign policy objectives" by providing "assistance targeted at key political transition and stabilization needs" through its international offices, and sponsors over 1,700 "activities" around the world each year.[23] In other words, the OTI was tasked with financing and grooming nominally "non-governmental organizations" and media outlets aligned with Washington's interests abroad. Operating under the guise of organic, grassroots movements, OTI's partners ultimately serve as the State Department's street muscle in foreign capitals, leading anti-government protest campaigns from Damascus to Kiev. Four months following Washington's unsuccessful April 2002 attempt to force a "transition" in Venezuela, USAID opened an OTI branch in Caracas and began doling out US tax dollars to groups it hoped could finish the job.[24]

To identify organizations fit for the task, the OTI contracted Development Alternatives Incorporated (DAI), a private DC-based firm that routinely raked in hefty federal contracts from the State Department and Pentagon.[25] Leading DAI's Venezuela team was none other than Vecchio's former Georgetown roommate, Antonio Iskandar (Vecchio 2018, 39). As luck would have it, the OTI quickly selected Vecchio's organization, Ciudadanía Activa, as one of the first beneficiaries of its multimillion-dollar initiative in Caracas, granting it $76,900 in 2003 alone (Golinger 2010). A young María Corina Machado, another signatory to the Carmona Decree, also wound up on Washington's

23   "Office of Transition Initiatives (OTI)," United States Agency for International Development, accessed April 12, 2023.

24   "Venezuela: Stabilization and Transitions," United States Agency for International Development, accessed April 12, 2023.

25   Philip Agee, "Use of a Private U.S. Corporate Structure to Disguise a Government Program," *Venezuelanalysis*, September 8, 2005.

payroll that year when her organization, Súmate, scored a $53,400 handout from the US-backed National Endowment for Democracy ("CHAVEZ ACCUSES . . ." 2023). When the US government initiated its next plot to overthrow Chávez, Ciudadanía Activa and Súmate labored to ensure Washington received a return on investment.

In 2004, Venezuela's opposition introduced a petition to subject Chávez to a recall, an effort that required over two million signatures to succeed. Ciudadanía Activa and Súmate led the drive to collect signatures, eventually gathering enough to schedule an August referendum on Chávez's leadership. A record number of Venezuelans participated in the recall, which delivered a resounding "no" vote by a 16 percent margin.[26] Lines at the polls were so long, in fact, that voting hours had to be extended twice, first from 5:00 p.m. to 8:00 p.m., and then from 8:00 p.m. to midnight.[27]

Despite Ciudadanía Activa and Súmate's best effort, Chavismo would remain undefeated at the polls until 2007. By then, Vecchio had established a lucrative career with ExxonMobil in Venezuela while moonlighting as a US-backed civil society activist. His path was upended that June, when Chávez drove ExxonMobil out of Venezuela as part of his effort to nationalize the country's oil reserves.[28] It was then that Vecchio emerged as the informal spokesman for Exxon and other foreign oil giants impacted by the reforms.

"I will be fired," Vecchio told *Marketplace*, reflecting on the industry upheaval. "The government will discriminate against me."[29] According to *Marketplace*, by then Vecchio had been "mount[ing] a fruitless legal challenge" against Chávez's effort to restructure Venezuela's oil sector "for years."

After losing his cushy post legally battling Venezuela's government on behalf of a multinational corporation, Vecchio turned to politics, announcing his bid for the mayoral seat in eastern Caracas's wealthy

---

26   Juan Forero, "Chávez Is Declared the Winner in Venezuela Referendum," *New York Times*, August 16, 2004.

27   "Record Turnout for Chavez Vote," CNN, August 16, 2004.

28   Brian Ellsworth, "Chavez Drives Exxon and ConocoPhillips from Venezuela," Reuters, June 26, 2007.

29   Dan Grech, "Venezuela's Oil Blacklist," *Marketplace*, May 1, 2007.

Chacao municipality. Though his candidacy flopped, it was during his mayoral campaign that Vecchio first met Leopoldo López, the aristocratic poster boy of Venezuela's US-backed opposition. In Vecchio's words, he and López swiftly became "political brothers" (Vecchio 2018, 64). Their friendship would leave Venezuela's pro-US opposition bloc forever changed—and deliver Chavismo its first official defeat at the ballot box.

In August 2007, Chávez introduced a proposal to amend thirty-three articles in Venezuela's 1999 constitution. Having won a third landslide victory the previous year that solidified his mandate until 2012, Chávez aimed to redirect the momentum behind his reelection into a campaign to legally codify the social gains made across nearly a decade of Chavista revolution. As detailed in chapter four, voters shot down the proposal following a months-long, foreign-backed street riot led by a group of students known as "Generation 2007."

Heralded in the foreign press as the greatest threat to Chavismo's continued reign, "Generation 2007" was hardly a natural phenomenon. Under the command of Vecchio's Georgetown roommate, USAID had actively trained and funded the movement's student leaders through its Caracas OTI (Gill and Hanson 2019). Meanwhile, USAID contracted the tax lawyer's own "civil society" front, Ciudadanía Activa, to produce information critical of Chávez's proposals in the lead-up to the vote (Golinger 2010).

After scoring the opposition's—and Washington's—first victory against Chavismo since its 1998 inception, Vecchio says he and López began to see themselves as leaders of "a political organization instead of a movement." In 2009, the duo formally merged the roiling energy of "Generation 2007" with Venezuela's covert network of foreign-backed NGOs to form an official political party, Voluntad Popular. United under López, the opposition's most charismatic and prominent national figure, Voluntad Popular provided a political home to several characters who would later serve in Venezuela's US-backed coup regime, including Guaidó himself. As was the case with nearly all Vecchio's endeavors, the hidden hand of the US government gave Voluntad Popular its first push.

"We gave them money," a former OTI Caracas employee divulged to US academics Tim Gill and Rebecca Hanson in 2019. "They were pulling people away from Chávez in a subtle manner" (Gill and Hanson 2019).

Gill and Hanson detailed the Caracas OTI's method:

> Since USAID/OTI could not directly fund political parties, they worked with party leaders, including those from Voluntad Popular, to help opposition activists set up community groups in neighborhoods where *Chavistas* were predominant. The groups, which claimed to promote and provide training related to participatory democracy, ultimately aimed to put opposition activists in contact with Chávez supporters in an effort to generate *Chavista* support for their political parties.

According to the OTI source, USAID labored to ensure these community groups appeared "very neutral in the eyes of [Venezuela's] government" while ultimately serving as proxies for Washington. On top of that, Voluntad Popular strategized to court middle and working-class Venezuelans who had benefited from Chavismo by adopting a "leftist" veneer. In 2014, the party was admitted into the Socialist International, status that enabled it to cast itself as progressive not only to Venezuelans, but self-proclaimed "leftists" in the West. When pressed to describe Voluntad Popular's platform, however, Vecchio struggled to offer anything beyond boilerplate commitments to "democracy" and "freedom." In fact, there is only one example of Vecchio clearly articulating the party's ideology in a coherent manner.

"We want oil to be a normal commodity in the international arena," the former ExxonMobil employee confessed in a 2013 interview with Yale's *Politic*.[30] So much for Voluntad Popular's supposed commitment to "socialism."

Since Voluntad Popular's inception, the party has performed poorly at the ballot box, most recently coming in fifth during parliamentary elections in 2015. The party boycotted subsequent elections, issuing baseless claims of vote rigging to justify their refusal to participate—and

---

30   Salaar Shaikh and Azad Amanat, "Yale World Fellow in Hiding: Carlos Vecchio and the Situation in Venezuela," *Yale Globalist*, November 9, 2013.

conceal their lack of appeal. Yet despite their failure to garner popular support, López and Vecchio demonstrated an uncanny ability to stoke chaos in times of national crisis.

Voluntad Popular's presence in Venezuela's streets reached its height during the 2014 guarimba riots that swept the country in the aftermath of Chávez's death. As explored in this book's introduction, the anarchy culminated with a López-led political march that concluded with his supporters attempting to set fire to Venezuela's Office of the Attorney General. Following the February incident, Venezuela's government issued arrest warrants for both Vecchio and López on charges of public incitement, property damage, arson, and conspiracy. Though authorities arrested López within a week, his partner had an escape plan. Vecchio materialized in New York City months later, explaining to media that his Voluntad Popular cohorts had decided that he could most effectively represent their party from within the United States.

"They considered that I am most useful in this moment denouncing the abuses which continue to exist against human rights in Venezuela at the international level," he told CNN en Español in June 2014, his first public appearance since fleeing Venezuela.[31]

Vecchio described the influence campaign he launched upon arriving in the United States in his memoir, writing: "I had to meet in the US Congress, the White House, the State Department, with professors in US universities, different ambassadors, [and] influential civil organizations in the States" (Vecchio 2018, 117).

From the comfort of Washington and Miami, Vecchio assumed the position of top lobbyist for Venezuela's extremist opposition. His arrival in the States directly coincided with the Obama administration's 2015 decision to classify Venezuela as a "national security threat," as well as subsequent escalations against Maduro's government at the OAS. In his memoir, Vecchio took credit for preparing the OAS report that inspired Venezuela's government to initiate its withdrawal from the organization in 2017. When the Trump administration announced its recognition of Guaidó two years later—effectively designating the decidedly unpopular Voluntad Popular bloc as Venezuela's ruling

31   "Exclusiva | Carlos Vecchio Da Sus 'Conclusiones' Sobre Venezuela," CNN en Español, June 6, 2014.

party—Vecchio was perfectly situated to take over as the coup regime's highest ranking official in the United States.

The pinnacle of Vecchio's career came on May 15, 2019, when US Secret Service agents raided Venezuela's DC embassy and arrested four peace activists who guarded the property from his unceremonious takeover. After enabling Vecchio's troops to deface Venezuela's diplomatic compound for weeks with zero repercussion, the US government ultimately charged the final four embassy protectors with the federal crime of "interfering" with Washington's ability to service the building. The defendants—veteran peace activists Kevin Zeese and Margaret Flowers, retired nurse David Paul, and anthropologist Adrienne Pine—each faced a maximum one-year prison sentence and fine of up to $100,000.

Kevin later described the EPC's trial, overseen by US district judge for the District of Columbia Beryl A. Howell, as a "through-the-looking-glass" experience. Indeed, Judge Howell barred their defense team from discussing the political situation in Venezuela, explaining the dynamics of the mutual protecting power agreement that served as justification for the EPC's entire existence, or even so much as *mentioning* international law in her court. The Obama appointee went on to play a critical role in the federal investigation of Donald Trump, taking the extreme decision to grant DOJ prosecutors access to the notes of his personal attorney, including private communications with the former president.[32]

In the end, Judge Howell's restrictions on the EPC's defense resulted in extreme confusion among the jury, which struggled to reach a decision in the case. The deadlock forced Howell to declare a mistrial in February 2020, and the four defendants eventually negotiated a plea deal with US authorities to avoid further prosecution.

"I proudly pleaded guilty to obstructing imperialism and neoliberal fascism," Pine told me hours after the agreement was announced.

---

32   Jose Pagliery, "Federal Judge Hands over Trump's Lawyer's Notes to DOJ," *Daily Beast*, March 18, 2023.

On September 6, 2020—seven months after the EPC's legal fight came to an end—Kevin Zeese passed away unexpectedly in his sleep. That afternoon, Max and I recalled our fondest memories of Kevin while gazing at the tiger lilies that bordered our backyard garden. Kevin and Margaret had uprooted the blossoms from their Baltimore home and gifted them to us in the summer months following the EPC struggle. David Paul, who happened to be housesitting for us at the time (and who also happened to be an avid gardener), promptly planted the flowers in our backyard and nursed them into a thriving patch of glowing orange and green flora.

I noticed the tangerine lilies were perpetually tilted toward the sun, straining themselves to make the most of the waning daylight. Like the peace movement Kevin dedicated his life to, the perennial flowers return year after year, eternally reaching for a light source far beyond their own roots. I still think of Kevin whenever they catch my eye.

TEN

THE GOOD, THE BAD, AND RICARDO HAUSMANN

Though Joanna Hausmann describes herself as a New York City-based nightclub comedian, she is best known for her work supporting Washington's coup against her family's homeland—no laughing matter. In the weeks immediately following the US recognition of Guaidó, Hausmann emerged as one of the most prominent pro-coup "Venezuelan voices" on the internet, packaging the policies of John Bolton and Elliott Abrams into quirky messages tailored for millennials.

Hausmann's first video on the subject, posted on her personal YouTube and Facebook pages within a week of Guaidó's "swearing in ceremony," racked up nearly four million views with its promise to explain "what is happening in Venezuela" by providing "just the facts."[1] Recorded in what appeared to be the living room of her apartment, the video opened with Hausmann's vow to dispel "misinformation" regarding the situation in her home country.

"I did a bunch of research to explain in the clearest way possible what is going on in a way that I hope people can understand," Hausmann announced, furrowing her harshly penciled-in brow to express deep concern.

Hausmann proceeded to rattle off a litany of Venezuelan opposition talking points used to justify regime change: Maduro was an illegitimate dictator who single-handedly squashed the opposition-controlled legislature, rounded up peaceful demonstrators, and ran the country's economy into the ground. Peculiarly, her account failed

1 Joanna Hausmann, "What's Happening in Venezuela? Just the Facts," Facebook, January 28, 2019.

to offer a thorough explanation of the National Assembly's legal status or chronicle of the brutal guarimba riots that prompted the arrest of US-backed opposition figures, as detailed in this book's introduction. Hausmann also completely erased the role US sanctions played in stunting Venezuela's economy, driving inflation, and harming the country's medical infrastructure, as documented in chapters one and three. Following her refrain of anti-Maduro arguments, Hausmann launched a whole-hearted defense of Guaidó, informing viewers that he "did not just declare himself president," was "not right-wing," and (somehow, despite never having run for president) was the "elected" leader of Venezuela.

Near the end of her carefully scripted rant, Hausmann's blue eyes swelled with tears as she delivered an emotional plea: "On a personal level . . . my father is exiled from going back home," she complained, concluding: "This is about people wanting their country back. That's it."

Based on Hausmann's performance, viewers may have been left with the impression that her father was an impoverished migrant forced to make the hellish trek from Venezuela to the US-Mexico border in search of political asylum. While that was far from the case, her commentary was an unintentional confession. Indeed, if any Venezuelan could be accused of "wanting their country back" it was Joanna Hausmann's father, Ricardo.

Ricardo Hausmann was no ordinary Venezuelan expat. He not only served as a high-ranking Venezuelan official in the pre-Chávez era, but established himself as an influential academic at Harvard's Kennedy School of Government after moving to the United States in the 1990s. By March 2019, Hausmann had also taken over as Guaidó's top economic advisor and representative before the Inter-American Development Bank (IDB), a regional equivalent of the International Monetary Fund.

Multiple sources who have worked with Hausmann over the years, including several with knowledge of his conduct during meetings with US government officials, have described him as unpleasant, "vindictive," and driven by "ideological blindness." A former colleague of his once recounted to me that during a lunch in the 1990s, Hausmann professed that he did not know anyone whose children went to public school. Were Hausmann's drivers and nannies not people in his eyes, the ex-colleague wondered?

Hausmann "had his fifteen seconds when US Venezuela policy was hijacked by the far right," a separate acquaintance remarked to me, adding, "he blew even that." That same source, who worked in the US financial sector, described Hausmann as an "academic with delusions of grandeur."

I became a target of Hausmann's volatile behavior myself when I questioned him regarding his professional conflicts of interest. In fact, Hausmann's late night tantrums against me eventually cost him his job in the Guaidó coup administration.

In March 2019, Guaidó selected Hausmann to serve as his representative at the IDB, a regional financial institution focused on promoting neoliberal development in Latin America and the Caribbean. A grandfatherly figure within Venezuela's opposition, Hausmann's addition to the Guaidó shadow government provided it an air of authority. Unlike diplomatic appointees such as Vecchio and Tarre, Hausmann was not a minor-league operative vying for influence, nor was he associated with the extreme wing of Venezuelan politics. Instead, Hausmann was regarded as one of the leading neoliberal thought leaders of his time.

Sporting a close-cut goatee and aviator-style, clear-framed spectacles, Hausmann was a prominent Harvard professor with a knack for boiling seemingly complex economic concepts down to simplistic tidbits that popular audiences could digest easily—the kind of pre-packaged policy wonk for which TED Talks were created. In 2006, he founded the Growth Lab at Harvard University, a policy research center that, according to its website, "works in the pursuit of inclusive prosperity and a quality of life for everyone that we know is achievable."[2]

"A country is, in this metaphor, a collection of monkeys that are living off some trees," Hausmann offered up in his degrading view of

---

2   About the Growth Lab, "About the Growth Lab," accessed March 21, 2023.

sovereign nations and their populations in a 2017 video promotion for the Growth Lab.[3]

Such penetrating insights secured Hausmann's place as a leading free-market scholar. Throughout the years leading up to his ascent within Guaidó's coup regime, Hausmann was ferried around the world to share his thoughts on global development, often punctuating analytical points with the rhetorical *"riiiight?"*—a needless interjection that academics tirelessly deploy to affirm the trust of suggestible audiences.

Hausmann delivered one such performance in November 2018, when he appeared to reveal prior knowledge of the impending regime change operation that would target his home country just two months later.

"The international community is now focused on the idea that . . . January 10 is the end of the presidential period of Nicolás Maduro." Hausmann presaged Guaidó's self-declared rule during a talk before the World Affairs Council of Greater Houston,[4] a foreign policy gathering funded by the local petroleum industry. During the meeting, Hausmann detailed his vision for the "morning after" regime change in Caracas, informing the crowd that based on his conversations with Venezuela's opposition, he was confident that a coup would result in "the opening up of the oil industry."

"We need to change the oil law so that we can allow private investment in the oil industry," the academic insisted.

Hausmann's "morning after" prescription for Venezuela represented a return to the country's cruel neoliberal period, when its government called in the military to repress massive bread riots in the capitol, disappeared and tortured protest leaders, and dug mass graves. For Hausmann, that era also happened to coincide with the height of his career as a Venezuelan government official.

Before joining Harvard in 2000, Hausmann served as a top economic advisor to Venezuelan president Carlos Andrés Pérez. Though he had

---

3   CID Harvard, "What Is the Product Space?" June 13, 2017.

4   World Affairs Council of Greater Houston, "Ricardo Hausmann on the Venezuela Crisis and The Road Ahead (11/01/18)," YouTube, November 7, 2018.

been elected on an anti-austerity platform,[5] Pérez accepted an IMF loan and implemented a series of reforms attached to it immediately upon taking office in 1989. Known as El Gran Viraje, or "The Great Turn," the reforms privatized state utilities and abolished price controls for basic supplies, policies that unsurprisingly spread despair and hunger among Venezuela's working class. As neoliberal Venezuelan economist Juan Cristóbal Nagel put it, El Gran Viraje represented "your basic Washington Consensus recipe."[6]

Venezuela's underclass erupted in February 1989, when the IMF reforms triggered a 30 percent hike in bus fares. Pérez ultimately unleashed the boot of the military to crush the week-long revolt, known as the Caracazo, resulting in the deaths of up to three thousand people.[7] Many were dumped in unmarked mass graves outside Caracas, their bodies marked with signs of death by execution.[8] Though Hausmann was working as a visiting fellow at Oxford University in the United Kingdom at the time, he had a key hand in crafting the policies that prompted the revolt.

"Hausmann will tell you that he was abroad at Oxford during the Caracazo rebellion," historian George Ciccariello-Maher told me in 2019. His book, *We Created Chávez: A People's History of the Venezuelan Revolution*, charted Chavismo's rise as the product of an IMF-prescribed, neoliberal economic program that ravaged Venezuela's working class.[9]

"While this may be true," Ciccariello-Maher continued, Hausmann "had already spent years in a number of government positions going back to the mid-1980s, and as a key 'IESA Boy,' spreading neoliberal doctrine from his professorship at the Institute."

5   Dan Fastenberg, "Carlos Andrés Pérez," *Time*, January 10, 2011.

6   Juan Cristobal Nagel, "El Gran Viraje, 25 Years On," *Caracas Chronicles*, February 16, 2014.

7   Sibylla Brodzinsky, "Venezuela President Maduro Announces Diplomatic Sanctions against US," *Guardian*, March 1, 2015.

8   Sarah Grainger, "Victims of Venezuela's Caracazo Clashes Reburied," BBC News, February 28, 2011.

9   George Ciccariello-Maher, *We Created Chávez: A People's History of the Venezuelan Revolution* (Durham, NC: Duke Univ. Press, 2013).

The term "IESA Boys" referred to a group of Venezuelan economists who taught and studied at the private Instituto de Estudios Superiores de Administración (IESA) in Caracas throughout the 1970s and '80s. Like their Chilean counterparts, the "Chicago Boys," who worked to liberalize Chile's economy under the military junta of Augusto Pinochet, the IESA Boys were synonymous with the kind of pro-capital, austere policies that Pérez implemented in the lead up to the Caracazo. In his book *Windfall to Curse: Oil and Industrialization in Venezuela*, economist Jonathan Di John wrote that "Pérez was greatly influenced" by IESA academics, including Hausmann, characterizing them as "an elite group . . . who had no party affiliation and were champions of radical, neoliberal reform."[10]

According to Di John, this group initiated "rapid liberalization reforms" under Pérez, opening Venezuela up for a pillaging at the hands of multinational corporations while gutting what remained of its meager welfare state. Many of Hausmann's disciples served in the Pérez administration, even if he did not rejoin them himself until 1992, when he took over as minister of planning. Within years, the widespread social and economic destruction that Hausmann and his fellow IESA Boys delivered had set the stage for Chávez's 1998 electoral victory.

"The Bolivarian Revolution was an indirect response to neoliberalism, born of mass resistance in the streets," Ciccariello-Maher explained. "In power, it remained largely faithful to that mission."

By the time of Chávez's 1998 triumph, Hausmann had been living outside of Venezuela for several years. In 1994, he relocated to Washington DC to work as chief economist at the IBD before moving to Boston in 2000 to further his academic career at Harvard. Even as they built their life in the United States, Hausmann and his family never gave up on overturning the revolution underway in their home country. His wife, Ana Julia Jatar, served on the executive committee of María Corina Machado's US-funded organization Súmate,[11] which

---

10   Jonathan Di John, *From Windfall to Curse? Oil and Industrialization in Venezuela, 1920 to the Present* (University Park, PA: Penn State University Press, 2015).

11   "Ana Julia Jatar Presenta 'Las Notas De Mi Vida,'" *Analítica*, February 26, 2010.

led the failed effort to remove Chávez through a recall vote in 2003 (chapter nine).

When the referendum delivered record turnout in support of Chávez, Hausmann used his lofty position at Harvard to defend his wife's futile effort, issuing a paper that undermined the official vote count by marring it with "hypotheses of fraud."[12] His argument was comprehensively debunked in a Center for Economic and Policy Research study that determined Hausmann and his co-author, MIT's Roberto Rigobon, ultimately "provid[ed] no evidence of fraud" in the recall.[13] Meanwhile, the Carter Center, which monitored the vote on the ground, released its own report asserting that it did not receive or observe any "credible evidence of fraud that would have changed the outcome,"[14] further eroding Hausmann's defense of Súmate.

For Hausmann and his wife, the tireless campaign to defeat progressivism within Venezuela's borders was family tradition. Hausmann's father-in-law, Braulio Jatar Dotti, was a high-level official in Venezuela's ruling Acción Democrática party when it waged a violent battle against leftist guerillas throughout the 1960s. According to the independent Chilean news site El Desconcierto, Jatar Dotti was "in charge of eliminating leftist groups" in the country at the time.[15] In 1963, he literally wrote the book on how to eradicate the guerillas, publishing a guide titled *Disabling the Extreme Left*.[16]

12   Ricardo Hausmann and Roberto Rigobon, "In Search of the Black Swan: Analysis of the Statistical Evidence of Electoral Fraud in Venezuela," Project Euclid (Institute of Mathematical Statistics, November 2011).

13   Mark Weisbrot, David Rosnick, and Todd Tucker, "Black Swans, Conspiracy Theories, and the Quixotic Search for Fraud: A Look at Hausmann and Rigobón's 1 Analysis of Venezuela's Referendum Vote," Center for Economic and Policy Research, September 20, 2004.

14   "Observing the Venezuela Presidential Recall Referendum," Carter Center, February 2005.

15   Cristian Hugo García, "¿Quién Es Braulio Jatar, El Supuesto Periodista Chileno-Venezolano?" *El Desconcierto* - Prensa digital libre, October 19, 2016.

16   Braulio Jatar Dotti, *Inhabilitacion De La Extrema Izquierda y Guerrillas Corionas* (Caracas: La Secretaria de Asuntos Parlamentarios y Municipales de Accion Democratica, 1963).

When Hausmann's daughter, Joanna, pledged to provide viewers with "the facts" on Venezuela in January 2019, she curiously omitted her family history; her father's role in Guaidó's coup government, her mother's US-backed campaign to remove Chávez from office, and her grandfather's dirty war on leftist guerillas. I uncovered the saga and put it on the record in a March 2019 piece titled "Ricardo Hausmann's 'Morning After' for Venezuela: The Neoliberal Brain Behind Juan Guaidó's Economic Agenda."[17] I noted that Joanna not only neglected to disclose her family ties to the coup government, but had merely parroted her father's own pro-regime change argument, which he outlined in a January 2018 opinion piece hauntingly titled "D-Day Venezuela."[18] Though much of Joanna's script tracked with her father's, the elder Hausmann added an open declaration of bloodlust for his homeland, insisting that "military intervention by a coalition of regional forces may be the only way" to resolve the country's crisis.

In publishing my Hausmann family exposé, I aimed to inform the public that the video racking up millions of views on social media had not been produced by a common Venezuelan, but one with a clear stake in regime change. Yet within weeks of my article's publication, Joanna was making the rounds on the internet once again—this time thanks to the *New York Times*.

On April 1, 2019, the *Times* published a fresh, slickly produced Hausmann harangue.[19] This time, Joanna's tirade took aim at the US left, which she complained was too focused on "what Trump is doing about Venezuela," and spreading "rumors" that "the US is considering military intervention" in the country—the very type of military intervention for which her father openly advocated.

"'Hands off' can actually mean 'blood on your hands,'" Joanna proclaimed, mocking the anti-war movement's "Hands off Venezuela" slogan before urging viewers to support Guaidó's effort to "restore

---

17   Anya Parampil, "Ricardo Hausmann: The Neoliberal Brain behind Juan Guaido's Agenda," *MintPress News*, March 15, 2019.

18   Ricardo Hausmann, "D-Day Venezuela: By Ricardo Hausmann," Project Syndicate, January 2, 2018.

19   Joanna Hausmann, Leah Varjacques, and Kristopher Knight, "What My Fellow Liberals Don't Get about Venezuela," *New York Times*, April 1, 2019.

democracy." Shockingly, the *Times* failed to disclose Joanna's familial link to Guaidó's US-backed coup regime, triggering a flood of comments from viewers outraged at the "paper of record's" flagrant disregard for basic journalistic ethics.

"As a Venezuelan, I agree with everything she has to say," one comment began. "That said, I think it's an ethical error of the *New York Times* to not disclose the fact that her father is Ricardo Hausmann." The commenter, Giorgio Angelini, went on: "His economic policy is likely the plan that will go into place should the opposition get control of the government. To say nothing of the merits of his plan, it should be noted that her father has a lot to gain politically and professionally should regime change happen."[20]

In response to public outcry, *Times* editor Adam Ellnick sought the cloak of feminist cant. Ellnick posted a swift reply to Angelini's comment, confessing that though his publication was "aware of her father's biography before publication," it opted not to disclose Joanna's relationship to the coup regime because she "is an independent adult woman who has built a popular following on her own."

Yet the paper's own ethics code explicitly stated that "staff members must be sensitive that perfectly proper political activity by their spouses, family or companions may nevertheless create conflicts of interest or the appearance of conflict."[21] Considering it was impossible to imagine the *Times* affording the same level of independence it granted Joanna to someone like Ivanka Trump, for example, Ellnick's argument fell flat. As criticism of Joanna's glorified ad for the coup regime that employed her father snowballed on social media, my article documenting the Hausmann family's dark history went viral. Joanna replied by blocking me on Twitter.

"I am proud of my dad," was all she could muster in response to the controversy.[22]

20   Giorgio Angelini, "Comment RE: What My Fellow Liberals Don't Get about Venezuela," *New York Times*, April 1, 2019.

21   "Ethical Journalism: A Handbook of Values and Practices for the News and Opinion Departments," *New York Times*, January 5, 2018.

22   Joanna Hausmann (@Joannahausmann), Twitter post, April 1, 2019, https:// twitter.com/Joannahausmann/status/1112800714252865536?s=20.

Rather than face me directly, the imperial nepo baby leaned on her father for defense. Like Joanna's editor at the *Times*, Professor Hausmann hid behind his daughter's gender to assert that my criticisms amounted to one of "the year's most sexist comments."[23]

"Since @Joannahausmann is my daughter, she is not entitled to her own opinion," the Harvard academic tweeted. "She must be speaking on behalf of some male figure that tells her what to say. Seriously?"

As with the task of penning her pro-coup diatribes, Joanna could count on her father to fight her Twitter battles. Meanwhile, Guaidó's shadow regime was relying on the professor to craft policies that would hand Venezuela's economy over to the highest foreign bidder. Unfortunately for the Hausmann clan, however, its patriarch's time in Venezuela's US-backed coup government would soon come to an end.

In August 2019, I discovered a financial disclosure form that Hausmann was required to file with Harvard in his capacity as a professor. The document revealed that throughout his time at the university, Hausmann raked in dozens of lucrative payments from major banking behemoths and global financial organizations, as well as repressive and theocratic governments in exchange for speaking engagements and consulting jobs.[24]

Between 2009 and 2019, Hausmann collected fees for a total of sixty-one "outside professional activities" while employed at Harvard, including paid speaking gigs for Wall Street titans JPMorgan Chase, Bank of America Merrill Lynch, and Citigroup. He also received compensation for speeches and consulting services performed for governments around the globe, including those in Peru, Brazil, Kazakhstan, Israel, and Saudi Arabia. Additionally, Hausmann participated in paid and unpaid engagements with the International Monetary Fund, the World Bank, and his future employer under Guaidó's shadow regime, the Inter-American Development Bank.

23   Ricardo Hausmann (@ricardo_hausman), Twitter post, April 2, 2019, https://twitter.com/ricardo_hausman/status/1113033158772101120?s=20.
24   Ricardo Hausmann public disclosure, accessed March 22, 2023.

How could someone who once criticized Goldman Sachs for its decision to purchase Venezuelan debt, an act he argued should make investors feel "morally queasy,"[25] justify collecting payments from the Wahhabi Kingdom of Saudi Arabia? Or the apartheid state of Israel, for that matter? Was Hausmann truly committed to the ideals of "freedom" and "democracy" he so frequently complained were lacking in his home country, or was he simply motivated by a paycheck?

On top of exposing his naked hypocrisy, Hausmann's disclosure form raised a serious ethical concern. Listed among the corporations, governments, and international financial institutions that had doled out cash to the professor was a mysterious benefactor: "Ricardo Hausmann Consulting." Starting in 2016, the firm was listed as having paid Hausmann for his work as its "consultant and principal investigator." Essentially, Hausmann had established his own private consulting firm through which to funnel unknown payment sums from anonymous clients. Because Harvard only required him to list the consulting firm on his disclosure form, the company effectively shielded Hausmann's clients from official transparency guidelines.[26]

The existence of Hausmann's private consulting firm cut to the core of the scandal surrounding his work for Guaidó's coup administration. Should a "government official" be allowed to maintain a private consulting firm and accept payments from anonymous clients? What's more, if Hausmann were indeed working as Venezuela's governor at the IDB, why was he still employed at Harvard? Other Guaidó appointees, such as PdVSA chair Alejandro Grisanti and OAS "ambassador" Gustavo Tarre, were required to quit their jobs before joining Venezuela's shadow regime. Similarly, Samantha Power was required to take "public service leave" from Harvard while fulfilling her duties as administrator of USAID. Why didn't Harvard apply those same standards to Hausmann? Or his underling at Harvard, Guaidó "attorney general" José Ignacio Hernández, for that matter?

25   Ricardo Hausmann, "The Hunger Bonds: By Ricardo Hausmann," Project Syndicate, May 26, 2017.

26   Anya Parampil, "Hausmann Hypocrisy: Guaido Coup Official Raked in Dollars from Dictators and Banking Behemoths While Promoting 'Democracy' for Venezuela," The Grayzone, August 31, 2019.

I contacted Harvard with these obvious ethical questions, inquiring whether it typically kept active government officials on its faculty or if there were rules against such dual employment. I also pressed Harvard to follow through on its supposed commitment to transparency and require Hausmann name the clients of his private consulting firm. Though the university failed to respond, I eventually received a much more consequential reply from the man at the center of the controversy.

On an afternoon in late August 2019, I obtained Hausmann's personal cell number and fired off a series of questions via WhatsApp. "I can't think of one example of someone who worked an academic job while serving in government. How do you have time for all your duties?" I asked the professor.

Hausmann's WhatsApp status indicated he was online, and he shot back almost immediately.

"I exercise no government functions. I do not run an organization, I am not paid by the Venezuelan government and I do not manage a public budget," Hausmann hastily explained.

With two sentences, the professor irreparably undermined Washington's Venezuela policy—and his own credibility. Though Hausmann claimed to exercise no government function, Guaidó had tapped him to represent Venezuela's shadow regime at the IDB five months prior. In addition to that role, Hausmann was overseeing Guaidó's $150 billion debt restructuring plan in his capacity as an official presidential "advisor."[27] If these activities did not constitute "government functions," then Hausmann was tacitly admitting what many critics of Washington's policy knew all along.

"Are you telling me Guaidó's administration does not constitute a legitimate government? I am sure the Venezuelan people will be surprised to hear that," I wrote.

Realizing his error, Hausmann conceded, "I am an advisor of Juan Guaidó, which I do on a pro bono basis. I have been named governor

---

27   Ben Bartenstein, "Adviser to Venezuela Guaido Has Harsh Message for Bondholders," *Bloomberg*, January 30, 2019.

of the IDB and a member of the restructuring commission. Neither involves any compensation."

"So you *do* exercise government function?" I replied to confirm Hausmann's self-contradiction, highlighting that Grisanti and Tarre were required to quit their jobs before joining Venezuela's shadow regime, regardless of whether they were getting paid.

"This isn't an issue of compensation," I argued, stressing the matter of his dual employment. At this point, Hausmann's defense devolved from logic, which seemed to be in low supply, to ad-hominem.

"You are not a journalist nor are you interested in the truth," he charged. "You are an advocate of a cause and you produce biased and untrue stuff that advances your political agenda."

"Ok, you are entitled to your opinion," I responded, inviting Hausmann to correct any inaccuracies in my reporting. "Have I said anything false?"

"I am not required to quit my job, according to Venezuelan law, US law or Harvard norms," the professor asserted.

"Ok," I accepted. "But shouldn't you disclose your private consulting clients if you are a government advisor?"

Rather than answer my question, Hausmann changed the subject: "You tried to disqualify my daughter just because she is my daughter, as if she was not an indipendent [*sic*] woman."

"Was anything I said false?" I asked. "Did she learn failure to disclose from you?"

Once again, Hausmann could only offer a deflection.

"Please diclose [*sic*] how much money you have received from Maduro. What have been your deslings [*sic*] with that dictatorship?" he wrote.

I noticed that as the Friday afternoon turned to evening and then night, the Harvard professor's spelling capabilities gradually deteriorated. Was it half-past cocktail hour in the Hausmann home?

The coup official's desperate devolution into accusations that Venezuela's government funded my work suggested that he had finally realized the grave error he made in engaging with me. While I openly worked as a correspondent and host for RT America between the years 2014 and 2019, since then I have never accepted payment from a state or state-funded institution. Unlike Hausmann, the *Grayzone* has never received funding or support from any government or state-backed group, and never will.

"So how much did the Wahhabi Kingdom pay you, again?" I asked Hausmann, apparently striking a nerve.

It was then that the esteemed academic and former Venezuelan government minister melted down, demanding I "Go to hell."

Considering his professional rank and "government" job, I was astonished by Hausmann's behavior. Yet his tantrum did not end there.

Our exchange, which began at roughly two in the afternoon on August 31, went on for over twelve hours. Throughout the evening, Hausmann descended deeper into the realm of absurdity, at one point even requesting that I disclose *my* father's identity. I proudly informed the professor that, unlike himself, my father spent his free time cooking Indian food and relaxing—not orchestrating a US-backed plot to overthrow the elected government of his homeland.

At precisely 3:31 a.m., Hausmann launched a final WhatsApp barrage demanding to see "one article" in which I "questioned or criticized any of Maduro's crimes and errors." I told him that I would leave that job to just about every Western journalist.

Ricardo Hausmann is typing …
…
…
…

The professor's manifesto never arrived. At around four in the morning, Hausmann blocked my number and prevented himself from issuing further insults. His self-restraint arrived too late, however. On September 6, I published the content of our highly revealing WhatsApp exchange at the *Grayzone*, screenshots included.[28] Eleven days later, Ricardo Hausmann resigned from Guaidó's shadow government.[29]

28   Anya Parampil, "'Go to Hell': Venezuelan Coup Leader Ricardo Hausmann Stages Whatsapp Meltdown When Confronted with His Own Hypocrisy and Lack of Transparency," *The Grayzone*, September 6, 2019.

29   Max Blumenthal, "Following Grayzone Exposé, Top Venezuelan Coup Official Ricardo Hausmann Is Forced to Resign," *The Grayzone*, September 27, 2019.

"Unfortunately, despite the honor and trust that this offer signified to me, I could not accept it at the moment due to the incompatibilities with my current obligations at Harvard University," Hausmann explained in his resignation, which he published on Twitter.[30]

As was customary with documents issued by Guaidó's shadow regime, Hausmann's letter contained a critical error. When he posted a screenshot of his resignation email online, Hausmann accidentally included the letter's recipient. Yet the name located in the top left corner of his screen was not "Juan" or "Guaidó." Instead, it simply read "Leopoldo."

Hausmann's mistake revealed that the true leader of Venezuela's coup regime was not Guaidó, but Leopoldo López, co-founder of the US-backed Voluntad Popular party. Atop the injury that Hausmann's departure exacted on Guaidó's doddering project, the professor had added a clumsy parting insult.

30   Ricardo Hausmann (@ricardo_hausman), Twitter post, September 26, 2019, https://twitter.com/ricardo_hausman/status/1177377601490477057?s=20.

ELEVEN

HUMAN RIGHTS, HUMAN WRONGS

In his memoirs, Soviet foreign minister Andrei Gromyko wrote that as he and fellow dignitaries endeavored to establish the United Nations in the aftermath of World War II, he voted for it to be headquartered in New York for a special reason.

"Moscow wanted to make sure Americans did not lose their interests in international affairs," Gromyko recalled telling US vice president Nelson Rockefeller.[1]

"We were afraid the USA would revert to isolationism," the Soviet diplomat, who served as foreign minister for nearly three decades (1957–1985), explained.

The US vice president's father, John D., ultimately donated the plot of prime Manhattan real estate where the UN General Assembly gathers to this day—a "charitable" gesture Gromyko interpreted as a possible ploy to increase the value of Rockefeller family property in the surrounding neighborhood.

Washington quickly assuaged Moscow's fears that it would withdraw from global affairs, adopting a decidedly interventionist foreign policy ever since the Second World War. Rather than disengage from the UN, US officials have instead treated it as a projector for their own worldview, as displayed when Trump's vice president Mike Pence addressed the Security Council in April 2019 to demand that it formally recognize Juan Guaidó as Venezuela's leader (Besheer 2019).

---

1   Gromyko, Andreĭ Andreevich, *Memoirs* (New York: Doubleday, 1990).

While Venezuela and other targets of Western hybrid war maintain confidence in the UN system and lean on it for legitimacy, the US and Europe's ability to manipulate the organization is transparent. The UN's limits are particularly clear in light of the increasingly politicized behavior of its Office of the High Commissioner for Human Rights, or OHCHR.

When it came to Venezuela, the OHCHR walked a fine line— maintaining official ties with Maduro's UN-recognized government while providing critical assistance to Washington's regime change offensive. Most notably, the OHCHR issued consequential reports in 2019 and 2020 that conveniently parroted Washington's anti-Maduro narrative, accusing Venezuela's government of "crimes against humanity" while completely overlooking abuses committed by the country's US-backed opposition.

The OHCHR reports fed a renewed wave of attacks on Venezuela's human rights record in the wake of Guaidó's coup. They were issued under the watch of a human rights commissioner who had suffered torture at the hands of a right-wing, US-backed dictatorship herself. Upon taking over the OHCHR in Geneva, however, she proved a begrudging servant of the Washington Consensus.

When UN high commissioner for human rights and former Chilean president Michelle Bachelet traveled to Caracas in June 2019, she met with numerous Venezuelans whose family members had fallen victim to US-backed extremist violence. Among them was Inés Esparragoza. During guarimba riots in 2017, an opposition mob attacked Esparragoza's twenty-two-year-old son, Orlando Figuera, in the street, doused him with gasoline, and lit him on fire.[2]

"He was stabbed, beaten, and cruelly burnt alive," Esparragoza, an Afro-Venezuelan, declared before Bachelet in March 2019. "Simply because of the color of his skin and because he said he was Chavista."

Video of Esparragoza's sorrowful testimony, which I published at the *Grayzone*, captured Bachelet scribbling down notes and glancing

2   "Venezuela Man Set Alight at Anti-Government Protest Dies," BBC, June 5, 2017.

over grisly photographs of Figuera's final moments.[3] One showed the anguished young man kneeling on the ground as a gang of anti-government thugs poured petrol all over him. Others depicted him running through the street in terror as flames engulfed his body.[4]

"I call on the United Nations high commissioner for human rights to make justice," Esparragoza pleaded between sobs. "These are not peaceful protesters, they are bloodthirsty."

Bachelet should have been able to relate to Esparragoza, and even Figuera himself. Long before her 2006 ascent to Chile's presidency, the US-backed military junta of Augusto Pinochet had detained and tortured Bachelet's own father, Alberto, after he refused to support the country's 1973 coup as a top air force officer.[5] When Alberto Bachelet died in a Santiago prison less than a year following his arrest, Chilean authorities turned their depraved attention to his family. In January 1975, Chile's secret police kidnapped then twenty-year-old Michelle and her mother, subjecting them to several weeks of torture before forcing them into exile in Australia.

"They put a hood over my head, threatened me and hit me," Bachelet later revealed, describing her experience in Chile's infamous Villa Grimaldi interrogation complex.[6]

Despite her family's own torment under the rule of Latin America's US-backed extremists, when Bachelet released her long-anticipated Venezuela report in July 2019, it was as though her meeting with Esparragoza never took place. Apparently unmoved by the testimony of Figuera's grieving mother and other casualties of anti-Chavista riots, Bachelet made no mention of opposition violence in her report. Instead, she focused her critique entirely on Venezuela's government,

3   Anya Parampil, "'Weaponizing Human Rights': UN Chief Bachelet's Venezuela Report Follows US Regime Change Script," *The Grayzone*, July 6, 2019.

4   Daniel García Marco, "Agresión a Orlando José Figuera: Lo Que Se Sabe Del Joven Al Que Prendieron Fuego Durante Una Protesta En Venezuela," BBC, May 22, 2017.

5   "Chile Charges Two over General Alberto Bachelet's Death," BBC, July 17, 2012.

6   "Torture Survivor Bachelet Takes Human Rights Lead at UN – DW – 09/01/2018," Deutsche Welle, September 1, 2018.

particularly its CLAP program and effort to defend itself through the establishment of nonstate civilian militias known as colectivos.[7]

According to Bachelet, the CLAP program initiated by Maduro was not an effort to feed his besieged population, but an "intelligence gathering" operation that spied on opposition families while blocking them from receiving benefits. Her evidence-free assertions are thoroughly dispelled in chapter two of this book, which established that CLAP not only helped avert a humanitarian catastrophe in Venezuela, but did so while largely avoiding partisan discrimination (Rodríguez June 2022).

In addition to CLAP, Bachelet directed her selective ire at Venezuela's colectivos, demanding Caracas "disarm and dismantle pro-government armed civilian groups" while accusing them of "exercising social control." As with CLAP, Bachelet's view of colectivos directly parroted claims of US officials like John Bolton and Marco Rubio, who branded the groups as disorderly terrorist gangs that Maduro personally commanded.[8] Such characterizations overlooked an obvious question: what kind of dictator promoted the arming of their civilian population beyond the state's authority?

Months before the publication of Bachelet's report, British journalist John McEvoy spent two weeks living with a colectivo in Caracas attempting to answer that question.[9] When I asked him about Bachelet's portrayal of colectivos as "pro-government civilian armed groups," McEvoy asserted such descriptions were "reductive and ahistorical." He explained her narrative discounted the fact that many colectivos were established decades before Chávez's rise, initially as guerilla movements in the 1960s, and then as "self-defense militias" in the 1990s. Though colectivos overwhelmingly lined up behind Chavismo in subsequent years, McEvoy insisted Bachelet's report "stripped the Venezuelan political situation of all of its historical context" while

7   "UN Human Rights Report on Venezuela Urges Immediate Measures to Halt and Remedy Grave Rights Violations," OHCHR, July 4, 2019

8   "Rubio Pide Que Régimen De Maduro y Colectivos Sean Designados Organizaciones Terroristas," Radio y Televisión Martí, April 5, 2019.

9   John McEvoy, "Two Weeks inside One of Venezuela's Notorious 'Colectivos'," *The Canary*, March 30, 2019.

"buttressing the US government's crude narrative of a criminal regime hanging on by criminal means."

As we will learn in chapter fifteen, colectivos played a key role in obstructing a foreign-directed mercenary invasion of Venezuela in May 2020. With this context, Bachelet's call for colectivos to disarm appeared equal to a demand that Venezuela surrender its last line of defense against an ongoing regime change operation that featured assassination attempts against the country's president and threats of a full-scale military intervention.

After undermining Venezuela's right to feed and defend itself, Bachelet issued a full-fledged defense of US sanctions on the country, dismissing criticism of the measures as Maduro "assign[ing] blame" for his own shortcomings. Her glib analysis was not only contradicted by copious evidence presented throughout this book, but by the US government itself.

Months before Bachelet released her report, the US State Department published an assessment of its Venezuela policy that openly touted Washington's central role in Guaidó's ongoing coup attempt. Posted in April 2019, the report boasted that sanctions had successfully cut Venezuela's government off from US financial markets and impaired its ability to generate oil revenue. Though the State Department deleted the fact sheet within hours of its publication, I obtained a copy of the document and published it on the *Grayzone*.[10]

Among the "key outcomes" of US-Venezuela policy in 2019, the State Department celebrated the following achievements:

- Juan Guaidó had announced his interim presidency
- $3.2 billion worth of Venezuela's overseas assets were frozen
- Maduro's government was cut off from US financial markets and unable to access credit
- Venezuelan oil production—and therefore, government revenue—had drastically reduced

10   Anya Parampil, "US State Department Publishes, Then Deletes Sadistic Venezuela Hit List Boasting of Economic Ruin," *The Grayzone*, May 6, 2019.

"It's a list of confessions," Venezuela's UN ambassador, Samuel Moncada, told me. He was not alone in expressing shock at the brazen document.

"If I were the State Department, I wouldn't brag about causing a cut in oil production," Mark Weisbrot, an economist and co-director of the Center for Economic and Policy Research (CEPR), remarked to me. "This means even more premature deaths than the tens of thousands that resulted from sanctions last year."

Indeed, the very month that the State Department released its Venezuela fact sheet, Weisbrot co-authored a report with economist Jeffrey Sachs concluding that US sanctions contributed to a 31 percent increase in Venezuelan mortality rates between the years 2017 and 2018 alone (Sachs and Weisbrot 2019). Yet just as she ignored the State Department's own sadistic admission that US policy was behind Venezuela's economic collapse, Bachelet completely discounted CEPR's assessment. Instead, she provided official UN cover for Washington's financial war and justified subsequent attacks on the CLAP program, including the extrajudicial kidnapping of its facilitator, Venezuelan diplomat Alex Saab, one year following her report's publication (chapter two).

"The U.S. deplores these human rights abuses in #Venezuela & calls on the international community to take steps to hold those responsible accountable," the State Department tweeted while promoting Bachelet's report, signaling Washington's satisfaction with her work.[11]

The UN Human Rights Council's obsession with Venezuela intensified in September 2020, when it published a report accusing the government in Caracas of "crimes against humanity."[12] Initiated the previous fall, the investigation was not only designed to undermine Caracas's official cooperation with the OHCHR, but to distract from rampant social upheaval that befell several of Venezuela's US-aligned neighbors throughout 2019 and 2020. During that period, neoliberal

11   State Department Spokesperson (@StateDeptSpox), Twitter post, July 5, 2019, https://twitter.com/StateDeptSpox/status/1147293203055312897?s=20.

12   "Venezuela: New UN Report Details Responsibilities for Crimes against Humanity to Repress Dissent and Highlights Situation in Remote Mining Areas," OHCHR, September 20, 2022.

governments in Chile,[13] Ecuador,[14] Colombia,[15] and Honduras[16] faced a wave of protests and labor strikes fueled by a popular rejection of austerity and increased state-sanctioned violence in the region. As millions poured into the streets, each government met their respective rebellions with their own flavor of vicious repression. Facing backlash in international media, these governments banded together at the UN human rights council to deflect attention onto their favorite regional bogeyman. In September 2019, they rammed through an initiative to investigate human rights abuses in Venezuela and quickly gathered a partisan team of "experts" to malign the country on the UN's behalf.[17]

To a critical eye, the resulting report was highly improper—if not entirely corrupt. None of the three "experts" tasked with leading the inquiry ever set foot in Venezuela, leading them to source their accusations of human rights abuses in the country to claims made by its compromised former intelligence chief, Manuel Cristopher Figuera. Less than one year into his stint at the helm of Venezuela's National Intelligence Service (SEBIN), Figuera sided with Guaidó amid the coup leader's botched military putsch in April 2019.[18] Exposed as the failed revolt's highest-level collaborator, Figuera fled to the United States after orchestrating opposition leader Leopoldo López's escape from house arrest. Days later, the US Treasury lifted personal financial sanctions that it had imposed on Figuera months prior.[19]

13   Brent McDonald, "A Bullet to the Eye Is the Price of Protesting in Chile," *The Independent*, November 21, 2019.

14   Dan Collyns, "Indigenous Ecuadorians Too Strong to Be Ignored after Deal to End Protests," *Guardian*, October 16, 2019.

15   "Colombia: At Least 17 Dead in Dayslong Protests – DW – 05/03/2021," Deutsche Welle, May 3, 2021.

16   Zoe Alexandra, "Hondurans Intensify Protests, Demand Resignation of President," *Peoples Dispatch*, June 20, 2019.

17   "Venezuela: UN Creates Independent Investigative Body," Human Rights Watch, September 27, 2019.

18   Anthony Faiola, "Maduro's Ex-Spy Chief Lands in U.S. Armed with Allegations against Venezuelan Government," *Washington Post*, June 24, 2019.

19   "Treasury Removes Sanctions Imposed on Former High-Ranking Venezuelan Intelligence Official after Public Break with Maduro and Dismissal," United States Department of the Treasury, May 7, 2019.

Though most Venezuelan officials do not maintain US bank accounts—therefore dodging the impact of such unilateral dictates—a June 2019 *Washington Post* report revealed that Figuera's wife was already living in Miami at the time of Guaidó's miscarried uprising, suggesting he was uniquely susceptible to the Treasury's attempt to coerce his defection (Faiola 2019).

Whilst reviewing the September 2020 Venezuela OHCHR report, I discovered that virtually every accusation of human rights abuse and torture was sourced to Figuera. Though they placed his testimony at the center of their "investigation," the authors omitted any mention of Figuera's defection to Washington under financial duress. The report's lack of credibility was further underscored by the fact that each of Figuera's examples of alleged widespread torture and abuse at SEBIN occurred between 2014 and 2018—a period that conveniently concluded when he took over the agency.

In addition to shoddy sourcing, the 2020 OHCHR relied on outright deception. At the heart of the accusations of political repression leveled against Caracas were the cases of US-backed opposition leader Leopoldo López and former police officer turned terrorist Óscar Pérez. While charging Venezuela's government with subjecting López to "cruel and inhuman punishment," the report avoided any mention of his role in the violent guarimba riots that paralyzed the country in 2014. It also failed to explain why it considered López's detention—which confined him to house arrest that he spent with his family[20]—to be "cruel and inhuman." Was his wife truly so unbearable?

Yet perhaps nothing in the 2020 OHCHR report was as farcical as its treatment of Óscar Pérez, a former helicopter pilot for the criminal investigation unit of Venezuela's police force. Pérez shot to international fame during the guarimba riots of 2017, when he hijacked his police helicopter and lodged grenades at Venezuela's Supreme Court in an apparent terrorist attack.[21] After fleeing the scene, Pérez released a statement in which he claimed to be leading a mutiny of police and

20   Reuters Staff, "Venezuela Restores Opposition Leader Lopez to House Arrest: Wife," Reuters, August 5, 2017.

21   Virginia López, "Venezuela: Police Helicopter Attacks Supreme Court with Grenades," *Guardian*, June 28, 2017.

military defectors in a "struggle for the liberation" of Venezuela.[22] Yet his uprising never materialized, and the militant was forced underground until January 2018, when a police raid on his hideaway resulted in a prolonged shootout that left Pérez, six of his men, and two law enforcement officers dead (Ellsworth and Chinea 2018). Though the 2020 OHCHR report acknowledged Pérez "commandeered a helicopter and flew it over the Supreme Court of Justice, in an attack," it somehow classified his death as an unjustified "extrajudicial killing."

So who exactly was behind this piece of propaganda dressed up as a clinical investigation? Among its three authors—none of whom set foot in Venezuela—was a lawyer named Francisco Cox Vial. Before he ventured to investigate human rights abuses in Venezuela, Cox worked as a defense attorney for Jovino Novoa, a Chilean official who served as the general undersecretary of Augusto Pinochet's notoriously brutal US-backed military junta between the years 1979 and 1982.[23]

"Francisco Cox Vial is not a lawyer who qualifies as an expert in human rights," Chilean sociologist Esteban Silva Cuadra told me in October 2020, arguing Cox's defense of figures like Novoa revealed him as a hypocrite.

"He is part of an operation against the government of Venezuela," Silva asserted.

The fact that Cox had previously defended a junta leader who oversaw the torture and execution of thousands of Chilean dissidents should have disqualified his UN "human rights" inquiry altogether. At the OHCHR, however, politicized perversion of human rights was par for the course.

Situated on the chilled banks of Lake Geneva, the UN Human Rights Office seems to have leapt from the illustrations of a fairytale. Stationed in a sprawling stone complex that was originally constructed to house the League of Nations, it is located in Ariana Park, a 113-acre greenspace that previously belonged to one of Switzerland's most preeminent

22   "Venezuela: Helicopter Pilot Appears in Video, Vows to Keep Fighting," NBC, July 5, 2017.
23   "Defensor De Novoa: Utilizan Al Sii Para Eliminar a UN Enemigo Político," Cooperativa, July 6, 2015.

ruling families, the Revilliods. According to UN lore, the Revilliods' last descendent donated the park to Geneva's local government in 1890 on the condition that his family's collection of wild peacocks remained on its grounds. As a result, visitors to the UN in Geneva are not only treated to views of its Alpine waters and distant Mountain peaks, but to the shimmery blue and green mating displays of the majestic birds that roam its premise to this very day.

I encountered these royal creatures myself when Max and I testified at the UN Human Rights Council on March 19, 2019. Speaking along-side UN special rapporteur Alfred de Zayas and Lucrecia Hernández, director of the Caracas-based human rights organization Sures, Max and I detailed our reporting from Venezuela at an event dedicated to exploring the impact of US sanctions in the country.

A soft-spoken yet forceful attorney with a background in human rights law, Hernández and her husband, attorney Cristóbal Cornieles Perret, founded Sures in 2016 to investigate the effects of US financial warfare on Venezuela's economy and population. As one of the country's leading experts on the matter, Hernández's presentation in Geneva thoroughly documented how Washington's sanctions had systematically undermined Venezuela's industrial capacity and, particularly, its health sector.[24]

De Zayas, meanwhile, used his speaking time to deliver a scorching indictment of the entire UN Human Rights Office, accusing its func-tionaries of violating "the most fundamental principles of methodol-ogy" in its approach to Venezuela.[25] Typically sporting a flamboyantly patterned bow tie and a delicately combed, salt-and-pepper coif, de Zayas was a rebel within the UN system. As a world-renowned special-ist in international law, he was uniquely qualified for such an insurgent role. De Zayas not only spent decades as a senior OHCHR official, but had visited Venezuela himself in 2017 in his capacity as a UN special rapporteur. Fluent in six languages, the dual US-Swiss citizen spoke in an indiscernible aristocratic accent as he addressed the room in Geneva.

24   "Derechos Humanos Y Medidas Coercitivas Unilaterales," Sures, September 26, 2021,

25   "Ex-UN Human Rights Expert Blasts 'Manipulation' on Venezuela: 'We Are Swimming in an Ocean of Lies'," *The Grayzone*, March 20, 2019.

"We are swimming in an ocean of lies," de Zayas informed the diplomats and lawyers gathered before us.

"When I went to Venezuela, I expected to find a humanitarian crisis—I was *predetermined* to find a humanitarian crisis," he continued, explaining that upon arriving in the country, he discovered "that's not the case."

"That meant I had been manipulated, I had been lied to, and I resent that!"

Though the situation de Zayas observed in Venezuela was not nearly as dire as he anticipated, the lawyer's 2018 UN inquiry still concluded that US sanctions amounted to a modern "Medieval siege" of the country (chapter one). The report was just one example of his work as a dissident legal scholar. Primarily known for his contributions to the UN, where he used his senior position to argue in defense of Palestinians, Sahrawis, and other marginalized groups, de Zayas's independence streak informed an unorthodox—and at times, controversial—approach to international law. In 1980, he published a historical review of the Wehrmacht War Crimes Bureau, a German initiative that investigated Nazi *and* Allied war crimes in the aftermath of World War II.[26] Though academic reviews, including the Cambridge Law Journal, praised his scholarship,[27] de Zayas's documentation of crimes committed *against* rank and file Nazi troops outraged others, including critics who absurdly equated his research with Holocaust denialism.

One of de Zayas's loudest detractors was UN Watch, a Geneva-based organization funded by the US Israel lobby.[28] Since its 1993 foundation, UN Watch served as Israel's most aggressive defender within the halls of the human rights council, weaponizing its role as a so-called "monitor" to viciously smear anyone who dared speak up for

---

26   Alfred M. de Zayas, *The Wehrmacht War Crimes Bureau 1939 - 1945* (Lincoln: University of Nebraska Press, 1989).

27   Christopher Greenwood, "The Wehrmacht War Crimes Bureau, 1939–1945. By Alfred M. De Zayas, with the Collaboration of Walter Rabus," Cambridge University Press, January 16, 2009.

28   "UN Watch," Militarist Monitor, December 1, 2011.

Palestinian rights or other causes opposed to Zionism as "antisemitic."[29] As such, UN Watch maintained an undying obsession with de Zayas throughout his career, and even issued a demand the OHCHR officially condemn the lawyer's Venezuela investigation on the basis that he was "a hero to Holocaust deniers."[30]

UN Watch's bullying tactics were palpable during my own visit to the human rights council. As we prepared to testify, a representative of the group arrived to inform our host, Italian lawyer Micòl Savia, that UN Watch had booked the room for a session immediately following our scheduled event. According to Savia, who represented the International Association of Democratic Lawyers before the UN, the maneuver was meant to ensure that the question-and-answer portion of our discussion was cut short. Sure enough, the UN Watch envoy sat through our entire testimony with a stopwatch in hand, leaping to displace us as soon as our reservation technically expired.

According to several people I met at the OHCHR, UN Watch was not the only special interest group with outsized influence over the United Nations. As I chatted with officials and lawyers gathered in the UN cafeteria, several complained that corporate and state-backed lobbying groups had strengthened their hold over the organization in recent years. One source specifically bemoaned the UN's increasing reliance on funding from the Bill & Melinda Gates Foundation, a development that undermined its ostensible role as forum for exchange between *states*. Such concerns are justified by the fact that the second largest donor to the UN's World Health Organization, for example, is not a sovereign government, but the Gates family's private foundation.[31]

Despite the UN's shortcomings, individuals like de Zayas and Savia have dedicated their careers to preserving what remains of its integrity. In de Zayas's case, that effort required a willingness to

---

29   Naomi Zeveloff, "U.N. Official Answers Questions about Fierce Criticism of Israel," The Forward, July 21, 2011.

30   "U.N. Chief Must Condemn Own Expert's 'Fake Investigation' of Venezuela Rights Record," UN Watch, November 29, 2017.

31   Annalisa Merelli, "The WHO Has a Worrisome Reliance on the Bill & Melinda Gates Foundation," Quartz, December 16, 2021.

publicly shame UN officials who failed to uphold the organization's founding principles.

"The lack of professionalism on the part of the UN secretariat is a disgrace and should be exposed by civil society," de Zayas said of UN high commissioner for human rights Michelle Bachelet when I reached out to him following the publication of her demonstrably biased Venezuela report in July 2019.

In de Zayas's view, reports like Bachelet's were "methodologically flawed" because they relied "overwhelmingly on unverified allegations by opposition politicians and advocates of regime change." He accused Bachelet and other UN officials of refusing to engage with Venezuela's government in good faith, arguing such breakdowns in communication eroded the OHCHR's supposed commitment to human rights.

Indeed, Bachelet's ideological approach to her job stood in stark contrast with de Zayas's pragmatic method. By establishing a rapport with Venezuela's government—rather than the US-backed forces working to overthrow it—he yielded tangible results. In 2019, de Zayas successfully lobbied Caracas to release twenty-three prisoners, including a German citizen, through a personal request filed with the country's foreign minister, Jorge Arreaza.

"I asked Arreaza personally for the release of the German journalist, Billy Six," de Zayas revealed during his March 2019 UN testimony, days after Six was released from a Venezuelan jail. "What does that tell you? That if you have good faith, if you want to mediate, if you want to have dialogue, the government is willing."

According to de Zayas, his success was rooted in his status as a special rapporteur, which afforded him a level of autonomy that figures like Bachelet did not enjoy.

"I was not a UN employee with a salary, and no one could give me instructions," de Zayas explained to me, adding "a high commissioner is not independent, and is subject to political pressures."

De Zayas encountered such pressure himself while conducting his own Venezuela inquiry, informing me that he experienced "pre-mission, during mission and post mission mobbing" aimed at influencing the report's outcome.

"I was pressured, intimidated, insulted by non-governmental organizations and even colleagues, but I was able to proceed with my investigation and reflect what I saw and learned on the ground," de Zayas recounted.

"I am not an ideologue," he continued. "There are many in the UN secretariat."

The politicized nature of its human rights council cast the UN's genuine commitment to its founding principles—sovereignty, territorial integrity, and self-determination—in a questionable light. Yet fatalistic views of the organization are discouraged by one important factor: most UN member states remain overwhelmingly dedicated to a defense of those ideals. I witnessed the strength of their resolve first-hand when I traveled to Caracas in the summer of 2019 to cover a high-level summit of the Non-Aligned Movement (NAM), the UN's largest member bloc.

TWELVE

THE BEGINNING OF HISTORY
AND THE FIRST MAN

If not for the international demonization campaign and economic siege waged against Venezuela, the country would be a hotspot for global tourism. Between its Caribbean coast, tropical islands, maritime mountains, slice of the Amazon rainforest, and site of the tallest waterfall in the world, Venezuela offers a medley of Earthly portals to the celestial realm. One such location is Isla Margarita, a moderately sized isle located just a few miles off Venezuela's northeastern coast. Margarita's alabaster beaches and lucent waters reflect the eternal equatorial sun so intensely that it is known as the "Pearl of the Caribbean."

Guaidó selected Isla Margarita as the backdrop for a "presidential" visit on July 18, 2019. Traveling aboard a small fishing boat, he arrived at the island waving a Venezuelan flag as a few dozen supporters cheered him on from the beach. Later, he stripped down to black swim trunks and dove headlong into the water with local fishermen. While Guaidó's backers, including some in Western media, celebrated his "heroic" stunt,[1] others on Venezuelan social media derided it as a humorously unpresidential photo-op.

At the time of Guaidó's Margarita tour, I was on my way back to the Venezuelan capital to cover a ministerial summit of the Non-Aligned Movement (NAM) hosted by the country's *actual* government. The UN chartered a plane for its New York-based ambassadors to make the journey down south as top diplomats from all over the world convened upon Caracas to finalize NAM's agenda for the coming years.

---

1   "Guaido Receives Hero's Welcome at Venezuela's Margarita Island Amid Peace Talks," Global News (July 19, 2019).

The NAM summit presented Venezuela's government with a timely opportunity to not only demonstrate that an overwhelming majority of the world's nations rejected Guaidó's US-backed coup effort, but that it was capable of hosting a high-level diplomatic conference even while under an international sanctions regime. Throughout the conference, I spoke with several UN dignitaries who expressed surprise at how normal Caracas was, explaining they expected a less hospitable, even hellish experience based on what they read about Venezuela in international media. One Yemeni diplomat was especially happy to discover a late-night hookah café in Caracas.

Among the most prominent guests in attendance was Iranian foreign minister Javad Zarif, who traveled to Caracas all the way from Tehran. Tapped as Iran's top diplomat in 2013, the Western-educated Zarif had guided his country's negotiations with the Obama administration on the JCPOA, or Iran Deal, up to its 2015 completion. Though the agreement was initially celebrated as a historic breakthrough in US-Iran relations, the zealously pro-Israel Trump administration withdrew from the JCPOA in 2018.

Upon Zarif's Caracas arrival on the eve of NAM's opening day, his Venezuelan counterpart, Jorge Arreaza, greeted him on the tarmac with a reverent embrace.

"The resistance of the people of Venezuela against the United States is very important for all the countries of the world," Zarif told reporters gathered nearby, adding, "today in the Middle East and the regions of South America and Latin America, the US is creating instability and insecurity."[2]

Zarif's remarks set a defiant tone for the gathering, which served as a formal rebuke to US and European attacks on the sovereignty of NAM member states. At no point was this clearer than during a session convened on the sidelines of the official summit by members of the UN group dedicated to reasserting the organization's founding principles, an initiative launched by Venezuela's Arreaza earlier that year (chapter five). Throughout the meeting, I watched foreign ministers and senior diplomats from all regions of the world take the floor, one

2   "Iranian Foreign Minister Lands in Venezuela," *Iran Press*, July 20, 2019.

after another, to articulate the plight their respective populations faced under Western sanctions.[3]

The most passionate intervention came from Zarif, who, in flawless English, implored his fellow diplomats to ditch the term "sanctions" when describing US and EU aggression toward their countries. He complained the word inadvertently legitimized the measures by framing them as punishment for wrongdoing. Zarif had another term in mind. Raising his mobile phone in the air, he urged his colleagues to "just Google 'terrorism.'"

"This is the definition that the dictionary will give you: 'unlawful use of violence or intimidation, especially against civilians, in pursuit of political gains,'" he continued, pausing to look around the room. "So please friends, stop using [the term] 'sanctions' . . . sanctions have a legal connotation. This is economic terrorism . . . we have to say it again and again."

Zarif characterized sanctions as a tool the US and its allies deployed against governments that resisted transatlantic hegemony, vowing the policy would fail in Iran, Syria, Cuba, Venezuela, and anywhere else it reared its head. Indeed, if I had one takeaway from the NAM summit, it was that a new system of international relations—one less dependent on the power centers of Washington, London, and Brussels—was forming before my eyes. While the West's global onslaught of war and sanctions had scarred invariable millions of citizens from NAM states, their leaders did not see themselves as helpless victims. Instead, these diplomats were energized to shepherd a revolution in global affairs.

***

The Non-Aligned Movement was born from the developing world's desire for sovereignty following the ostensible collapse of European empires brought about by the Second World War. Founded in 1961 by postcolonial icons such as Egypt's Gamal Abdel Nasser, Ghanaian president Kwame Nkrumah, Indian prime minister Jawaharlal Nehru,

---

3   Anya Parampil, "'We Are the Vaccine against Unilateralism': Non-Aligned Movement Gathers in Venezuela to Resist Dictatorship of Dollar," *The Grayzone*, July 28, 2019.

and Josip Tito of Yugoslavia, NAM originally comprised an alliance of countries that sought independence from the US and Soviet power blocs at the height of the Cold War. Though the Soviet Union had since collapsed, NAM's 2019 reunion in Caracas underscored the group's modern role as an alliance of powerful nations that wished to exist without interference from the US or Europe—a level of sovereignty that many countries in Asia, Africa, Latin America, and the Middle East have yet to fully realize despite the end of traditional colonialism.

All of the diplomats I spoke with at the NAM summit agreed that modern transatlantic hegemony was enabled by the US and Europe's outsized control of the global financial system. That grip was largely based on two factors: dependence on the US dollar for international trade, and the politicization of the Society for Worldwide Interbank Financial Telecommunication (SWIFT) system, the Belgian-based network that has processed nearly all messaging for global financial transactions since its 1971 foundation. It's unlikely that average US citizens regularly consider SWIFT's existence, or their dollar's status as the world's reserve currency. For foreign leaders struggling against US and European economic war, however, the push to overturn these systems was the natural subject of longtime obsession.

As noted in chapters three and five, for decades the US dollar's standing as the world's reserve currency has permitted Washington to implement unilateral sanctions against countries like Venezuela and Iran without UN approval. The dollar's privileged status was rooted in Washington's historic relationship with the Kingdom of Saudi Arabia, which enabled it to form what is known as the Petrodollar system following an unprecedented international oil crisis in 1973. Throughout the '70s and '80s, Saudi Arabia began overtaking the United States and Soviet Union as the world's largest oil producer.[4] When Riyadh joined Arab Nations in boycotting crude sales to the US over Washington's support for Israel in the 1973 Yom Kippur War, it triggered a global oil shock. Within a matter of months, the US was rocked by a sudden 40

4 "Rankings, Total Energy Production," United States Energy Information Administration, accessed April 13, 2023.

percent surge in gas prices and fears of nationwide shortages that sent the middle class into a panic.[5]

In the summer of 1974, President Richard Nixon dispatched US Treasury Secretary William Simon and Secretary of State Henry Kissinger to Saudi Arabia on a mission to end the crisis. The resulting landmark arrangement saw Riyadh lift its oil embargo and purchase US Treasury bonds in exchange for US-supplied military equipment.[6] More importantly for Washington, however, was that from 1974 on, Saudi Arabia agreed to sell its oil exclusively in US dollars. Due to Riyadh's significant share of the international crude market and resulting influence over the Organization of Petroleum Exporting Countries (OPEC), that Petrodollar arrangement has protected the greenback's status as the world's reserve currency to this day by ensuring that any government purchasing oil (i.e., all of them) is forced to maintain a steady supply of US dollars.

Alongside the dollarization of global trade, SWIFT's historic willingness to act as an enforcer of US policy—rather than an autonomous institution—compounded Washington's command of the international financial system. Often described as a "global post office for banks," SWIFT is connected to over 11,000 financial institutions spanning across 200 countries and territories, and is responsible for issuing transactional orders between banks, corporations, and other entities.[7] Though billed as an independent financial institution, over the years SWIFT has fallen under Washington's sanctions spell.

"During the war on terror, the United States quietly turned the world financial system into a hidden empire," the *New York Times* explained in a rare critique of US financial warfare.[8] According to the *Times*, Washington used "the power of the dollar and its influence over obscure organizations such as the SWIFT financial messaging service

5   "Timeline: Oil Dependence and U.S. Foreign Policy," Council on Foreign Relations, accessed March 24, 2023.

6   Andrea Wong, "The Untold Story behind Saudi Arabia's 41-Year U.S. Debt Secret," *Bloomberg*, May 30, 2016.

7   "Discover Swift," Swift, accessed March 24, 2023.

8   Henry J. Farrell and Abraham L. Newman, "The Wrong Way to Punish Iran," *New York Times*, November 1, 2018.

to monitor" its enemies and, "in some cases, to cut entire states, such as North Korea, out of world financial flows."

"These policies effectively pressed foreign banks into service as agents of American influence and helped bring states like Iran to the negotiating table," the *Times* continued.

This "maximum pressure" strategy reached its height following the Trump administration's May 2018 withdrawal from the JCPOA, or Iran Nuclear Deal. A product of Trump's subservience to pro-Israel allies including his son-in-law, Jared Kushner, and top donor, Sheldon Adelson, the decision to crush the agreement and reimpose hostile, unilateral sanctions on Tehran aimed to undercut Iran's rise as a regional bulwark.[9] The policy quickly put SWIFT's supposed independence to the test. In November 2018, the US Treasury issued a threatening directive advising "providers of specialized financial messaging services," like SWIFT, to "discontinue the provision of such services to the Central Bank of Iran" and other Iranian institutions or risk incurring sanctions themselves.[10] SWIFT complied with the demand and unlinked Iran's Central Bank from its network days later, handing the US a victory in its financial war games that would prove pyrrhic.[11]

Though Washington succeeded in transforming SWIFT into a political weapon, it ultimately undermined the system's long-term viability as other countries—including US allies—sought alternate routes to Iranian bank accounts. In January 2019, Germany, Britain, and France established the Instrument in Support of Trade Exchanges (INSTEX), a SWIFT alternative specifically designed to bypass Washington's unilateral Iran sanctions. By July 2021, a total of ten European nations had officially joined the INSTEX project.[12]

At the NAM Caracas summit, it was obvious that Washington's overreliance on unilateral sanctions—particularly against oil producers such as Venezuela, Russia, and Iran—had backfired. A push to

---

9   Eli Clifton, "Follow the Money: Three Billionaires Paved Way for Trump's Iran Deal Withdrawal," LobeLog, May 8, 2018.

10   "Iran Sanctions FAQ," United States Department of the Treasury, November 5, 2018.

11   "SWIFT Unlinks Iran's Central Bank," *Financial Tribune*, November 13, 2018.

12   INSTEX, "About Us," January 31, 2022.

trade in currencies other than the dollar and build viable alternatives to SWIFT dominated the meeting's agenda. NAM's position was succinctly articulated by Russia's deputy foreign minister Sergei Ryabkov when he addressed the diplomatic roundtable on the importance of the UN charter.

"Let's turn dependence into independence," Ryabkov advised his colleagues, emphasizing the need to craft a global financial system beyond the West's grip.

I approached Ryabkov for an interview shortly following the session, hoping to gain insight into Russia's perspective on global affairs from the country's second most powerful diplomat.

"I think it's very real when people here talk a lot about the policies of regime change," Ryabkov reflected as we chatted on the summit's sidelines. "I hate finger pointing, but that sense of danger is very real."[13]

Ryabkov was well acquainted with the modern legacy of Western imperial rampage. Having entered the Soviet diplomatic corps in 1982 at just twenty-two years old, Ryabkov had weathered a tumultuous four decades in his country's history that spanned the Soviet Union's 1991 collapse; Russia's subsequent pillaging at the hands of international capital under the watch of a US-backed drunk called Boris Yeltsin; devastating NATO-led wars from Yugoslavia to Afghanistan; and eventually, President Vladimir Putin's effort to reclaim Russia's great power status. After a four-year stint at Russia's embassy in Washington, Ryabkov returned to Moscow in 2006 and was appointed deputy foreign minister two years later.

Though his tenure began with the Obama administration's fleeting attempt to "reset" US-Russia ties, the West's quest for world dominance soon drove relations between Washington and Moscow to new lows. Under Obama's watch, the US and its allies launched a series of regime change operations, including those targeting the governments of Libya, Syria, and Ukraine. The aggressive policy not only ousted sovereign governments in Tripoli and Kiev—both of which previously

---

13   Anya Parampil, "World 'Will Diminish Role of Dollar and US Banking System': Russian Minister at Non-Aligned Movement," *The Grayzone*, July 26, 2019.

enjoyed hospitable relations with Moscow—but successfully embroiled Russia in costly military ventures in Syria and Ukraine.

By the time Trump arrived in the White House, the Syria and Ukraine fronts threatened to spark direct military confrontation between Russia and the United States at any moment. Unfortunately, despite Trump's try for détente, the "Russiagate" hysteria that gripped the US media and political establishment throughout his presidency ultimately squashed all hope for a negotiated resolution to either conflict, as I discovered whilst covering the president's July 2018 meeting with Putin in Helsinki (chapter eight). Trump adopted a shockingly belligerent policy toward Moscow following the Helsinki summit, culminating with his decision to unilaterally withdraw the US from a series of Cold War-era treaties limiting nuclear arms procurement and military surveillance. As previously established, the about-face appeared to be the handiwork of Trump national security advisor John Bolton.

To Ryabkov, who specialized in arms reduction policy, Trump's decision to abandon the promise of Helsinki was a shock.

"We couldn't believe our own eyes and ears when we heard, point after point, how understandings between the leaders were literally dismantled in Washington," Ryabkov recalled during our conversation in Caracas.

In conjunction with his Iran deal reversal, Trump's actions sent a message to Moscow and other foreign capitals that good faith engagement with the US was a fool's errand. Rather than wrestle with Washington's erratic behavior, these countries looked to each other for stability—a fact Ryabkov knew well. Throughout our discussion, the seasoned diplomat offered his analysis of the emerging multipolar world with cheerful matter-of-factness.

"China, Russia, others—we at the moment are creating alternatives" to the Western-controlled financial system, he explained.

According to Ryabkov, countries he described as the "historic West"—the US and its European partners—deployed sanctions to prevent developing nations—such as Iran and Venezuela—from emerging as regional powers. Rather than surrender, however, targeted countries have formed a diverse alliance dedicated to subverting transatlantic hegemony once and for all.

"I will reject the idea that countries like Venezuela, Iran, Syria, North Korea, China, Russia, or whoever, are unified through ideology," Ryabkov explained, stressing that each country had its own unique system of government. "We only work together as closely as we do because we face similar challenges, and similar threats to sovereignty."

Ryabkov disclosed that according to his government's internal calculations, the United States had sanctioned roughly seventy countries in recent decades, subjecting up to one-third of the global population to its hybrid financial war.

"I think it will backfire, it cannot be sustained in this way," the dignitary forecasted, insisting "people will bypass [the measures] in literal terms, and people will find ways to defend themselves and to protect themselves."

Russia developed its own alternative payment outlet, the System for Transfer of Financial Messages (SPFS), in 2014, after the US threatened to block Moscow's access to SWIFT in response to the Ukraine conflict. By establishing a financial messaging system outside of Washington and London's reach, SPFS provided a lifeline to other sanctioned countries, including Venezuela. Days before my July 2019 conversation with Ryabkov, Caracas initiated SPFS membership.[14]

After establishing alternative financial networks, "we will probably move to [use] not just national currencies, but baskets of currencies" when conducting trade, Ryabkov continued, adding: "We will use ways that will diminish the role of the dollar and US banking system."

Ryabkov's prediction has proven correct. In December 2021, a joint parliamentary committee in India, an ostensible US ally, recommended New Delhi develop its own SWIFT alternative to avoid interference from Washington.[15] The following March, *Bloomberg* reported India was officially considering a Russian proposal to join SPFS,[16] a move that would allow its government to purchase weapons and oil from Moscow

---

14   Patricia Laya and Anya Andrianova, "Weary of Sanctions, Venezuela Mulls Using Russian Payment System," *Bloomberg*, July 16, 2019.

15   Rishikesh Kumar, "Indian Government Urged to Set up Alternative to Swift Payment System over US Misuse," Sputnik International, December 8, 2022.

16   Shruti Srivastava and Vrishti Beniwal, "Russia Offers Swift Payment System Alternative to India for Buying Oil in Rubles," *Bloomberg*, March 30, 2022.

in rupee-ruble denominated payments.[17] Four months later, Turkey, a NATO member, announced its intent to join the Russian and Chinese-led Shanghai Cooperation Organization,[18] an economic and defense alliance of European and Asian nations that represents 40 percent of the world's population and more than 20 percent of global GDP.[19] Meanwhile, diplomatic sources informed journalist Pepe Escobar in December 2021 that Russia and China planned to launch a jointly operated SWIFT alternative in coming years.[20]

These same countries are moving away from dollar-dependence. In recent years, governments in Russia,[21] India,[22] Turkey,[23] and China[24] have sold off staggering portions of their US debt holdings while simultaneously increasing their central bank stockpiles of gold. Meanwhile, US sanctions drove Iran and Venezuela to formally ditch the dollar while conducting international trade. Tehran halted use of the greenback in January 2015.[25] Roughly three years later, Caracas dropped the dollar and replaced it with the euro.[26]

Such developments have had an observable impact on global trade. In 2017, Turkey and Iran committed to trade in local currencies, including

17   India signed an agreement to join SPFS in April 2023.

18   Baris Balci and Selcan Hacaoglu, "Turkey Seeks to Be First NATO Member to Join China-Led SCO," *Bloomberg*, September 17, 2022.

19   "Iran Looks East after China-Led Bloc Oks Entry," France 24, September 18, 2021.

20   Pepe Escobar, "Putin and XI Plot Their Swift Escape," *The Cradle*, December 17, 2021

21   Michael Selby-Green, "Russia Is Dumping US Debt and Buying Gold Instead," *Business Insider*, July 19, 2018.

22   Gayatri Nayak and Saikat Das, "India Sold $11 Billion Worth US Treasury Securities since October," *Economic Times*, March 17, 2021.

23   "Turkish Central Bank Sells off Half of US Government Bonds in 6 Months," Daily Sabah, August 15, 2018.

24   Yuta Saito and Iori Kawate, "China's U.S. Treasury Holdings Hit 12-Year Low on Rate Hikes, Tensions," *Nikkei Asia*, February 17, 2023.

25   Iran Joins Growing List of Countries to Ditch Dollar in Foreign Trade," Sputnik International, January 24, 2015.

26   Rachael King, "Venezuela Says It Will Drop US Dollar for Euros," Central Banking, October 19, 2018.

for gas and oil deals.[27] Two years later, Moscow and Ankara created a joint-investment fund bankrolled entirely in euros.[28] The following month, Venezuela sold $570 million worth of gold to the United Arab Emirates that Abu Dhabi paid for in cash—yet in euros, not dollars.[29]

These agreements represented a tectonic shift in global relations. Never before had the "developing" world, which includes Russia, China, and former Western colonies, acquired the capacity to participate in the globalized economy independent of the United States and Europe. Its rise has upended the once consensus view that the Soviet Union's collapse would usher in an era of US-led, unipolar dominance.

"After the end of the Cold War, it took particularly long for the US to realize there is no such thing as everyone agreeing to what the US asks or demands," Ryabkov remarked when I asked him about Russia's role in NAM.

Indeed, though NAM historically provided a space for formerly colonized nations to act as a unified league in pursuit of common interests—initially established to circumvent US *and* Soviet influence— both China and Russia had joined the group as observer states by 2019. Meanwhile the US, Canada, and European nations make up the bulk of the seventy-three states that remain excluded from the UN's largest member bloc.

On the second day of the NAM Caracas gathering, the most senior diplomats in attendance took an official group photo. I looked on as they arranged themselves on the stone steps of Hotel Alba, the former Caracas Hilton that Chávez expropriated in 2007.[30] One Arab diplomat donned a *thobe* and *keffiyeh*, others wore suits; one official sported a *song-kok*, another wore a bowler hat. There in Caracas, countries typically understood to be mortal enemies such as India and Pakistan, or Saudi

27   Reuters Staff, "Update 1-Turkey-Iran Central Banks Agree to Trade in Local Currencies - Turkish PM," Reuters, October 19, 2017.

28   "Russia, Turkey to Create Joint Investment Fund for 900 MLN Euro," TASS, April 8, 2019.

29   "Venezuela Sells Additional $570mln in Gold, Skirts US Sanctions – Report," Sputnik International, May 18, 2019.

30   Rory Carrol, "Workers of the World, Relax! Chávez Takes over Hilton," *Guardian*, October 22, 2009.

Arabia and Iran, stood shoulder to shoulder in an expression of unity. For these nations, their alliance was an acknowledgment that their continued survival as sovereign states, regardless of conflicting ideologies, required more cooperation than ever before. With Venezuela's Arreaza and Iran's Zarif at the center, the NAM dignitaries projected confidence—assured their combined force represented the majority of the world's population, rising nations, and therefore, the future.

Venezuela's president articulated that conviction during his formal address to NAM several hours later.

"This twenty-first century is our century," Maduro proclaimed with enthusiasm. "It is the century of freedom, it is the century of the end of empires, and it is just beginning in 2019. Although the battle is hard . . . no matter how bloody or criminal the attacks are, if we are determined to be free, nothing, nor anyone, will stop us. Brothers and sisters of the world, no one can stop the course of the new story that is making its way."

At the conclusion of the NAM summit, the bloc unanimously adopted a final document that officially established a working group to investigate the impact of sanctions on populations around the world, a task that Venezuela would lead (Parampil July 2019). The Caracas declaration also officially denounced US efforts to overthrow Venezuela's government and emphasized NAM's recognition of President Maduro as the country's leader.

Speaking before the NAM delegates, Venezuela's UN ambassador Samuel Moncada announced, "In the world there are 193 countries, and the United States cites only 55" that have recognized Guaidó's authority. "Here, there are 120 nations. Two-thirds of the United Nations believes that the government of Nicolás Maduro is the legitimate government of Venezuela."

As Moncada and his colleagues hosted international dignitaries in Caracas, Guaidó splashed away in the Caribbean.

"We have the support of the world," he assured *Foreign Policy* days before the NAM meeting began.[31]

When the UN General Assembly convened in New York two months later, Guaidó's confidence would be put to the test.

---

31   Annika Hernroth-Rothstein, "'We Are Going to Continue to Fight,'" *Foreign Policy*, July 16, 2019.

THIRTEEN

SWING FOR THE FENCES

In the months leading up to the September 2019 UN General Assembly session, a covert diplomatic war unfolded in the halls of its New York headquarters.

"We are battling," Venezuela's UN ambassador, Samuel Moncada, told me that April. As detailed in chapter seven, US vice president Mike Pence had addressed the Security Council earlier that month and implored its members to replace Moncada with a representative of Guaidó's coup regime.

"Battling, meaning campaigning," Moncada said of his team's effort. "We are talking, persuading, convincing all the world, and we are right now pretty sure that they don't have the numbers."

Even as the US lobbied his colleagues to betray him, Moncada kept a level of faith in the UN system. He asserted most countries understood that if the US achieved his removal, the absurd precedent for regime change would apply to any sovereign government going forward. What would stop the US from then imposing an unelected puppet regime on Tehran, Moscow, or Beijing? What's more, considering only about 55 of the UN 193 member states recognized Guaidó's legitimacy, it was unlikely the US would succeed in dismissing Moncada. To remove him and install Guaidó's representative, Washington would have to rally support from two-thirds of the voting delegates who attended the UN General Assembly meeting in September.

Yet precedent offered the US a possible opening: in 2009, Madagascar's then president, Andry Rajoelina, was prevented from addressing the UNGA after a *simple* majority of delegates present when

he took the floor voted to block his right to speak.[1] Moncada anticipated the US would try to obstruct his government's UNGA participation in a similar fashion, triggering a game of numbers between Caracas
and Washington in the months leading up to the September gathering.

Throughout this period, Washington worked to ensure that delegates from all 55 pro-Guaidó member states would be present on the
General Assembly floor at the time of Venezuela's UNGA address.
This meant that Caracas had to guarantee at least 55 of its own friends
also attended the speech, or the US would call for a vote to block
Venezuela's representative from speaking, win by simple majority, and
initiate the process of removing Maduro's government from the UN.

Venezuela's moment arrived on the afternoon of Friday, September
27, 2019. Tasked with addressing the UNGA on the country's behalf
was Vice President Delcy Rodríguez. As with Arreaza and his staff, who
arrived in New York days prior, US sanctions had barred Rodríguez
from chartering a plane to the US and forced her to fly commercial-
ly—an inconvenience that other foreign dignitaries of her rank could
hardly imagine.

Rodríguez was fit for the task before her, making up for what
she lacked in height with abounding personality. Usually dressed in
a brightly colored, well-tailored monochrome suit, Rodríguez was a
uniquely effective communicator, regularly spouting off rapid-fire statistics to reinforce her fiery political rhetoric before official podiums
and television cameras alike. When she entered UN headquarters on
the afternoon of her General Assembly address adorned in a trim royal
blue pantsuit accented with white stripes, she was upbeat and resolute.

As Rodríguez greeted those of us in the UN press gaggle with a
smile, we noticed she was holding a large photograph.

"Tell us about this photo!" shouted a male reporter who stood
to my right.

"We're going to talk about this photo," Rodríguez assured us while
continuing her waltz beyond the press's view.

I immediately recognized the photograph. Days before the UNGA
kicked off, images of Guaidó posing with members of a Colombian

---

1   "Rajoelina Stopped from Addressing UN General Assembly," France 24,
September 26, 2009.

drug gang called Los Rastrojos had surfaced online. Subsequent media reports revealed that the notoriously violent narco-paramilitary group had arranged Guaidó's illegal passage to Colombia in February 2019, when he participated in the US military's botched attempt to ram "humanitarian aid" across Venezuela's border.[2] For the coup leader and his backers in Washington, the images could not have come at a more inconvenient time.

I arrived at the press box above the General Assembly floor moments before Rodríguez was set to speak. In a hopeful sign for Venezuela, international delegates packed the gallery below. When Rodríguez finally took the podium, US officials were forced to confront reality: the world had rejected their fantastical Venezuela regime change scheme. Rather than call for a vote to block Rodríguez from speaking, US representatives and their allies stood up and marched out of the room in vain protest of her presence.[3] And that was all they could do.

In her distinctively raspy voice, Rodríguez proceeded to denounce US interference in her country and charge governments that had recognized Guaidó's authority with committing "one of the worst mistakes" in diplomatic history.[4] Characterizing the coup leader as "a criminal element who has been introduced to breach the peace" in Venezuela, she held a photograph of Guaidó palling around with Colombian narco-traffickers before the world.

"This Member of Congress is an imperial puppet," she informed the room. "He does not exist in Venezuelan politics."

Rodríguez's address marked the formal defeat of Guaidó's coup at the United Nations. Moments following its conclusion, a normally subdued Arreaza was uncharacteristically emotive as he recorded a video message to Venezuelans back home.

---

2   "Guaidó Habría Entrado a Colombia Apoyado Por 'Los Rastrojos'," *Portafolio*, September 12, 2019.

3   U.S. Mission to the UN (@USUN), Twitter post, September 27, 2019, https://twitter.com/USUN/status/1177686281112801280?s=20.

4   "Venezuela - Vice-President Addresses General Debate, 74th Session," United Nations, September 27, 2019.

"They could not, nor will they," Venezuela's foreign minister declared with an abandoned grin, invoking the traditional Chavista rallying cry in its more alliterative, original Spanish: *"No pudieron, ni podrán."* [5]

"They could not with Chávez, they cannot with Maduro, and they cannot with the Venezuelan people. Not Trump, not anyone."

Indeed, though US officials often referred to the "international community" as united in support for Guaidó, the 2019 UNGA session told a different story. At the UN, it turned out, the "international community" consisted of much more than Europe and Washington's allies in the Americas.

Africa's role in defending Venezuela was particularly significant. The fifty-four nations of the African continent account for roughly one-third of UN member states, and they have remained unified in their rejection of Guaidó. Following Caracas's win at the UN, I spoke with Venezuela's vice minister for African affairs, Yuri Pimentel, about his government's relationship with the continent.

"The relations of the Bolivarian Revolution with the African continent are very strong, and it's not something that began two days ago," Pimentel told me. "Since the beginning of the revolution, the late president, Commander Hugo Chávez, always told us that we had to strengthen relations with Africa."[6]

For Chávez, establishing ties with the continent he routinely described as "Mother Africa" was a top priority. When he took office in 1999, Venezuela had official diplomatic relations with just twenty African states. By 2019, that number had more than doubled to fifty-five.

"I speak about fifty-five [countries], even though one of them is not recognized in the United Nations, because we recognize the Western Sahara as an independent country," Pimentel explained, referring to the northwest African territory that has struggled against Moroccan occupation since the 1970s (it was formerly a Spanish colony). In Pimentel's

5   Jorge Arreaza (@jaarreaza.ve), Instagram post, September 27, 2019, https://www.instagram.com/p/B27t4YtgBus/?igshid=MDJmNzVkMjY%3D.

6   Anya Parampil, "How Venezuela Defeated Washington's Coup Attempt at the United Nations," *The Grayzone*, October 2, 2019.

view, the legacy of Chávez's "Bolivarian diplomacy" had enabled Venezuela's triumph at the UN.

"The defeat was a huge, huge defeat," Pimentel reflected on the moment US diplomats and their allies exited the UNGA floor. "They couldn't achieve what they wanted to do."

"Clearly they underestimated all the work that the diplomats of Venezuela have been doing in regard to the situation we are facing and the threat they were trying to impose on us," the diplomat continued. "The majority of UN countries clearly understand what the US is trying to do in Venezuela and they cannot support it, because they know that today it is Venezuela, and tomorrow it can be any one of them."

Though the US failed to officially install Guaidó allies at the UN, a handful of his representatives were granted UNGA credentials by US-allied Latin American countries including Colombia, Brazil, and Honduras. Among them was Diego Arria, a pre-revolution Venezuelan politician who once represented Caracas at the United Nations, and who accused late president Hugo Chávez of crimes against humanity at the International Criminal Court in 2011,[7] one year after Venezuela's government moved to expropriate his private ranch as part of an effort to expand domestic agricultural capacity.[8] Also present was Guaidó's US "ambassador," former Exxon lawyer and opposition consigliere Carlos Vecchio.

"This is really incredible, how some countries, by US instructions, agreed to accredit Venezuelan opposition members in their delegations," Pimentel remarked.

One member of the *actual* Venezuelan delegation, Gessy González, tweeted a photo of Arria seated behind the "Honduras" placard. She juxtaposed the image of the vanquished former diplomat with one showing Venezuelan Vice President Rodríguez, UN Ambassador Moncada, and Foreign Minister Arreaza smiling proudly in Venezuela's seat.

"For those who had any doubt about who represents Venezuela, here is its true delegation to the UNGA, while on the other hand we

7   Isabel Ferrer, "Diego Arria Demanda a Chávez Por Crímenes Contra La Humanidad," *El País*, November 21, 2011.

8   "Expropian Una Segunda Hacienda a Un Ex Embajador Venezolano Ante La Onu," *elEconomista*, June 22, 2010.

see lackeys of the opposition shaming the positions of other countries," González commented.[9]

"They are wandering like ghosts at the United Nations," Arreaza told reporters, referencing figures like Arria and Vecchio. "They are wandering around with credentials through the missions of other countries. It's the most absurd thing. Absolute desperation."[10]

Three days before Venezuela took the UNGA floor, US president Donald Trump delivered his own address to international dignitaries gathered in New York, inflating the importance of Washington's pro-Guaidó minority coalition.

"Since I last spoke in this hall, the United States and our partners have built a historic coalition of fifty-five countries that recognize the legitimate government of Venezuela," Trump bellowed.[11]

Throughout the entirety of the US president's speech, Venezuelan diplomat Daniela Rodríguez sat behind her country's placard on the General Assembly floor, her eyes fixed on a biography of Latin America's anti-colonial liberator, Simón Bolívar.[12]

In the aftermath of Venezuela's September victory at the United Nations, it seemed Washington forgot all about its maladroit coup in Caracas. In October, the US set its sights on Bolivia and supported the ouster of its longtime president, Evo Morales, through a military putsch. Venezuela's extremist opposition welcomed the development, even as it underscored their own failure to seize power.

"Bolivia took eighteen days, we have been at it for years," Guaidó assured supporters during a rally following the coup in La Paz.[13]

9   Gessy González (@gessy_ve), Twitter post, September 27, 2019, https://twitter.com/gessy_ve/status/1177677861941059584?s=20.

10   Associated Press, "At UN, Venezuela's Rival Delegations Circle Each Other," Voice of America, September 26, 2019.

11   "Remarks by President Trump to the 74th Session of the United Nations General Assembly," National Archives and Records Administration, September 25, 2019.

12   Tom O'Connor, "Venezuela Diplomat Reads Book during Trump's U.N. Speech Attacking Country," Newsweek, September 24, 2019.

13   "Venezuela Rivals Seek to Capitalise on Bolivia Crisis," TRTWorld, November 16, 2019.

By then, his future in the fast-approaching New Year looked bleak. Each day that President Maduro remained in Miraflores Palace weakened Guaidó's position even among the ranks of Venezuela's opposition. As his star faded in the final months of 2019, he renewed a call for street protests.

"If we are not going to have Christmas, neither will they," he said of Venezuela's government in early November,[14] just as *el espíritu de la Navidad* took hold of the country's streets.

Yet Santa found his way to Venezuela after all. Lights went up around the country and *gaitas*, the traditional holiday folk songs originating from Estado Zulia, emanated from storefronts nationwide. The cheerfully fast-paced maraca and drum-heavy beats blared as Venezuelans purchased their holiday *pan de jamón* and ingredients for *hallacas*, the Venezuelan take on *tamales* that adds raisins and green olives to traditional meat fillings. Families received their government-subsidized Christmas ham via the CLAP food program as 2019 came and went alongside a year of failed US regime change policy.

Even mainstream media were forced to acknowledge Guaidó's abating popularity in the final months of 2019. Reuters described one of his November rallies as "significantly smaller than those earlier in the year" with "participants [seeming] less optimistic about change."[15] The Associated Press made similar observations, noting the gatherings "lacked the size and combativeness of demonstrations in January" while openly stating "it was not clear [Guaidó] would be able to sustain momentum."[16]

That question would be answered on January 5, 2020, when Guaidó's term as president of Venezuela's National Assembly (AN) was set to expire. Considering he based his entire claim to Venezuela's presidency on his role at the helm of the country's legislature, the date represented a turning point in the legitimacy of Guaidó's coup project.

---

14   "Guaidó: Si No Vamos a Tener Navidad, Que Tampoco La Tenga El Régimen," *El Nacional*, November 9, 2019.

15   Brian Ellsworth and Deisy Buitrago, "Venezuela Opposition Rallies against Maduro to Revive Momentum," Reuters, November 16, 2019.

16   Scott Smith, "Venezuela's Guaidó Leads Thousands in Anti-Maduro Protest," Associated Press, November 16, 2019.

Unless he extended his mandate as AN president, Guaidó's shaky US-backed regime change venture risked altogether collapse.

The scenes that emerged from the January 5 vote for AN president were some of the most infamous of the entire Guaidó saga. As legislators gathered to elect their leader, an opposition lawmaker named Luis Parra declared his last-minute candidacy for president. A member of the Primero Justicia party, Parra's eleventh-hour challenge from within the halls of the Palacio Federal Legislativo came as a surprise to fellow legislators and outside observers alike, especially Guaidó and his allies. Along with Guaidó's Voluntad Popular party, Un Nuevo Tiempo, and Acción Democrática, Primero Justicia was part of the "G4" coalition that represented the most extreme bloc of Venezuela's opposition. G4 not only historically aligned itself with US objectives in the country, but provided the base of Guaidó's support in the legislature following the initiation of his self-declared presidency. Though Primero Justicia had expelled Parra weeks before the AN vote, his willingness to break with Guaidó suggested that nearly a year into Washington's failed coup project, Venezuela's opposition was less unified than ever.

It is important here to understand the rules and numbers that dictated Venezuela's legislature. In 2020, the National Assembly consisted of 167 lawmakers and required an 84-person quorum to carry out its function. To secure the AN presidency, either Guaidó or Parra had to win a *simple* majority of votes present once a quorum was established.

Seeing as Parra announced his candidacy mere minutes before the scheduled vote, however, Guaidó did not have time to take the temperature of his peers or whip up support for his own leadership bid. Of course, simply refusing to show up for the election would have displayed major weakness on Guaidó's part. Rather than openly boycott the vote, he attempted to sabotage it by staging a made-for-foreign media stunt designed to cast himself as the victim of a repressive regime rather than a politically insecure showman. Faced with possible defeat, he launched a panicked attempt to deny his colleagues the eighty-four-person quorum needed to proceed with the election.

As the vote approached, Guaidó materialized outside of the Palacio Federal Legislativo alongside two legislators from Estado Amazonas who had been banned from the National Assembly over allegations of voter fraud in their region (introduction). When security forces predictably blocked the banned lawmakers from entering the legislature, Guaidó's plan went into effect.

In video of the incident, Guaidó jostled his way toward the Palacio Federal Legislativo with his shoulders squished together, body swaying from side to side, as a sea of supporters, journalists, and concerned citizens engulfed him from all directions. He rolled his eyes and shook his head, appearing miffed when a reporter asked why he was trying to enter the National Assembly with disqualified legislators.

"Don't even reply," he defiantly instructed his cohorts. "Either we all go in or no one goes in."[17]

Guaidó's strategy was obvious: by insisting to enter the legislature alongside banned lawmakers, he directed a scene that appeared to prove Maduro's government was preventing him from seeking a second term as AN president. The drama reached its unintentionally hilarious apex when Guaidó ran along the perimeter of the Palacio Federal Legislativo and attempted to climb over its protective fence. Supporters boosted the politician's feet as he clung to the iron barrier and struggled to mount it. Security services yanked the wannabe president's coattails while their colleagues on the other side of the fence blocked him from leaping into the National Assembly grounds.[18]

While Guaidó scaled the fence outside, the scene within the AN chamber was equally chaotic as warring lawmakers exchanged charged words and, at times, physical blows. Parra declared victory amid the mayhem, claiming to have secured 81 out of 150 votes cast.

Parra's swearing-in was less than ceremonial. As he raised a hand and made his stately vows, nearly every lawmaker present was screaming at someone else in the room.[19] Parra's promise to uphold his civic duties were drowned out by the howls of disorderly colleagues who, locked in fiery debates with their peers, failed to even notice his rushed

17   Madelein Garcia (@madeleintlSUR), Twitter post, January 5, 2020, https://twitter.com/madeleintlSUR/status/1213937918701711362?s=20.

18   Factores de Poder, Twitter post [VIDEO], January 5, 2020, https://x.com/FactoresdePoder/status/1213886166304481280?s=20.

19   VIVOplay (@vivoplaynet), Twitter post, January 5, 2020, https://twitter.com/vivoplaynet/status/1213877037187944452?s=20.

confirmation. Amid the chaos, one lawmaker even leapt atop a desk to shout unintelligible declarations before the room.

Though Guaidó's attempt to prevent the vote was unsuccessful, his degrading clamber up the National Assembly fence achieved a more important objective. Below are samples of foreign media headlines summarizing the events of January 5, 2020:

"Guaidó says Venezuela police block access to parliament" (France 24)[20]

"Venezuela's Guaidó Blocked from Congress as Rival Lawmaker Claims Speaker Post" (Voice of America)[21]

"Venezuela's Last Democratic Institution Falls as Maduro Attempts De Facto Takeover of National Assembly" (*Washington Post*)[22]

Yet video of the incident demonstrated without question that Venezuelan authorities had not prevented Guaidó from entering the National Assembly. As he approached the building's front door with a banned Amazonas legislator, security guards instructed Guaidó's compromised companion to wait outside.

"In the meantime, the rest of you can get in," a guard clearly told Guaidó on video.[23]

"No, no one is going in unless you let him in with us," Guaidó responded, referring to the sanctioned lawmaker.

Acción Democrática legislator Williams Dávila further contradicted Guaidó's narrative, telling media later that afternoon that "only Calzadilla and a congressman from Amazonas were not allowed inside. Other than that, everyone else got in."[24]

20   "Guaido Says Venezuela Police Block Access to Parliament," France 24, January 5, 2020.

21   "Venezuela's Guaido Blocked from Congress as Rival Lawmaker Claims Speaker Post," Voice of America, January 6, 2020.

22   Rachelle Krygier and Anthony Faiola, "Venezuela's Last Democratic Institution Falls as Maduro Attempts De Facto Takeover of National Assembly," *Washington Post*, January 6, 2020.

23   Orlenys OV (@OrlenysOV), Twitter post, January 5, 2020, https://twitter.com/OrlenysOV/status/1213955849535807490?s=20.

24   Tania Díaz (@taniapsuv), Twitter post, January 5, 2020, https://twitter.com/taniapsuv/status/1213915399038873603?s=20.

The lawmaker's lack of sympathy for Guaidó was revealing. Like Parra, Dávila was a member of the once solidly pro-Guaidó G4 coalition.

"We have it all precisely done," Dávila said of the vote that elected Parra.

Yet as is customary with Venezuelan politics, the AN leadership vote was a complicated affair. Opposition analyst Francisco Rodríguez produced a thorough investigation of the election days later, noting that while Parra declared victory, he did not provide attendance records to certify his claim to the AN presidency. Rodríguez thus determined that "since no roll call vote was taken (the vote was by show of hands), there is no direct way to verify the number of legislators present or the number of votes obtained by Parra."[25]

Guaidó and his allies capitalized on the sloppiness of the vote within minutes of its conclusion, accusing Parra of collaborating with Maduro and his socialist party to carry out a "parliamentary coup" against Venezuela's opposition bloc.[26] Hours after Parra's hasty swearing-in, they convened their own shadow session of the National Assembly in the offices of *El Nacional*, an anti-Chavista newspaper, and held a separate vote that Guaidó won with ease.[27]

Though 100 legislators participated in the *El Nacional* vote, several were in fact substitute lawmakers who were only authorized to vote in the event of their principal member's absence, adding another layer of complexity to the AN leadership battle. Rodríguez broke through the confusion by analyzing both vote counts to determine who would have won if the election had been held under ordinary circumstances.

"Based on the public statements of lawmakers ahead of the vote, I estimate that under normal conditions, Guaidó would have won re-election as National Assembly president with 86 votes to Parra's 71," he later told me. However, he noted that three of those votes came from

25   Francisco Rodríguez, "¿Cuál Es La Verdadera Relación De Fuerzas En La Asamblea Nacional De Venezuela?" January 11, 2020.

26   "Guaido and Rival Perra Both Declare Selves Speaker of Venezuelan Parliament," France 24, January 5, 2020.

27   "En Vivo - Elección De La Nueva Directiva De La Asamblea Nacional 2020," VPItv, January 5, 2020.

the banned Amazonas legislators, meaning without them, Guaidó ulti-mately lacked the quorum needed to validate his victory.

The 2020 vote for AN president left Venezuela's opposition perma-nently disfigured. Following the events of January 5, 2020, contradic-tions between its competing factions were on permanent display within the legislature. From that point on, lawmakers outside the hardcore G4 coalition launched an official boycott of committee hearings in explicit protest of Guaidó's claim to authority.

While generating sympathy from the international press, Guaidó's exhibition on the National Assembly fence left his colleagues in Venezuela's opposition unimpressed. In fact, any self-respecting per-son who watched the scene unfold must have wondered what thoughts crossed Guaidó's mind as he gracelessly wobbled atop the pokey iron barrier. Perhaps he hoped that the foreign media eagerly documenting his humiliation from below might, at the very least, still consider him president of *something* when all was said and done.

Soon enough, the US-backed coup leader lost his balance and crashed to the ground.

FOURTEEN

THE CITGO CONSPIRACY

"¡Exprópiese!"

So went one of Hugo Chávez's most recognizable catchphrases, an order he handed down in reference to private shopping centers, foreign-owned mining operations, banks, and utility companies alike.

"Expropriate it!"

Chávez's commands to nationalize the property of foreign companies and Venezuela's domestic oligarchy were often dictated on his weekly Sunday program, *Aló Presidente*, which broadcast on state television and radio throughout his presidency. The show kicked off at 11:00 a.m. and ended whenever Chávez decided it was over.

"And this building?" he asked his local government companions during an episode transmitted on February 7, 2010.[1] Chávez pointed toward a multistory storefront situated on the corner of central Caracas's Plaza Bolívar, emblazoned with the words "The Gold Market" in English. His colleagues informed him the building was the site of several jewelry stores.

"Expropriate it!" the president instructed without hesitation. His government later alleged the building was the site of a black-market gold and money exchange.[2]

Television was a central means of communication for Chávez—a medium through which he unveiled policy initiatives, engaged with constituents, and articulated his agenda directly to the public.

1   "7 Feb 2010 Hugo Chávez En Aló Presidente N° 351," andresoasis, December 22, 2012.

2   Kiraz Janicke, "Venezuelan Government Closes Illegal Gold Trading and Money Laundering Racket," *Venezuelanalysis*, February 11, 2010.

A platform for unscripted fireside chats, *Aló Presidente* typically featured Chávez visiting public work sites, meeting with ministers, and fielding live phone calls from Venezuelan voters. The show produced a total of 378 episodes between the years 1999 and 2012, each one running anywhere between four and eight hours long.

When Chávez died in March 2013, most analysts focused on determining his political successor. While Maduro quickly rose to the occasion and won Venezuela's presidency, the void left by Chávez's stamina and enthusiasm before the media's klieg lights remained wide open—at least until February 2014, when a square-jawed military captain turned Chavista politician named Diosdado Cabello established *Con El Mazo Dando*. In launching the program, Cabello inherited the task of communicating the actions of Venezuela's government—and dispelling propaganda deployed against it—to its constituents.

Like Chávez before him, Cabello relied on blue-collar charisma, saucy humor, and a seemingly endless supply of effusive energy to fuel marathon live broadcasts that typically ran for over four hours. Rather than maintain a fixed studio, the weekly program set up shop in a variety of public venues such as state universities, local elementary schools, and the national military academy. In between Cabello's politically charged rants, *Con El Mazo Dando* featured on-set music performances interspersed with dramatic clips of Chávez's most revered speeches as cameras panned across a live studio audience of jubilant Chavistas.

One of *Con El Mazo Dando*'s regular segments featured Cabello standing before a bulletin board decorated with dozens of printed tweets and headlines. The tidbits typically consisted of Twitter declarations from opposition politicians, attacks on the Maduro government in international media, and news updates on US foreign policy. Cabello dissected the stories one by one, relentlessly mocking political opponents to the delight of his audience.

"*El Nuevo Herald*," Cabello underlined the media outlet's logo with a red pen during one such segment, reading the headline: "The United States considers sanctioning Russia for its support of Maduro."

Cabello paused for dramatic effect and looked toward his audience, which whistled and booed in response.

"And it must be causing tremors in Putin!" he quipped.

I attended a live taping of *Con El Mazo Dando* on July 31, 2019. The set, constructed in the headquarters of Venezuela's state oil company, Petróleos de Venezuela (PdVSA), showcased a large red desk emblazoned with the show's logo and the phrase "loyal always, traitors never," placed before towering portraits of Chávez and Maduro. The program opened with a live performance from El Colectivo Patria Nueva, a government-sponsored youth band that cranked out fast-paced llanero tunes traditional to Venezuela's rural plains as Cabello shimmied on the sidelines.[3]

When he appeared onstage for his opening monologue, Cabello took aim at US media for their portrayal of Venezuela's colectivos as criminal gangs that kidnapped and intimidated Chavista opponents. Pointing toward the fresh-faced vocalists on stage, he sarcastically bellowed: "El Colectivo Patria Nueva. Are you afraid of this colectivo yet?"

It was during this episode of *Con El Mazo Dando,* during Cabello's bulletin board segment, that I first heard the name José Ignacio Hernández. Though Guaidó had tapped the young lawyer as his "attorney general" in the initial days of his self-declared presidency, Hernández avoided media scrutiny throughout the early months of Washington's coup attempt. His distaste for public examination was well founded. I soon discovered that behind his sheepish demeanor, Hernández served as the most consequential member of Venezuela's US-backed shadow administration. While chronicling his role in Guaidó's puppet regime, I uncovered a hidden motivation behind Washington's seemingly failed regime change push: a conspiracy to rob Venezuela of its most prized international asset.

Amid the global economic crash of 2008, Venezuela's government moved to expropriate its Las Cristinas gold mine located in the southeastern Estado Bolívar.

"Due to the financial crisis that has expanded on a worldwide scale, it is necessary to recuperate our gold and increase our international reserves," then minister of basic industries and mining Rodolfo Sanz explained while making the announcement.[4]

The decision dealt a major blow to a Canadian mining company called Crystallex, which had signed an exclusive contract to develop and exploit Las Cristinas in 2002. On its website, Crystallex boasted that Las Cristinas was "one of the largest undeveloped gold deposits in the world" and home to an estimated 20.8 million ounces of gold valued at $550 per ounce.[5] When Venezuela's government rejected final approval for the Cristinas project in 2008 and proceeded to cancel the contract altogether three years later, Crystallex took Caracas to court.

For multinational corporations seeking favorable rulings against sovereign governments for the "crime" of reclaiming their land and resources, the venue of choice was the DC-based International Center for Settlement of Investment Disputes tribunal (ICSID). Though ICSID described itself as "an independent, depoliticized and effective" institution,[6] it was overwhelmingly partial to Western financial interests in practice. Andrés Arauz, an economist and former Ecuadorian presidential candidate who narrowly lost to millionaire banker Guillermo Lasso in 2021, became well acquainted with ICSID's inner workings during his tenure in the leftist government of Rafael Correa.

"ICSID is not an independent arbitrator of justice," he explained to me. "ICSID is a neocolonial gatekeeper of transnational corporate impunity."

The tribunal's deference to international capital was baked into its structure. The ICSID was established in 1966 as a subsidiary of the World Bank Group, and the president of the World Bank—historically a former US official or banking executive—also served as president of the tribunal. At ICSID, investor-state disputes were overseen and resolved by three arbitrators: one selected by the state, one selected by the investor, and a third typically selected by the World Bank president.

---

4   James Suggett, "Venezuela to Nationalize Country's Largest Gold Mine Las Cristinas," *Venezuelanalysis*, November 6, 2008.

5   "Projects - Las Cristinas," Crystallex International Corporation, accessed March 28, 2023.

6   ICSID, "About ICSID," accessed March 28, 2023.

"Arbitrators are heavily biased toward commercial—not public—law, and are mostly from law firms heavily associated with transnational corporations," explained Arauz. "The cases are almost always against states of the Global South."

Arauz noted that according to ICSID treaties, corporate entities are allowed to initiate arbitration against states, yet states cannot file arbitrations against corporations, arguing such rules "structurally demonstrated that ICSID is intentionally designed to exclusively attend to the interests of transnational corporations."

Crystallex initiated arbitration against Venezuela's government at ICSID in February 2011, asserting Caracas owed it $3.16 billion plus interest for its expropriation of Las Cristinas despite the fact that the mine was never operational. ICSID sided with Crystallex and ordered Venezuela's government to pay the company $1.2 billion plus interest in April 2016, declaring Caracas's decision to nationalize its natural gold supply was made "for purely political reasons."[7]

When Venezuela's government failed to comply with the decision, Crystallex's claim was placed in jeopardy. Even with the favorable ICSID ruling, Crystallex had no authority to force Caracas to satisfy the debt and no legal avenue through which to seize Venezuela's financial assets as payment. That is, until Guaidó's gang took over.

Unlike his colleagues in Guaidó's shadow administration, "Attorney General" José Ignacio Hernández avoided the limelight. While former Exxon lawyer and Guaidó "ambassador" Carlos Vecchio was a social media butterfly, regularly posting photographs of himself schmoozing with US officials and Venezuelan expats, Hernández's Instagram page was private. The only insight it offered into his (super original) personality was the revelation: "I listen to The Beatles." Though he was an underling of the notoriously outspoken and attention-hungry neoliberal economic guru Ricardo Hausmann, Hernández dodged the international speaking circuit and rarely, if ever, spoke to the media in the early months of Guaidó's coup.

7 "Crystallex International Corporation v. Bolivarian Republic of Venezuela, ICSID Case No. ARB(AF)/11/2," Italaw, April 4, 2016.

Hernández's name first made international headlines in July 2019, days after a US court ruled that Crystallex could collect upon its 2016 ICSID award by seizing shares belonging to Citgo Petroleum, the US-based private subsidiary of Venezuela's state oil company.[8] Following the ruling, news reports revealed that before Hernández took over as Guaidó's top prosecutor, he had served as an expert witness in Crystallex's legal pursuit of Citgo.[9] In other words, Hernández had provided material support for a lawsuit filed against the very government whose legal strategy he would go on to direct.

"It's exactly like the case of Carlos Vecchio," Diosdado Cabello told his audience during the July 31 *Con El Mazo Dando* broadcast I attended in-studio. "He is also over there, in the United States. Carlos Vecchio is a functionary of ExxonMobil. Carlos Vecchio is not an ambassador of Guaidó, but of Exxon."

Cabello gestured toward his bulletin board and placed a hand on Hernández's photo. "Just like this man is not the attorney general of Guaidó, he's the attorney general of Crystallex."

I first spoke with Jorge Alejandro Rodríguez, a Venezuelan engineer based in Switzerland, in August 2019.

"I am 110 percent against Maduro and against Chávez," he explained, adding that his "intention was not to make a scandal out of this, but to make a warning as private as possible."

But Rodríguez, an influential member of Venezuela's moderate opposition party, Avanzada Progresista, had uncovered a scandal brewing within Guaidó's camp. He told me that in the early months of 2019, he warned Venezuelan lawmakers about the conduct of Guaidó officials, above all José Ignacio Hernández, on matters related to the Crystallex case. According to Rodríguez, throughout that time Hernández appeared to quietly set the stage for Crystallex's July 2019 legal victory in US courts, a ruling that placed Citgo, Venezuela's most valuable international asset, on the verge of liquidation.

8   Alexandra Jones, "Third Circuit: Crystallex Can Seize Venezuela's Citgo Shares," Courthouse News Service, July 29, 2019.

9   "Procurador Especial Designado Por Guaidó Desmiente Haber Participado En Caso Crystallex," *La Patilla*, August 1, 2019.

For those of us in the United States, Citgo was just another gas station—a place to fill the tank or pick up a Slim Jim while cruising about our Great Frontier. For Venezuelans, however, the company was a symbol of national patrimony. Venezuela's state oil company, Petróleos de Venezuela (PdVSA), has owned and operated Citgo since 1990. By 2021, experts placed Citgo's value at approximately $7.8 billion.[10]

As the crown jewel of Venezuela's internationally stored wealth, Citgo's predicament began just before the initiation of Guaidó's coup. In August 2017, President Trump issued an executive order that banned all transactions with Venezuela's government and PdVSA within US financial markets (McNabb and Caine 2017). By preventing Citgo from issuing dividends back to its parent company, PdVSA, the order effectively blocked the government in Caracas from accessing its lucrative stream of US revenue.

Washington turned up its assault on Venezuela's oil industry within days of recognizing Guaidó, unrolling sweeping sanctions targeting PdVSA's US assets in January 2019 (Wong and Casey 2019). The restrictions not only banned the sale of Venezuelan oil in US markets, but officially placed the country's US-based financial accounts, including those belonging to Citgo, under the authority of Guaidó's shadow regime. Venezuela's government hastily condemned the action, accusing the US of trying to "steal" Citgo.[11] Yet even as Caracas denounced a plot to pilfer its internationally stored wealth, the full depths of the Citgo Conspiracy remained far from public view.

By the time I began investigating the Crystallex case in August 2019, Citgo's survival was officially on the line. The previous month, a Delaware court had authorized Crystallex to seize $1.2 billion worth of the company's assets to satisfy ICSID's 2016 arbitration order against Venezuela's government (Jones 2019). Following the Delaware decision, I became acquainted with Rodríguez and other members of Venezuela's opposition who helped me understand the link between Guaidó's coup and Crystallex's billion-dollar triumph. I discovered that

10   Fabiola Zerpa and Ezra Fieser, "Creditors Close in on Citgo, the Last Asset Guaido Has Left," *Bloomberg*, August 5, 2021.

11   Reuters Staff, "Maduro Says U.S. Seeks to Steal Citgo from Venezuela," Reuters, January 29, 2019.

while Guaidó's US-based representatives were nominally tasked with fighting Crystallex in court, they had actively enabled its legal victory over the government they claimed to represent.

At this point in our story, readers should know that the rest of this chapter contains a crash course in business law that, at times, is overly technical, if not dull. If they can resist the urge to glaze the eyes and mind, however, they will find the information is not only beneficial, but vital to understanding the corporate coup directed against the Venezuelan state and people in 2019.

Though ICSID ordered Venezuela's government to pay Crystallex $1.2 billion in April 2016, the firm's ability to collect that debt was constrained. Due to the legal concept of "limited liability," a claimant like Crystallex could not foreclose upon the assets of a state-run entity to satisfy debt owed by the state, and vice versa. This precedent was well established in international law by a high-profile incident involving billionaire US hedge funder Paul Singer's firm, Elliott Capital Management, and Argentina's government.

In October 2012, Ghana's government apprehended an Argentine warship called *La Libertad* as it passed through its territorial waters.[12] The seizure came after a local Ghanaian court ruled in favor of an Elliott Capital Management subsidiary that had claimed the ship as collateral for a $370 million debt owed by the government in Buenos Aires. *La Libertad* spent two months in Ghanaian custody before a UN tribunal ordered Accra to release the ship, leaving Elliott Capital empty-handed.

In theory, the concept of "limited liability" applied to Citgo as well. Crystallex should not have been allowed to seize assets belonging to Citgo—a private, US-based company—to satisfy debt owed by the Venezuelan state. To win the favorable Delaware ruling, Crystallex had to persuade a judge that Citgo's assets were fair game through a legal concept known as "alter ego."

In business law, alter ego is understood as "lifting the corporate veil," or proving the "instrumentality" of an entity. It is the doctrine through which a court determines that a private corporation, in this

12   Joe Weisenthal, "A Hedge Fund Has Physically Taken Control of a Ship Belonging to Argentina's Navy," *Business Insider*, October 4, 2012.

case Citgo, merely serves as cover for an individual or group, in this case Venezuela's government. In other words, Crystallex could only justify seizing assets belonging to Citgo as compensation for money owed by the Venezuelan state if it could "lift the corporate veil" and prove that the private, US-based company was merely an instrument of the Caracas government.

In the Delaware court, that job was left to a forty-three-year-old Venezuelan lawyer and professor of administrative law. He filed a sworn declaration in April 2017 asserting his country's government had instrumentalized PdVSA, Citgo's majority shareholder, into "a political tool to achieve its domestic and international objectives."[13] That expert witness was none other than José Ignacio Hernández, the man who went on to serve as Venezuela's top legal representative in the eyes of US courts following the initiation of Guaidó's coup.

At the time of Hernández's 2017 testimony, Citgo was technically shielded from accusations of "instrumentality." Under Venezuelan law, the president of the Republic only appointed the board of PdVSA. The PdVSA board in turn selected the board of the company's Delaware subsidiary, PdVSA Holding, which then chose the board of Citgo Holding. Finally, Citgo Holding appointed the board of Citgo Petroleum. These rules placed a comfortable distance between the Venezuelan state and Citgo's day-to-day operations, making it difficult to claim the US-based company was simply an "instrument" of Maduro.

That whole chain of command was upended immediately following the launch of Guaidó's self-declared presidency. In February 2019, Venezuela's opposition-controlled National Assembly directly appointed not only an ad-hoc PdVSA board but also the top executives of all three of its US subsidiaries.[14] This meant that under Guaidó's leadership, Venezuela's National Assembly placed a government hand smack in the middle of three private, US-based corporations. In doing

---

13   "Declaration of José Ignacio Hernández," Italaw, April 7, 2017.

14   Fabiola Zerpa and Alex Vasquez, "Venezuela's Guaido Names PDVSA Board in Haste to Seize Assets," *Bloomberg*, February 12, 2019.

so, they legitimized Crystallex's legal argument that Citgo was, in fact, an "alter ego" of the Venezuelan state.[15]

Critics like opposition-aligned engineer Jorge Alejandro Rodríguez argued that, as Guaidó's top legal advisor, it was up to Hernández to prevent the National Assembly from appointing Citgo's board, thereby jeopardizing Venezuela's defense in the Crystallex case.

"It was absolutely unacceptable for him to proceed with the appointment, no matter what the National Assembly would have said," Rodríguez contended. "You are the attorney general. You have duties. You can't do something that goes against the rules of the nation. If somebody in the whole world knew that action was wrong, it was him."

On July 29, 2019, a US district court in Delaware ruled in favor of Crystallex's alter ego argument, legitimizing the Canadian corporation's claim to $1.2 billion worth of Citgo's assets (Jones 2019). Two days later, Venezuela's government announced a criminal investigation into Hernández over his ties to Crystallex, accusing the lawyer of "a conflict of interest that violates all judicial ethics" and "treason toward his fellow citizens."[16]

Outrage toward Hernández was not confined to Venezuela's government. Having squandered their country's most valuable international asset less than a year into their fledgling political project, Guaidó officials began to draw heat from their own opposition allies. In an attempt at damage control, Hernández turned to TVV Noticias, a Spanish-language television channel based in Miami. Sporting an unkempt beard and nervously rumpled brow, the normally camera-shy Hernández dismissed the accusations against him as "false" and asserted that by the time he entered Guaidó's shadow regime, the Crystallex case was "practically in its final stage."[17]

15   On pg. 242 of his memoir, *The Room Where It Happened*, Trump National Security Advisor John Bolton boasted that he and other US officials personally counseled Guaidó on his Citgo board selections.

16   Luc Cohen, "Corrected-Update 3-Crystallex Would Need Sanctions Waiver to Seize Citgo Shares -Guaido Adviser," Reuters, July 31, 2019.

17   TVV Noticias (@TVVnoticias), Twitter post, July 31, 2019, https://twitter.com/TVVnoticias/status/1156735765239324672.

According to Hernández it was Maduro's government, not Guaidó's, that had crafted Venezuela's legal strategy in the Crystallex case. While that claim was technically true, Hernández's version of events overlooked salient facts presented before the court. On April 10, 2019, Crystallex submitted a court filing lambasting "the Guaidó-led National Assembly's complete disregard for corporate formalities" when it directly appointed "the boards of PdVSA's subsidiary." Underlining their argument that Citgo was an instrument of the Venezuelan state, lawyers representing Crystallex noted the National Assembly's failure to follow basic procedure was "hardly a sign of [the subsidiaries'] independence from government control."[18]

The filing demonstrated that even Crystallex recognized Hernández had helped prove the crux of their alter ego argument—an argument that he himself previously made on the company's behalf—when he allowed Venezuela's National Assembly to illegally appoint the board of PdVSA's US subsidiaries.

"It was not until Hernández did what he did, or allowed the Assembly to do what it did, that it became so clear for the Delaware courts to say: 'Ok, it makes no sense to keep Crystallex waiting,'" Rodríguez explained.

In addition to presenting a dishonest timeline, Hernández deflected responsibility by claiming that he had recused himself from the Crystallex case back in March 2019. While the lawyer produced no evidence to back up that claim in public, he privately forwarded his supposed recusal letter, dated March 13, to Venezuelan lawmakers. Though Hernández hoped the document would salvage his reputation among the country's opposition, it ultimately produced more controversy after a group of skeptics, led by Rodríguez, analyzed its metadata and determined the file had not been created in March, but on July 31—the very day they received it.

Guaidó officials accounted for the inconsistency by claiming the document's metadata merely reflected the time that they converted it into a PDF for circulation among Venezuela's opposition, not the date it was actually submitted. According to standard government practice,

18   Appellee Crystallex International Corp, "Electronic Supplemental Brief 003113208533 in 18-2797," PacerMonitor, April 10, 2019.

however, a document of such importance should have been signed as a hard copy and stamped with the date and time it was received. If Guaidó's team had been maintaining government records according to Venezuelan law, they should have been able to verify the letter's March submission with ease. Yet they repeatedly failed to do so, even after I obtained a copy of the document and published it at the *Grayzone*.[19] On top of that, an individual with personal knowledge of internal Guaidó regime meetings has since informed me that Hernández was actively directing their legal strategy in defense of PdVSA and its assets as of April 2019—categorically invalidating the lawyer's claim that he recused himself from the Crystallex case the previous month.

Regardless, the letter itself contained a significant detail offering a glimpse into the coup regime's bizarre chain of command. Oddly, Hernández did not address his supposed recusal letter to "President" Guaidó, but to his DC-based envoy, Carlos Vecchio. The curious act was tantamount to the attorney general of the United States submitting a recusal letter to Washington's ambassador in London rather than the US president.

Hernández and Vecchio provided no explanation for the oversight, prompting speculation the two men were coordinating behind Guaidó's back. By claiming to have received Hernández's recusal letter in March, Vecchio provided cover for the lawyer's apparent double dealing with Crystallex. According to Hernández's own account, Vecchio had always been a trusted confidant.

"When my name started to float as attorney general, I spoke with Ambassador Carlos Vecchio," Hernández told *Hispano Post* in August 2019. "I prepared him a memo in which I informed him that until December 2018, I was a partner at a law firm, then I quit and told him of the cases which I knew of, and that I had been an independent witness in cases that were problematic, like that of Crystallex."[20]

19   Anya Parampil, "The Citgo Conspiracy: Opposition Figures Accuse Guaidó Officials of 'Scam' to Liquidate Venezuela's Most Prized International Asset," *The Grayzone*, September 3, 2019.

20   Andrés Rojas Jiménez, "José Ignacio Hernández: He Sido Difamado y Sometido Al Escarnio Público," HispanoPost, August 9, 2019.

As news of Hernández's "problematic" relationships surfaced, Vecchio—the Exxon lawyer turned coup operative—emerged among his most prominent defenders.

Hours after Venezuela's attorney general opened a criminal investigation into Hernández's relationship with Crystallex, Guaidó's US-based entourage circled the wagons for their embattled colleague. Ricardo Hausmann, the Harvard professor who worked as Guaidó's representative at the Inter-American Development Bank, was the first to leap to Hernández's defense.

"In my professional career I have never worked with someone more capable, more hardworking, more dedicated, more knowledgeable about legislation, and more honest than Attorney General Hernández," Hausmann declared in an August 3 tweet. "The attacks against him are based on lies and false conflicts of interest."[21]

Hausmann was hardly an objective source. Having worked directly under the Harvard professor since 2017, Hernández was essentially Hausmann's protégé.[22]

"Venezuela must thank Nacho a lot for his contributions to the decisions of the National Assembly since 2015, for the many legal decisions of the Presidency of Juan Guaidó, [and] for his defense of more than 40 lawsuits against the Republic," Hausmann insisted, referring to Hernández by an affectionate nickname.

Vecchio echoed Hausmann's adoring tribute, adding, "The Attorney General has been an honest professional who has contributed greatly to protect our assets and join efforts to cease usurpation."[23]

Considering Hernández had done the complete opposite of protecting Venezuela's assets—instead taking deliberate actions that placed

21   Ricardo Hausmann (@ricardo_hausman), Twitter post, August 3, 2019, https://twitter.com/ricardo_hausman/status/1157642322479321088.

22   Jose Ignacio Hernández, LinkedIn, accessed March 28, 2023, https://www.linkedin.com/in/jose-ignacio-hernandez-g-2845ba29/en?trk=people-guest_people_search-card.

23   Carlos Vecchio (@carlosvecchio), Twitter post, August 3, 2019, https://twitter.com/carlosvecchio/status/1157652745274449921?s=20.

Citgo's entire existence on the line—Vecchio and Hausmann's homage to the lawyer was comically obtuse at best, and deeply deceitful at worst.

"The fraud of Mr. Hernández is against Guaidó and the National Assembly," Jorge Alejandro Rodríguez, the opposition-aligned Venezuelan engineer, told me. "Vecchio has backed Hernández in all situations, and that is something I also do not understand."

Though it was impossible to prove the motivation behind Vecchio's deceptive acts, a closer look at Citgo's legal wrangling offered a potential clue. When a court rules that one corporation, such as Crystallex, can seize shares belonging to another, such as Citgo, as a debt payment, the shares are not directly transferred from company to company. Rather, the court sells off a portion of the indebted company's assets and uses funds raised from the sale to pay the claimant.

"They're auctioned," Rodríguez explained, referring to the indebted company's assets.

In Citgo's case, this meant the court would oversee the fire sale of roughly $1.2 billion worth of its assets—including gas stations, oil pipelines, oil terminals, and refineries throughout the United States—in order to satisfy Venezuela's debt to Crystallex. Through that process, oil industry rivals including Shell, British Petroleum, and ExxonMobil would gain a chance to expand their share of the US oil market by swallowing up Citgo's infrastructure.

As established in chapter nine, though he posed as a disgruntled opposition figure, Vecchio was in fact a leading functionary of the US oil industry in Venezuela and spent much of his career employed as a top lawyer for ExxonMobil. Vecchio's intimate ties to Exxon provided a possible explanation for his consistent defense of Hernández—it was not hard to imagine a scenario in which the oil giant profited from Citgo's liquidation.

"I was not aware of any of his relationships," Rodríguez said of Vecchio, telling me he was "quite annoyed" when he read my exposé of the lawyer's past. "Not that I criticize anybody for working for Exxon, but to me this sounds like the lawyers of Standard Oil Company of New Jersey, one hundred years back, writing Venezuelan laws. For me, it's no fun. It's unacceptable."

Though Hernández endeavored to distance himself from Crystallex, his actions as Venezuela's top legal representative in the eyes of US courts reverberated beyond one singular case. A quick review of the ICSID website reveals there are roughly a dozen cases against Venezuela pending before the tribunal at the time of this book's publication. Meanwhile, since Crystallex's victory in Delaware, ICSID has granted additional corporate behemoths, including Koch Industries and Air Canada,[24] favorable rulings against Venezuela's government. Taken together, these interests threaten to kill Citgo once and for all. With the Crystallex precedent in hand, Koch Industries immediately headed to Delaware to collect its debt by claiming its own stake in Citgo.[25]

"The Crystallex case has a lot of implications because it completely opens the door to the whole list of companies that are suing" Venezuela's government, Rodríguez cautioned.

Remarkably, Crystallex was not the only corporate vulture that weaponized Hernández in its legal hunt for Citgo. According to ICSID records, US glassmaker Owens-Illinois retained Hernández as an expert witness in its own arbitration claim filed against the Venezuelan state.[26] The World Bank ruled in favor of Owens-Illinois in 2015, determining Venezuela's government owed it more than $455 million over a 2010 decision to nationalize two plants owned by the Ohio-based company.[27]

Owens-Illinois proceeded to mimic Crystallex's legal strategy against Citgo. On February 11, 2019, Owens-Illinois filed suit against Venezuela's government, PdVSA, and PdVSA's US subsidiaries in a Delaware court. The essence of the complaint was familiar: though PdVSA Holding, Citgo Holding, and Citgo Petroleum were "nominally Delaware corporations," they were actually "alter egos, and mere

---

24 Cosmo Sanderson, "Air Canada Lands Win against Venezuela," *Global Arbitration Review*, September 14, 2021.

25 Caroline Simpson, "Koch's $400m Dispute with Venezuela Heads to Delaware," Law360, February 22, 2022.

26 ICSID, "Centro Internacional De Arreglo De Diferencias Relativas a Inversiones," March 10, 2015.

27 "O-I Prevails in International Arbitration against Venezuela," O-I, March 12, 2015.

instrumentalities of Venezuela itself."[28] Within days, Guaidó's National Assembly appointed the board of PdVSA and its three US subsidiaries.

Like Crystallex, it seemed Owens-Illinois had directly benefited from Hernández's failure to ensure Venezuela's coup regime followed proper procedure while managing PdVSA and Citgo's affairs. When confronted about his relationship with Owens-Illinois by *Hispano Post*, Hernández simply remarked: "I was not a lawyer for the company, nor did I promote their interests" (Rojas Jiménez 2019).

Public court documents directly contradicted that claim, revealing Owens-Illinois had in fact paid Hernández $163,720 in exchange for his expert witness testimony (ICSID 2015). Yet the lawyer's dishonesty did not end with questions over his compensation. Stunningly, in a bid to skirt responsibility for Citgo's imminent destruction, Hernández even claimed that he "never analyzed the alter ego thesis nor its merits" on behalf of corporate clients like Owens-Illinois and Crystallex.

Crystallex characterized his contribution to their lawsuit quite differently, explicitly stating in a March 2019 court filing that "before assuming his current position, José Ignacio Hernández—Special Counsel to the Venezuelan National Assembly tasked with evaluating creditor claims against Venezuela—provided expert testimony supporting Crystallex's alter ego arguments."[29]

Easily dispelled by a winding trail of court records, Hernández's lies were apparent not only to me but to Venezuela's government and opposition alike. On October 1, 2019, Vice President Delcy Rodríguez delivered a nationally televised press conference based on my investigation into the Crystallex case, detailing what she described as "a grand plot of organized transnational crime."[30]

Before a crowd of reporters gathered in her office, Rodríguez summarized my Crystallex chronicle, explaining the legal concept of "alter ego" and Hernández's role in proving it applied to Citgo. While

---

28   "OI European's Complaint against Venezuela and Others (US Court Proceedings)," Italaw, February 11, 2019.

29   "Crystallex's Opposition to the Motion of the Interim President of Venezuela," Arbitration, March 11, 2019.

30   Luigino Bracci Roa, "Vicepresidenta Delcy Rodríguez Sobre Embargo De Citgo, 1 Octubre 2019," October 1, 2019.

detailing the corporate conspiracy, Rodríguez accompanied her denunciations of Hernández, Vecchio, and Guaidó with handheld photos of each coup official plastered with text reading "*LADRÓN*" (thief).

"José Ignacio Hernández is the criminal mastermind behind a whole process to deprive Venezuela of its assets and resources abroad," Rodríguez declared with indignation.

Despite the well-deserved public shaming, Hernández did not resign from Guaidó's shadow government until June 2020. Though the lawyer offered no explanation for his sudden departure, it came on the heels of yet another scandal regarding his conduct as "attorney general."

On June 18, Vice President Rodríguez's office published an audio recording of Hernández's testimony before the opposition-controlled National Assembly's energy commission earlier that month, during which the lawyer boasted of "directing a strategy" for Venezuela's legal fights with multinational corporations at the World Bank.[31]

"I personally oversaw a strategy directly with the World Bank president," Hernández disclosed.

Hernández's remarks compromised not only his authority but that of World Bank president (and former US treasury official) David Malpass. Malpass's alleged coordination with Hernández flew in the face of World Bank rules, which stipulated "its officers shall not interfere in the political affairs of any member" nor "be influenced in their decisions by the political character of the member or members concerned."[32]

While Malpass's office ignored the leak, Hernández announced his resignation from Guaidó's shadow regime hours after the recording surfaced.[33] Like his mentor, Ricardo Hausmann, before him, Hernández completely bungled his departure from Venezuela's faltering coup project. Though he publicly announced his exit from Guaidó's team on

31 VTV Canal 8 (@VTVcanal8), Twitter post, June 18, 2020, https://twitter.com/VTVcanal8/status/1273678037662474245.

32 "IBRD Articles of Agreement: Article IV," World Bank, accessed March 28, 2023.

33 Jose Ignacio Hernández (@ignandez), Twitter post, June 18, 2020, https://twitter.com/ignandez/status/1273757278961836032.

June 18, Hernández claimed to have submitted his resignation on May 28—a clear attempt to downplay the significance of the embarrassing audio leak. (Jorge Alejandro Rodríguez, the Guaidó critic among Venezuela's opposition, personally offered a $1,000 prize to anyone who could prove the lawyer did, in fact, resign in May).

The circumstances surrounding Hernández's resignation demonstrated the anti-Chavista opposition's growing discontent with Guaidó's coup regime. At the time of Hernández's testimony in June 2020, several opposition parties were boycotting legislative committee hearings in protest of Guaidó, having recognized opposition lawmaker Luis Parra as National Assembly president that January (chapter 13). As a result, the only parties present for Hernández's statement were those representing the extremist, US-aligned G4 coalition: Un Nuevo Tiempo, Primero Justicia, Acción Democrática, and Guaidó's Voluntad Popular.

This meant that unless Venezuela's government spied on the meeting, Hernández's comments had been leaked to the vice president's office by his own supposed allies. The lawyer acknowledged the betrayal moments after the recording surfaced, complaining on Twitter that the leak was "only possible if there is internal complicity."[34]

To fully illustrate José Ignacio Hernández's corrupt character within the single chapter of a single book represented a Sisyphean task. Following his resignation from Guaidó's shadow regime, I discovered yet another nefarious mark on the lawyer's record—this time related to his work on behalf of foreign oil giants that had successfully defrauded Venezuela's government out of billions of dollars.[35]

The investigation was an arduous slog, requiring me to trudge through heaps of court documents containing arcane corporate and legal jargon until I reached the inner workings of a multibillion-dollar fraud racket. From there, I traced the blueprints of a scheme that saw foreign oil companies coordinate with corrupt PdVSA functionaries in

34   Jose Ignacio Hernández (@ignandez), Twitter post, June 18, 2020, https://twitter.com/ignandez/status/1273677399725613056.

35   Anya Parampil, "Blockbuster Oil Bribery Scandal Exposes Corrupt Double-Dealing of Guaidó 'Attorney General'," The Grayzone, July 14, 2020.

order to win favorable contracts with the state-run company, bilking Venezuela's government out of untold billions along the way.

The plot centered around a shady Panama-based "consulting firm" called Helsinge Inc.

Having established Helsinge amid Chávez's effort to reform Venezuela's oil sector in the early 2000s, former PdVSA functionaries Francisco Morillo and Leonardo Baquero officially fled the country for Miami in 2004. From there, the pair leveraged their contacts within PdVSA's Caracas office to gain confidential information regarding Venezuela's future oil contracts. Helsinge then shared that information with its corporate oil industry clients, including Russia's Lukoil and Singapore's Trafigura, enabling them to crush competing bids with ease.

Essentially, Helsinge provided cover for a textbook insider trading conspiracy. The "consulting fees" it collected were simply bribes its corporate patrons furnished in exchange for an unauthorized peak at PdVSA's internal operation. Clients like Lukoil compensated Helsinge through the firm's Panama bank accounts, which served as a money wash for funds that Morillo and Baquero then transferred to their corrupt PdVSA collaborators in Caracas.

As a result of the contract-rigging ploy, PdVSA purchased products from its international partners at an inflated price while selling its oil at a below-market rate for years. One oil industry source familiar with the case estimated the scheme resulted in upwards of $15 billion in losses for PdVSA. Venezuela's government eventually caught wind of the racket and established a US-based legal trust to investigate it. Headed by hotshot corporate attorney David Boies, in 2018 that trust filed a lawsuit against Helsinge, its oil industry clients, its PdVSA collaborators, and the international financial institutions that facilitated their conspiracy.[36]

Despite a mountain of evidence presented to the Florida court—including emails, bank ledgers, and sworn witness testimony detailing the mammoth fraud—Magistrate Judge Alicia M. Otazo-Reyes ultimately dismissed the suit just one year after it was filed. Her decision

36   Brian Ellsworth, "Venezuela's PDVSA Sues Oil Traders over Corruption Scheme - Lawyer," Reuters, March 9, 2018.

was not based on the merits of the case itself, however, but on a technical argument put forward by its corporate defendants.

Perhaps at this point in the tale of Venezuela's *Corporate Coup*, readers will be unsurprised to learn that José Ignacio Hernández supplied the main line of defense for the multinational enterprises accused in the Helsinge scheme. In August 2018—just five months before Guaidó tapped the lawyer as his top legal representative in the United States— the oil companies charged in the contract-rigging scheme sought Hernández's expertise to save their skins in court.

Hernández's task was not to prove his clients' innocence, but to invalidate the case brought against them by arguing the litigation trust that assembled the lawsuit "was not valid under Venezuelan law."[37] His strategy was a smashing success. On March 8, 2019, the Florida court announced that "relying on the testimony of Professor José Ignacio Hernández," it "found that the Trust Agreement was void under Venezuelan law."[38]

Hernández was handsomely rewarded for his corporate collaboration. Amid the pages of his August 2018 witness testimony, Hernández disclosed that he received $350 an hour for his work on behalf of the suit's defendants. As with Crystallex and Owens-Illinois, their investment in Hernández proved money well spent.

Prior to his ascent within Guaidó's coup regime, Hernández served as the opposing team's star witness in at least three separate legal battles involving Venezuela's government in US courts and international arbitration tribunals. Hernández demonstrated habitual fealty to his corporate clients after gaining nominal status as Venezuela's "attorney general" in US courts, a perverted allegiance that ultimately placed his country's most valuable asset, Citgo Petroleum, in peril.

A Delaware court confirmed this fact in March 2023, when it ruled that four additional foreign corporations could collect debt owed by

37   "Expert Report of Jose Ignacio Hernández," Florida Southern District, August 3, 2018.

38   "Lukoil Dismissal," Court House News, March 8, 2019.

the Venezuelan state by seizing assets belonging to Citgo.[39] Though the "alter ego" argument that informed the judgment was nothing new, this time the court explicitly cited the actions of Guaidó's government as justification for its decision. The court specifically asserted that Guaidó's policy of treating Venezuela's sovereign debt as equal to debt incurred by its state oil company, PdVSA, in negotiations with foreign creditors—terms crafted by Harvard economic wizard Ricardo Hausmann himself—proved that Citgo's assets were, in fact, indistinguishable from those of the state.

Beneficiaries of the March 2023 ruling included US defense manufacturer Northrop Grumman and Ohio-based glassmaker Owens-Illinois—the latter of which contracted Hernández as an expert witness in its legal pursuit of Citgo, as detailed above. Days after the Delaware decision, members of Venezuela's once solidly pro-Guaidó G4 coalition called for a formal investigation into the conduct of his US-based functionaries. [40]

Though Hernández's venal manner eventually forced his departure from official public life, his critics among Venezuela's opposition assured me their fight to hold him accountable did not end alongside the lawyer's service in Guaidó's shadow regime.

"We have reasons to believe that Hernández's conduct is something to be investigated," Jorge Alejandro Rodríguez, the opposition-aligned engineer, told me in July 2020. The previous summer, Rodríguez and his Avanzada Progresista party filed a formal complaint with the US Justice Department urging it to investigate Hernández under the Foreign Corrupt Practices Act, which barred US citizens and entities from bribing foreign government officials in pursuit of business interests.[41]

39   "Opinion of the United States District Court for the District of Delaware," Italaw, March 23, 2023.

40   El Político, Twitter post [VIDEO], April 11, 2023; "Piden a Estados Unidos Investigar Actos Del Procurador Especial." TalCual, August 8, 2019. https://talcualdigital.com/piden-a-estados-unidos-investigar-actos-del-procurador-especial/.

41   "Piden a Estados Unidos Investigar Actos Del Procurador Especial," TalCual, August 8, 2019.

Hernández's brazen behavior also appeared to violate the American Bar Association's Rules of Professional Conduct for Attorneys, which stipulated "a lawyer shall not represent a client if the representation involves a concurrent conflict of interest."[42] At the time of this book's publication, Washington continues to ignore Hernández's probable violation of US legal standards.

"Knowing that political instability in countries usually brings about white-collar crimes—which we saw in Russia and other former communist republics—in the case of Venezuela right now, with this political turmoil, it's obvious the DOJ has to investigate Hernández," Rodríguez argued.

"There is a case here, I am positive about it," he insisted.

Washington's continued refusal to investigate Hernández raises the irresistible question: was the *Corporate Coup* enabled by Washington's recognition of Guaidó merely a side effect of its failed Venezuela regime change gambit, or its intended result?

42   "Model Rules Of Professional Conduct," American Bar Association, accessed March 28, 2023.

FIFTEEN

OPERATION GIDEON

Oil, gold, and iron ore are the natural riches with which Venezuela is widely associated. Yet the country is also home to a delicacy that remains virtually unknown on the modern international market: Venezuelan cacao. This was not always the case. Before the discovery of its vast oil reserves in the 1920s, Venezuela was the chocolatey crop's top global producer.[1] Some even claim the world's first cocoa plant sprouted in the country's oil-rich Orinoco-Amazon region.[2]

Though Venezuela is no longer a leading cacao exporter, luxury chocolatiers still covet its crop, and its centers of production are among the country's top tourist destinations. Spend enough time in Venezuela and a local will eventually try to convince you to visit Choroní, a Caribbean beach town that is only accessible via a two-hour ride down a dirt road winding through a cloud forest located in the country's oldest national park, Henri Pittier. The steamy mountain ranges that envelope Choroní provide the perfect climate for cacao plants to thrive, and Venezuelans speak of the fruity chocolate that comes from the region with observable pride.

Choroní's neighbor, Chuao, is also a base of cacao production nestled between dense mountain rainforests and the Caribbean Sea. The lush peaks surrounding Chuao are so impenetrable, in fact, that the village is only accessible by boat.

1   Kaoru Yonekura, "The Miracle of Producing the World's Best Cocoa," *Caracas Chronicles*, August 2, 2022.
2   J C Motamayor et al., "Cacao Domestication I: The Origin of the Cacao Cultivated by the Mayas," *Nature*, October 28, 2002.

Early in the morning of May 4, 2020, local *pescadores* in Chuao noticed a suspicious vessel bobbing in the distant sea. The fishermen alerted local colectivos and Venezuelan state security forces, which coordinated to apprehend the boat. On board, they discovered a cache of military equipment as well as eight apparent mercenaries, among them two US citizens.[3]

The raid was part of Venezuela's response to what is known as Operation Gideon, a foiled plot to capture or kill President Nicolás Maduro led by a former US Green Beret named Jordan Goudreau. While the conspiracy is subject to routine popular ridicule (often dubbed the "Bay of Piglets" in reference to the bungled CIA-directed invasion of Cuba in 1961), Operation Gideon reminded ordinary Venezuelans of the extreme threat they faced as the US actively sought their government's overthrow—and raised questions about how far ideologues in Washington would go to achieve regime change in Caracas.

Perhaps one day there will be a dramatic biopic about Jordan Goudreau. His character was beyond parody, an archetypical huckster who, by inflating personal and professional ties, confidently climbed society's ladder to rungs far beyond his reach. Between his blonde buzzcut, cartoonishly chiseled physique, and symmetrical face, Goudreau practically begged for Hollywood's spotlight.

Goudreau's entry to the world of made-for-TV intelligence ops began with a childhood admiration of the US military. Though he was Canadian by birth, he moved south as a young man so that he could enlist in the US Armed Forces, telling a family friend that he believed it "would give him more challenges" than the military back home.[4] Goudreau fought in the Iraq and Afghanistan Wars as part of the elite Charlie Company of the First Battalion, 10th Special Forces Group, before injury forced him to retire from combat in 2016. Two years later he founded a private, Florida-based security firm called Silvercorp USA.

3   Scott Smith and Joshua Goodman, "Venezuela: 2 Us 'Mercenaries' among Those Nabbed after Raid," Associated Press, May 5, 2020.

4   Anthony Faiola, Shawn Boburg, and Ana Vanessa Herrero, "Venezuela Raid: How an Ex-Green Beret and a Defecting General Planned to Capture Maduro," *Washington Post*, May 10, 2020.

Silvercorp's early promotional material had nothing to do with Latin America or mercenary missions. The first video posted on its Instagram page featured audio of news reports and 911 calls filed from the scenes of high-profile US school shootings—from Stoneman Douglas to Sandy Hook—playing over grainy video of flashing police lights and traumatizing rescue footage.[5]

"Last year, more than 750,000 instances of violent crime took place within the US school system," Goudreau narrated, his all-American accent cutting through the panic with strident annunciation.

After portraying US school children as sitting ducks surrounded by psychotic mass shooters, Goudreau offered his solution to the bloodshed. The slow, eerie background music suddenly faded to synth-fueled, electronic optimism as Goudreau informed viewers that Silvercorp USA existed "to remove threats, keep your family safe, and create opportunities for those who protect and serve our country."

Goudreau's pitch was simple. Silvercorp would employ US military veterans to train teachers, police, and others "within the school system" to neutralize active shooter threats. From his perspective, he was solving two problems at once: fighting gun violence in schools while providing jobs to fellow former military men still longing for the thrill of combat.

Through Silvercorp, Goudreau hoped to cash in on elevated parental anxiety while bringing the counter-insurgency tactics he learned fighting the so-called "War on Terror" abroad back to the US homeland. In Goudreau's mind, his employees would apply their experience in Kabul to Columbine, and move on from their search for Bin Laden to a search for the next Uvalde shooter.

"Silvercorp USA is there for you," Goudreau vowed as the ad flashed images of soldiers in full combat gear leaping out of planes interspersed with stock footage of happy families and studious school children.

Beyond the slickly produced promotional video, it was unclear how far Goudreau took his school security venture. His business model was half-baked, at best.

---

5   Silvercorp USA (@silvercoupusa), Instagram post, March 21, 2018, https://www.instagram.com/p/BgmlCTsnf_V/?igshid=MDJmNzVkMjY%3D.

"The beauty of it is it's all for the price of a Netflix subscription," the strapping vet mused as he pitched Silvercorp to the *Washington Post* during a 2018 school security expo in Orlando, Florida.[6]

According to Goudreau's vision, parents would pay Silvercorp $8.99 a month to obtain its security services in their children's schools. On campus, Silvercorp employees would not only train school staff in military tactics, but embed themselves with faculty and deploy counter-intelligence tactics against students. Speaking with the *Post*, Goudreau conjured up a highly implausible scenario during which he rooted out a potential school shooter by pretending to be a teacher.

"He's just a—he's a cool shop teacher: 'Hey, what's up, fellas.' I go sit down with a kid who's alone, playing *Dungeons and Dragons*, and I just try to see whether there's any problems," he imagined.

Goudreau's madcap fantasies reflected a mentality that would soon lead him to direct an undermanned, undersupplied invasion of a country that he had never visited and hardly understood. Though no schools nor parents had contracted his services at the time of his November 2018 rendezvous with the *Post*, Goudreau and Silvercorp would soon attain the international notoriety he desperately craved.

When Goudreau's name first surfaced in media reports connected to Venezuela, the story was almost too absurd to believe. On May 1, 2020, the Associated Press's Joshua Goodman published a stunning investigation revealing the existence of a covert plan to "ignite a popular rebellion" in Venezuela that would culminate with the arrest of President Maduro.[7] The plot, dubbed "Operation Gideon," was to be carried out by three hundred volunteer combatants, many of them Venezuelan defectors, who planned to sneak into the country from Colombia, raid military bases in an effort to turn soldiers to their cause, and march toward Caracas in pursuit of the president. At the center of the blueprint was Goudreau's private security company, Silvercorp

6   John Woodrow Cox and Steven Rich, "Billions Are Now Spent to Protect Kids from School Shootings. Has It Made Them Safer?" *Washington Post*, November 13, 2018.

7   Joshua Goodman, "Ex-Green Beret Led Failed Attempt to Oust Venezuela's Maduro," Associated Press, May 1, 2020.

USA, which had reportedly been contracted to oversee training and weapons procurement for the operation.

Goodman based his report on interviews with over two dozen opposition activists and would-be mercenaries with direct knowledge of, or involvement in, Operation Gideon. According to their account, Goudreau first linked up with Venezuela's opposition in February 2019, when he traveled to Cúcuta, Colombia to provide security for Virgin CEO Richard Branson's Venezuela Aid Live concert (chapter six). Following his Cúcuta gig, Goudreau made contacts within Guaidó's team that eventually led him to a Venezuelan military vet named Clíver Alcalá.

A former army general, Alcalá had been organizing low-level Venezuelan military deserters in Colombia since his own defection from Caracas in early 2019. Over the course of a two-day meeting at the Bogotá JW Marriott that spring, Alcalá informed Goudreau that he was overseeing roughly three hundred men, including participants in previously botched assassination attempts against Maduro, in camps scattered across Colombia's border with Venezuela. Hoping "to capitalize on the Trump administration's growing interest in toppling Maduro," Goodman explained that Goudreau and Alcalá hatched a plan to train and equip those men for the plot that became Operation Gideon. Goudreau told his new Venezuelan friends that the plan to kidnap or kill their country's president came with a high cost—what he estimated to be around $1.5 million. Thankfully, the gun-for-hire claimed his "high-level" contacts in the Trump administration would help iron out operational kinks.

Indeed, Goudreau had previously made contact with the president's personal bodyguard, Keith Schiller, through industry connections, and won a single Silvercorp contract to provide security for Trump in November 2018.[8] Still, no evidence ever materialized to prove the Oval Office had any role in Operation Gideon. In fact, sources close to Schiller told Goodman that he ended all contact with the ex-Green Beret after a May 2019 meeting in Miami because he "thought Goudreau was naive and in over his head."

8   Ben Makuch, "Mercenaries Behind Failed Venezuela Coup Claim to Have Done Trump Security," *VICE*, May 5, 2020.

Despite limited resources and waning interest from would-be patrons, Goudreau and Alcalá pushed ahead with their plot. Ephraim Mattos, a retired Navy Seal who spent two weeks training Goudreau's men in September 2019, told Goodman that the soldiers lived in squalid conditions with no running water. They rationed food, slept on the floor, and were even forced to train with "sawed-off broomsticks in place of assault rifles."

"Unfortunately, there's a lot of cowboys in this business who try to peddle their military credentials into a big pay day," Mattos told Goodman, reflecting on Goudreau's conduct.

Though Goudreau declined to speak on the record for Goodman's report, Operation Gideon came to life within hours of the report's May 1 publication.

Goudreau's day in the sun finally arrived in the early morning hours of May 3, when Venezuela's government announced it had repelled an attempted maritime invasion of its borders.[9] In a video statement posted to Twitter that evening, Goudreau sported a New York Yankees baseball cap as he knelt on one leg before a backdrop of fluttering trees.[10]

"At 17:00 hours, a daring amphibious raid was launched from the border of Colombia deep into the heart of Caracas," the life-size G.I. Joe announced, his biceps bulging from the sleeves of a slate-blue polo.

To Goudreau's left, a Venezuelan military defector named Javier Nieto Quintero mimicked the former Green Beret's manufactured pose. Clad in a flak vest and costume complete with a rolled up Venezuelan flag pinned to his shoulder, Nieto appeared to be auditioning for a supporting role in Amazon's next *Jack Ryan* installation.

"Our units have been activated in the south, west, and east of Venezuela," Goudreau declared with contrived confidence before turning to Quintero, who proceeded to deliver a Spanish-language appeal to Venezuela's armed forces, urging them to join Operation Gideon.

9   Scott Smith, "Venezuela Says It Foiled Attack by Armed Men on Boat, Blames Plot on Colombia, US," Associated Press (*Chicago Tribune*, May 3, 2020).

10   Érika Ortega Sanoja (@ErikaOSanoja), Twitter post, May 3, 2020, https://twitter.com/ErikaOSanoja/status/1257078346367762432.

"The number one objective is the capture of the criminal organization that today unfortunately directs the destiny of the nation," Quintero explained.

According to Goudreau, a Venezuelan national guard captain named Antonio José Sequea Torres was commanding the ongoing raid. Sequea fled Venezuela in April 2019 after he participated in Guaidó's failed military rebellion and helped coordinate opposition leader Leopoldo López's escape from house arrest.[11]

Goudreau and Quintero's decision to publicize Operation Gideon's launch was bizarre. By the time they published their statement, Venezuelan authorities had already captured two of their men and killed at least six others. Yet they pressed ahead, undeterred by obvious signs of defeat.

Juan José, or J.J., Rendón was a smooth operator—at least according to the mythology he built around himself as the Latin American right's most coveted political consultant. Known as "Latin America's Karl Rove,"[12] Rendón's infamous gutter-level tactics have led the region's most notorious US-collaborators to political victory in Mexico, Colombia, Honduras, and the Dominican Republic.

During Colombia's 2010 presidential campaign, a left-of-center Green Party contender threatened to defeat Washington's preferred candidate, Juan Manuel Santos. Faced with sinking poll numbers, the Santos team hired Rendón just twenty-one days before the election. In that short time, Rendón was credited with converting what had been a split race into a comfortable victory for Santos, who walked away with 69 percent of the vote.[13] Colombian and US media claimed the result was delivered by a Rendón-directed internet whisper campaign

11   Sebastiana Barráez, "El Inexplicable Origen Del Poder y El Dinero Del Capitán Sequea, El Hombre Que Comandó La Operación Gedeón," *Infobae*, June 8, 2020.

12   Tim Elfrink, "J.J. Rendon Is Latin America's Karl Rove," *Miami New Times*, July 1, 2010.

13   "Political Mastermind and Strategist JJ Rendon Once Again the Driving Force Behind Juan Manuel Santos' Land-Slide Victory in Colombian Presidential Election," Cision PR Newswire, June 22, 2010.

that spread rumors asserting Santos's opponent was a gay, foreign-born atheist (Elfrink 2010). Though Rendón denied fueling Colombia's toxic rumor mill, he counted a number of high-profile clients beyond Bogotá, including Mexican president Enrique Peña Nieto, who won office in 2012, and Honduras's Porfirio Lobo Sosa, who came to power in 2010 after a US-backed coup removed the country's democratically elected leader, José Manuel Zelaya.

A psychologist by training, Rendón received two postdoctorates in ontopsychology,[14] an obscure brand of thought that links one's physical well-being to their subconscious, positing that diseases like cancer are the product of an individual's inner manifestations. He presented himself as a political mystic, typically accenting his soft, spherical features with designer bottleneck eyeglasses and dark, Mandarin-collared dress shirts more suitable for Mao Zedong than a Miami-based consultant.

Journalists granted the privilege of visiting Rendón's residence in Miami's financial center tend to produce fawning profiles describing the luxurious gold trinkets, samurai swords, and Buddhist shrine (complete with a flowing fountain) that decorate his ocean-view estate. Throughout 2019, that condo in the upscale Brickell district provided the backdrop for Operation Gideon's planning phase.

The political consultant's involvement in Operation Gideon came to light in the botched raid's immediate aftermath, when Goudreau turned to media to blame the plot's failure on Rendón and his colleagues in Guaidó's shadow regime. Around the time that Goudreau took responsibility for the attack via Twitter, he hopped online for an interview with Miami-based YouTuber Patricia Poleo, a popular personality among Venezuela's anti-Chavista expat community. In a since-deleted livestream titled "PROOF THAT GUAIDÓ SIGNED THE CONTRACT," Goudreau shared his side of the Operation Gideon saga for the first time, explaining that while he initially refused AP's offer to discuss his contract with Venezuela's opposition out of professionalism, he decided it was time to publicize the agreement after his associates failed to uphold their end of the bargain.

---

14   Marlene Valero, "¿Quién Es J.J. Rendón y Para Quién Trabaja?" La Silla Rota, January 15, 2018.

"Typically, I'm never going to come out and share a contract, but men's lives are at stake," Goudreau told Poleo, sporting the same Yankees baseball cap and gray polo worn in his Twitter statement. He appeared to be in the same mystery outdoor location as well, with the early evening sun shining through the foliage behind him.

The contract, later partially published online, established a "General Services Agreement" to, in Goudreau's words, "help the liberation" of Venezuela.[15] The former Green Beret claimed that dozens of his men had spent preceding weeks living in a cemetery located near Colombia's border with Venezuela, evading local police while preparing to carry out Operation Gideon.

"You had sixty Venezuelans who were hungry, still training, thinking about liberation," Goudreau lamented. His men's dire condition was the fault of Guaidó and his allies, who, Goudreau claimed, failed to follow through on their contractual obligation to finance and support the operation.

"Who violated it?" Poleo demanded to know whose names appeared on the contract.

Goudreau flipped through a stack of papers and held a singular sheet up to the camera, revealing four signatures: his own; Rendón's; that of Guaidó advisor, Sergio Vergara; and one purportedly scribbled by Guaidó himself. A fifth signature ascribed to a lawyer named as a "witness" to the contract signing, Manuel J. Retureta, also appeared on the document.

"I have never seen the level of backstabbing and complete disregard for men in the field," an incensed Goudreau said of his Venezuelan associates, denouncing AP's report as a "hit piece" because it described Operation Gideon's troops as "mercenaries."

"Mercenaries get paid," he complained. "No one paid me or my team a cent," he whined, claiming he ultimately "crowd-funded" the operation by soliciting support from average Venezuelans around the world, including "Uber drivers."

"I want these guys to live, and I want them to succeed," Goudreau said of his men carrying out Operation Gideon in real time.

---

15   Ricardo Vaz, "Venezuelan Armed Forces: Paramilitary Incursion Neutralized," *Venezuelanalysis*, May 3, 2020.

Within hours of the Poleo interview, on the early morning of May 4, a second group of Goudreau's men attempted to invade Venezuela via the remote, northern coastal city of Chuao. These were the ones apprehended by local fisherman militias and police as described at the beginning of this chapter. By the time Operation Gideon ended, Venezuelan authorities had killed at least six of Goudreau's troops and captured forty-seven more,[16] including Sequea and two US citizens, Luke Denman and Airan Berry. A second high-level Venezuelan military defector, Army Captain Robert Colina Ybarra, was among those killed.

Venezuela's government published images of the equipment it recovered during the botched raid, including rifles, satellite phones, and a helmet emblazoned with the US flag, on state television.[17] Photographs of the arrests in Chuao showed several of Goudreau's grunts—including Denman and Berry—face down on the pavement of the small fishing village with their hands tied behind their backs. In another image, members of the Servicio Bolivariano de Inteligencia Nacional (SEBIN), Venezuela's top intelligence agency, stood with the detainees—also including Denman and Berry—on the beach next to a police van. The photos provided a morale boost to the besieged Venezuelan population, which disseminated the images on social media as proof that their nation was capable of defending its borders, even amid a prolonged standoff with Washington.

"Speedboats, mercenaries, large-caliber weapons, vehicles with machine guns installed," said television host and Venezuelan army captain Diosdado Cabello, describing a "scene to assassinate a people that only asks for peace."[18]

"They underestimated us again," he added. "We will win!"

16   Antonio Maria Delgado, Kevin G. Hall, and Shirsho Dasgupta, "Venezuelan Insurgent Describes How Betrayal in Ranks Produced Failure, Summary Executions," *Miami Herald*, November 18, 2010.

17   "Somos Revolucionarios y Profundamente Patriotas," Prensa Presidencial, May 7, 2020.

18   Diosdado Cabello (@dcabellor), Twitter post, May 3, 2020, https://twitter.com/dcabellor/status/1256996901532073990?s=20.

According to Cabello, Venezuelan intelligence had penetrated Operation Gideon to the highest level.

"We knew everything," he told the Associated Press (Goodman 2020). "Some of their meetings we had to pay for. That's how infiltrated they were."

Goudreau himself contended that Operation Gideon had been compromised, making vague references to "Cubans from the regime" who had "infiltrated" the plot throughout his interview with Poleo.

Meanwhile, Goudreau's claim to an alleged contract with Guaidó and his advisors placed Rendón on the defensive. With the responsibility for dead men and captured gringos placed directly on his high-rent doorstep, the political spinmeister launched into damage control.

Rendón's version of events appeared in a May 6 *Washington Post* report detailing how Venezuelan opposition leaders had schmoozed with Goudreau at the consultant's "glittering Miami high-rise."[19] Complete with an obligatory mention of Rendón's "room adorned with samurai swords," the *Post* revealed that in August 2019, Guaidó tapped Rendón—a Venezuelan native—to lead a covert "Strategic Committee" tasked with investigating ways to forcibly remove Maduro from power.

"We went through every law possible," Rendón later told *Vice*. "In our process, we discovered we cannot use the law. So we studied what is the possibility of someone else—a third party, the French Legion, whoever—to pick him up, like they have bounty hunters in the United States, and present him to justice."[20]

Rendón's search for a bounty hunter eventually led him to Goudreau, who claimed to be training hundreds of men in Colombia for a mission to capture Maduro. Though he admitted to signing the Silvercorp contract and paying Goudreau $50,000, Rendón said he ceased all communication with the former Green Beret after he demanded a $1.5 million retainer fee. Rendón insisted that he and others within Guaidó's circle—including the "interim president" himself—eventually grew suspicious

19   Anthony Faiola, Karen DeYoung, and Ana Vanessa Herrero, "From a Miami Condo to the Venezuelan Coast, How a Plan to 'Capture' Maduro Went Rogue," *Washington Post*, May 6, 2020.

20   "Inside the World's Most Spectacularly Failed Coup," *VICE*, October 27, 2021.

of Goudreau and began to doubt key elements of his pitch. Rendón told the *Post* that as of November 2019, he and his allies believed Operation Gideon was defunct.

"I thought, are these guys crazy?" Rendón recalled his reaction to hearing that Operation Gideon was underway in May 2020. "They were blackmailing us [for the money]. I thought, wow, are you really going to take it this deep?"

While much of Rendón's story matched up with Goudreau's version of events, he contradicted one key element of the ex-Green Beret's tale. Though Goudreau had published a contract that included Guaidó's signature, Rendón insisted Venezuela's coup leader never signed the agreement, and only had limited information regarding its cursory outline. Even this admission undermined Guaidó's official statement on Operation Gideon, which not only asserted he did not sign the contract, but that his "government" had no link to the plot whatsoever. Rendón officially took the fall for Operation Gideon within days of the *Post* report, when he and Sergio Vergara resigned from Guaidó's shadow regime.[21]

In response to Guaidó's cries of innocence, Goudreau produced an audio recording purporting to document the moment Venezuela's US-backed shadow leader, whom he referred to as "President Guy-doh," signed the agreement.

"I do have concerns, but we are doing the right thing for our country," the voice allegedly belonging to Guaidó declared in a familiarly cringey cadence and forced low-pitch.[22]

Who was telling the truth? To find out, I tried to reach as many of the characters involved in Operation Gideon as possible.

The phone rang once. Goudreau answered on my first attempt to reach him. It was May 4, hardly a day since Venezuelan authorities first responded to Operation Gideon, and hours after they had detained a second group of Goudreau's men, including two US citizens, in Chuao.

21   "Man Who Paid for Failed Invasion of Venezuela Resigns," Newsroom Panama, May 11, 2020.

22   Factores de Poder (@FactoresdePoder), Twitter post, May 3, 2020, https://twitter.com/FactoresdePoder/status/1257088954165268481?s=20.

"They were my guys," Goudreau woefully conceded the moment I mentioned the arrests.

In light of the open disdain he expressed for Venezuelan opposition figures while speaking with Patricia Poleo hours prior, I tried to establish a connection with Goudreau based on our shared experience dealing with Guaidó's unsavory apparatchiks.

"I would definitely talk to you tomorrow, it's just that I am kind of in the middle of containing this crisis," he told me.[23]

The former Special Ops soldier sounded stressed, and who could blame him? I agreed to call back the next day. But by then, Goudreau was off the radar. The following afternoon, AP revealed the US government had opened a federal investigation into the former Green Beret for arms trafficking, a move that virtually muzzled him from future discussions with the media, including our scheduled conversation.[24]

I was disappointed. Though I was interested in Goudreau's dealings with Guaidó et al., I was far more preoccupied with his relationship to Washington. Which US officials knew about Operation Gideon? Had any of them provided logistical support? Considering these obvious queries, Washington picked a convenient time to gag Goudreau. With Operation Gideon's central character incommunicado, I sought out the next best thing: his business partner.

Drew White was listed as Silvercorp's chief operating officer on company tax files. On May 5, 2020, I spoke with White for roughly seventeen minutes. According to White, Goudreau was a "great guy" whom he considered "a brother" (Parampil May 2010).

"He was the best man at my wedding," White said of Goudreau. "Love the guy."

Like Goudreau, White was an ex-US Special Forces operative who served in Iraq and Afghanistan. He told me that he fought alongside Goudreau overseas as a "teammate," then partnered with him to launch Silvercorp following their respective departures from the military.

---

23   Anya Parampil, "Silvercorp Co-Founder Speaks with *The Grayzone*: What Did State Department Know about Failed Venezuela Invasion?" *The Grayzone*, May 7, 2020.

24   Joshua Goodman, "Sources: US Investigating Ex-Green Beret for Venezuela Raid," Associated Press, May 6, 2020.

Yet at its inception, Silvercorp's mission was a far cry from providing operational support to US regime change ops in foreign lands. As far as White was concerned, he had founded a private school security company—not a mercenary firm. Like many of Goudreau's friends and allies, White said he declined his colleague's proposal to participate in Operation Gideon. By the time I spoke with White, he was running a home inspection company in Colorado Springs.

"I own several companies around here, and, you know, I have my wife and kid," White told me. "They're my priority."

Reflecting on Goudreau's pitch for Operation Gideon, White recalled: "My gut check was like, 'I don't want to be a part of this.'"

White explained that Goudreau originally contacted him with an offer to participate in a "State Department operation." He said his friend produced what "was presented as a State Department contract," that, upon further review, "didn't line up." As a result, White said he tapped out of Silvercorp in the early days of Operation Gideon's planning phase.

Though he confessed prior knowledge of the harebrained plot, like Rendón, White expressed surprise at Goudreau's decision to follow through with it. He was especially preoccupied with the fate of Luke Denman and Airan Berry, who had served as White's Special Forces teammates overseas alongside Goudreau.

"I just wish the guys went back to doing the school security shit," White muttered wistfully as we wrapped our call.

Why did Jordan Goudreau claim to have a State Department contract? Was he a completely delusional fraud, or a patsy placed in the line of fire to conceal more powerful forces behind Operation Gideon? Though Venezuela's government charged Washington with overseeing the scheme and had arrested two US citizens involved in it, the Trump administration played coy in its immediate aftermath.

"There was no US government direct involvement." Secretary of State Mike Pompeo was characteristically obtuse when reporters asked him about Operation Gideon during a May 6 press conference.[25]

25   Matt Spetalnick and Humeyra Pamuk, "U.S. Will Use 'Every Tool' to Secure Release If Any Americans Held in Venezuela: Pompeo," Reuters, May 6, 2020.

"[If] we had been involved, it would have gone differently," the stiff politician joked, making his best attempt at dark humor. When asked specifically about the US detainees in Venezuela, Pompeo refused to concede they were citizens.

"If these are in fact Americans that are there, then we can figure a path forward," Washington's top diplomat declared enigmatically (curiously, Pompeo, who once famously declared "we lied, we cheated, we stole," while reflecting on his work at the CIA,[26] neglected to discuss the botched Gideon plot in his 2023 memoir).

At the time of Pompeo's press conference, Venezuela had already published images of Airan Berry and Luke Denman's US government-issued passports.[27] On the same afternoon that Pompeo fielded questions from reporters in DC, Venezuelan authorities broadcast video statements from the two Americans on state television.

In their confessions, Berry and Denman discussed their respective experiences in the US military and explained that they met Goudreau while serving abroad. Both men told their interrogators they traveled to Colombia in January 2020 to carry out a job on behalf of their former Special Ops teammate. According to Denman, their agenda was to "meet a group of Venezuelans in Colombia, train them, and come with them to Venezuela to secure Caracas and secure the airport."[28] Then, the US government would dispatch a plane to collect Maduro.

When Denman and Berry departed from the Colombian coast aboard fishing dinghies accompanied by a shabby team of sixty or so hungry men, they genuinely expected to be greeted as liberators in Venezuela. Upon their arrival, high-level military commanders, rank and file soldiers, and average citizens would join their march to the Venezuelan capital, sweeping the country up in an anti-Maduro riot. By the time their mutiny arrived at Miraflores Palace, the president would have no choice but to offer his wrists to Washington's handcuffs.

26 "'We Lied, Cheated and Stole': Pompeo Comes Clean About CIA," Telesur English, April 24, 2019.

27 Reuters Staff, "Presidente De Venezuela Dice Que Hay Dos Estadounidenses En Grupo 'Mercenario,'" Reuters, May 4, 2020.

28 "Nicolás Maduro | Luke Denman, Confesión De Mercenario Estadounidense," Nicolás Maduro (YouTube, May 6, 2020).

The former Special Ops soldiers' apparitions of glory must have been sincere. Otherwise, it is difficult explain why they went ahead with what many neutral observers considered a suicide mission. If not for Venezuela's prior knowledge of the plot and those involved, there is a good chance both men could have been killed during the operation. Fortunately for them, armed fishermen militias and intelligence units had prepared for their arrival long before the hulls of their boats even scraped Venezuela's shore.

According to Drew White, Denman and Berry had been "pretty closed" about their preparations for Operation Gideon. Still, he insisted he told everyone involved with the plan that it "did not seem viable." Shortly after I published my phone call with White, Luke Denman's younger brother, Mark, reached out to me via Twitter. Though the Denman and Berry families opted to avoid the public spotlight in the days following Operation Gideon, Mark wanted to talk with me.

"As far as I knew, my brother Luke was deep-sea diving," he recalled. "Obviously, I know my brother's history and background, and when I saw [Operation Gideon] in the news, it piqued my interest. And then it *really* piqued my interest when I saw Jordan's name attached to it, because he was one of Luke's unit buddies."

During our May 8 phone call, Mark said he was relieved to know that Luke and Airan were alive and that they appeared to be healthy in the video confessions aired on Venezuelan television. He related that although he came from a large family that included six siblings, Luke talked about Airan and Jordan as if they were his brothers, too.

"These are like, six-man teams," Mark said of the special units in which his brother and the other men served. "They learn to work in tandem very closely, and that's why they build that bond of trust."

According to Mark, that trust ultimately convinced his big brother to travel down to Colombia when Goudreau offered him the Gideon job in early December 2019. Airan, meanwhile, left his wife and kids behind in Schweinfurt, Germany, where he settled following his 2013 departure from the military, to join the mission.[29]

---

29   Jorge Fitz-Gibbon, "Wife of Ex-Green Beret Pleads for His Release from Venezuelan Jail after Coup Attempt," *New York Post*, May 12, 2020.

Luke Denman told Venezuelan authorities that he expected to receive somewhere between $50,000 and $100,000 from Goudreau once Operation Gideon was completed. Instead, he and Berry received charges of terrorism, illegal weapons trafficking, and conspiracy, and each faced up to thirty-five years in prison, the maximum sentence under Venezuelan law, for their involvement in the plot. They were found guilty in August 2020 and each sentenced to twenty years behind bars.[30]

In October 2020, Goudreau filed a $1.4 million suit against J.J. Rendón in a Florida court, accusing the Venezuelan political consultant of a contract breach. As part of the lawsuit, Goudreau revealed more details to support his claim that Operation Gideon was a US government plot, naming two mid-level federal officials he said were aware of the plan before it went into effect.[31]

Goudreau contended that Silvercorp beat out competing proposals for a private military operation to oust Maduro, including one put forward by Erik Prince, founder of the infamous Blackwater mercenary firm—a charge Prince denied. He also insisted that knowledge of the plot permeated the highest level of Venezuela's US-backed opposition. According to Goudreau, not only was Guaidó involved, but Leopoldo López, the ringleader of Venezuela's US-backed opposition, had been briefed on the operation as well.

Was Goudreau being honest? His lawsuit was designed to make Operation Gideon seem as legitimate as possible, yet the only US government officials he claimed to have met with were Jason Beardsley, an advisor to the Department of Veterans Affairs, and Andrew Horn, an advisor to Vice President Mike Pence. Both men refused to speak with the media, while Pence's office denied knowledge of Horn's involvement and asserted he worked on "the domestic policy team."

Regardless of their relationship with Goudreau, neither man held the rank of someone who would be tasked with overseeing a covert military operation on behalf of the US government. They were,

---

30   Scott Smith and Joshua Goodman, "Ex-Green Berets Sentenced to 20 Years for Venezuela Attack," Associated Press, August 8, 2020.

31   Antonio Maria Delgado et al., "How a Venezuela Coup Attempt, Plotted in Miami, Unraveled," *Miami Herald*, October 20, 2020.

however, the kind of peripheral figures who may have linked up with Goudreau to prove their worth to Trump administration higher-ups. It was conceivable that they may have met with Goudreau, made promises to arrange future summits with President Trump himself at Mar-a-Lago (as the lawsuit alleged), and then dropped off as it became clear the plot was unrealistic.

Yet Goudreau was not the only player swept up in the Gideon drama who claimed the US government had operational knowledge of the plan. Clíver Alcalá, the retired Venezuelan general who initially hatched the plot alongside Goudreau, also asserted the CIA and other US agencies were aware of their conspiracy. According to his attorneys, Alcalá's "efforts to overthrow [Maduro's government] were reported to the highest levels of the Central Intelligence Agency, National Security Council, and the Department of the Treasury."[32]

Alcalá's character arc climaxed weeks before details of Operation Gideon even surfaced in the media. On March 23, 2020, Colombian authorities intercepted a truck carrying arms that appeared destined for the Venezuelan border (Delgado et al. 2020). While authorities initially believed the supplies were meant for local guerillas or gangs, Alcalá posted a video statement on March 26 claiming responsibility for the weapons shipment.[33] Filing his Twitter testimony from his apartment in Colombia, Alcalá proceeded to announce his involvement in a military operation against Maduro's government, which he claimed to have planned alongside Guaidó and Rendón.

On the day of Alcalá's extraordinary confession, the US State Department just happened to indict President Maduro on drug trafficking charges and announce a $15 million reward for information leading to his "arrest and/or conviction."[34] In conjunction with its prize on Maduro's head, the State Department issued bounties for other Chavista officials including Diosdado Cabello; Tarek El-Aissami,

---

32   Joshua Goodman, "Alleged Maduro Co-Conspirator Says CIA Knew about Coup Plans," Associated Press, January 28, 2022.

33   Misión Verdad (@Mision_Verdad), Twitter post, March 26, 2020, https://twitter.com/Mision_Verdad/status/1243251030445494273?s=20.

34   "Nicolás Maduro Moros - New Target," United States Department of State, March 26, 2020.

the minister of industry and production; and, oddly, Clíver Alcalá.[35] The following day, Alcalá surrendered to the US Drug Enforcement Agency in Barranquilla, Colombia.[36]

The episode intensified intelligence intrigues surrounding Gideon. Why did the US file charges against Alcalá even though he had already defected from Venezuela's government? Why did Alcalá reveal details of Operation Gideon, including the involvement of Guaidó and Rendón, before turning himself in to US authorities? Most puzzlingly: why did Operation Gideon move forward even after Alcalá, its commander, had been arrested and taken to the United States? These are some of the most bewildering questions to emerge from the plotline of Operation Gideon, an event that marked perhaps the singularly most fantastic chapter in the already exceptionally weird saga of Guaidó's failed coup.

A Venezuelan government source once posited to me that a faction of Colombia's intelligence services opposed Operation Gideon and had set out to sabotage the plot with its March 23 weapons seizure. If that were the case, perhaps Alcalá saw the writing on the wall: Operation Gideon was doomed. On top of possible reservations in Bogotá, a *Vice* investigation later asserted the CIA gained prior knowledge of the operation and had dispatched a representative to advise Goudreau against proceeding with it.[37] These details suggested that some figures involved in Gideon, such as Alcalá, may have gotten cold feet as the mission approached. But why would US authorities charge and detain Alcalá if he had cooperated with them all along? And where did the State Department fit into the picture?

Images of Alcalá's "arrest" may provide an answer to the first question. In video footage of the moment the former Venezuelan general boarded a DEA plane in Colombia, he is seen wearing a light blue dress

35   "US Indicts Venezuela's Maduro for 'Narco-Terrorism', Offer $15 Million for Arrest," France 24, March 26, 2020.

36   Angus Berwick, Luis Jaime Acosta, and Sarah Kinosian, "Alleged Maduro Accomplice Surrenders to U.S. Agents, Will Help Prosecution: Sources," Reuters, March 27, 2020.

37   Ben Makuch, "Maga, the CIA, and Silvercorp: The Bizarre Backstory of the World's Most Disastrous Coup," *VICE*, October 26, 2021.

shirt and black slacks as he shakes hands with, and even hugs, a group of suited up men who accompanied him to the tarmac.[38] The identities of the men were unknown, but considering Alcalá was in DEA custody at that point, we can assume they were DEA agents.

Following his emotional goodbye, Alcalá carried his own luggage aboard the DEA plane and set off for New York City. Though they had charged him with conspiracy to commit narco-terrorism and other drug-related crimes, US authorities did not handcuff their prisoner, instead presenting a perplexing image of bonhomie. Had Alcalá's US government handlers merely offered him a comfortable exit from Colombia and Operation Gideon as the plot fell apart? Although the mystifying images invited speculation, we may never know their full backstory.

Then there was the question of the State Department's involvement.

At the center of the State Department's operation in Venezuela was James Story, a career foreign service officer from South Carolina who took over as Washington's Caracas chargé d'affaires in July 2018. Puffed in a February 2019 AP profile as the "steely huntsman at helm of embattled US embassy in Caracas,"[39] Story arrived in Venezuela just five months before the US recognition of Guaidó sent diplomatic relations between the two countries into free fall. In his memoir, Pompeo personally credited Story with spearheading the campaign to whip up Venezuelan opposition support for Guaidó in the lead up to his self-declared presidency (chapter four).

Though Story served in a global array of US embassies—including in Mozambique and Afghanistan—the diplomat's fluency in Spanish and Portuguese eventually grounded him in Latin America. Story held a variety of high-level posts in the region before moving to Caracas, including consul general in Rio, Brazil. His other résumé highlights included a stint as director of the Bureau of International Narcotics and Law Enforcement Affairs (INL) Office for the Western Hemisphere,

38   Gabriel Bastidas (@Gbastidas), Twitter post, March 26, 2020, https://twitter.com/Gbastidas/status/1243855852077015041?s=20.

39   Joshua Goodman, "Steely Huntsman at Helm of Embattled US Embassy in Caracas," Associated Press, February 1, 2019.

as well as an assignment directing local INL operations in Colombia.[40] Founded in 1978, the INL was a division of the State Department that monitored international narcotics trafficking in close coordination with other US agencies, including the DEA.

During his time with the INL in Bogotá, Story oversaw the US government's controversial aerial fumigation program in Colombia, an initiative that doused roughly 4.4 million acres of the country's farmland with the cancer-causing herbicide known as glyphosate over the course of twenty-one years.[41] Billed as an effort to eradicate narcotic crops, the policy was widely associated with the destruction of Colombia's farmland and biodiversity as well as a rise in health defects among its population.

"They've destroyed our food," Avelardo Joya, one of Colombia's 3.5 million internally displaced drug war refugees, explained to filmmakers in a 2011 CNN report. "That's the only thing they destroy, because our food crops cannot resist the poison they drop."[42]

Moments after Joya's heart-wrenching testimony, a bespectacled diplomatic functionary seated beside the US tricolor appeared on screen to sing the program's praises.

"The aerial eradication program run by the government of Colombia has been extraordinarily successful," a young James Story enthused from within his office at the US embassy in Bogotá.

Upon landing in Caracas years later, Story's strong command of the Spanish language and disarming Southern charm enabled him to insinuate himself into Venezuelan opposition circles with ease. Throughout his brief stay in Venezuela, Story was unashamed of his close collaboration with the country's anti-Chavista forces. In a Facebook post from March 3, 2019, for example, he shared a photo of himself hiking with former opposition presidential candidate Henrique Capriles Radonski. "The Venezuelan people love him," the US diplomat raved.[43]

40   "Ambassador James 'Jimmy' Story," U.S. Embassy in Venezuela, April 15, 2021.

41   "U.S.-Colombia Anti-Drug Plan Pushes Failed Policy of Aerial Fumigation," Washington Office on Latin America, March 6, 2020.

42   Ann Colwell, "Documentary Shines Light on Farmers Displaced by Accidental Fumigation," CNN, October 19, 2011.

43   Anya Parampil and Max Blumenthal, "US 'Virtual Ambassador' to Venezuela Hosts Insurrectionist Summit Ahead of Biden's Guaidó Recognition," *The Grayzone*, March 3, 2021.

When Guaidó returned to Venezuela from a regional tour the following afternoon, Story was on the freshly minted coup leader's heels—almost literally.

"Venezuela's Interim President Juan Guaidó is back," the diplomat chirped in a Facebook post accompanying a photo of Guaidó standing atop a car surrounded by supporters (Parampil and Blumenthal 2021).

Story's overtly partisan activity represented the kind of behavior considered uncouth for diplomats on foreign assignment. As such, Venezuela's actual government kicked Story out of the country shortly following Washington's recognition of Guaidó.[44] Bizarrely, "Venezuela's Interim President" had no power to ensure Story remained in the country.

After a brief return to the States, Story established a "virtual US embassy" to Venezuela housed within Washington's diplomatic offices in Bogotá. From there, he managed a command post for Venezuela's US-backed opposition as they mapped out paths to regime change in Caracas.

Story was so fond of Venezuela's extremist opposition, in fact, that he eventually hosted a private gathering of Guaidó allies at his Bogotá residence. In February 2021, Venezuelan opposition leaders, including Leopoldo López and Carlos Vecchio, traveled to the Colombian capital to attend a closed-door summit at the local Marriott hotel. There, over the course of several days, they enjoyed valuable face time with US government officials and mulled options for a political "transition" in Caracas (Parampil and Blumenthal 2021). The secret meeting's agenda was subsequently leaked to Venezuela's government and published online. According to the leaked details, the summit kicked off with a welcome barbeque at Story's private home. Story later confirmed the party took place, boasting on his weekly YouTube livestream *Aló Embajador*—a twisted homage to Chávez's *Aló Presidente* program—that he roasted an entire pig for the Venezuelan putschists in attendance.[45]

---

44   Jorge Arreaza (@jaarreaza), Twitter post, March 12, 2019, https://twitter.com/jaarreaza/status/1105454380248154114?s=20.

45   "Aló Embajador, 25 De Febrero De 2021," US Embassy Venezuela, February 25, 2021.

Story complemented his open affection for Washington's anti-democratic Venezuelan shock troops with raging contempt for sovereign governments in the surrounding region. When a military coup ousted Bolivia's elected president, Evo Morales, in 2019, Story took to Facebook in celebration.

"Proud of the brave people of Bolivia," the diplomat declared (Parampil and Blumenthal 2021), vowing: "Venezuela will also one day be free of tyranny."

Several months following Story's forecast of regime change in Venezuela, Goudreau's ragtag band made its way to the country's coastline on a quest to capture or kill its president.

As we know, Alcalá and Goudreau planned Operation Gideon in Bogotá, and Goudreau claimed to his business partner that he had secured a State Department contract. What gave Goudreau that impression? Did Story ever meet with Goudreau? Did Story have any knowledge of Operation Gideon? Then there is the obvious question: how were US citizens able to travel to Colombia, ship arms into the country, and oversee military training camps on its territory without the knowledge of US embassy staff in Bogotá?

Now consider the ominous statement Secretary of State Pompeo delivered on April 29—days before Operation Gideon went into effect.

"In Venezuela, I am pleased to report that the multilateral effort to restore democracy is continuing to build momentum," Pompeo informed reporters. "I've asked my team to update our plans to reopen the US embassy in Caracas so we are ready to go. As soon as Maduro steps aside, I am confident that we will raise [our] flag again in Caracas."[46]

What made Pompeo so optimistic in Maduro's imminent ouster that he was actively preparing State Department staff for a return to Caracas? Considering Story's past work in the State Department's narcotics division, did he have any role in its decision to offer a $15 million reward for information leading to Maduro's capture days before Gideon's launch—providing a direct incentive for wannabe bounty hunters like Goudreau to target Venezuela's president?

---

46   U.S. Mission Italy, "Secretary Michael R. Pompeo at a Press Availability, April 29, 2020," U.S. Embassy & Consulates in Italy, April 29, 2020.

We may never know the true Story of Operation Gideon. We do know, however, that the US diplomat earned a promotion in the plot's immediate aftermath. On May 6, 2020, President Trump nominated Story to serve as Washington's "ambassador" to Venezuela[47]—a superficial gesture that upgraded his chargé d'affaires status despite his lack of a physical embassy in Caracas. Story remains in command of a Bogotá-based "virtual" US embassy to Venezuela at the time of this book's publication.

Though the deepest questions regarding Operation Gideon remain unanswered, there is increasing evidence that, at the very least, high-level US officials had prior knowledge of the ill-fated plan. In his memoir, *A Sacred Oath*, former defense secretary Mark Esper shared his impression that members of Trump's National Security Council (NSC) were collaborating with Venezuela's extremist opposition on a mysterious plot. He described a February 2020 White House Cabinet Room meeting during which US and Guaidó officials discussed possible scenarios for a "smaller, special operation directly targeted directly at Maduro" (Esper 2022, 301).

"Then, out of the blue, one of Guaidó's colleagues looked at me from across the table and said something like, 'We have some plans you [the US government] know we are working on, they're just not ready yet,'" the Raytheon executive turned defense secretary recalled, noting the Guaidó ally made "some quick reference to Florida" before making eye contact with Mauricio Claver-Carone, the Cuban American hawk whom John Bolton selected to manage Western Hemisphere affairs on Trump's NSC (Bolton 2020, 250).

"Claver-Carone smiled and nodded back," Esper continued in his description of the meeting: "I looked directly at him about fifteen feet away from me, down the table to my left. He turned to me, and as our eyes met, his face immediately went blank. Something was up."

Esper let his suspicions pass, relating that he proceeded to dismiss himself from the meeting to tend to obligations at the Pentagon. Yet other participants in the Venezuela NSC summit "stayed for quite some

47   "President Donald J. Trump Announces Intent to Nominate and Appoint Individuals to Key Administration Posts," National Archives and Records Administration, May 6, 2020.

time," the defense secretary recounted before admitting: "I probably should have too." When Operation Gideon went into effect roughly three months later, Esper said he "wondered if this was the plan referred to by Guaidó's team at the White House back in February and, if so, to what degree was the NSC aware and involved."

Though Venezuela's government and its sympathizers characterized Esper's narrative as a confession of US involvement in Operation Gideon,[48] his words could just as easily be interpreted as careful spin. By emphasizing his exit from the meeting once discussions turned to the topic of covert Venezuela ops, Esper separated himself—a representative of official Washington and the military—from ideological figures like Claver-Carone. Esper previously described Claver-Carone as "pushing a hard line" on Venezuela and expressed his concern the Cuban American's role at the NSC was "too personal for him" (Esper 2022, 298). If that were the case, then it was Esper's responsibility as defense secretary to find out exactly what Claver-Carone and Guaidó officials were planning. Rather than apply due diligence, however, Esper fled the room and maintained a shield of plausible deniability when their conspiracy (predictably) failed. As a result, two former US Green Berets spent three and a half years in Venezuelan custody (Venezuela released Denman and Berry as part of a prisoner swap with the US in December 2023).

Regardless of whether Washington was directly involved in Operation Gideon, there is no question that US policy toward Venezuela drove Goudreau and his friends to follow through with their reckless plot. What purpose did the State Department's decision to offer a $15 million reward for Maduro's arrest otherwise serve? According to Esper, the narco-trafficking charges against Maduro were the brainchild of Trump attorney general William Barr, who convinced the US president that a renewed focus on Washington's drug war in Latin America was the most effective way to pressure Venezuela's government—a proposal the defense secretary accepted as a reasonable alternative to direct military intervention in the country.

Barr's hand in crafting the premium on Maduro's head was revealing. In 1989, Barr, then an advisor to the Justice Department, authored

48   Alan MacLeod, "Mark Esper's Tell-Some Reveals US Plans for War and Terror against Venezuela," *MintPress News*, May 23, 2022.

a legal memo that provided justification for the US invasion of Panama.[49] The ensuing "Operation Just Cause," which George H. W. Bush's administration launched on December 20, 1989, resulted in the arrest of Panama's then president, Manuel Noriega, on drug trafficking charges. Over thirty years later, Barr redeployed his Panama playbook to provide legal cover for Washington's imperial interventions in Latin America once again.

Discounting the preceding chapter, only one plausible explanation for Operation Gideon remains: a desperate and delusional man hired US mercenaries to invade his homeland and arrest its sitting president, all because Washington convinced him he was the country's chosen leader.

49   Mattathias Schwartz, "William Barr's State of Emergency," *New York Times*, June 1, 2020.

SIXTEEN

ELECTION EXCEPTIONALISM

I last visited Venezuela in December 2020, when Max and I covered its first legislative election since the opposition won control of the National Assembly (AN) in 2015. The December 6 vote not only presented the Maduro-aligned Gran Polo Patriótico Simón Bolívar (GPP) coalition with an opportunity to regain a majority in the legislature, but marked the formal conclusion of Juan Guaidó's imagined presidency. With his Voluntad Popular party officially boycotting the election, Guaidó was guaranteed to lose his AN seat, his already dubious position as AN chief, and therefore, his claim to Venezuela's presidency.

By refusing to take part in the vote,[1] Guaidó and other members of the US-backed extremist bloc intensified their tried-and-true strategy of delegitimizing Venezuela's democratic process in international media, which spun their lack of participation as evidence of Maduro's authoritarian rule. The push to sabotage the vote was overseen by Leopoldo López, who coordinated the radical opposition's public relations campaign from the comfort of Spain. After spending roughly a year in Madrid's Caracas embassy, where they found sanctuary following Guaidó's failed military uprising of April 2019, López and his family finally relocated to the capital of Venezuela's former European colonizer in October 2020.[2]

López escalated the opposition's delegitimization effort on November 30, when he tweeted a video of Chavista official Diosdado

---

1   Reuters Staff, "Venezuela's Major Opposition Parties Pledge to Boycott December Election," Reuters, August 2, 2020.

2   Reuters Staff, "Venezuelan Opposition Politician Lopez Arrives in Madrid, Spain Says," Reuters, October 25, 2020.

Cabello proclaiming before a campaign rally: "Those who don't vote, don't eat."[3]

"The culprits of the humanitarian catastrophe that Venezuela is experiencing . . . blackmail the hungry people with food," López wrote in a message accompanying the six second clip, accusing Cabello of bribing Venezuelans to participate in the upcoming vote.

López's allegations were promptly repeated by a bipartisan group of US lawmakers, who issued a since-deleted December 4 letter accusing Venezuela's government of threatening to withhold food from citizens who refused to participate in what they characterized as a "sham" election.[4] Their denunciation was parroted in a subsequent *Wall Street Journal* report that similarly described Venezuela's upcoming vote as a "sham" merely designed to "challenge" incoming US president Joe Biden[5] (never mind that the country's constitution mandated legislative elections occur every five years).

In their haste to undermine Venezuela's democratic process, US officials and their loyal lackies overlooked the cultural—and comical—context of Cabello's remarks. Though Cabello did in fact utter the words "those who don't vote, don't eat" in the short clip López deceptively posted to Twitter, a full review of his statement revealed the notoriously sarcastic military captain was making a sexually charged joke.

"Women are going to be at the forefront of this battle," Cabello announced, explaining he believed Venezuelan females would lead the effort to get out the vote on election day.[6] Only then did he declare that "those who don't vote, don't eat"—a double entendre that was obvious to most Venezuelans who heard it. In Venezuelan culture, the verb *comer* not only means "to eat," but is also slang for "to have sex." In

---

3   Leopoldo López (@leopoldolopez), Twitter post, November 30, 2020, https://twitter.com/leopoldolopez/status/1333537348123037698?s=20.

4   Max Blumenthal and Anya Parampil, "US Congress and Corporate Media Deploy Massive Lie, Claiming Venezuela's Gov't Threatened to Starve Non-Voters," *The Grayzone*, December 6, 2020.

5   Ryan Dube, "Venezuela's Regime Challenges Biden with Sham Election," *Wall Street Journal*, December 5, 2020.

6   "Diosdado Cabello: Este 6D El Pueblo De Bolívar Le Dará Una Lección De Democracia Al Imperialismo," Multimedios VTV, November 30, 2020.

their full context, Cabello's words were not a threat to withhold food, but merely a Chavista-style reference to Aristophanes's *Lysistrata*—the ancient Greek comedy in which women launched a sex strike to force an end to the Peloponnesian War.

Though López himself may have understood his deceit, the Venezuelan slang and literary innuendo at play in Cabello's comments were too advanced for US lawmakers and international media to process. For them, the narrative of a socialist party official openly announcing his intent to starve his own population at a public campaign rally was a sufficient—and somehow, believable—account.

In conjunction with dishonest attacks in the press, the US government launched a pressure campaign against members of Venezuela's opposition who refused to concede their right to run for office. As with previous attempts to implement a nationwide electoral boycott, the extremist bloc's zero-sum strategy was complicated by the fact that moderate forces within the opposition actually *wanted* to engage with their country's democratic process.[7] As one Avanzada Progresista party source explained to me, many opposition lawmakers were poised to keep their AN seats. As a result, they saw no value in sitting on the sidelines and allowing the Chavista coalition to sweep the election unchallenged.

To intimidate candidates into complying with its boycott strategy, Washington levied sanctions against a variety of opposition figures who dared challenge it. Among those personally targeted were Luis Parra,[8] the anti-Chavista lawmaker and former Guaidó ally who was elected leader of Venezuela's National Assembly in a disputed January 2020 vote, as well as members of the opposition Mesa de la Unidad Democrática (MUD) coalition.[9] While announcing the MUD sanc-

---

7   Mariana Martínez and Anatoly Kurmanaev, "Venezuela's Opposition Splits over Taking Part in Coming Elections," *New York Times*, September 6, 2020.

8   "Treasury Sanctions Maduro Regime Officials for Undermining Democratic Order in Venezuela," United States Department of the Treasury, September 4, 2020.

9   "The United States Sanctions Additional Individuals Involved in the Illegitimate Maduro Regime's Attempts to Corrupt Democratic Elections in Venezuela," United States Embassy in Georgia, September 22, 2020.

tions, US secretary of state Mike Pompeo accused the targeted lawmakers of "enabling Maduro's efforts to rob the people of Venezuela of their right to choose their leaders in free and fair elections." Yes, according to Pompeo's logic, opposition legislators had robbed Venezuelans of the "right to choose their leaders" by agreeing to participate in elections and providing them with more choices at the ballot box.

Washington's boycott campaign ultimately failed, as more than one hundred parties fielded candidates for the December 6 vote.[10] To obscure this reality, Reuters openly asserted that opposition candidates who participated in the election were secretly collaborating with Maduro, running a December 3 article accusing those who defied the boycott of "suspected of ties" to Venezuela's ruling socialist party.[11]

Efforts to undermine the vote's validity extended far beyond those launched by Venezuela's US-backed opposition and their media allies. Though Venezuela's government invited European Union officials to observe the vote in the summer of 2020, Brussels rejected the offer and called on Caracas to delay its constitutionally mandated election.[12] Critics of the EU decision claimed it was meant to deny Caracas the ability to legitimize the vote with the presence of international observers. Regardless, over three hundred foreign observers from thirty-four countries traveled to Venezuela to monitor the vote,[13] which went ahead on December 6. As with Venezuela's presidential election in 2018, US officials leapt to disqualify its results before polls had even closed.

"Venezuela's electoral fraud has already been committed," Pompeo tweeted on the afternoon of the vote. "The results announced by the illegitimate Maduro regime will not reflect the will of the Venezuelan people."[14]

10   "Venezuela's Guaido Vows to Challenge Maduro's Congress Win," Al Jazeera, December 7, 2020.

11   Brian Ellsworth and Vivian Sequera, "Opposition Candidates Suspected of Ties to Venezuela's Ruling Party Defy Call for Vote Boycott," Reuters, December 3, 2020.

12   "EU Refuses to Monitor Venezuelan Election, Urges Delay," Associated Press, August 11, 2020.

13   Leonardo Flores, "Free Elections in Venezuela Are a Blow to Regime Change," Code Pink, December 9, 2020.

14   Mike Pompeo (@secpompeo), Twitter post, December 6, 2020, https://twitter.com/SecPompeo/status/1335672345894268938?s=20.

Yet the vote concluded without incident, as more than 14,000 candidates from over 100 parties—that majority of which opposed Maduro's government (Flores 2020)—competed for 277 seats in Venezuela's legislature. Though the radical opposition's boycott resulted in lower voter participation rates—which dropped from roughly 75 percent in 2015 to 31 percent in 2020—Venezuelan American political analyst, Leonardo Flores, noted turnout was not drastically lower than rates seen in US midterm elections, which averaged around 40 percent (Flores 2020). The PSUV's GPP coalition won 68 percent of votes cast, securing a legislative supermajority. Beyond the material triumph of Chavismo, the vote was touted as the final defeat of US regime change policy, as it left Washington's coup leader without a legitimate claim to any government office whatsoever.

By the time of the election, US president Donald Trump's mandate was in its final days. Roughly a month before Venezuelans cast their ballots, former vice president Joe Biden declared victory over Trump in a presidential vote marred by accusations of fraud typically unheard of in the United States. For the first time in modern US history, the winner of the presidential vote had not been declared on election night, but nearly four days after polls closed.

Though many US citizens, me included, went to bed on November 3 believing that Trump had secured a second term in office, delayed ballot counting later overturned his projected victory in the key states of Pennsylvania, Michigan, and Wisconsin. According to election officials, the delay was caused by a record submission of mail-in ballots spurred by the outbreak of COVID-19. Though mail-in ballots were cast in advance, they were not counted until election day—resulting in an electoral system overload on the night of November 3. Biden's vote count steadily increased as authorities processed mail-in ballots, and he was declared the winner on November 7—an extraordinary turn of events that prompted large swaths of Trump's base to question the final tally.[15] According to the US census, 69 percent of ballots cast in

---

15   Mark Murray, "Poll: 61% of Republicans Still Believe Biden Didn't Win Fair and Square in 2020," NBC, September 27, 2022.

2020 were submitted by mail or before election day, a nearly 30 percent increase from the previous vote.[16]

Regardless of one's personal view of the vote, there was no denying that its unprecedented circumstances prompted millions of US citizens to lose faith in their country's electoral system, and by extension, exceptionalist ideals of US democracy. This was not lost on foreign populations subject to Washington's regime change exploits, including the people of Venezuela. As Max and I visited polling stations and chatted with voters throughout election day on December 6, one talking point reigned supreme.

"We're used to voting," a white-haired gentleman whom I encountered outside of a polling station in Petare, a bastion of Chavista support in Caracas, declared. "On the other hand, if we consider the US elections, they held a vote and Trump still claims there was fraud," he continued. "No one knows who the president is, but Biden, the winner, is on stand-by."[17]

Inside the polling center, a middle-aged brunette noted the extreme delay in the 2020 US presidential vote before boasting: "Tonight, most certainly, we will know who the winning candidates are."

The Venezuelans we spoke with were not only confident in their electoral process but considered it superior to that in the United States. Based on my own experience covering the 2020 legislative election in the country, such comparisons were not unfounded. In Venezuela, voting machines were activated through a two-step verification process consisting of a physical check of the voter's national identity card and a digital scan of their fingerprint. After casting their vote, the voter received a physical receipt of their ballot which they then personally dropped in a secure box on site. The voter then signed their name and stamped their thumbprint on a physical electoral registry to certify their participation. When polls closed, authorities assuaged fears of digital vote tampering by checking their final electronic tally against a

16   Zachary Scherer, "Majority of Voters Used Nontraditional Methods to Cast Ballots in 2020," United States Census, April 8, 2021.

17   Anya Parampil, "Venezuelan Voters Hit Back at US Election Hypocrisy," *The Grayzone*, December 9, 2020.

random sampling of 54 percent of the physical ballot receipts submitted by voters at polling stations.

This multistep process is what once prompted former US president Jimmy Carter to characterize Venezuela's elections as "the best in the world."[18] It was also comparable to the electoral process I observed in Bolivia, which similarly included an in-person ID check and issuing of a physical ballot receipt to enable multiple audits of the electronic vote tally. I even watched local poll workers in the Franco Boliviano school in southern La Paz physically count votes by holding up every ballot for the public to see, vocally declaring the chosen candidate, and marking the selection on a publicly displayed tally sheet.[19] Such transparency stood in stark contrast to the system in the US, where just a few months prior, vote counts in several Iowa Democratic Party caucuses had been determined via a literal coin toss.[20]

Venezuelans and Bolivians alike spoke of their respective systems with pride, specifically pointing to the physical ID check as proof of their electoral processes' infallibility. This flew in the face of conventional wisdom in the United States, where strict election laws and voter ID checks are largely considered "right-wing" initiatives.

"I think if the US government believes there is fraud in Venezuela, then they should reflect on themselves and their own elections before giving an opinion on ours," a middle-aged man told me on the streets of Petare. "There is no bigger fraud than the one committed in the US."

When the victors of Venezuela's 2020 legislative vote were sworn-in on January 5, 2021, Juan Guaidó's short-lived—albeit turbulent—career in government reached its official end. Even so, his swan song was not broadcast in the foreign press until December 2022, when outlets from

18   Smartmatic, "Carter: 'The Electoral System in Venezuela Is the Best in the World,'" September 26, 2012.

19   Anya Parampil (@anyaparampil), Twitter post [VIDEO], October 19, 2020, https://twitter.com/anyaparampil/status/1318247885125857284?s=20.

20   Kelly McLaughlin, "Several Iowa Caucus Votes Ended in Coin Tosses When Delegate Counts Were Too Close to Call," *Business Insider*, February 4, 2020.

Reuters[21] to the *New York Times*[22] finally declared the US-backed coup leader had been "voted out" as leader of Venezuela's opposition.

The reports emerged after opposition lawmakers from the 2015 National Assembly—which continued to meet and "legislate" via video conference well beyond their constitutionally mandated five-year term—voted to formally dissolve Guaidó's "interim government" on December 30, 2022.

"To annul [this government] is to leap into the void," Guaidó warned his colleagues. "Who is going to take over the power vacuum?"

The December 30 vote represented a monumental shift in the strategy of Venezuela's US-backed opposition, by then under the stewardship of Biden administration functionaries. After backing his regime change effort for nearly four years—even as moderate forces within the opposition mounted an official challenge to his authority—Guaidó's allies within the hardline G4 coalition had ultimately spearheaded the effort to dissolve his government. Their wish to oust Maduro, however, endured.

"Everything we are doing has to do with laying the foundations for a new stage of a more effective democratic struggle," Juan Miguel Matheus, a member of G4's Primero Justicia party, told the *New York Times* after voting to remove Guaidó, stressing the opposition's goal was still "to defeat Maduro as soon as possible" (Herrera and Glatsky 2022).

Considering G4's deep financial and political links to the US (as one Venezuelan source joked to me, its members could hardly breathe without seeking permission from the White House), their move to drop Guaidó reflected a decision made in Washington. Though the Biden administration has yet to reverse the US's formal recognition of Guaidó—or Treasury's aggressive Venezuela sanctions, for that matter—at the time of this book's publication, the radical opposition's break with the failed coup leader was not a mere act of symbolism.

---

21   Mayela Armas, "Venezuela Opposition Removes Interim President Guaido," Reuters, December 30, 2022.

22   Isayen Herrera and Genevieve Glatsky, "Juan Guaidó Is Voted out as Leader of Venezuela's Opposition," *New York Times*, December 30, 2022.

While media reports focused on the civic implications of Guaidó's loss, the material focus of Venezuela's Washington-aligned political faction remained unchanged. In addition to dissolving Guaidó's non-existent government, opposition lawmakers voted to establish a commission dedicated to managing Venezuela's international financial assets, most importantly those belonging to its state oil company, PdVSA. In other words, the vote appeared to be an effort by G4 and their US backers to reassert command over those assets, particularly Citgo, in light of Guaidó's undeniable descent into the depths of political irrelevance.

Leading up to the opposition's vote to remove Guaidó, the US government hosted the Ninth Summit of the Americas in Los Angeles. The State Department–led gathering served as a roundtable on Biden administration policy toward Latin America and the Caribbean, featuring esteemed guests including Salvadoran president Nayib Bukele, Bolivian president Luis Arce, and other regional dignitaries. Washington formally excluded three governments from the June summit, however: those representing Cuba, Nicaragua, and Venezuela— the trio Trump NSC chief John Bolton infamously characterized as a "Troika of Tyranny."

"The person that you recognize as the leader, democratic leader in Venezuela, is not here," a female reporter complained during a press conference convened by then US House Speaker Nancy Pelosi.[23]

"What do you think about the absence of Juan Guaidó here?" the reporter inquired.

Pelosi, the veteran Democratic Party leader who had momentarily adjourned from her partisan posturing to eagerly applaud Guaidó's presence at President Trump's State of the Union address just two years prior,[24] looked confused.

"By whom?" the octogenarian, multimillionaire US official replied.

23   "Nancy Pelosi Doesn't Remember Juan Guaido," *Kawsachun News*, June 15, 2022.

24   Jake Johnson, "'No Better Distillation of Washington': Democrats and GOP Join Trump in Standing Ovation for Failed Venezuelan Coup Leader Juan Guaido," Common Dreams, February 5, 2020.

SEVENTEEN

THE ECSTASY OF GOLD

In a country brimming with natural beauty, perhaps the most marvelous region in Venezuela is La Gran Sabana. Spanning over 4,000 square miles in southeastern Estado Bolívar, the grand savanna is replete with flowing rivers, table-top mountains (*tepuis,* in the indigenous Pemón language), and flourishing tropical foliage. It is home to a section of Venezuela's most renowned national park, Canaima, a gigantic territory that stretches over 11,000 square miles of protected natural land.

Within Canaima sits Angel Falls (Kerepakupai Merú), a towering, uninterrupted waterfall that cascades down a 3,212-foot summit. Pouring from the edge of a table-top mountain called Auyán-tepui situated in the midst of an untamed jungle, Angel Falls is the tallest waterfall in the world, with a drop nineteen times higher than that of Niagara Falls. The pristine water that flows down Angel Falls spills directly from the clouds circling above Auyán-tepui. Tourists visit the cascade with the help of indigenous Pemón guides who lead river trips to its base, and daring climbers even venture to abseil its face.

A Venezuelan friend who climbed a neighboring tepui mountain called Roraima told me its summit was covered with crystalline pools of pure rainwater. She described how, after hiking for several days, she developed pain in her knee and complained to her guide, who advised her to soak in the pools and experience their "medicinal properties." Relaxing in a sinkhole below a waterfall on the mountaintop, surrounded by rocks containing veins of gold, raw quartz, and other precious minerals, she felt her aches miraculously subside. She was not the first to tell of Canaima's healing abilities. A Venezuelan official once related to me that in the later years of his life, Cuban leader Fidel

Castro sought water from Angel Falls to drink, believing the *agua pura* possessed magical qualities.

The mythical power of Angel Falls may be rooted in its lack of industrial contamination, or perhaps the cosmic energy flowing from the precious minerals and metals that enrich the earth below it. Either way, Canaima's unquantifiable natural wealth explains why corporate conglomerates and their government collaborators in Washington and London have worked to install a puppet regime in Caracas by any means necessary—sacrificing their already feeble grip on reality along the way. Venezuela hosts the largest untapped gold deposits in the world, with much of its supply of the precious metal concentrated in La Gran Sabana's home state of Bolívar.[1]

Gold is man's most eternal and universal fixation. After all, the Spanish conquistadors who pillaged the Americas first set out for the continent in search of El Dorado, the city of lost gold. Indeed, a thirst for Venezuela's gold has maintained the West's obsession with the country to this very day.

To fully understand gold's significance in the *Corporate Coup* against Venezuela, it is necessary to grasp the precious metal's importance to the international financial system. Man's lust for the gilded chemical element stretches millennia—all the way back to the days of ancient Egypt. Despite centuries of technological, economic, and political advancement, modern monetary policy has still largely revolved around gold's undying value.

Even as the US emerged from World War II as the dominant great power, the Bretton Woods system established in 1944 enabled competition between national currencies through its incorporation of the gold standard. While the US dollar became the principal fiat currency for international trade, the greenback's fixed exchange rate under Bretton Woods ($35 per ounce of gold) allowed governments to easily convert their national currencies into dollars, and vice versa. This was possible thanks to the US Treasury's "gold window," where foreign governments

---

1   Valentina Ruiz Leotaud, "Maduro Exhorts Venezuelan Army to Combat Environmental Destruction . . . ," *Mining*, December 29, 2022.

exchanged unwanted US dollars into physical gold bullion maintained by the Federal Reserve.[2]

This system, in which US dollars effectively served as banknotes representing Washington's physical gold supply, was not challenged until the mid-1960s, when former imperial governments in Japan and Europe began to recover from the destruction of the war. After nearly twenty years of Bretton Woods, it was evident the financial arrangement disproportionately benefited the United States—and that Washington had violated the deal's basic terms.

According to economists Michael J. Graetz and Olivia Briffault, by 1965 the international "gold supply had not increased to match the growing supply of dollars, the US deficit had ballooned, and US inflation was increasing as a result of spending on both social programs and the Vietnam War."[3] That year, French president General Charles de Gaulle delivered a landmark speech in which he declared "the convention that gives the dollar an overriding value as an international currency no longer has its initial basis."[4]

De Gaulle's assertion was not unfounded. According to the IMF, by 1966 foreign central banks held more than fourteen billion US dollars, yet the US Federal Reserve maintained gold deposits valued at just $13.2 billion.[5] Of that deposit, only $3.2 billion was available to pay out foreign dollar holdings, meaning the US had printed and issued billions upon billions of paper dollars that it could not physically back in gold bullion. As a result, US dollars stashed in the central banks of Paris, Frankfurt, Tokyo, and beyond represented a gold supply that did not materially exist.

De Gaulle, the leader of French resistance to Nazi occupation and father of the country's Fifth Republic, continued his 1965 address:

2   BullionStar, "British Requests for $3 Billion in US Treasury Gold – the Trigger That Closed the Gold Window," August 16, 2021.

3   Naomi R. Lamoreaux and Ian Shapiro, *The Bretton Woods Agreements* (New Heaven: Yale University Press, 2019).

4   USA Gold, "De Gaulle Criterion Speech," accessed March 30, 2023.

5   "The Incredible Shrinking Gold Supply," International Monetary Fund, accessed March 31, 2023.

> We cannot see that, in this respect, there can be any other
> criterion, any other standard, than gold. Oh, yes! Gold,
> which never changes its nature, which can be shaped into
> bars, ingots, or coins, which has no nationality, and which
> is eternally and universally accepted as the unalterable
> fiduciary value, par excellence.

The French president promptly endeavored to reassert his country's
financial independence by launching an initiative to convert Paris's US
dollars into gold, but his effort was cut short. De Gaulle resigned on
April 28, 1969, following months of widespread student and worker
protests against his leadership. Though he died the following year, the
dream of ending Bretton Woods was not buried alongside de Gaulle.

By 1971, Washington's allies in Europe were officially fed up with
the system. West Germany dropped the dollar on May 5, effectively
withdrawing from Bretton Woods, and immediately convened a meeting of regional finance ministers to explore alternative monetary
arrangements.[6] That July, Switzerland redeemed $50 million worth of
gold from the US Treasury.[7] The following month, French president
Georges Pompidou deployed a warship to New York Harbor alongside
a demand that the US repatriate $191 million worth of Paris's gold.
When Washington obliged, US gold reserves plunged to their lowest
level since 1938.[8]

When Britain's ambassador to Washington implored the US
Treasury to convert $3 billion worth of London's dollar holdings into
gold within days of the Paris payout,[9] the fragility of the US Federal
Reserve system was laid bare. Faced with soaring domestic inflation
and an evident international run on Washington's over-leveraged gold

6 "The Implementation of the First Stage against a Backdrop of European
and International Monetary Difficulties," Centre Virtuel de la Connaissance sur
l'Europe, accessed March 31, 2023.

7 The Staff of the Board of Governors of the Federal Reserve System,
"CURRENT ECONOMIC AND FINANCIAL CONDITIONS," The United
States Federal Reserve, July 21, 1971.

8 David Frum, *How We Got Here* (New York, NY: Basic Books, 2007).

9 "The Burden of Bretton Woods," Richard Nixon Foundation, February 26,
2016.

supply, President Richard Nixon gathered Federal Reserve chairman Arthur Burns, Treasury secretary John Connally, and thirteen other US officials for a watershed summit at Camp David. When Nixon emerged from the Catoctin Mountains two days later, he announced "a new economic policy for the United States" that stunned the world.

"We must protect the position of the American dollar as a pillar of monetary stability around the world," Nixon declared in a nationally televised address on the evening of August 15, 1971, accusing foreign "speculators" of "waging an all-out war on the American dollar."[10]

"Accordingly, I have directed the secretary of the Treasury to take the action necessary to defend the dollar," the US president continued, announcing he had "directed Secretary Connally to suspend temporarily the convertibility of the American dollar except in amounts and conditions determined to be in the interest of monetary stability and in the best interests of the United States."

Known as the "Nixon Shock," Washington's redesigned exchange policy unilaterally ended the international monetary system that had reigned for nearly three decades. By suspending the dollar's convertibility, the US government formally shuttered the Treasury's "gold window" that served as the basis of Bretton Woods. No longer able to exchange their US banknotes for gold, foreign governments were finally forced to accept that the billions of US dollars stored in their central banks were utterly worthless. When US, European, and Japanese officials gathered in Rome for a summit of the IMF's Group of Ten that November, Treasury Secretary Connally famously informed his colleagues: "The dollar is our currency, but it's your problem."[11]

Yet Nixon's 1971 surprise did not mark the end of the US dollar's global supremacy. As established in chapter twelve, his administration resurrected the dollar's status as the world's reserve currency just three years later, when US officials, including then secretary of state Henry Kissinger, negotiated a deal with Saudi Arabia through which Riyadh agreed to exclusively trade its oil in US dollars, giving birth to

---

10   "Speech by Richard Nixon (15 August 1971)," Centre Virtuel de la Connaissance sur l'Europe, accessed March 31, 2023.

11   "The Fed's Hikes Are a New Version of 'Our Dollar, Your Problem'," *Barron's*, June 15, 2022.

the modern Petrodollar system. Because the US and Saudi Kingdom were by far the leading oil producers in the world at the time,[12] the 1974 arrangement ensured the US dollar's continued status as the world's reserve currency.

Roughly fifty years since the Petrodollar's inception, the system is facing a crisis of legitimacy similar to that which Bretton Woods experienced throughout the 1960s. As documented throughout this book, Washington's weaponization of the international financial system against sovereign nations that refuse to submit to its will has revived a global push to dump the dollar. Meanwhile, the US Federal Reserve has increased its money-printing effort to unprecedented rates, minting more new dollars in the single month of June 2020 than it did throughout the first two hundred years of its existence.[13] Coupled with soaring international oil prices, the increased dollar flow gave way to record US inflation[14] and, subsequently, calls for a return to the gold standard. US Representative Alex Mooney introduced a bill to peg the US dollar to the value of gold in October 2022,[15] formally proposing a return to the monetary standard that even former President Trump himself once endorsed.[16]

The dollar's uncertain future has renewed a global gold rush of epic proportions. International demand for the gilded asset climbed by close to 20 percent in 2022 alone,[17] and gold's market price is on track to shatter all-time highs of $2,075 per ounce, established in August 2020, at the time of this book's publication.[18] It's no surprise then that

12   "Oil Production," Our World in Data, accessed March 31, 2023.

13   Turner Wright, "US Printed More Money in One Month than in Two Centuries," Cointelegraph, July 31, 2020.

14   Christopher Rugaber, "U.S. Inflation at 9.1 Percent, a Record High," PBS, July 13, 2022.

15   "U.S. Congressman Introduces Gold Standard Bill as Inflation Spirals out of Control," Yahoo! Finance, October 9, 2022.

16   Jim Zarroli, "Trump Favors Returning to the Gold Standard, Few Economists Agree," NPR, June 16, 2016.

17   Stacey Vanek Smith, "The New Global Gold Rush," NPR, February 3, 2023.

18   Lee Ying Shan, "Gold Prices Could Notch an All-Time High Soon - and Stay There," CNBC, March 23, 2023.

foreign corporate and government interests alike are keen to exploit Venezuela's vast gold supply—be it glistening in untapped domestic mines or stored in offshore bank accounts.

As previously established, the Trump administration transferred control of Venezuela's US-based financial accounts to representatives of Guaidó's shadow government immediately following its January 2019 coup attempt. As the US lobbied its allies to do the same, it found no accomplice more zealous than the United Kingdom. Within days of Guaidó's self-directed "swearing in" ceremony, the Bank of England blocked Venezuela's attempt to repatriate its London-stored gold bullion, then worth an estimated $1.2 billion.[19] The Bank of England's decision came despite the fact Caracas lodged its repatriation request in November 2018[20]—months before anyone in London or elsewhere had ever heard of Guaidó.

The US-backed coup leader inserted himself into the drama on January 27, when he published an extraordinary letter begging UK officials not to repatriate Venezuela's gold.

"I am writing to ask you to stop this illegitimate transaction," read the message, addressed to then UK prime minister Theresa May, and Bank of England governor Mark Karney. "If the money is transferred . . . it will be used by the illegitimate and kleptocratic regime of Nicolás Maduro to repress and brutalize the Venezuelan people."[21]

London officially recognized Guaidó as Venezuela's president days later,[22] further complicating the situation by calling into question which government—Guaidó's or Maduro's—could claim rightful ownership of Venezuela's foreign assets. The reality that Maduro's government controlled every single federal institution, including Venezuela's

19   Rob Picheta, "Bank of England Blocks Maduro's $1.2B Gold Withdrawal - Report," CNN, January 26, 2019.

20   Mayela Armas, "Exclusive: Venezuela Seeks to Repatriate $550 Million of Gold from Britain - Sources," Reuters, November 5, 2018.

21   Deisy Buitrago, "Venezuela Opposition Leader Urges Britain Not to Give Gold to Maduro," Reuters, January 27, 2019.

22   "UK Recognises Juan Guaido as Interim President of Venezuela," Government of the United Kingdom, February 4, 2019.

Central Bank, apparently did not matter to British authorities. In fact, according to Trump NSC chief John Bolton, UK foreign minister Jeremy Hunt visited Washington in the early days of Guaidó's coup attempt and expressed that London "was delighted to cooperate on steps they could take" to support the regime change policy, including "freezing Venezuelan gold deposits" (Bolton 2020, 257).

The UK Foreign & Commonwealth Office (FCO) was so enthusiastic about the prospect of regime change in Caracas, in fact, that it quickly prepared plans to further exploit Venezuela's natural wealth in the event of the coup's success. In May 2020, British journalist John McEvoy obtained UK government documents via a Freedom of Information Act request that revealed the FCO had created a clandestine unit tasked with planning Venezuela's economic "reconstruction" under a hypothetical Guaidó presidency.[23] Though the FCO established its "Venezuela Reconstruction Unit," led by Britain's former ambassador to Caracas, in the fall of 2019, it had kept the initiative secret.

"We cannot understand why they created this unit to 'reconstruct' Venezuela, which is not destroyed," then Venezuelan foreign minister Jorge Arreaza told McEvoy in response to the findings.[24] Following McEvoy's exposé, Arreaza summoned the British chargé d'affaires in Caracas, Duncan Hill, to demand details of the unit's purpose.

"I asked him, 'what's the meaning, what's the sense of the unit?' If they wanted to bomb and attack Venezuela like they did in Iraq, like they did in Afghanistan, like they did in Syria, to reconstruct Venezuela with their companies and win profit out of Venezuelan tragedy and bloodshed?" Venezuela's foreign minister recalled his conversation with Hill. According to Arreaza, the British diplomat's only line of defense was to insist the unit had been "misnamed."

At the time of this book's publication, Caracas's UK-stored gold reserves remain in legal limbo. Regardless, UK authorities have already allowed Venezuela's opposition to loot a portion of their country's assets in London. In August 2021, McEvoy uncovered court documents

23   John McEvoy, "Revealed: Secretive British Unit Planning for 'Reconstruction' of Venezuela," *The Canary*, May 13, 2020.

24   John McEvoy, "'I Was Outraged': Venezuelan Foreign Minister Responds to Secretive British 'Reconstruction' Plans," *The Canary*, May 19, 2020.

revealing that Guaidó officials tapped into Venezuela's UK bank accounts to satisfy roughly £400,000 worth of attorney fees stemming from the Bank of England gold case.[25] Fortunately for UK authorities, the unresolved legal fight enabled their continued blockage of Caracas's repatriation request, ensuring Venezuela's gold remained in the Bank of England's vaults indefinitely—a convenient development as London grappled with a potential bullion shortage.[26]

What's more, the market price of gold has skyrocketed so sharply in recent years that Venezuela's UK-stored reserve is worth upwards of $2 billion at the time of this book's publication, compared to its estimated value of $1.2 billion in 2018. In other words, Guaidó effectively facilitated London's indefinite seizure of Venezuela's gilded assets in contravention of an explicit repatriation request from the country's elected government. London's modern treatment of Venezuela recalled the strategy the British crown deployed to establish its empire centuries ago, when it contracted high seas pirates to maraud ships and New World territories controlled by rival European powers.[27]

"They invent a government of Narnia, a government of fantasy, to steal companies, money, accounts, and to steal gold from Venezuela," Maduro said in July 2021, describing the UK gold heist as "twenty-first-century piracy."[28]

Across the Atlantic, meanwhile, Guaidó's coup attempt yielded similarly lucrative results for US financial interests. As in the UK, Guaidó's rise directly coincided with a US effort to hold Venezuela's New York-stored gold reserves hostage.

In March 2019, Citigroup announced it would sell off $1.3 billion worth of Venezuelan gold bullion housed in its vaults after the

25   John McEvoy, "Exclusive: Juan Guaidó Paid UK Legal Fees with Looted Venezuelan Money," *The Canary*, August 3, 2021.

26   Eddie Spence, "London Gold Dealer Runs Out of Bullion as Truss Budget Shocks," *Bloomberg*, October 1, 2022.

27   Trevor John Whitaker, "The Economic and Military Impact of Privateers and Pirates on Britain's Rise as a World Power," Arizona State University Library, April 2020.

28   BullionStar, "British Requests for $3 Billion in US Treasury Gold – the Trigger That Closed the Gold Window," August 16, 2021.

government in Caracas failed to make a $1.1 billion debt payment to the bank.[29] Caracas's default was by design. Trump sanctions introduced in 2017 banned all transactions with Venezuela's government in US financial markets (McNabb and Caine 2017), literally blocking Caracas from servicing its debt and, in turn, forcing the nonpayment.

According to Reuters, Citi planned to deposit surplus cash raised from its sale of Venezuela's gold, an estimated $258 million, into "a bank account in New York."[30] While Reuters failed to disclose its beneficiary, it was eventually revealed that Citi dropped the funds into an account owned by Venezuela's Central Bank—which by then had been turned over to representatives of Guaidó's shadow regime. Though sanctions officially rendered the money frozen, Venezuela's opposition later approved a US Treasury request to transfer the funds out of Citi's vaults and into an account maintained at the New York Federal Reserve bank.[31] Venezuela's government denounced the decision, accusing Guaidó operatives of coordinating with the US Treasury to enable "the vulgar plunder" of their country's wealth.[32]

As with London's indefinite seizure of Venezuela's gold bullion, the US Treasury-Citi swindle was entirely enabled by Guaidó's seemingly botched attempt at regime change. Though the highest profile, these cases did not constitute the bulk of the international heist committed against Venezuela thanks to Guaidó's US-directed coup effort. Portugal's Novo Banco, which is majority-owned by a US private equity fund,[33] similarly blocked the transfer of $1.2 billion worth of Venezuelan funds to Maduro's government in February 2019.[34]

29   Patricia Laya and Jennifer Surane, "Citigroup Settles Venezuela Gold Swap Transaction," *Bloomberg*, March 20, 2019.

30   Mayela Armas and Corina Pons, "Citigroup to Sell Venezuelan Gold in Setback to President Maduro: Sources," Reuters, March 20, 2019.

31   AFP, "Venezuela Slams US over 'Vulgar' Central Bank Funds Seizure," *Barron's*, April 17, 2020.

32   Jorge Arreaza (@jaarreaza), Twitter post, April 17, 2020, https://twitter.com/jaarreaza/status/1251183730510659586.

33   Sergio Goncalves, "Portugal's Novo Banco Never Sold Assets to Lone Star, Says CEO," Reuters, September 2, 2020.

34   Reuters Staff, "Portuguese Bank Halted $1.2 Billion Transfer of Venezuela Funds: Lawmaker," Reuters, February 5, 2019.

Months later, a Congressional Research Institute report found the US Treasury attempted to divert millions of dollars raised from its prosecution of allegedly corrupt Venezuelan functionaries to bankroll the construction of the US-Mexico border wall.[35] That June, the Miami-based *PanAm Post* published an investigation extensively documenting how Guaidó envoys in Colombia blew thousands of dollars earmarked for Venezuelan refugees on luxury shopping sprees and hotel stays (Avendaño 2019). That same month, Venezuela's government accused Guaidó's US representatives, namely Carlos Vecchio, of personally pocketing a $70 million payment destined for US bondholders with a stake in the country's state oil company, PdVSA.[36] The following April, AP's Joshua Goodman revealed Venezuelan opposition lawmakers appropriated a portion of their country's seized assets to pay themselves a $5,000 monthly salary after the Trump administration transferred them $80 million to finance Guaidó's fight against COVID-19.[37]

Finally, as detailed in chapter 14, the actions of Guaidó officials directly enabled a gang of corporate bandits to loot Citgo, Venezuela's most prized international asset. It is worth recalling that the company's peril is primarily the result of maneuverings coordinated by Guaidó's top legal advisor, José Ignacio Hernández, and a Canadian mining firm, Crystallex, to seize Citgo's assets as payment for debt owed by the Venezuelan state. And for what was that debt determined to be owed? As financial retribution for Venezuela's decision to nationalize its Las Cristinas mine in Estado Bolívar, home to the most abundant untapped gold deposit on the planet. With international demand for gold surging, Las Cristinas will no doubt incur even more value—and attract more foreign interest—in years to come.

Though the total cost of this hybrid financial war on Venezuela is impossible to tally, one fact is certain: it could have never occurred without the advent of Guaidó's presidency. Nearly fifty years after

35   David C. Adams, "Legal Battle over Venezuela's Looted Billions Heats Up," Univision, June 12, 2020.

36   Anya Parampil, "Did Venezuelan Coup Leaders Pocket $70 Million from Citgo's Stolen US Assets?" *The Grayzone*, June 19, 2019.

37   Joshua Goodman, "Sources: Guaido Allies Take Slice of First Venezuela Budget," Associated Press, April 23, 2020.

Nixon seized the world's gold supply seemingly overnight, the US and its allies made off with billions of dollars' worth of Venezuelan assets through the simple—and absurd—act of appointing a parallel government in Caracas. Despite short-term gains, these actions ultimately sent a message to the world that financial institutions in the US and Europe are not to be trusted.

Today, physical regime change in Caracas remains a morbid fantasy relegated to the minds of Bolton and his crazed contemporaries— whom, thankfully, will soon be fixtures of the past. Even so, Guaidó's imagined authority provided Washington and its allies perfect cover for their brazen theft of Venezuela's internationally stored wealth. In the end, this *Corporate Coup* will be Guaidó's only legacy.

Incapable of winning elections, Venezuela's US-backed opposition exploited Guaidó's ascent to establish a shadow network of so-called "ambassadors" and "officials" in key international capitals and multilateral institutions. Their legitimacy was not rooted in Venezuelan law or the country's sovereign democratic process. Rather, Guaidó's ability to take control of Venezuela's foreign bank accounts, diplomatic compounds, and seats before institutions such as the Organization of American States was facilitated by the brute force of Western imperial might. Whether it was handing Venezuela's Washington embassy over to a former Exxon lawyer or installing a Harvard professor and lackey for global finance before the Inter-American Development Bank, the US government repeatedly demonstrated its total disregard for international law throughout its quest to legitimize Guaidó's coup regime.

And whom did these officials serve? Though Guaidó's project claimed to represent the true interests of Venezuela's population, it revealed itself as nothing more than a vassal for the same foreign and commercial interests that have worked to overthrow Chavismo since its inception—and which pillaged Venezuela throughout most of its history. The top functionaries of this US-backed shadow regime were mere alter-egos of the oil titans, mining giants, and neoliberal financial institutions that pilfered Venezuela for decades preceding Chavismo's rise. The tales of Carlos Vecchio, Ricardo Hausmann, José Ignacio Hernández, and other leading figures in this unprecedented, fantastical regime change saga reveal the real face of Washington's *Corporate Coup* in Venezuela.

What have they achieved? Thanks to their actions, Venezuela's most valuable international asset, Citgo Petroleum, is slated for liquidation at the time of this book's publication. Competing oil companies will buy up Citgo's assets while Crystallex, the Canadian mining company that once dreamed of exploiting Venezuela's gold deposits, makes off with billions raised from its court-ordered execution. The US oil market will further monopolize so that Crystallex can cash in on a gold mine that was never even operational. If nothing else, Citgo's destruction serves as a lesson in Imperialism 101: revealing the machinations of an international financial system rigged to favor transnational corporate interests over the will of sovereign states.

José Ignacio Hernández, Guaidó's "attorney general" who never argued a single case on behalf of his "government" in Venezuelan courts, served his corporate paymasters well. He will fade into the academic machinery of Harvard alongside his mentor, Ricardo Hausmann, who remains forever encased in an Ivory Tower of neoliberal delusion. Hausmann will never again have the chance to test his failed economic vision on the Venezuelan population and is instead left in Boston with his Saudi-sponsored professorship and stewing rage.

Carlos Vecchio's future is a bit brighter. Though the US government assumed official control of Venezuela's US embassy in March 2023,[38] he will continue to serve as the de facto liaison between Venezuela's radical diaspora and opportunistic US politicians vying for votes in south Florida. Meanwhile, until Washington restores official diplomatic ties with the actual government in Caracas, Venezuelans living in the US will have to travel to Mexico, Canada, or elsewhere to procure passports and other consular services. Venezuela's embassy in Washington remains empty at the time of this book's publication, with crummy cardboard panels blocking the view of its expansive, ground floor windows overlooking Georgetown's flowing canal.

As for Juan Guaidó? Well, he was never much of anything to begin with, was he?

---

38   Joshua Goodman (@APjoshgoodman), Twitter post, March 31, 2023, https://twitter.com/APjoshgoodman/status/1641974593018646531?s=20.

AFTERWORD

THE MULTIDIMENSIONAL CHESSBOARD

When I set out to write *Corporate Coup* in November 2021, the multipolar world envisioned throughout its pages was, though detectable, still in its gestational period. Around the time I submitted my first draft in July 2022, however, that world experienced an abrupt and extraordinary birth. It was delivered via a military conflict that did not include Venezuela as a belligerent, yet it unleashed monumental shifts in the international order that reverberated in Caracas and, quite frankly, across capitals the world over. That conflict took shape on the icy borderlands that once separated Russia from its western neighbor and former territory, Ukraine.

When Russia launched its special military operation in east Ukraine on February 24, 2022, Washington and its European allies responded with an all-out economic war. Within a year, the US government and its partners levied over 11,000 sanctions against Moscow,[1] boasting of their ability to "isolate" Russia from the global economy, restrict its access to key tech and industry imports, and "impose severe costs" on its main financial entities. The US and EU promptly banned the sale of Russian energy on their respective markets and pressured the international SWIFT payment messaging network to unlink Moscow's premier banking institutions. Meanwhile, roughly 1,000 multinational corporations[2] including McDonalds,

---

1   "Western Countries Imposed Some 11,000 Sanctions on Russia - Diplomat," TASS, September 8, 2022.

2   "Over 1,000 Companies Have Curtailed Operations in Russia—But Some Remain," Yale School of Management, August 18, 2023.

Netflix, and Ikea announced plans to either curtail or completely suspend operations in Russia alongside a laundry list of international airlines, banking giants, and clothing brands, as US president Joe Biden openly declared Washington's intent to overthrow the government in Moscow.

"For God's sake, this man cannot remain in power," the gaffe-prone Biden proclaimed during a March 2022 speech in Poland, referring to Russian president Vladimir Putin. The White House later claimed the US president's impassioned battle cry had been vocalized in error.[3]

Caracas felt the implications of the 2022 transatlantic economic war on Moscow almost immediately. On the weekend of March 5, the Biden administration dispatched a team of envoys to the Venezuelan capital for meetings with local officials, including the country's president, Nicolás Maduro. It marked the first time US authorities participated in direct negotiations with Maduro since Washington's 2019 recognition of a shadow government in Venezuela. According to the *New York Times*, the US delegation aimed to restart oil trade with Caracas and represented Washington's effort "to separate Russia from its remaining international allies amid a widening standoff over Ukraine."

Washington's self-serving objectives in Caracas were transparent. When the Trump administration launched a domestic boycott of Venezuelan oil—personally crafted by then NSC chief John Bolton (chapter one)—in January 2019, Caracas supplied roughly 7 percent of US oil imports. In the aftermath of the Venezuela ban, Russia increased its crude imports to the US by 7 percent virtually overnight. In other words, as illustrated below, Moscow swallowed up the share of the US oil market that Caracas lost in 2019 due to Washington's sanctions.[4]

3   Chris Megerian, Vanessa Gera, and Aamer Madhani, "Biden Says Putin 'Cannot Remain in Power,'" PBS, March 26, 2022.

4   Philip Bump, "The Complicated Question of Ending Imports of Russian Oil," *Washington Post*, March 8, 2022.

From Venezuela to Russia

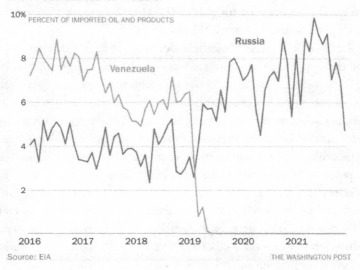

Source: EIA   THE WASHINGTON POST

Within days of the March 2022 Caracas summit, the Biden administration implemented their own domestic oil embargo, this time against Moscow.[5] This meant that over the course of three years, the United States had restricted its access to two foreign oil exporters with a combined 10 percent hold on its domestic market. Did Biden's White House hope to account for their self-imposed oil embargo on Russia by reversing that delivered by Trump's administration against Venezuela in 2019?

The Biden team ultimately failed to revoke Washington's blanket ban on Venezuelan oil imports, lift financial sanctions targeting Maduro's government, or even reverse its nakedly futile recognition of an unknown opposition lawmaker—who by then did not even occupy a legislative seat (chapter sixteen)—as the country's president. US Treasury did, however, grant Chevron an expanded license to restart its Venezuela-based oil operations in a bid to shore up imports. This action enabled the US to import an estimated 100,000 barrels per day (bpd) of

---

5   "Fact Sheet: United States Bans Imports of Russian Oil, Liquefied Natural Gas, and Coal," The White House, March 8, 2022.

Venezuelan oil by February 2023,[6] a meager showing compared to the (historically low) rate of roughly 500,000 bpd Caracas shipped to the US just prior to the January 2019 embargo.[7]

Chevron's marginal Venezuela operation was insufficient to supplant the gap in US oil imports wrought by Washington's combined embargos on Caracas and Moscow, amounting to less than half of Russia's average daily crude exports to the US in 2021. What's more, the Biden administration's wider geopolitical objective in Caracas—to drive a wedge between Venezuela and its Russian ally—was patently unattainable. After withstanding years of Washington-backed military putsches, covert destabilization campaigns, economic war, and a *Corporate Coup*, Venezuela's leaders are unlikely to betray their faithful friends in Moscow even as they reengage with US business interests.

Throughout the first two decades of the twenty-first century, Washington banned the sale of US arms to Venezuela, funded its violent political opposition, and inflicted financial terror upon its population. During that same period, Putin courted the Latin American powerhouse as a strategic partner in Russia's quest to establish a multipolar world order. Today, as that world finds its first steps, the notion that Washington could successfully peel Caracas back into its outdated orbit can only be entertained within the think tanks, elite university campuses, and corporate offices that sustain an increasingly isolated and delusional US imperial guard.

"We fully support our Venezuelan friends," veteran Russian dignitary Sergey Lavrov, who has served as Moscow's chief diplomat since 2004, declared while on an official state visit to Caracas in April 2023.[8] The Russian foreign minister made the trip to Venezuela, which he described as one of Moscow's "most reliable" allies, during a regional Latin America tour that included stops in Brazil, Cuba, and Nicaragua.

---

6   Marianna Parraga, "Chevron to Send over 100,000 Bpd of Venezuelan Oil to U.S. This Month," Reuters, February 17, 2023.

7   "U.S. Imports from Venezuela of Crude Oil (Thousand Barrels per Day)," U.S. Energy Information Administration, accessed August 22, 2023.

8   Regina Garcia Cano, "Russian Foreign Minister Visits Venezuela, Offers Support," Associated Press, April 19, 2023.

"It is their country," Foreign Minister Lavrov added. "We are going to support it in any way so that the Venezuelan economy becomes independent, depending less and less on the whims and geopolitical games of the United States or other Western actors."

"The Grand Chessboard" of Washington-led global hegemony once prophesied by the architects of US Cold War policy was turned upside down in 2022. Less than a year into the transatlantic economic war on Moscow, it was evident the offensive was not nearly as effective as US and European officials hoped. Big Macs reappeared throughout Russia under new branding and ownership,[9] while e-commerce sites and import work-arounds enabled Russians' continued access to nominally banned products including Coca-Cola, Ikea furniture, and cheap clothing brands like Zara.[10] Rather than stoke outrage at Putin, the luxury Chanel brand's decision to boycott their homeland led Russian social media influencers to destroy their designer handbags on camera, all while denouncing corporate "Russophobia."[11] As Russia's population trudged on despite sanctions, by January 2023 the IMF predicted their country's economy was on track to outperform the US within two years.[12]

"Is America the Real Victim of Anti-Russia Sanctions?"[13] posed a May 2022 report in *Tablet Magazine*. Authored by China-based analyst Arnaud Bertrand, the piece argued that US and European officials grossly underestimated the strength of Russia's economy when crafting their sanctions regime, particularly by failing to adjust their calculations of Moscow's Gross Domestic Product (GDP) for purchasing

9   "Tasty Name but No Big Mac: Russia Opens Rebranded McDonald's Restaurants," Reuters, June 13, 2022.

10   "Coca-Cola, Zara, Ikea: Rusia Se Las Ingenia Para Seguir Accediendo a Las Grandes Marcas Internacionales," *elEconomista*, February 23, 2023.

11   Jennifer Hassan, "Russian Influencers Cut up Chanel Handbags, Claiming 'Russophobia,'" *Washington Post*, April 7, 2022.

12   Brendan Cole, "Russia's Economy Forecast to Outperform U.S. within Two Years," *Newsweek*, January 31, 2023.

13   Arnaud Bertrand, "Is America the Real Victim of Anti-Russia Sanctions?" *Tablet Magazine*, May 25, 2022.

power parity (PPP), which factored in productivity rates and per capita living standards when evaluating a country's fiscal strength. As a result, Western officials were prone to repeat misleading comparisons like US senator Lindsey Graham's assertion that Russia's economy was as insignificant as Spain's—a superficial observation rooted in Moscow's unadjusted GDP that overlooked its key role in the global commodities exchange, including its 19.5 percent hold on the international wheat market; significant exports of semi-finished iron and other metals; and position as the world's leading exporter of oil.

Fresh off their federal government's years-long, coronavirus-induced money printing and spending spree, the US public faced soaring food and fuel expenses within months of the transatlantic war on Moscow. According to the Biden administration,[14] the unprecedented costs were the product of actions taken by Russia's government—what the US president dubbed "Putin's price hike"—not Washington's decision to further restrict its own access to international oil streams or impose costs on the global commodities market via sanctions. Biden's narrative ignored the reality that US and EU sanctions on Russian natural gas and other inputs central to the production of agricultural products had prompted an exorbitant surge in the market price of fertilizer.[15] In addition to the overall campaign of economic aggression against Moscow—the world's top grain exporter—the rise in fertilizer costs inspired the UN to declare the Ukraine war had spurred a global food crisis by June 2022.[16]

Meanwhile, in Europe, which was previously dependent on Russian imports to meet demand, self-imposed bans on Moscow-supplied fuel fostered a continent-wide energy crisis that saw wholesale electricity and gas prices increase fifteen-fold in 2022.[17] Catastrophic human suffering and large-scale, government-directed energy rations were only averted

14   "Remarks by President Biden on Gas Prices and Putin's Price Hike," The White House, June 22, 2022.

15   "Russia-Ukraine Crisis Ignites Fertilizer Prices at Critical Time for World Crops," Gro Intelligence, accessed August 22, 2023.

16   "War in Ukraine Drives Global Food Crisis," UN World Food Programme, June 24, 2022.

17   "Beating the European Energy Crisis," IMF, December 1, 2022.

thanks to an unseasonably warm European winter. On top of sanctions, Europe's energy security was critically damaged following Moscow's shutdown of the Nord Stream pipelines that transported Russian natural gas to northeastern Germany via the Baltic Sea. Moscow was forced to close the Nord Stream 1 pipeline in September 2022, after a pair of underwater explosions caused massive gas leaks at the site. At the time of the blasts, Russia supplied roughly 45 percent of EU gas imports via Nord Stream 1[18] and was poised to double its European export capacity pending German regulatory approval of Nord Stream 2.

As noted in chapter 8, the Nord Stream network posed a direct threat to US hegemonic interests in Europe by enabling EU nations to supplant Washington-supplied natural gas with locally sourced (and therefore, cheaper) Russian energy. Washington's bloodlust to maintain a grip on Europe's energy market stretched back decades, something the Biden administration knew well. Coincidentally, Biden secretary of state Antony Blinken's 1984 Harvard thesis detailed Washington's Reagan-era effort to undermine construction of the Trans-Siberian pipeline, which allowed the Soviet Union to export natural gas to Europe via Ukraine. He published the contents of his thesis in a 1987 book, aptly titled *Ally Versus Ally*.

The US ultimately denied responsibility for the September 2022 Nord Stream attacks and officially accused Russia of blowing up its own vital infrastructure project. Washington's narrative unraveled in February 2023, when veteran journalist Seymour Hersh published a blockbuster report that charged Biden officials and UK intelligence with directing a conspiracy to bomb the pipelines. Hersh based his claims on confidential (and impressively thorough) details furnished by a US government source with direct knowledge of the plot. The German Bundestag blocked an initiative to formally investigate the Nord Stream incident the following month. Meanwhile, in 2022, the EU imported more natural gas from the United States than it did from Russia for the first time in history.

Short term gains in the natural gas sector are insufficient to declare Washington's victory in its hybrid war on Moscow, particularly as US

18   IEA, "How Europe Can Cut Natural Gas Imports from Russia Significantly within a Year - News," IEA, March 1, 2022.

officials struggle to define their actual mission in Ukraine—that is, when they are willing to admit they are fighting there at all. Though President Biden insisted the Ukrainian theater did not represent a proxy war between his government and Russia, classified Pentagon documents leaked in March 2023 confirmed the US provided not only logistical support but on-the-ground Special Forces troops to assist Kiev's military in its confrontation with Moscow.[19] Regardless, Washington contended its interest in Ukraine was not geopolitical, but entirely charitable, necessitating a blank check from the US tax-payer so that Kiev could continue an indefinite fight to preserve the abstract concepts of freedom and liberal democracy once threatened on the front lines of Vietnam and Iraq. Or, as US vice president Kamala Harris put it: "Russia is a bigger country. Russia is a powerful country. Russia decided to invade a smaller country called Ukraine. So, basically, that's wrong."[20]

Moscow's mission, however, was defined from the outset of its February 2022 incursion into Ukraine: this war was to ensure Russia's continued survival as a sovereign nation in the face of intensifying NATO encroachment. Contrary to popular belief in the West, the war in Ukraine did not begin in 2022, but over eight years prior when US-backed protests in the country—much like the violent, foreign-sponsored Venezuelan guarimbas detailed throughout this book—overthrew the elected government in Kiev and established a decidedly pro-EU, pro-Washington regime in its place. Civil war officially broke out in February 2014, when ethnically Russian, Moscow-backed separatists in Ukraine's east took up arms against the coup regime in Kiev that swiftly banned their language, criminalized their religion, and bestowed state honors upon the country's Nazi collaborators of dark decades past.

After eight years of failed diplomatic engagement with Ukraine and its transatlantic backers—a ruse that both former German chancellor

---

19   Luis Martinez, "US Special Operations Team Working out of Embassy in Ukraine: Sources," ABC, April 12, 2023.

20   "US VP Kamala Harris Mocked over Simplistic Answer on Russia's Invasion of Ukraine," Al Arabiya English, March 4, 2022.

Angela Merkel[21] and former French president François Hollande[22] have since acknowledged was designed solely to buy time for Kiev's combat preparations—Moscow formally entered Ukraine's civil conflict in February 2022 and sent a message to the West: your collective empire stops here. By then, the UN estimated at least 15,000 people had already perished on the Ukrainian battlefield.

Putin's red line in Ukraine was decades in the making. The era of transatlantic unipolar dominance ushered in by the Soviet Union's 1991 collapse left oozing scars that transcended the limits of Russia's own borders—from the NATO-ravaged battlegrounds of Yugoslavia, Afghanistan, Iraq, Libya, and Syria to the economically besieged territories of Iran, Venezuela, and beyond. Between its State Department-funded grassroots "democracy" initiatives and sheer military force, by 2022 Washington and its allies had marched all the way to Russia's doorstep. From there, where was left to go?

The economic defense Moscow crafted in the lead-up to 2022 was just as vital as its military preparation for the Ukraine front. As insulated ideologues in the Obama and Trump administrations ratcheted up Washington's dependence on unilateral sanctions as a form of hybrid war (chapter five), officials from Russia, China, India, Venezuela, Iran, South Africa, Turkey, and other developing nations quietly established a global financial network that shattered the foundation of US-led, transatlantic supremacy (chapter twelve). This is precisely why US and EU sanctions on Russia failed to achieve their desired effect throughout the Ukraine conflict, just as a nearly decade-long concerted economic war failed to dislodge Venezuela's elected government. The newfound strength and independence of these emerging powers means that US and European sanctions increasingly amount to a policy of economic warfare directed against their *own* domestic populations.

Take Washington's ban on Russian oil, for example. While wreaking havoc on the domestic US gas market, the policy failed to inflict significant damage on Moscow. In fact, Russia managed to recuperate

---

21   "Attempt to 'Give Ukraine Time': Merkel on Minsk Agreements," TASS, December 7, 2022.

22   "Hollande Confirms Merkel's Remark Minsk Agreements Let Kiev Build up Military Muscle," TASS, December 30, 2022.

oil earnings by August 2022,[23] offsetting the US embargo by selling its products to China and India, the first- and third-largest oil importers in the world. Inert when it comes to Beijing, Washington is similarly unable to block New Delhi's continued exchange with Moscow, a lesson demonstrated by Air India's continued refusal to join a boycott of Russian airspace in response to the Ukraine war. It seems the Indians (who command the world's fastest-growing economy) are not in the mood to endure Western dictates regarding their sovereign affairs, rendering the US and EU embargo of Moscow's oil sector practically moot. This reality mirrored Caracas's ability to combat the 2019 US embargo on Venezuelan oil by prioritizing trade partnerships with Beijing and New Delhi, as detailed in chapter five.

As established in chapter twelve, this unprecedented exchange between developing nations was facilitated by the Russian and Chinese-led effort to form alternatives to SWIFT, the West's premier international payment messaging network. Even as SWIFT complied with demands that it discontinue services to Russian entities, Western analysts were forced to consider whether the emergence of competing networks would soon close the chapter on "the golden age of US sanctions."[24] Yet even if the blunt force of SWIFT's weaponization waned, Washington's most lethal hold over the international financial system—the Petrodollar arrangement—remained intact. Or did it?

Though a delicate dance, ever since the 1974 Petrodollar agreement between the US and Saudi Arabia, Washington has depended on allies in Riyadh to play the international oil market according to its interests. As established in chapter one, for example, the global oil crash of 2014 began after US secretary of state John Kerry visited Riyadh and nudged the Saudis to increase petroleum production, flooding the international exchange and driving prices down as a result. While Iran was the primary target of this strategy, the market manipulation also inflicted pain on the governments of other oil-dependent, designated US-enemy countries including Russia, Venezuela, and Iraq.

---

23   Joe Wallace and Anna Hirtenstein, "Russia Confounds the West by Recapturing Its Oil Riches," *Wall Street Journal*, August 30, 2022.

24   Agathe Demaris, "The End of the Age of Sanctions?" *Foreign Affairs*, December 27, 2022.

Fast-forward eight years and witness US leadership prepare to implement a domestic oil embargo on Moscow—a policy that was guaranteed to increase domestic gas prices according to the basic laws of economy. While readying his ban on Russian crude in March 2022, Biden placed a phone call to Saudi prince Mohammed bin Salman that should have been routine for a US president. His message: Please, pump more oil. Yet Riyadh refused to answer the phone.

One can deduce the US president's response based on what we know happened next: "Well then, get the Emiratis on the line, damnit!"

Radio silence in Abu Dhabi, too. The *Wall Street Journal* later revealed that Prince Salman and UAE Sheikh Mohamed bin Zayed al Nahyan had deliberately shunned the US president, anticipating his request that they boost oil production in light of the Ukraine escalation.[25] Within months of the March 2022 snub, Saudi and other OPEC nations demonstrated their total disregard for US concerns over rising crude costs and moved to slash collective output, signaling further gas hikes on the horizon. Across the board, Western media characterized the OPEC cuts as a "surprise."[26] To those familiar with the revolution in modern international relations detailed throughout this book, however, Saudi's newfound independence was to be expected.

As we learned in chapter twelve, Washington's sanctions have prevented Iran and Venezuela—two oil producers—from accessing US dollars in recent years, forcing their respective governments to ditch the greenback while conducting international trade. In the meantime, the West's prolonged currency war inspired other powerful states including China, Turkey, and India to move away from dollar dependence, dump their US debt holdings, and begin trading in local currencies. The UAE even brokered a 2019 gold swap with Venezuela that it satisfied entirely in euros. Meanwhile, Russia initiated a domestic gold standard to mitigate effects of its 2022 economic confrontation with the West.

25   Dion Nissenbaum, Stephen Kalin, and David S. Cloud, "Saudi, Emirati Leaders Decline Calls with Biden during Ukraine Crisis," *Wall Street Journal*, March 8, 2022.

26   Maha Dahan and Ahmed Rasheed, "OPEC+ Announces Surprise Oil Output Cuts," Reuters, April 2, 2023.

It is important to understand that the global push to de-dollarize occurred alongside Russian, Chinese, and Iranian efforts to revive Venezuelan oil production. Having struggled against Western sanctions ever since its own revolution in 1979, Iran had decades to adapt its oil sector to the conditions of foreign-directed economic war. When the US placed Venezuela under a similar sanction regime in 2015, the government in Tehran came to Caracas's defense. Though Iranian interventions in Venezuela's oil sector have already delivered tangible results (chapter two and five), we have yet to experience the Tehran-Caracas partnership's long-term impact on the global crude market at the time of this book's publication. What happens when Iran-supplied technology and repairs enable Venezuela to revamp its sanctions-ravaged Paraguana oil refinery, the largest in the country? Or when Russian and Chinese financial support, which has replaced US-sourced foreign investment in recent years, gives way to a flourishing Venezuelan oil sector?

Considering US sanctions drastically curbed Caracas's production capacity in recent years, it is easy to forget that for most of the twentieth century, Venezuela consistently ranked as a leading, if not the top, international exporter of crude. As we learned in this book's introduction, the US and UK militaries quite literally fueled their fight in the Second World War with Venezuelan oil. Still home to the planet's largest crude reserves, there is no reason to doubt Venezuela's ability to reclaim its status as a premier oil producer in the near future.

A global oil exchange that includes healthy export sectors in Venezuela, Russia, and Iran while counting China and India among its greatest import markets will render the US-Saudi Petrodollar arrangement irrelevant. These countries will not trade in the dollar and, for the first time in history, wield more influence within OPEC than the US-Saudi bloc. Perhaps that is why the Kingdom has already indicated its break with Washington runs far deeper than a one-off decision to ignore a single phone call from the US president.

In December 2022, Riyadh entered a series of landmark investment deals with Beijing over the course of Chinese president Xi Jinping's three-day visit to the Saudi Kingdom. After greeting Xi with a grandiose exhibition that even Western media recognized as having historically been reserved for US state visits, Saudi officials proceeded to sign over thirty agreements with China's government. Valued at over $50 billion, the investment package spanned a variety of Saudi industries including its finance, energy, housing, health, and technology sectors.[27]

In a joint declaration issued upon the summit's conclusion, Saudi Arabia and China "reaffirmed that they will continue to firmly support each other's core interests, support each other in maintaining their sovereignty and territorial integrity, and exert joint efforts to defend the principle of non-interference in the internal affairs of states."

Within months of Xi's visit to the Saudi Kingdom, Riyadh moved to join the Shanghai Cooperation Organization, a Chinese-led initiative to integrate Eurasian coordination on regional development and security. Saudi Arabia also reestablished diplomatic ties with Syria,[28] whose government Riyadh previously sought to overthrow via a multibillion dollar, US-backed dirty war; and Iran, a neighboring oil producer historically considered the Wahhabi Kingdom's arch ideological nemesis.[29] Like Riyadh, Tehran entered a series of long-term investment deals with China (totaling an estimated $400 billion) in the months leading up to the diplomatic breakthrough.[30]

The Chinese-brokered Middle East détente spelled disaster for Washington's only genuine ally in the region. Since its UN-mandated inception, Israel's survival as a European settler-colonial, and now openly apartheid, state has depended on the West's ability to foment sectarian divisions between Tel Aviv's Muslim neighbors. Israel's decades-long subjugation of non-Jewish civilians and continued occupation of territories belonging to Syria and an imagined "Palestinian Authority" was only possible thanks to a parochial local order established by the

27   Fahad Abuljadayel and Abeer Abu Omar, "Saudi Arabia Says $50 Billion Investments Agreed With China," *Bloomberg*, December 11, 2022.

28   Eyad Kourdi and Hande Atay Alam, "Saudi Arabia and Syria to Resume Diplomatic Missions after Decade-Long Freeze: State Media," CNN, May 10, 2023.

29   Patrick Wintour, "Iran and Saudi Arabia Agree to Restore Ties after China-Brokered Talks," *Guardian*, March 10, 2023.

30   Farnaz Fassihi and Steven Lee Myers, "China, With $400 Billion Iran Deal, Could Deepen Influence in Mideast," *New York Times*, March 27, 2021.

ever-fading transatlantic empire (and US taxpayer–supplied weapons worth untold billions). As regional powers realign according to the nascent multipolar world, the fragile, US-brokered "normalization" agreement established between Israel and its Arab neighbors in 2020 looks trivial. Is it possible that the superficial unity projected by Jared Kushner's regional business partners provided an inadequate foundation for lasting Middle East peace?[31]

As China offered developing countries, including our own allies, the chance to fortify their national economies, US leadership not only doubled down on foreign aggressions, but animated their domestic political scene with sights beyond parody. Following years of media hysteria casting Donald Trump as an agent of Moscow, the FBI's multimillion-dollar investigation into his ties to Russia finally scored its first legal indictment in March 2023. The alleged crime? A misdemeanor bookkeeping charge stemming from his personal lawyer's payment of a legal settlement to a porn star who threatened to go public with claims that she and Trump had an affair.[32]

As the Uniparty establishment in the US salivated over the prospect of Trump's arrest, they entrenched their position as an international laughingstock. To a world still reeling from the carnage of US-directed crimes like the Wars on Iraq, the fact that the first criminal prosecution of a former president to occur in US history concerned legal settlements delivered to an adult film star was comical. It also exposed the fallacies of American exceptionalism upon which Washington based its entire approach to world affairs.

"Just imagine if this happened in any other country, where a government arrested the main opposition candidate," Salvadoran president Nayyib Bukele tweeted following Trump's April 4 arraignment. "The United States ability to use 'democracy' as foreign policy is gone."[33]

---

31   Stephen Kalin, "Jared Kushner's New Fund Looks to Profit from His Middle East Diplomacy," *Wall Street Journal*, February 25, 2022.

32   Brooke Singman, "Trump Targeted: A Look at Probes Involving the Former President; from Stormy Daniels to Russia to Mar-a-Lago," Fox News, March 31, 2023.

33   Nayib Bukele (@nayibbukele), Twitter post, April 4, 2023, https://twitter.com/nayibbukele/status/1643334584082345986?s=20.

Considering the instability wrought by Washington's conduct abroad alongside its increasingly palpable political crisis in the home front, it is easy to see why our friends have pursued communion with rising alternative powers. In fact, the greatest mystery of modern international relations may be why Europe, which is slated for years of popular strife aroused by attacks on its energy sector, remains wedded to transatlanticism despite demonstrative adverse effects. Is the continued subsidization of their national militaries at the expense of the US taxpayer truly worth sacrificing the continent's future independence? How would Charles de Gaulle, Helmut Schmidt, or Margaret Thatcher regard their successors among Europe's contemporary political leadership, as their populations freeze to sustain a war over immaterial concepts? Western democracy and freedom, indeed.

Regardless, Europe cannot insulate itself, nor Washington, from changes ahead. While adjusting to the pushes and pulls of the emerging multipolar order, the most arduous challenge US businesses, officials, and, most importantly, citizens will face is how to manage the inevitable death of the Petrodollar. Amid his government's realignment with its eastern neighbors, Saudi economy minister Mohammed Al-Jadaan made a stunning declaration to US media.

"There are no issues with discussing how we settle our trade arrangements," Al-Jadaan informed *Bloomberg TV* during the annual Davos summit of global financial elites in January 2023.[34]

"Whether it is in the US dollar, whether it is the euro, whether it is the Saudi riyal," Al-Jadaan continued. "I don't think we are waving away or ruling out any discussion that will help improve trade around the world."

The dollar's link to gold bullion was severed decades ago. Without the backing of liquid gold, what is the foundation of its worth?

The John Boltons and Elliot Abramses of the world, perhaps due to psychological defects not even they fully understand, will respond to the arrival of a multipolar international order with unrestrained agony. The

34   Abeer Abu Omar and Manus Cranny, "Saudi Arabia Says Open to Settling Trade in Other Currencies (2)," *Bloomberg Law*, January 17, 2023.

neoliberal inheritors of their disordered world view—including Biden officials Jake Sullivan, Anthony Blinken, and Victoria Nuland—may even spark direct military conflict with Russia, a rival nuclear power, to preserve an evanescent unipolar order that has failed to benefit anyone other than an increasingly belligerent and borderless transatlantic elite. The representatives of Venezuela's vanquished coup regime cast their lot with this decaying force, laughing all the way to the bank.

If our leaders can resist mutually assured nuclear destruction, however, the US public will reflect on this paradigm shift with a collective sigh of relief. The time for Washington to break from its transatlantic obsession and accept its status as a great world pole—not dominant over others, but equal to them—has arrived. Like all dramatic break-ups, this period provides an opportunity for internal reflection. What could the US achieve if it stopped leeching off its public to sustain an infinite web of foreign military bases, aid-dependent outposts like Israel and Ukraine, State Department-backed regime change fronts like USAID, and rogue intelligence agencies? What if we accepted that NATO—and transatlanticism itself—is indeed obsolete? What if we stopped seeing enemies in every direction and pursued diplomatic engagement based on mutual respect and pragmatic dealmaking? What if the United States were to apply Alaska's policy of distributing funds raised off state oil reserves directly to its citizens at the national level? What if the US public were allowed to prosper from their country's vast natural wealth themselves, rather than lose their sons and daughters to wars waged by the very transnational elite exploiting the soil beneath their feet?

Unless US citizens consider these questions, that elite will continue to sacrifice the conditions of our republic on the altar of their global empire. A true "America First" foreign policy, if it entails an audit of the Pentagon, State Department, intelligence networks, and US government money-laundering fronts like USAID, offers Washington its only path forward amid the current global realignment—other than nuclear holocaust. Perhaps by drawing down our international presence and refocusing on the home front, we can mount a position within the multipolar order that is more comfortable and attractive than our imperial status ever was. As long as international financial interests and disgruntled expat communities in key battleground states dictate US foreign policy, however, there can be no "America First."

In our own hemisphere, we should recognize that the radical Florida Cubans and Venezuelans agitating for Washington's aggressive regional posture are never going to reclaim power in their homelands—and they should accept that, too. It is unwise to craft foreign policy based on short-term domestic political calculations and the impulses of a vengeful Latin American expat class. This is especially the case with Venezuela, which has treated us as a kindred nation ever since their anti-colonial liberator, Francisco de Miranda, commanded troops to assist our own revolutionary war against an empire on the other side of the Atlantic. Continuing to alienate a Caracas government that has stood the test of time will only make the US weaker, particularly as the emergent multipolar order bestows power upon Venezuela that it has never truly enjoyed as a sovereign state.

The United States is a rich nation. Unlike the European empires that spawned our own (and survive today by leeching US tax dollars via NATO), we will be able to sustain ourselves long after surrendering our quest for total world domination. Much of what we seek abroad can be found between sea and shining sea—and if we behaved like a respectable country, our friends would happily cut mutually beneficial deals to supply the rest.

The future international landscape will not tolerate phony ideological posturing and zero-sum power plays between states. It leaves no space for interventionist zealots such as Mike Pompeo, Antony Blinken, or Hillary Clinton at the helm of US foreign policy. Their Project for a New American Century was dead upon arrival: despite the new century, it offered nothing more than the same, worn-out imperial America. The inexorable transformation taking place in our world today should not be viewed as an attack on our nation, however, but an opportunity to reorient ourselves as a self-contained, willing participant in a world governed by the basic principles of sovereignty, self-determination, and territorial integrity. Would that really be so awful?

The people I've met in Seoul, Damascus, the Gaza Strip, Caracas, and beyond do not hold the US public responsible for the crimes of their ruling elite. In fact, the wisest among them understand the US citizen is, in many ways, the original victim of Washington's imperial sin. If there's one thing I know for certain, it is that no one can resist the genuine charm of a genuinely decent American. If we put our best face forward and conduct our affairs in good faith, the world will not turn its back to us.

On a Monday in March 2023, I got to work on this book's citations while sipping coffee at La Famosa, the Puerto Rican café bordering Washington's Navy Yard where I wrote much of the preceding manuscript. Amid the mid-morning lunch rush, a fellow patron leaned over my shoulder to ask what I was typing so ferociously. He then inquired about the book's subject and title.

"Why is it called *Corporate Coup*?"

I had answered that question many times before, explaining that my reporting on US-Venezuela policy exposed Washington's main collaborators in the country as agents of a transnational corporate elite. This time, however, the title's true significance revealed itself to me.

"I suppose you could say the *Corporate Coup* refers to something that took place within our own government long ago," I suddenly realized aloud.

The man, who worked as an analyst at the Navy Yard, wholeheartedly concurred. I wager that most US citizens would agree, too.

ACKNOWLEDGEMENTS

To my parents, siblings, and extended family—your love and support gave me the confidence to approach the world with an open mind and heart. Thank you for teaching me to believe not only in myself, but all people who stand for truth and justice regardless of national or perceived political boundary. Max and T—you are my foundation; I can only thank God for the blessing that is our life and family. Diego and my extended Venezuelan family—thank you for graciously welcoming me to your country and trusting me to enter a world beyond the conventional media feedback loop. I look forward to the day when my own country respects our shared continent as its immediate neighborhood, rife with a rebel American spirit that has yet to realize its full potential. Francisco—thank you for patiently enduring my ceaseless barrage of questions and for being the university professor I never had. I forever admire your integrity and objectivity.

I also want to acknowledge the sources—named and unnamed—who guided my reporting; friends who thoughtfully reviewed drafts (especially you, Naila); and media colleagues (particularly the team at *Venezuelanalysis*) whom I cite throughout this book.

To the staff at La Famosa, Yellow, and everywhere else I set up shop while writing this book—thank you for always putting up with the crazy woman pounding away on her laptop, you made the day to day stress bearable. To Colin and the OR team—thank you for taking a chance on me and being patient while I completed this "50,000-word book." Finally, to all who have supported the *Grayzone* over the years, particularly Len, Roger, Reza, Fritzi and the Tabard family—thank you for making it possible for me to do what I love with true independence. Onward and upward!

BIBLIOGRAPHY

"180° Keys of the Truth | Chapter IX: Bismarck Martínez - Abduction, Torture and Murder." *JP+*, July 8, 2019. https://www.youtube.com/watch?v=qpqot_IzV30.

"1991: Nelson Mandela Visitó a Venezuela." *Con El Mazo Dando*, July 22, 2021. https://mazo4f.com/1991-nelson-mandela-visito-a-venezuela.

"7 Feb 2010 Hugo Chávez En Aló Presidente N° 351." andresoasis. YouTube, December 22, 2012. https://www.youtube.com/watch?v=7PwRClYjr2M&t=8315s.

About the Growth Lab. "About the Growth Lab." Accessed March 21, 2023. https://growthlab.cid.harvard.edu/about.

Abuljadayel, Fahad, and Abeer Abu Omar. "Saudi Arabia Says $50 Billion Investments Agreed With China." *Bloomberg*, December 11, 2022. https://www.bloomberg.com/news/articles/2022-12-11/saudi-arabia-says-50-billion-investments-agreed-at-china-summit.

Achtenberg, Emily. "Bolivia: USAID out, Morales in for Re-Election Bid." NACLA, May 11, 2013. https://nacla.org/blog/2013/5/11/bolivia-usaid-out-morales-re-election-bid.

Adams, David C. "Legal Battle over Venezuela' s Looted Billions Heats Up." Univision, June 12, 2020. https://www.univision.com/univision-news/latin-america/legal-battle-over-venezuelas-looted-billions-heats-up.

Adenekan, Samson. "Ex-INTERPOL Director Faults Arrest of Venezuelan Diplomat in Cape Verde." *Premium Times*, January 30, 2021. https://www.premiumtimesng.com/news/more-news/439608-ex-interpol-director-faults-arrest-of-venezuelan-diplomat-in-cape-verde.html?tztc=1.

AFP. "Venezuela Slams US over 'Vulgar' Central Bank Funds Seizure." *Barron's*, April 17, 2020. https://www.barrons.com/news/venezuela-slams-us-over-vulgar-central-bank-funds-seizure-01587160807.

Agee, Philip. "Use of a Private U.S. Corporate Structure to Disguise a Government Program." *Venezuelanalysis*, September 8, 2005. https://venezuelanalysis.com/analysis/1350.

Alexandra, Zoe. "Hondurans Intensify Protests, Demand Resignation of President." *Peoples Dispatch*, June 20, 2019. https://peoplesdispatch.org/2019/06/20/hondurans-intensify-protests-demand-resignation-of-president/.

Almagro, Luis (@Almagro_OEA2015). Twitter post, June 14, 2019. https://twitter.com/Almagro_OEA2015/status/1139658418573234179?s=20.

Almagro, Luis (@Almagro_OEA2015). Twitter post [PHOTO], December 11, 2019. https://twitter.com/Almagro_OEA2015/status/1204872145660239872.

Almagro, Luis (@Almagro_OEA2015). Twitter post, October 12, 2021. https://twitter.com/Almagro_OEA2015/status/1447956560945221642?s=20.

"Aló Embajador, 25 De Febrero De 2021." US Embassy Venezuela, February 25, 2021. https://www.youtube.com/watch?v=0g9YzN8ulBk.

"Ambassador Bolton Remarks to the Bay of Pigs Veterans Association – Brigade 2506." United States Embassy in Cuba, April 17, 2019. https://cu.usembassy.gov/ambassador-bolton-bay-of-pigs-veterans-association-brigade-2506/.

"Ambassador James 'Jimmy' Story." U.S. Embassy in Venezuela, April 15, 2021. https://ve.usembassy.gov/ambassador-james-jimmy-story/.

America Reports. "Trump: A New Day Is Coming in Venezuela and Latin America." Fox News, February 18, 2019. https://www.foxnews.com/video/6003599082001?ts=%7Bseek_to_second_number%7D.

"Ana Julia Jatar Presenta 'Las Notas De Mi Vida.'" *Analítica*, February 26, 2010. https://www.analitica.com/entretenimiento/ana-julia-jatar-presenta-las-notas-de-mi-vida/.

Anderson, Jon Lee. "Is the President of Honduras a Narco-Trafficker?" *New Yorker*, November 8, 2021. https://www.newyorker.com/magazine/2021/11/15/is-the-president-of-honduras-a-narco-trafficker.

"Áñez Acude Al Fmi Por Crédito De $US 320 Mm y Al BM Para Financiar Bonos." *La Razón*, April 16, 2020. https://www.la-razon.com/economia/2020/04/16/anez-acude-al-fmi-por-credito-de-us-320-mm-y-al-bm-para-financiar-bonos/?fbclid=IwAR1eN1xPn_ymk9HthjQZKDXDlrMXqUAw1RjzBxMCI6d-8PjcmYD7uZD9Hngw.

Angelini, Giorgio. "Comment RE: What My Fellow Liberals Don't Get about Venezuela." *New York Times*, April 1, 2019. https://www.nytimes.com/2019/04/01/opinion/contributors/venezuela-us-hands-off-joanna-hausmann.html#permid=31333315.

AP, Special to the *New York Times*. "Abrams Denies Wrongdoing In Shipping Arms to Contras." *New York Times*, August 17, 1987. https://www.nytimes.com/1987/08/17/world/abrams-denies-wrongdoing-in-shipping-arms-to-contras.html.

Appellee Crystallex International Corp. "Electronic Supplemental Brief 003113208533 in 18-2797." PacerMonitor, April 10, 2019. https://www.

pacermonitor.com/case/25369289/Crystallex_International_Corp_v_
Bolivarian_Republic_of_Venezue?period=all&order=.

Armando.info (@ArmandoInfo). "Dos Apoderados Manejan a Group Gran
Limited En México. Uno De Ellos Sería Hijo De Álvaro Pulido Vargas."
Twitter post, September 3, 2017. https://twitter.com/ArmandoInfo/
status/916800313377427457?s=20.

Armas, Mayela, and Corina Pons. "Citigroup to Sell Venezuelan Gold in Setback
to President Maduro: Sources." Reuters, March 20, 2019. https://www.reuters.
com/article/us-venezuela-politics-gold-idUSKCN1R12GR.

Armas, Mayela, and Deisy Buitrago. "Venezuelan Government
Suspends Negotiations with Opposition." Reuters, October
17, 2021. https://www.reuters.com/world/americas/
maduro-envoy-alex-saab-extradited-us-cape-verde-radio-2021-10-16/.

Armas, Mayela. "Venezuela Opposition Removes Interim President Guaido."
Reuters, December 30, 2022. https://www.reuters.com/world/americas/
venezuela-opposition-removes-interim-president-guaido-2022-12-31/.

Armas, Mayela. "Exclusive: Venezuela Seeks to Repatriate $550 Million of Gold
from Britain - Sources." Reuters, November 5, 2018. https://www.reuters.com/
article/us-venezuela-gold-exclusive-idUSKCN1NA1Q7.

Arreaza, Jorge (@jaarreaza.ve). Instagram post, September 27, 2019. https://www.
instagram.com/p/B27t4YtgBus/?igshid=MDJmNzVkMjY%3D.

Arreaza, Jorge (@jaarreaza). Twitter post, April 4, 2019. https://twitter.com/
jaarreaza/status/1113831506781384704?s=20.

Arreaza, Jorge (@jaarreaza). Twitter post, April 17, 2020. https://twitter.com/
jaarreaza/status/1251183730510659586.

Arreaza, Jorge (@jaarreaza). Twitter post, March 12, 2019. https://twitter.com/
jaarreaza/status/1105454380248154114?s=20.

Associated Press. "Venezuela Crushes Army Coup Attempt." New York Times,
February 5, 1992. https://www.nytimes.com/1992/02/05/world/venezuela-
crushes-army-coup-attempt.html.

Associated Press. "At UN, Venezuela's Rival Delegations Circle Each Other."
Voice of America, September 26, 2019. https://www.voanews.com/a/usa_un-
venezuelas-rival-delegations-circle-each-other/6176551.html.

Associated Press. "Bolivians Back Morales in Recall Vote." NBC, August 10, 2008.
https://www.nbcnews.com/id/wbna26127208.

Associated Press. "Honduras President Seeks 2nd Term despite Constitutional
Ban." Fox News, November, 23, 2017. https://www.foxnews.com/world/
honduras-president-seeks-2nd-term-despite-constitutional-ban.

Avendaño, Orlando. "Enviados De Guaidó Se Apropian De Fondos Para Ayuda
Humanitaria En Colombia." PanAm Post, June 14, 2019. https://es.panampost.

com/orlando-avendano/2019/06/14/enviados-de-guaido-se-apropian-de-fondos-para-ayuda-humanitaria-en-colombia/?cn-reloaded=1.

"Backfire: The Global Ripple Effects of U.S. Sanctions." Carnegie Endowment, February 28, 2023. https://www.youtube.com/watch?v=KLdssfNrBbg.

Bahar, Dany, and Douglas Barrios. "How Many More Migrants and Refugees Can We Expect out of Venezuela?" Brookings, December 10, 2018. https://www.brookings.edu/blog/up-front/2018/12/10/how-many-more-migrants-and-refugees-can-we-expect-out-of-venezuela/.

Baker, Peter, Maggie Haberman, and Thomas Gibbons-Neff. "Urged to Launch an Attack, Trump Listened to the Skeptics Who Said It Would Be a Costly Mistake." *New York Times*, June 21, 2019. www.nytimes.com/2019/06/21/us/politics/trump-iran-strike.html.

Balci, Baris, and Selcan Hacaoglu. "Turkey Seeks to Be First NATO Member to Join China-Led SCO." *Bloomberg*, September 17, 2022. https://www.bloomberg.com/news/articles/2022-09-17/turkey-seeks-china-led-bloc-membership-in-threat-to-nato-allies.

Barráez, Sebastiana. "El Inexplicable Origen Del Poder y El Dinero Del Capitán Sequea, El Hombre Que Comandó La Operación Gedeón." *Infobae*, June 8, 2020. https://www.infobae.com/america/venezuela/2020/06/08/el-inexplicable-origen-del-poder-y-el-dinero-del-capitan-sequea-el-hombre-que-comando-la-operacion-gedeon/.

Barráez, Sebastiana. "Grupos Delictivos Reclutan En Cúcuta a Militares Venezolanos Desertores: 'Lo Que Esconde La Oferta Final Es La Muerte.'" *Infobae*, April 18, 2019. https://www.infobae.com/america/venezuela/2019/04/18/grupos-delictivos-reclutan-en-cucuta-a-militares-venezolanos-desertores-lo-que-esconde-la-oferta-final-es-la-muerte/.

Barry, Tom. "The New Politics of Political Aid in Venezuela." Militarist Monitor, July 17, 2007. https://militarist-monitor.org/the_new_politics_of_political_aid_in_venezuela/.

Bartenstein, Ben. "Adviser to Venezuela Guaido Has Harsh Message for Bondholders." *Bloomberg*, January 30, 2019. https://www.bloomberg.com/news/articles/2019-01-30/harvard-guru-advising-guaido-has-harsh-message-for-bondholders?leadSource=uverify+wall.

Bastidas, Gabriel (@Gbastidas). Twitter post, March 26, 2020. https://twitter.com/Gbastidas/status/1243855852077015041?s=20.

Beeton, Dan. "The Venezuela Coup, 20 Years Later." Center for Economic and Policy Research, April 12, 2022. https://cepr.net/the-venezuela-coup-20-years-later/.

Beller, Nadia (@nadia_beller). Twitter post [PHOTO], October 14, 2020. https://twitter.com/nadia_beller/status/1316441590664253440?s=20.

Benjamin, Medea (@medeabenjamin). Twitter post, May 20, 2019.
https://twitter.com/medeabenjamin/status/1108344878700904449.

Bertrand, Arnaud. "Is America the Real Victim of Anti-Russia Sanctions?" *Tablet Magazine*, May 25, 2022. https://www.tabletmag.com/sections/news/articles/is-america-the-real-victim-of-anti-russia-sanctions.

Besheer, Margaret. "US Vice President Urges UN to Recognize Venezuela's Guaido." Voice of America, April 10, 2019. https://www.voanews.com/a/us-vice-president-mike-pence-urges-un-to-recognize-venezuela-juan-guaido/4870087.html.

Berwick, Angus, Luis Jaime Acosta, and Sarah Kinosian. "Alleged Maduro Accomplice Surrenders to U.S. Agents, Will Help Prosecution: Sources." Reuters, March 27, 2020. https://www.reuters.com/article/us-usa-venezuela-dea-exclusive-idUSKBN21E3IQ.

Bielik, Stefan. "The Great Virgin Train Robbery." *Tribune*, April 19, 2020. https://tribunemag.co.uk/2020/04/the-great-virgin-train-robbery.

Blumenthal, Max, and Anya Parampil. "US Congress and Corporate Media Deploy Massive Lie, Claiming Venezuela's Gov't Threatened to Starve Non-Voters." *The Grayzone*, December 6, 2020. https://thegrayzone.com/2020/12/06/congress-corporate-media-venezuelas-government-food-voters/.

Blumenthal, Max. "Bolivia Coup Led by Christian Fascist Paramilitary Leader and Millionaire – with Foreign Support." *The Grayzone*, November 11, 2019. https://thegrayzone.com/2019/11/11/bolivia-coup-fascist-foreign-support-fernando-camacho/.

Blumenthal, Max. "Burning Aid: An Interventionist Deception on Colombia-Venezuela Bridge?" *The Grayzone*, February 24, 2019. https://thegrayzone.com/2019/02/24/burning-aid-colombia-venezuela-bridge/.

Blumenthal, Max. "Following Grayzone Exposé, Top Venezuelan Coup Official Ricardo Hausmann Is Forced to Resign." *The Grayzone*, September 27, 2019. https://thegrayzone.com/2019/09/27/following-grayzone-expose-top-venezuelan-coup-official-ricardo-hausmann-is-forced-to-resign/.

Blumenthal, Max. "How Bolivia's New Socialist Senator Resisted Coup Terror: Meet MAS Party Leader Patricia Arce." *The Grayzone*, October 25, 2020. https://thegrayzone.com/2020/10/25/bolivia-coup-interview-patricia-arce/.

Blumenthal, Max. "How US Govt-Funded Media Fueled a Violent Coup in Nicaragua." *The Grayzone*, June 12, 2021. https://thegrayzone.com/2021/06/12/coup-nicaragua-cpj-100-noticias/.

Blumenthal, Max. "How Washington and Soft Power NGOs Manipulated Nicaragua's Death Toll to Drive Regime Change and Sanctions." *The Grayzone*, July 30, 2018. https://thegrayzone.com/2018/07/30/

how-washington-and-soft-power-ngos-manipulated-nicaraguas-death-toll-to-drive-regime-change-and-sanctions/.

Blumenthal, Max. "'John Bolton Tried to Assassinate Me': Interview with Venezuelan President Nicolás Maduro." *The Grayzone*, August 6, 2019. https://thegrayzone.com/2019/08/06/interview-venezuelan-president-nicolas-maduro/.

Blumenthal, Max. "The Making of Juan Guaidó: How the US Regime Change Laboratory Created Venezuela's Coup Leader." *The Grayzone*, January 29, 2019. https://thegrayzone.com/2019/01/29/the-making-of-juan-guaido-how-the-us-regime-change-laboratory-created-venezuelas-coup-leader/.

Blumenthal, Max. "The Real Humanitarian Aid: Inside Venezuela's State-Subsidized Communal Markets." *The Grayzone*, February 24, 2019. https://www.youtube.com/watch?v=qlX3yfXNX_g&t=18s.

Blumenthal, Max (@MaxBlumenthal). Twitter post, February 26, 2019. https://twitter.com/MaxBlumenthal/status/1100485398353113088?s=20&t=qSsRoFN_WY3JoPgOT7cJ9w.

Blumenthal, Max (@MaxBlumenthal). Twitter post [PHOTO], July 22, 2018. https://twitter.com/MaxBlumenthal/status/1020930881656061952?s=20.

Blumenthal, Max (@MaxBlumenthal). Twitter post [VIDEO], October 17, 2020. https://twitter.com/MaxBlumenthal/status/1317616982641049600?s=20.

Blumenthal, Max (@MaxBlumenthal). Twitter post [VIDEO], October 19, 2020. https://twitter.com/MaxBlumenthal/status/1318043809998131201?s=20.

Blumenthal, Max (@MaxBlumenthal). Twitter post, May 12, 2019. https://twitter.com/MaxBlumenthal/status/1127658105045753858?s=20.

Blumenthal, Max. "US Military Attack on Venezuela Mulled by Top Trump Advisors and Latin American Officials at Private DC Meeting." *The Grayzone*, April 13, 2019. https://thegrayzone.com/2019/04/13/us-military-attack-venezuela-trump-csis-invasion/.

Blumenthal, Max. "US Regime-Change Blueprint Proposed Venezuelan Electricity Blackouts as 'Watershed Event' for 'Galvanizing Public Unrest.'" *The Grayzone*, March 11, 2019. https://thegrayzone.com/2019/03/11/us-regime-change-blueprint-proposed-venezuelan-electricity-blackouts-as-watershed-event-for-galvanizing-public-unrest/.

Blumenthal, Max. "Venezuela's Opposition Pleads for US Intervention - Max Blumenthal Reports from Caracas March." *The Grayzone*, February 15, 2019. https://www.youtube.com/watch?v=vI8_JoGzwjk.

"BOLIVIA FORECAST: LEADING UP TO MAY 4." Cablegate, WikiLeaks. March 28, 2018. https://web.archive.org/web/20191112072339/http://wl.1-s.es/cable/2008/03/08LAPAZ693.html.

"Bolivia: Pursuing Sustainable Lithium Mining: Development Dispatch." Center for Strategic and International Studies. Accessed April

13, 2023. https://www.csis.org/blogs/development-dispatches/
bolivia-pursuing-sustainable-lithium-mining.

"Bolivian Army Chief Urges Morales to Step Down." BBC, November 10, 2019.
https://www.bbc.com/news/world-latin-america-50369591.

Bolton, John. "Beyond the Axis of Evil: Additional Threats from
Weapons of Mass Destruction." The Heritage Foundation,
May 6, 2002. https://www.heritage.org/defense/report/
beyond-the-axis-evil-additional-threats-weapons-mass-destruction-0.

Bolton, John. *The Room Where It Happened*. New York, NY: Simon & Schuster, 2020.

Bolton, John (@AmbJohnBolton). Twitter post, April 30, 2019. https://twitter.com/
AmbJohnBolton/status/1123298012145516545?s=20.

Bolton, John (@AmbJohnBolton). Twitter post, February 2, 2019. https://twitter.
com/AmbJohnBolton/status/1091769750068305921?s=20.

Boothroyd Rojas, Rachel, and Ryan Mallett-Outtrim. "Has Maduro Really Dissolved
the National Assembly in Venezuela?" *Venezuelanalysis*, March 31, 2017. https://
venezuelanalysis.com/analysis/13018.

Boothroyd-Rojas, Rachel. "Guarimba Victims Pursue New Charges Against
Leopoldo Lopez as Opposition Marches." *Venezuelanlysis*, February 20, 2017.
https://venezuelanalysis.com/news/12939.

Boothroyd Rojas, Rachel. "Venezuelan Opposition Abandons Talks in Dominican
Republic, Dismisses Deal with Gov't." *Venezuelanalysis*, February 8, 2018.
https://venezuelanalysis.com/news/13647.

Boothroyd Rojas, Rachael. "Venezuelan Supreme Court: 'National Assembly
Is Void.'" *Venezuelanalysis*, January 12, 2016. https://venezuelanalysis.com/
news/11813.

Borger, Julian. "Donald Trump Confirms US Withdrawal from INF Nuclear
Treaty." *Guardian*, February 1, 2019. https://www.theguardian.com/world/2019/
feb/01/inf-donald-trump-confirms-us-withdrawal-nuclear-treaty.

Borger, Julian. "US Diplomat Convicted over Iran-Contra Appointed Special Envoy
for Venezuela." *Guardian*, January 26, 2019. https://www.theguardian.com/
us-news/2019/jan/26/elliott-abrams-venezuela-us-special-envoy.

Borges, Anelise. "Maduro Declares Challenge to His Leadership 'over' as He Attacks
EU." Euronews, March 13, 2019. https://www.euronews.com/2019/02/13/
maduro-declares-challenge-to-his-leadership-over-as-he-attacks-eu.

Bowden, John. "Protesters Arrested Outside Venezuelan Embassy in DC." *The Hill*,
May 3, 2019. https://thehill.com/policy/international/441952-three-protesters-
arrested-outside-venezuelan-embassy-in-dc/.

Bowman, Charles H. "The Activities of Manuel Torres as Purchasing Agent,
1820-1821." *Hispanic American Historical Review*. Duke University Press,

May 1, 1968. https://read.dukeupress.edu/hahr/article/48/2/234/157707/
The-Activities-of-Manuel-Torres-As-Purchasing.

Bowman, Michael. "US Lawmakers Warn Maduro Loyalists in Venezuela." Voice
of America, March 7, 2019. https://www.voanews.com/a/us-lawmakers-warn-
maduro-loyalists-in-venezuela/4817812.html.

Bracci Roa, Luigino. "Discurso Completo De Nicolás Maduro Ante Gran Marcha
Este 23 Febrero 2019." February 23, 2019. https://www.youtube.com/
watch?v=_qfKWW5DWYA&t=441s.

Bracci Roa, Luigino. "Vicepresidenta Delcy Rodríguez Sobre Embargo De
Citgo, 1 Octubre 2019." October 1, 2019. https://www.youtube.com/
watch?v=BvRKn8K0sfY.

Branson, Richard (@richardbranson). Twitter post, February 25, 2019. https://twit-
ter.com/richardbranson/status/1096401760476909568?s=20.

"Bringing Venezuela's Economic Crisis Into Focus." Stratfor,
August 27, 2015. https://worldview.stratfor.com/article/
bringing-venezuelas-economic-crisis-focus.

Brodzinsky, Sibylla. "Venezuela President Maduro Announces
Diplomatic Sanctions against US." *Guardian*, March 1,
2015. https://www.theguardian.com/world/2015/feb/28/
venezuela-president-nicolas-maduro-diplomatic-sanctions-us.

Buitrago, Deisy. "Venezuela Opposition Leader Urges Britain Not to Give Gold
to Maduro." Reuters, January 27, 2019. https://www.reuters.com/article/us-
venezuela-gold/venezuela-opposition-leader-urges-britain-not-to-give-gold-to-
maduro-idUSKCN1PM02F.

BullionStar. "British Requests for $3 Billion in US Treasury Gold – the Trigger That
Closed the Gold Window." August 16, 2021. https://www.bullionstar.us/blogs/
ronan-manly/british-requests-for-3-billion-in-us-treasury-gold-the-trigger-that-
closed-the-gold-window/.

BullionStar Singapore. "The Saga Continues: Venezuela's 31 Tonnes of Seized Gold
at the Bank of England." July 28, 2021. https://www.bullionstar.com/blogs/
ronan-manly/the-saga-continues-venezuelas-31-tonnes-of-seized-gold-at-the-
bank-of-england/.

"The Burden of Bretton Woods." Richard Nixon Foundation, February 26, 2016.
https://www.nixonfoundation.org/2016/02/the-burden-of-bretton-woods.

Bukele, Nayib (@nayibbukele). Twitter post, April 4, 2023. https://twitter.com/
nayibbukele/status/1643334584082345986?s=20.

Bump, Philip. "The Complicated Question of Ending Imports of Russian
Oil." *Washington Post*, March 8, 2022. https://www.washingtonpost.com/
politics/2022/03/04/complicated-question-ending-imports-russian-oil/.

Caballero Carrizos, Esteban. *Venezuela*. International Foundation for Electoral
Systems, 1993. Google Books. shorturl.at/kwz19.

Cabello, Diosdado (@dcabellor). Twitter post, May 3, 2020. https://twitter.com/
dcabellor/status/1256996901532073990?s=20.

"Camacho Reconoce Que Coordinó Las Protestas Con Policía y Ejército Para Forzar
La Salida De Evo Morales." *Europa Press*, December 19, 2019. https://www.euro-
papress.es/internacional/noticia-camacho-reconoce-coordino-protestas-policia-
ejercito-forzar-salida-evo-morales-20191229214636.html.

"Can the Rio Treaty Help Venezuela?" The Center for Strategic and
International Studies, January 21, 2020. https://www.csis.org/events/
can-rio-treaty-help-venezuela.

Cano, Regina Garcia. "Russian Foreign Minister Visits Venezuela, Offers
Support." The Associated Press, April 19, 2023. https://apnews.com/article/
venezuela-russia-lavrov-latin-america-c6c863514c9588bd6dadb4462aab538e.

Carasik, Lauren. "Opinion: Obama Continues Bush's Policies in Venezuela." Al
Jazeera America, April 8, 2014. http://america.aljazeera.com/opinions/2014/4/
nicolas-maduro-onobamaandbushspoliciesinvenezuela.html.

Cardona, Roberto. "As It Happens: Venezuela Live Aid Kicks Off
Amid Calls For Liberty, Richard Branson Comments." *Billboard*,
February 22, 2019. https://www.billboard.com/music/latin/
venezuela-live-aid-kicks-off-calls-liberty-richard-branson-interview-8499597/.

Carlson, Chris. "Capriles Falsifies Evidence in Order to Claim Fraud in Venezuela's
Elections." *Venezuelanalysis*, April 17, 2013. https://venezuelanalysis.com/
news/8665.

Carlson, Chris. "Maduro Wins Venezuelan Presidential Election with 50.66 Percent
of the Vote [Updated]." *Venezuelanalysis*, April 15, 2013. https://venezuelanalysis.
com/news/8626.

Carlson, Tucker. "The League Of Extraordinary Gentlemen." *Esquire*, July 14, 2009.
https://www.esquire.com/news-politics/a450/esq1103-nov-liberia-rev/.

Carlson, Tucker. "Tucker Carlson: A Few Quick Questions We Should Ask before
the U.S. Decides to Meddle in Venezuela's Affairs." Fox News, May 1, 2019.
https://www.foxnews.com/opinion/tucker-carlson-a-few-quick-questions-we-
should-ask-before-the-u-s-decides-to-meddle-in-venezuelas-affairs.

Carroll, Rory. "Workers of the World, Relax! Chávez Takes over Hilton." *Guardian*,
October 22, 2009. https://www.theguardian.com/world/2009/oct/22/
chavez-seizes-hilton-caracas.

Carroll, Rory. "Nobel Economist Endorses Chávez Regional Bank Plan." *Guardian*,
October 11, 2007. https://www.theguardian.com/business/2007/oct/12/vene-
zuela.banking.

"The Case of Leopoldo Lopez." Global Freedom of Expression. Accessed
    August 15, 2023. https://globalfreedomofexpression.columbia.edu/cases/
    el-caso-de-leopoldo-lopez/.

Casey, Nicholas, Christoph Koettl, and Deborah Acosta. "Footage Contradicts U.S.
    Claim That Nicolás Maduro Burned Aid Convoy." *New York Times*, March 10,
    2019. https://www.nytimes.com/2019/03/10/world/americas/venezuela-aid-
    fire-video.html.

Casey, Nicholas. "Will the Real Simón Bolívar Please Stand up?" *New York
    Times*, January 13, 2016. https://www.nytimes.com/interactive/projects/cp/
    reporters-notebook/moving-to-venezuela/simon-bolivar-posters.

Cawthorne, Andrew. "Venezuela Sues Black Market Currency Website in United
    States." Reuters, October 23, 2015. https://www.reuters.com/article/venezuela-
    currency/venezuela-sues-black-market-currency-website-in-united-states-
    idUSL1N12N2LG20151023.

Center for Strategic and International Studies. "About CSIS." Accessed April 11,
    2023. https://www.csis.org/about.

"CHARTER OF THE ORGANIZATION OF AMERICAN STATES."
    Organization of American States, 1967. https://www.oas.org/en/sla/dil/inter_
    american_treaties_a-41_charter_oas.asp.

"CHAVEZ ACCUSES USG OF FUNDING 'COUPMONGERS.'" Cablegate,
    WikiLeaks. Accessed April 5, 2023. https://wikileaks.org/plusd/cables/04CA-
    RACAS634_a.html.

"Chile Charges Two over General Alberto Bachelet's Death." BBC, July 17, 2012.
    https://www.bbc.com/news/world-latin-america-18879593.

"Chile Court Confirms Salvador Allende Committed Suicide." BBC, September 12,
    2012. https://www.bbc.com/news/world-latin-america-19567445.

Cho, Emmy M. "Federal Judge Upholds Ruling Against Former Bolivian
    President in Human Rights Case Brought by HLS Clinic." Harvard
    Crimson, April 14, 2021. https://www.thecrimson.com/article/2021/4/14/
    bolivian-president-ruling-upheld/.

Chávez, Ailyn. "A 45 Años Del Asesinato Del Mártir Revolucionario Jorge
    Rodríguez, Su Ejemplo De Lucha Prevalece En La Patria." Ministerio del Poder
    Popular de Economía y Finanzas, July 25, 2021. http://www.mppef.gob.ve/a-45-
    anos-del-asesinato-del-martir-revolucionario-jorge-rodriguez-su-ejemplo-de-
    lucha-prevalece-en-la-patria/.

Chávez, Ailyn. "Movimiento Bolivariano Revolucionario 200, Organización Que
    Nació Para ..." Ministerio del Poder Popular de Economía y Finanzas, July 24,
    2021. http://www.mppef.gob.ve/movimiento-bolivariano-revolucionario-200-
    organizacion-que-nacio-para-combatir-el-modelo-neoliberal-que-oprimia-
    al-pueblo/.

Ciccariello-Maher, George. *We Created Chávez: A People's History of the Venezuelan Revolution.* Durham, NC: Duke Univ. Press, 2013.

CID Harvard. "What Is the Product Space?" June 13, 2017. https://www.youtube.com/watch?v=HLK_xE2P_XI&t=136s.

Clifton, Eli. "Follow the Money: Three Billionaires Paved Way for Trump's Iran Deal Withdrawal." LobeLog, May 8, 2018. https://lobelog.com/three-billionaires-paved-way-for-trumps-iran-deal-withdrawal/.

Clinton, Hillary Rodham. *Hard Choices.* New York: Simon & Schuster, 2014.

"Coca-Cola, Zara, Ikea: Rusia Se Las Ingenia Para Seguir Accediendo a Las Grandes Marcas Internacionales." *eEconomista*, February 23, 2023. https://www.eleconomista.es/retail-consumo/noticias/12160850/02/23/CocaCola-Zara-Ikea-Rusia-se-las-ingenia-para-seguir-accediendo-a-las-grandes-marcas-internacionales.html.

Cohen, Luc. "Corrected-Update 3-Crystallex Would Need Sanctions Waiver to Seize Citgo Shares -Guaido Adviser." Reuters, July 31, 2019. https://www.reuters.com/article/venezuela-oil-crystallex-idLTAL2N24W14X.

Cohen, Roger. "Who Really Brought Down Milosevic?" *New York Times*, November 26, 2000. https://archive.nytimes.com/www.nytimes.com/library/magazine/home/20001126mag-serbia.html.

Collyns, Dan. "Indigenous Ecuadorians Too Strong to Be Ignored after Deal to End Protests." *Guardian*, October 16, 2019. https://www.theguardian.com/world/2019/oct/16/ecuador-indigenous-protesters-bittersweet-triumph.

"Colombia: At Least 17 Dead in Dayslong Protests – DW – 05/03/2021." Deutsche Welle, May 3, 2021. https://www.dw.com/en/colombia-at-least-17-dead-in-dayslong-protests/a-57416473.

"Colombian Businessman Charged with Money Laundering Extradited to the United States from Cabo Verde." United States Department of Justice. Southern District of Florida, October 19, 2021. https://www.justice.gov/usao-sdfl/pr/colombian-businessman-charged-money-laundering-extradited-united-states-cabo-verde.

Colwell, Ann. "Documentary Shines Light on Farmers Displaced by Accidental Fumigation." CNN, October 19, 2011. https://www.cnn.com/2011/10/19/world/americas/colombia-displacement/index.html.

"Con El Mazo Dando | 31/07/2019." Noticias24, July 31, 2019. https://www.youtube.com/watch?v=uaenpYFwvBM.

Conflicts News Worldwide (@ConflictsW). Twitter post, January 5, 2020. https://twitter.com/ConflictsW/status/1213888813522653184?s=20.

"Contributions to OAS Funds." Organization of American States, 2022. https://www.oas.org/saf/DFAMS/2022/08/SF_TABLE_CONTOAS_20220831_EN.pdf.

"Corporations: Our Donors." Center for Strategic and International Studies. Accessed April 11, 2023. https://www.csis.org/about/financial-information/donors/corporations.

"Costa Rica Demands Maduro-Accredited Diplomats Leave Country." *The Tico Times*, February 16, 2019. https://ticotimes.net/2019/02/16/costa-rica-demands-maduro-accredited-diplomats-leave-country.

Cotovio, Vasco, and Isa Soares. "Alleged Financier for Venezuelan President Nicolas Maduro Says He Fears Being Extradited to the US." CNN, June 18, 2021. https://www.cnn.com/2021/06/18/americas/alex-saab-maduro-detention-interview/index.html.

"Crude Oil Prices - 70 Year Historical Chart." Macrotrends. Accessed April 4, 2023. https://www.macrotrends.net/1369/crude-oil-price-history-chart.

"Crystallex International Corporation v. Bolivarian Republic of Venezuela, ICSID Case No. ARB(AF)/11/2." Italaw, April 4, 2016. https://www.italaw.com/cases/1530#:~:text=APR%202016-,Award%20(English),-EditSign.

"Crystallex's Opposition to the Motion of the Interim President of Venezuela." Arbitration, March 11, 2019. https://arbitration.org/award/509/6043.

Cuffe, Sandra. "Ten Years after Coup, Hondurans Flee amid Violence and Repression." Al Jazeera, June 28, 2019. https://www.aljazeera.com/news/2019/6/28/ten-years-after-coup-hondurans-flee-amid-violence-and-repression.

Cupos en La Haya (@jcajias). Twitter post [VIDEO], January 6, 2016. https://twitter.com/jcajias/status/684793428140515328.

Curiel, John, and Jack R. Williams. "Bolivia Dismissed Its October Elections as Fraudulent. Our Research Found No Reason to Suspect Fraud." *Washington Post*, February 27, 2020. https://www.washingtonpost.com/politics/2020/02/26/bolivia-dismissed-its-october-elections-fraudulent-our-research-found-no-reason-suspect-fraud/.

Dahan, Maha, and Ahmed Rasheed. "OPEC+ Announces Surprise Oil Output Cuts." Reuters, April 2, 2023. https://www.reuters.com/business/energy/sarabia-other-opec-producers-announce-voluntary-oil-output-cuts-2023-04-02/.

Davis, Seana, Emmanuelle Saliba, and Alex Morgan. "Venezuela: 1 Litre of Milk Could Cost a Third of Your Wage." Euronews, July 26, 2019. https://www.euronews.com/my-europe/2019/02/15/venezuela-all-my-life-s-savings-were-destroyed-by-hyperinflation-thecube.

Dawkins, David. "Moneyman for Venezuela-Accused of Looting Billions-Nears Extradition to the U.S." *Forbes*, October 1, 2021. https://www.forbes.com/sites/daviddawkins/2021/10/01/money-man-for-venezuelaaccused-of-looting-billionsnears-extradition-to-the-us/?sh=49593fb96a5f.

"Defensa Presenta Cartas De Misión Aceptadas Por Irán En Inicio De Audiencia Probatoria De Alex Saab." *Fuser News*, December 12, 2022.

"Dem: Why My Fellow Democrats Are Wrong on Russia." Fox News, July 17, 2017. https://www.youtube.com/watch?v=LMq2PKjl6fc.

Department of State (@StateDept). Twitter post, February 8, 2018. https://twitter.com/StateDept/status/961699730710564865.

De Zayas, Alfred M. *The Wehrmacht War Crimes Bureau 1939 - 1945*. Lincoln: University of Nebraska Press, 1989.

De Zayas, Alfred. "Report of the Independent Expert on the Promotion of a Democratic and Equitable International Order on His Mission to the Bolivarian Republic of Venezuela and Ecuador." United Nations Digital Library, August 3, 2018. https://digitallibrary.un.org/record/1640958?ln=es.

"Declaration of José Ignacio Hernández." Italaw, April 7, 2017. https://www.italaw.com/cases/1530#:~:text=Declaration%20of%20Jos%C3%A9%20Ignacio%20Hern%C3%A1ndez.

"Defensor De Novoa: Utilizan Al Sii Para Eliminar a UN Enemigo Político." Cooperativa, July 6, 2015. https://www.cooperativa.cl/noticias/pais/politica/caso-penta/defensor-de-novoa-utilizan-al-sii-para-eliminar-a-un-enemigo-politico/2015-07-06/131000.html.

Delgado, Antonio Maria, Kevin G. Hall, and Shirsho Dasgupta. "Venezuelan Insurgent Describes How Betrayal in Ranks Produced Failure, Summary Executions." *Miami Herald*, November 18, 2010. https://www.miamiherald.com/news/nation-world/world/americas/article247237189.html.

Delgado, Antonio Maria, Kevin G. Hall, Shirsho Dasgupta, and Ben Wieder. "How a Venezuela Coup Attempt, Plotted in Miami, Unraveled." *Miami Herald*, October 20, 2020. https://www.miamiherald.com/news/nation-world/world/americas/article246819562.html.

Demaris, Agathe. "The End of the Age of Sanctions?" *Foreign Affairs*, December 27, 2022. https://www.foreignaffairs.com/united-states/end-age-sanctions.

"Dem: Why My Fellow Democrats Are Wrong on Russia." Fox News, July 17, 2017. https://www.youtube.com/watch?v=LMq2PKjl6fc.

"Derechos Humanos Y Medidas Coercitivas Unilaterales." Sures, September 26, 2021. https://sures.org.ve/bloqueo/.

Diálogo Américas. "Social Control: Maduro's CLAP." January 24, 2020. https://dialogo-americas.com/articles/social-control-maduros-clap/#.Y_51Ry1h1N1.

Di John, Jonathan. *From Windfall to Curse? Oil and Industrialization in Venezuela, 1920 to the Present*. University Park, PA: Penn State University Press, 2015.

"Diosdado Cabello: Este 6D El Pueblo De Bolívar Le Dará Una Lección De Democracia Al Imperialismo." Multimedios VTV, November 30, 2020. https://www.youtube.com/watch?v=I96Q3wCQYLU&t=553s.

"Diputado Venezolano Grave y Su Primo Muerto Por Burundanga." *La Opinión*, February 23, 2019. https://www.laopinion.com.co/judicial/diputado-venezolano-grave-y-su-primo-muerto-por-burundanga.

Dobson, Paul. "Venezuela's Defunct National Assembly Attempts to Privatise Oil Industry." *Venezuelanalysis*, July 12, 2018. https://venezuelanalysis.com/news/13935.

"Does the Bakken Formation Contain More Oil than Saudi Arabia?" United States Geological Survey. Accessed April 6, 2023. https://www.usgs.gov/faqs/does-bakken-formation-contain-more-oil-saudi-arabia.

Doğantekin, Vakkas. "Venezuela Slams Regional Efforts to Invoke Rio Treaty." Anadolu Agency, December 9, 2019. https://www.aa.com.tr/en/americas/venezuela-slams-regional-efforts-to-invoke-rio-treaty/1580145.

Donati, Jessica, and Vivian Salama. "Pence Pledged U.S. Backing Before Venezuela Opposition Leader's Move." *Wall Street Journal*, January 25, 2019.

Dotti, Braulio Jatar. *Inhabilitacion De La Extrema Izquierda y Guerrillas Corionas*. Caracas: La Secretaria de Asuntos Parlamentarios y Municipales de Accion Democratica, 1963.

Dube, Ryan. "Venezuela's Regime Challenges Biden with Sham Election." *Wall Street Journal*, December 5, 2020. https://www.wsj.com/articles/venezuelas-regime-challenges-biden-with-sham-election-11607180401.

Díaz, Tania (@taniapsuv). Twitter post, January 5, 2020. https://twitter.com/taniapsuv/status/1213915399038873603?s=20.

"'Drug Dealers, Criminals, Rapists': What Trump Thinks of Mexicans." BBC, August 31, 2016. https://www.bbc.com/news/av/world-us-canada-37230916.

Dutka, Z.C. "Venezuelan Government Exposes Plot to Assassinate President Maduro, Opposition Rejects Charges." *Venezuelanalysis*, May 31, 2014. https://venezuelanalysis.com/news/10712.

The Editors. "The U.S. Should Back New Elections in Honduras." *Bloomberg*, December 20, 2017. https://www.bloomberg.com/opinion/articles/2017-12-20/the-u-s-should-back-new-elections-in-honduras.

Ehrlich, Jamie, and Kate Sullivan. "Rubio Visits Venezuela-Colombia Border, Says Aid Will Get Through." CNN, February 17, 2019. https://www.cnn.com/2019/02/17/politics/marco-rubio-venezuela-aid-border/index.html.

"El Exdirector De Migración Marcel Rivas Es Enviado a La Cárcel Por Cinco Meses Por Caso Alertas Migratorias." *La Razón*, May 27, 2021. https://www.la-razon.com/nacional/2021/05/27/el-exdirector-de-migracion-marcel-rivas-es-enviado-a-la-carcel-por-cinco-meses-por-caso-alertas-migratorias/.

Elfrink, Tim. "Marco Rubio's Ties to a Drug-Smuggling Brother-in-Law Were Closer Than Advertised." *Miami New Times*, October 26, 2016. https://www.miaminewtimes.com/news/

marco-rubios-ties-to-a-drug-smuggling-brother-in-law-were-closer-than-advertised-8873774.

"El Listado De Los Artistas Del Concierto Chavista En La Frontera." Blu Radio, February 22, 2019. https://www.bluradio.com/mundo/el-listado-de-los-artistas-del-concierto-chavista-en-la-frontera.

"El Papá De Nicolás Maduro Se Hizo Bachiller En Colombia." *El Heraldo*, March 30, 2013. https://revistas.elheraldo.co/latitud/el-papa-de-nicolas-maduro-se-hizo-bachiller-en-colombia-105132.

Elfrink, Tim. "J.J. Rendon Is Latin America's Karl Rove." *Miami New Times*, July 1, 2010. https://www.miaminewtimes.com/news/jj-rendon-is-latin-americas-karl-rove-6380975.

Ellsworth, Brian, and Deisy Buitrago. "Venezuela Opposition Rallies against Maduro to Revive Momentum." Reuters, November 16, 2019. https://www.reuters.com/article/uk-venezuela-politics-idUKKBN1XQ0FQ.

Ellsworth, Brian, and Eyanir Chinea. "Rogue Ex-Policeman, Six Others Die in Venezuela Forces Raid." Reuters, January 16, 2018. https://www.reuters.com/article/us-venezuela-politics-perez-idUSKBN1F5245.

Ellsworth, Brian, and Vivian Sequera. "Opposition Candidates Suspected of Ties to Venezuela's Ruling Party Defy Call for Vote Boycott." Reuters, December 3, 2020. https://www.reuters.com/article/uk-venezuela-election-idUKKBN28D34S.

Ellsworth, Brian. "Chavez Drives Exxon and ConocoPhillips from Venezuela." Reuters, June 26, 2007. https://www.reuters.com/article/uk-venezuela-nationalization-oil-idUKN2637895020070626.

Ellsworth, Brian. "Venezuelans March against Closure of TV Station." Reuters, May 26, 2007. https://www.reuters.com/article/us-venezuela-television-march-idUSN2621739620070526.

Ellsworth, Brian. "Venezuela's PDVSA Sues Oil Traders over Corruption Scheme - Lawyer." Reuters, March 9, 2018. https://www.reuters.com/article/uk-venezuela-oil-idUKKCN1GL08J.

Elving, Ron. "Trump's Helsinki Bow To Putin Leaves World Wondering: Why?" NPR, July 17, 2018. https://www.npr.org/2018/07/17/629601233/trumps-helsinki-bow-to-putin-leaves-world-wondering-whats-up.

"En Vivo - Elección De La Nueva Directiva De La Asamblea Nacional 2020." VPItv, January 5, 2020. https://www.youtube.com/watch?v=-tC_6Qt8MfA&t=24175s.

"Enhanced Processes and Implementer Requirements Are Needed To Address Challenges and Fraud Risks in USAID's Venezuela Response." USAID Office of Inspector General, April 16, 2021. https://oig.usaid.gov/node/4688.

Entrambasaguas, Alejandro. "Los 'Observadores' De Podemos En Las Elecciones Bolivianas Dicen a La Policía Que Viajan Por «Negocios»." Okdiario, October 16, 2020. https://okdiario.com/investigacion/observadores-podemos-elecciones-bolivianas-dicen-policia-que-viajan-negocios-6288188.

Escobar, Pepe. "Putin and XI Plot Their Swift Escape." *The Cradle*, December 17, 2021. https://thecradle.co/article-view/4857.

Esper, Mark T. *Sacred Oath: Memoirs of a Secretary of Defense during Extraordinary Times.* New York, NY: HarperCollins, 2022.

"An Estimate of Recoverable Heavy Oil Resources of the Orinoco Oil Belt, Venezuela." United States Geological Survey. Accessed April 6, 2023. https://pubs.usgs.gov/fs/2009/3028/pdf/FS09-3028.pdf.

"Está En Vías De Consolidarse La Victoria Del Pueblo Al Restituirse En Todo El País El Suministro Eléctrico." Ministerio del Poder Popular del Despacho de la Presidencia, March 12, 2019. http://presidencia.gob.ve/Site/Web/Principal/paginas/classMostrarEvento3.php?id_evento=12992.

"Ethical Journalism: A Handbook of Values and Practices for the News and Opinion Departments." *New York Times*, January 5, 2018. https://www.nytimes.com/editorial-standards/ethical-journalism.html#sortingOutFamilyTies.

"EU Refuses to Monitor Venezuelan Election, Urges Delay." Associated Press, August 11, 2020. https://apnews.com/article/venezuela-foreign-policy-elections-latin-america-caribbean-995d28ca71a43b95a66acc5b452f95b9.

"Ex-UN Human Rights Expert Blasts 'Manipulation' on Venezuela: 'We Are Swimming in an Ocean of Lies'." *The Grayzone*, March 20, 2019. https://thegrayzone.com/2019/03/20/un-human-rights-expert-blasts-manipulation-on-venezuela-we-are-swimming-in-an-ocean-of-lies/.

"Exclusiva | Carlos Vecchio Da Sus 'Conclusiones' Sobre Venezuela." CNN en Español, June 6, 2014. https://www.youtube.com/watch?v=A8WqCgaZvfU.

"Expert Report of Jose Ignacio Hernández." Florida Southern District, August 3, 2018. https://ecf.flsd.uscourts.gov/doc1/051119651036.

"Expropian Una Segunda Hacienda a Un Ex Embajador Venezolano Ante La Onu." *elEconomista*, June 22, 2010. https://www.eleconomista.es/materias-primas/noticias/2249922/06/10/Expropian-una-segunda-hacienda-a-un-ex-embajador-venezolano-ante-la-ONU.html.

"Fact Sheet: United States Bans Imports of Russian Oil, Liquefied Natural Gas, and Coal." The White House, March 8, 2022. https://www.whitehouse.gov/briefing-room/statements-releases/2022/03/08/fact-sheet-united-states-bans-imports-of-russian-oil-liquefied-natural-gas-and-coal/.

"Fact Sheet: Venezuela Executive Order." National Archives and Records Administration, March 9, 2015. https://obamawhitehouse.archives.gov/the-press-office/2015/03/09/fact-sheet-venezuela-executive-order.

Factores de Poder (@FactoresdePoder). Twitter post, May 3, 2020. https://twitter.com/FactoresdePoder/status/1257088954165268481?s=20.

Factores de Poder (@FactoresdePoder). Twitter post, January 5, 2020. https://x.com/FactoresdePoder/status/1213886166304481280?s=20

Faiola, Anthony, Karen DeYoung, and Ana Vanessa Herrero. "From a Miami Condo to the Venezuelan Coast, How a Plan to 'Capture' Maduro Went Rogue." *Washington Post*, May 6, 2020. https://www.washingtonpost.com/world/the_americas/from-a-miami-condo-to-the-venezuelan-coast-how-a-plan-to-capture-maduro-went-rogue/2020/05/06/046222bc-8e4a-11ea-9322-a29e75ef-fc93_story.html.

Faiola, Anthony, Shawn Boburg, and Ana Vanessa Herrero. "Venezuela Raid: How an Ex-Green Beret and a Defecting General Planned to Capture Maduro." *Washington Post*, May 10, 2020. https://www.washingtonpost.com/world/the_americas/venezuela-raid-jordan-goudreau-cliver-alcala-maduro/2020/05/10/767c3386-9194-11ea-9322-a29e75effc93_story.html.

Faiola, Anthony. "How a Plot Filled with Intrigue and Betrayal Failed to Oust Venezuela's President." *Washington Post*, May 3, 2019. https://www.washington-post.com/world/the_americas/how-a-plot-filled-with-intrigue-and-betrayal-failed-to-oust-venezuelas-president/2019/05/03/4b46ca30-6db1-11e9-a66d-a82d3f3d96d5_story.html.

Faiola, Anthony. "Maduro's Ex-Spy Chief Lands in U.S. Armed with Allegations against Venezuelan Government." *Washington Post*, June 24, 2019. https://www.washingtonpost.com/world/the_americas/maduros-ex-spy-chief-lands-in-us-armed-with-allegations-against-venezuelan-government/2019/06/24/b20ad508-9477-11e9-956a-88c291ab5c38_story.html.

Faría Faría, Maria (@MariaFariaVE). Twitter post, February 20, 2019. https://twitter.com/MariaFariaVE/status/1098192617295237120.

Farrell, Henry J., and Abraham L. Newman. "The Wrong Way to Punish Iran." *New York Times*, November 1, 2018. https://www.nytimes.com/2018/11/01/opinion/swift-iran-sanctions.html.

Fassihi, Farnaz, and Steven Lee Myers. "China, With $400 Billion Iran Deal, Could Deepen Influence in Mideast." *New York Times*, March 27, 2021. https://www.nytimes.com/2021/03/27/world/middleeast/china-iran-deal.html.

Fastenberg, Dan. "Carlos Andrés Pérez." *Time*, January 10, 2011. https://content.time.com/time/magazine/article/0,9171,2040189,00.html.

"The Fed's Hikes Are a New Version of 'Our Dollar, Your Problem'."
    Barron's, June 15, 2022. https://www.barrons.com/articles/
    things-to-know-today-51655290030.

Ferchen, Matt. "China, Venezuela, and the Illusion of Debt-
    Trap Diplomacy." Carnegie Endowment, August 16,
    2018. https://carnegieendowment.org/2018/08/16/
    china-venezuela-and-illusion-of-debt-trap-diplomacy-pub-77089.

Ferrer, Isabel. "Diego Arria Demanda a Chávez Por Crímenes Contra La
    Humanidad." *El País*, November 21, 2011. https://elpais.com/internac-
    ional/2011/11/21/actualidad/1321908448_227631.html.

Fischer, Ford (@FordFischer). Twitter post [VIDEO], May 15, 2019. https://twitter.
    com/FordFischer/status/1128764020494950401?s=20.

Fischer, Ford (@FordFischer). Twitter post, May 9, 2019. https://twitter.com/
    FordFischer/status/1126659217681788928?s=20.

Fisher, Toby. "Koch's Award against Venezuela Upheld at ICSID." *Global
    Arbitration Review*, May 26, 2022. https://globalarbitrationreview.com/article/
    kochs-award-against-venezuela-upheld-icsid.

Fischer-Hoffman, Cory. "Venezuelan Officials Seize Warehouse with Enormous
    Cache of Hoarded Items as Opposition Calls for Strike." *Venezuelanalysis*, January
    14, 2015. https://venezuelanalysis.com/news/11158.

Fitz-Gibbon, Jorge. "Wife of Ex-Green Beret Pleads for His
    Release from Venezuelan Jail after Coup Attempt." *New
    York Post*, May 12, 2020. https://nypost.com/2020/05/12/
    ex-green-berets-wife-begs-for-his-release-from-venezuelan-jail/.

Flores, Leonardo. "Free Elections in Venezuela Are a Blow to Regime
    Change." Code Pink, December 9, 2020. https://www.codepink.org/
    free_elections_in_venezuela_are_a_blow_to_regime_change.

Foran, Clare. "Putin Gave Trump a Soccer Ball That May Have a Transmitter Chip."
    CNN, July 26, 2018. https://www.cnn.com/2018/07/25/politics/trump-putin-
    soccer-ball-chip-transmitter/index.html.

"Foreign Minister Responds to Escalated Assault and Media Demonization
    of Nicaragua." *The Grayzone*, October 5, 2021. https://www.youtube.com/
    watch?v=lOEGVekuHzA&t=604s.

Forero, Juan. "Chávez Is Declared the Winner in Venezuela Referendum." *New York
    Times*, August 16, 2004. https://www.nytimes.com/2004/08/16/international/
    americas/chvez-is-declared-the-winner-in-venezuela-referendum.html.

Forero, Juan. "Even in Death, Chavez Dominates Venezuelan Election."
    NPR, April 13, 2013. https://www.npr.org/2013/04/13/177061399/
    even-in-death-chavez-dominates-venezuelan-election.

Forero, Juan. "UPRISING IN VENEZUELA: MAN IN THE NEWS; Manager and Conciliator -- Pedro Carmona Estanga." *New York Times*, April 13, 2002. https://www.nytimes.com/2002/04/20/world/venezuela-s-2-fateful-days-leader-is-out-and-in-again.html.

France 24. "Bolivia Reanuda Su Participación En UNASUR, CELAC y ALBA." France 24, November 20, 2020. https://www.france24.com/es/minuto-a-minuto/20201120-bolivia-reanuda-su-participaci%C3%B3n-en-unasur-celac-y-alba.

France 24. "Security Forces 'Thwart Assassination Plot' against Morales." France 24, April 16, 2009. https://www.france24.com/en/20090416-security-forces-thwart-assassination-plot-against-morales-.

Frantzman, Seth J. "Roger Waters Slams Syria Intervention, Attacks 'White Helmets' as 'Fake'." *Jerusalem Post*, April 17, 2018. https://www.jpost.com/international/roger-waters-slams-syria-intervention-attacks-white-helmets-as-fake-549894.

Frum, David. *How We Got Here*. New York, NY: Basic Books, 2007.

Fuentes, Fred. "Dramatic Escalation in Campaign against Constitutional Reform." *Venezuelanalysis*, November 5, 2007. https://venezuelanalysis.com/blog/fred/2803.

"FULL Donald Trump, Vladimir Putin Press Conference." Global News. July 17, 2018. https://www.youtube.com/watch?v=MP2zt_buXNk.

Gaouette, Nicole, and Jennifer Hansler. "Pompeo Claims Russia Stopped Maduro Leaving Venezuela for Cuba." CNN, May 1, 2019. https://www.cnn.com/2019/04/30/politics/pompeo-maduro-russia/index.html.

García, Cristian Hugo. "¿Quién Es Braulio Jatar, El Supuesto Periodista Chileno-Venezolano?" *El Desconcierto* - Prensa digital libre, October 19, 2016. https://www.eldesconcierto.cl/opinion/2016/10/19/quien-es-braulio-jatar-el-supuesto-periodista-chileno-venezolano.html.

Garcia, Madelein (@madeleintlSUR). Twitter post, February 23, 2019. https://twitter.com/madeleintlSUR/status/1099429021857861633?s=20.

Garcia, Madelein (@madeleintlSUR). Twitter post, January 5, 2020. https://twitter.com/madeleintlSUR/status/1213937918701711362?s=20.

García Marco, Daniel. "Agresión a Orlando José Figuera: Lo Que Se Sabe Del Joven Al Que Prendieron Fuego Durante Una Protesta En Venezuela." BBC, May 22, 2017. https://www.bbc.com/mundo/noticias-america-latina-40007635.

Garcia Rawlins, Carlos. "Univision Team Deported from Venezuela after Maduro Interview." Reuters, February 26, 2019. https://www.reuters.com/article/uk-venezuela-politics-deportation-idUKKCN1QF2Z8.

Gearan, Anne, Josh Dawsey, and Seung Min Kim. "A Frustrated Trump Questions His Administration's Venezuela Strategy." *Washington Post*, May 8, 2019.

https://www.washingtonpost.com/politics/a-frustrated-trump-questions-his-administrations-venezuela-strategy/2019/05/08/ad51561a-71a7-11e9-9f06-5fc2ee80027a_story.html.

Gibson, Carl, and Steve Horn. "EXPOSED: GLOBALLY RENOWNED ACTIVIST COLLABORATED WITH INTELLIGENCE FIRM STRATFOR." Occupy.com, December 2, 2012. https://www.occupy.com/article/exposed-globally-renowned-activist-collaborated-intelligence-firm-stratfor#sthash.6qo3VWIK.qUuj2YKQ.dpbs.

Gibson, Dunn & Crutcher. Rep. *2019 Year-End Sanctions Update*. Gibson, Dunn & Crutcher, January 23, 2020. https://www.gibsondunn.com/2019-year-end-sanctions-update/.

Gill, Tim, and Rebecca Hanson. "How Washington Funded the Counterrevolution in Venezuela." *The Nation*, February 8, 2019. https://www.thenation.com/article/archive/venezuela-washington-funded-counterrevolution/.

Gilsinan, Kathy. "A Boom Time for U.S. Sanctions." *The Atlantic*, May 3, 2019. https://www.theatlantic.com/politics/archive/2019/05/why-united-states-uses-sanctions-so-much/588625/.

"'Goebbels Would Be Proud': Twitter Users Expose Jake Tapper's Misleading Maduro Message." RT, May 1, 2019. https://www.rt.com/news/458028-tapper-venezuela-fake-news-tweet/.

Goldmacher, Shane, and Jeremy Herb. "DNC Crowd Erupts at Panetta: 'No More War.'" *Politico*, July 27, 2016. https://www.politico.com/story/2016/07/dnc-2016-leon-panetta-chant-226335.

Golinger, Eva. *The Chavez Code: Cracking U.S. Intervention in Venezuela*. Northampton, MA: Olive Branch Press, 2006.

Golinger, Eva. "Documento Evidencia Un Plan De Desestabilización Contra Venezuela." Actualidad RT, November 5, 2013. https://actualidad.rt.com/opinion/eva_golinger/view/110489-documento-evidencia-plan-desestabilizacion-venezuela-golinger.

Golinger, Eva. "¿Quién Es Ciudadanía Activa?" Aporrea, August 27, 2010. https://www.aporrea.org/oposicion/a106826.html.

"Golpe De Posgrado De Soa / Whinsec En Bolivia: Régimen Respaldado Por Estados Unidos Masacra a Manifestantes." School of the Americas Watch, November 22, 2019. https://soaw.org/golpe-en-bolivia.

Goncalves, Sergio. "Portugal's Novo Banco Never Sold Assets to Lone Star, Says CEO." Reuters, September 2, 2020. https://www.reuters.com/article/portugal-banks-novobanco-idINL8N2FZ3QO.

González, David. "Coronel Jesus Rodriguez 'Salio a Buscar La Libertad'." Venezuela Awareness, August 15, 2006. https://www.venezuelaawareness.com/2006/08/

coronel-jesus-rodriguez-salio-a-buscar-la-libertad/?fbclid=IwAR0ZdGTaWrJ8G
eAXZ7VsZJn8PdYbnu-Lgzglu-3mnndUfCRCpu8YWvLrwL0.

González, Elyangelica (@ElyangelicaNews). Twitter post, February 20, 2019.
https://twitter.com/ElyangelicaNews/status/1098273951627833346?s=20.

González, Gessy (@gessy_ve). Twitter post, September 27, 2019. https://twitter.
com/gessy_ve/status/1177677861941059584?s=20.

Goodman, Joshua. "Alleged Maduro Co-Conspirator Says CIA Knew about Coup
Plans." Associated Press, January 28, 2022. https://apnews.com/article/
venezuela-miami-united-states-united-states-government-cia-7b0dba046661501c
859e1358f591a839.

Goodman, Joshua, and Ian Phillips. "AP Interview: Maduro Reveals
Secret Meetings with US Envoy." Associated Press, February 15,
2019. https://apnews.com/article/donald-trump-caribbean-ap-top-
news-venezuela-international-news-21b641f6def1400894125e3a8117f
66c.

Goodman, Joshua. "AP Breaks Global News with Unprecedented Maduro
Interview." Associated Press, February 22, 2019. https://leads.ap.org/
best-of-the-week/exclusive-interview-with-maduro-breaks-news.

Goodman, Joshua. "Ex-Green Beret Led Failed Attempt to Oust Venezuela's
Maduro." Associated Press, May 1, 2020. https://apnews.com/article/miami-
us-news-ap-top-news-venezuela-south-america-79346b4e428676424c0e5669c8
0fc310.

Goodman, Joshua. "Sources: Guaido Allies Take Slice of First Venezuela Budget."
Associated Press, April 23, 2020. https://apnews.com/article/latin-america-
virus-outbreak-caribbean-ap-top-news-venezuela-bd68454e33c7cf5a57fe7bdfa3
2fe5a7.

Goodman, Joshua. "Sources: US Investigating Ex-Green Beret for Venezuela
Raid." Associated Press, May 6, 2020. https://apnews.com/article/miami-us-
news-ap-top-news-venezuela-virus-outbreak-038e966350a9d7e8ec7a38341f0ef
eac.

Goodman, Joshua. "Steely Huntsman at Helm of Embattled US Embassy
in Caracas." Associated Press, February 1, 2019. https://apnews.com/
article/02829adf5429497f9720a748d85681b7.

Goodman, Joshua (@APjoshgoodman). Twitter post, March 31, 2023. https://twit-
ter.com/APjoshgoodman/status/1641974593018646531?s=20.

Goodman, Joshua (@APjoshgoodman). Twitter post, October 16, 2021. https://
twitter.com/APjoshgoodman/status/1449459796151840776.

Goodman, Joshua. "US Judge Rejects Maduro Ally's Claim of Diplomatic
Immunity." Associated Press, December 23, 2022. https://apnews.com/article/

venezuela-money-laundering-nicolas-maduro-de68f1818a40554304f34d686
f8f2691.

Goodman, Joshua. "Venezuela Demands Release of Businessman Connected
to Maduro." Associated Press, June 15, 2020. https://apnews.com/article/
colombia-miami-caribbean-ap-top-news-venezuela-6b20d5164e76243138e211d
4eb45da79.

Gosztola, Kevin. "Police Tried to Arrest Code Pink Activist Medea Benjamin
for 'Assault'." Shadowproof, November 13, 2019. https://shadowproof.
com/2019/11/13/without-proof-dc-police-attempted-to-arrest-code-pink-
activist-medea-benjamin-for-allegedly-assaulting-congresswoman-debbie-wass-
erman-schultz/.

Grainger, Sarah. "Victims of Venezuela's Caracazo Clashes Reburied." BBC,
February 28, 2011. https://www.bbc.com/news/world-latin-america-12593085.

Grech, Dan. "Venezuela's Oil Blacklist." *Marketplace*, May 1, 2007. https://www.mar-
ketplace.org/2007/05/01/venezuelas-oil-blacklist/.

Greenwood, Christopher. "The Wehrmacht War Crimes Bureau, 1939–1945. By
Alfred M. De Zayas, with the Collaboration of Walter Rabus." Cambridge
University Press, January 16, 2009. https://www.cambridge.org/core/journals/
cambridge-law-journal/article/abs/wehrmacht-war-crimes-bureau-19391945-by-
alfred-m-de-zayas-with-the-collaboration-of-walter-rabus-lincoln-and-london-
university-of-nebraska-press-1989-xix-328-bibliography-23-and-index-12-pp-har
dback-3865-paperback-1435-net/03D2FE1CB5093ED46C64D3A87D70171B.

Gromyko, Andreiĭ Andreevich. *Memoirs*. New York: Doubleday, 1990.

"Guaido and Rival Perra Both Declare Selves Speaker of Venezuelan Parliament."
France 24, January 5, 2020. https://www.france24.com/en/20200105-
venezuelan-opposition-denounces-parliamentary-coup-as-guaido-rival-names-
himself-speaker.

Guaidó, Juan. Periscope Stream, April 30, 2019. https://www.pscp.
tv/w/1rmxPejBrvXKN.

"Obituary: General Marcos Pérez Jiménez." *Guardian*, September 20, 2021. https://
www.theguardian.com/news/2001/sep/21/guardianobituaries1.

"Guaido Loyalists Seize Diplomatic Properties in US."
Deutsche Welle, March 19, 2019. https://www.dw.com/en/
venezuela-guaido-loyalists-seize-diplomatic-properties-in-us/a-47970126.

"Guaido Receives Hero's Welcome at Venezuela's Margarita Island Amid Peace
Talks." Global News. YouTube, July 19, 2019. https://www.youtube.com/
watch?v=2h3kHGeqlxs.

"Guaido Says Venezuela Police Block Access to Parliament."
France 24, January 5, 2020. https://www.france24.com/
en/20200105-guaido-says-venezuela-police-block-access-to-parliament.

"Guaidó Habría Entrado a Colombia Apoyado Por 'Los Rastrojos'."
    Portafolio, September 12, 2019. https://www.portafolio.co/internacional/
    guaido-habria-entrado-a-colombia-apoyado-por-los-rastrojos-533516.
Guaidó, Juan (@jguaido). Twitter post, March 7, 2019. https://twitter.com/jguaido/
    status/1103798495587287040?s=20.
"Guaidó: Si No Vamos a Tener Navidad, Que Tampoco La Tenga El Régimen."
    El Nacional, November 9, 2019. https://www.elnacional.com/venezuela/
    guaido-si-nosotros-no-vamos-a-tener-navidad-que-tampoco-la-tenga-
    el-regimen/.
Guerin, Orla. "Venezuela President Nicolás Maduro Interview: Full Transcript,"
    February 12, 2019. https://www.bbc.com/news/world-latin-america-47211509.
Gupta, Girish, and Brian Ellsworth. "Venezuela Movie Actor behind Helicopter
    Attack on Government Buildings." Reuters, June 28, 2017. https://www.reuters.
    com/article/us-venezuela-politics-actor-idUSKBN19J2EZ.
Hauser, Christine. "Bolivia Nationalizes Natural Gas Industry." *New York Times*,
    May 1, 2006. https://www.nytimes.com/2006/05/01/world/americas/01cnd-
    bolivia.html.
Hanke, Steve. "Venezuela's Hyperinflation, 29 Months and Counting." Jewish
    Policy Center, 2019. https://www.jewishpolicycenter.org/2019/04/04/
    venezuelas-hyperinflation-29-months-and-counting/.
"A Harvard-Henry Kissinger Détente?" *Harvard Magazine*, March 28, 2012. https://
    www.harvardmagazine.com/2012/03/henry-kissinger-returns-to-harvard.
Hausmann, Joanna, Leah Varjacques, and Kristopher Knight. "What My Fellow
    Liberals Don't Get about Venezuela." *New York Times*, April 1, 2019. https://
    www.nytimes.com/video/opinion/100000006424693/venezuela-us-hands-off-
    joanna-hausmann.html.
Hausmann, Joanna (@Joannahausmann). Twitter post, April 1, 2019. https://twitter.
    com/Joannahausmann/status/1112800714252865536?s=20.
Hausmann, Joanna, "What's Happening in Venezuela? Just the Facts," Facebook
    post, January 28, 2019, https://www.facebook.com/joannahausmanncomedy/
    videos/357443151754380/.
Hausmann, Ricardo, and Roberto Rigobon. "In Search of the Black Swan: Analysis
    of the Statistical Evidence of Electoral Fraud in Venezuela." Project Euclid.
    Institute of Mathematical Statistics, November 2011. https://projecteuclid.org/
    journals/statistical-science/volume-26/issue-4/In-Search-of-the-Black-Swan--
    Analysis-of-the/10.1214/11-STS373.full.
Hausmann, Ricardo. "D-Day Venezuela: By Ricardo Hausmann." Project
    Syndicate, January 2, 2018. https://www.project-syndicate.org/commentary/
    venezuela-catastrophe-military-intervention-by-ricardo-hausmann-2018-01.

Hausmann, Ricardo. "The Hunger Bonds: By Ricardo Hausmann." Project
    Syndicate, May 26, 2017. https://www.project-syndicate.org/commentary/
    maduro-venezuela-hunger-bonds-by-ricardo-hausmann-2017-05.
Hausmann, Ricardo (@ricardo_hausman). Twitter post, April 2, 2019. https://twit-
    ter.com/ricardo_hausman/status/1113033158772101120?s=20.
Hausmann, Ricardo (@ricardo_hausman). Twitter post, August 3, 2019. https://
    twitter.com/ricardo_hausman/status/1157642322479321088.
Hausmann, Ricardo (@ricardo_hausman). Twitter post, September 26, 2019. https://
    twitter.com/ricardo_hausman/status/1177377601490477057?s=20.
Hernández Navarro, Luis. "Nicolás Maduro, El Conductor." *La Jornada*, March 19,
    2013. https://www.jornada.com.mx/2013/03/19/opinion/023a2pol.
Hernroth-Rothstein, Annika. "'We Are Going to Continue to Fight.'"
    Foreign Policy, July 16, 2019. https://foreignpolicy.com/2019/07/16/
    we-are-going-to-continue-to-fight-juan-guaido-.
Herrera, Isayen, and Anatoly Kurmanaev. "Bouncy Castles and Grenades: Gangs
    Erode Maduro's Grip on Caracas." *New York Times*, May 30, 2021. https://www.
    nytimes.com/2021/05/30/world/americas/venezuela-gang-maduro.html.
Herrera, Isayen, and Genevieve Glatsky. "Juan Guaidó Is Voted out as Leader
    of Venezuela's Opposition." *New York Times*, December 30, 2022. https://
    www.nytimes.com/2022/12/30/world/americas/venezuela-opposition-juan-
    guaido.html.
Herrero, Ana Vanessa. "After U.S. Backs Juan Guaidó as Venezuela's Leader,
    Maduro Cuts Ties." *New York Times*, January 23, 2019. https://www.nytimes.
    com/2019/01/23/world/americas/venezuela-protests-guaido-maduro.html.
"Hinterlaces: 81% De Los Venezolanos Desconoce a Guaidó Como
    Líder Político." VTV, January 20, 2019. https://www.vtv.gob.ve/
    hinterlaces-81-venezolanos-desconoce-a-guaido-como-lider-politico/.
Hirschfeld Davis, Julie. "U.S. Places New Sanctions on Venezuela Day
    After Election." *New York Times*, May 21, 2018. https://www.nytimes.
    com/2018/05/21/us/politics/trump-maduro-venezuela-sanctions.html.
"Hollande Confirms Merkel's Remark Minsk Agreements Let Kiev Build up
    Military Muscle." TASS, December 30, 2022. https://tass.com/world/1558075.
Holland, Steve. "Trump Urges Venezuelan Military to Abandon Maduro or 'Lose
    Everything'." Reuters, February 18, 2019. https://www.reuters.com/article/
    cnews-us-venezuela-politics-trump-idCAKCN1Q71G8-OCATP.
Huang, Eustance. "A 'Growing Club' of 'Very Powerful Countries' Is Steering
    Away from Using the Dollar." CNBC, October 30, 2019. https://www.cnbc.
    com/2019/10/31/de-dollarization-russia-china-eu-are-motivated-to-shift-from-
    using-usd.html.

Hu, Caitlin, and Bianca Britton. "El Gobierno De Maduro Rechaza La Ayuda Humanitaria y Anuncia Envío De Alimentos a Colombia." CNN En Español, February 19, 2019. https://cnnespanol.cnn.com/2019/02/19/el-gobierno-de-maduro-rechaza-la-ayuda-humanitaria-y-anuncia-envio-de-alimentos-a-colombia/.

"IBRD Articles of Agreement: Article IV." World Bank. Accessed March 28, 2023. https://www.worldbank.org/en/about/articles-of-agreement/ibrd-articles-of-agreement/article-IV.

ICSID. "About ICSID." Accessed March 28, 2023. https://icsid.worldbank.org/About/ICSID.

ICSID. "Centro Internacional De Arreglo De Diferencias Relativas a Inversiones." March 10, 2015. http://icsidfiles.worldbank.org/icsid/ICSIDBLOBS/OnlineAwards/C1800/DC5643_sp.pdf.

Idrobo, Nicolás, Dorothy Kronick, and Francisco Rodríguez. "Do Shifts in Late-Counted Votes Signal Fraud? Evidence From Bolivia." Social Science Research Network, July 1, 2020. https://papers.ssrn.com/sol3/papers.cfm?abstract_id=3621475.

Ignacio Hernández, Jose (@ignandez). Twitter post, June 18, 2020. https://twitter.com/ignandez/status/1273757278961836032.

IEA. "How Europe Can Cut Natural Gas Imports from Russia Significantly within a Year - News." IEA, March 1, 2022. https://www.iea.org/news/how-europe-can-cut-natural-gas-imports-from-russia-significantly-within-a-year.

Ignacio Hernández, Jose. LinkedIn, accessed March 28, 2023. https://www.linkedin.com/in/jose-ignacio-hernandez-g-2845ba29/en?trk=people-guest_people_search-card.

Ignacio Hernández, Jose (@ignandez). Twitter post, June 18, 2020. https://twitter.com/ignandez/status/1273677399725613056.

"The Implementation of the First Stage against a Backdrop of European and International Monetary Difficulties." Centre Virtuel de la Connaissance sur l'Europe. Accessed March 31, 2023. https://www.cvce.eu/en/collections/unit-content/-/unit/56d70f17-5054-49fc-bb9b-5d90735167d0/81eb1248-502f-45ed-af0d-cef256056022.

"Incendian La Casa De Una Hermana De Evo Morales y De Dos Gobernadores." El Mundo, November 10, 2019. https://www.elmundo.es/internacional/2019/11/10/5dc7bb5921efa05c788b4627.html.

"The Incredible Shrinking Gold Supply." International Monetary Fund. Accessed March 31, 2023. https://www.imf.org/external/np/exr/center/mm/eng/sc_sub_3.htm.

"Indefinite Strike Begins in Bolivia against Postponement of General Elections." Peoples Dispatch, August 4, 2020. https://peoplesdispatch.org/2020/08/04/indefinite-strike-begins-in-bolivia-against-postponement-of-general-elections/.

"Information on CANVAS." The Global Intelligence Files, WikiLeaks. February 13, 2013. https://search.wikileaks.org/gifiles/emailid/1792423.

"Inside the World's Most Spectacularly Failed Coup." *VICE*, October 27, 2021. https://www.youtube.com/watch?v=D2jtiQpxUH4.

INSTEX. "About Us." Accessed January 31, 2022. https://instex-europe.com/about-us/.

Inter-American Development Bank. *Venezolano No Botes Tu Voto*. Queremos Elegit. Accessed March 20, 2023. https://web.archive.org/web/20171203195239/https://www.ifes.org/sites/default/files/ce02706_0.pdf.

Intercepted. "NEOLIBERALISM OR DEATH: THE U.S. ECONOMIC WAR AGAINST VENEZUELA." *The Intercept*, February 13, 2019. https://theintercept.com/2019/02/13/neoliberalism-or-death-the-u-s-economic-war-against-venezuela/.

"Intervención Del Comandante Presidente Hugo Chávez Durante Encuentro Con Partidos Aliados Por El Sí a La Enmienda Constitucional." Todo Chávez, January 15, 2009. http://todochavez.gob.ve/todochavez/919-intervencion-del-comandante-presidente-hugo-chavez-durante-encuentro-con-partidos-aliados-por-el-si-a-la-enmienda-constitucional.

"Interview with Man Tortured by Catholic Priest —Nicaragua." *Nicaragua Golpe De Estado*, June 30, 2018. https://www.youtube.com/watch?v=mzg7Z-0vQjM.

"Iranian Firm Planning to Repair Power Plants in Venezuela," Press TV, November 22, 2022, https://en.otaghiranonline.ir/news/34255.

"Iran Joins Growing List of Countries to Ditch Dollar in Foreign Trade." Sputnik International, January 24, 2015. https://sputniknews.com/20150124/1017299147.html.

"Iran Looks East after China-Led Bloc Oks Entry." France 24, September 18, 2021. https://www.france24.com/en/live-news/20210918-iran-looks-east-after-china-led-bloc-oks-entry.

"Iran Sanctions FAQ." United States Department of the Treasury, November 5, 2018. https://ofac.treasury.gov/faqs/645.

"Iranian Foreign Minister Lands in Venezuela." *Iran Press*, July 20, 2019. https://iran-press.com/content/12564/iranian-foreign-minister-lands-venezuela.

Janicke, Kiraz. "Venezuelan Government Closes Illegal Gold Trading and Money Laundering Racket." *Venezuelanalysis*, February 11, 2010. https://venezuelanalysis.com/news/5129.

Janicke, Kiraz. "Venezuelan Opposition Protesters Shoot Chavez Supporter." *Venezuelanalysis*, November 28, 2007. https://venezuelanalysis.com/news/2913.

"John Bolton's Divorce – Group Sex Allegations." Scoop, May 13, 2019. https://www.scoop.co.nz/stories/WO0505/S00240/john-boltons-divorce-group-sex-allegations.htm.

Johnson, Jake, and Sara Kozameh. "Venezuelan Economic and
Social Performance under Hugo Chávez, in Graphs." Center for
Economic and Policy Research, March 7, 2013. https://cepr.net/
venezuelan-economic-and-social-performance-under-hugo-chavez-in-graphs/.

Johnson, Jake. "'No Better Distillation of Washington': Democrats and GOP Join
Trump in Standing Ovation for Failed Venezuelan Coup Leader Juan Guaido."
Common Dreams, February 5, 2020. https://www.commondreams.org/
news/2020/02/05/no-better-distillation-washington-democrats-and-gop-join-
trump-standing-ovation.

Johnston, Jake. "How Pentagon Officials May Have Encouraged a 2009 Coup in
Honduras." *The Intercept*, August 29, 2017. https://theintercept.com/2017/08/29/
honduras-coup-us-defense-departmetnt-center-hemispheric-defense-
studies-chds/.

Jones, Alexandra. "Third Circuit: Crystallex Can Seize Venezuela's Citgo Shares."
Courthouse News Service, July 29, 2019. https://www.courthousenews.com/
third-circuit-crystallex-can-seize-venezuelas-citgo-shares/.

"Jorge Ramos Explains What Happened during the Interview with Maduro and in
His Detention." Univision Noticias, February 26, 2019. https://www.youtube.
com/watch?v=IkXAUfWwq-c.

"Journalist: Fake News Media Are Lying about the Situation in Venezuela."
Fox News, April 30, 2019. https://www.foxnews.com/transcript/
journalist-fake-news-media-are-lying-about-the-situation-in-venezuela.

"Juan Orlando Hernández, Former President of Honduras, Indicted on Drug-
Trafficking and Firearms Charges, Extradited to the United States from
Honduras." United States Department of Justice, April 21, 2022. https://
www.justice.gov/opa/pr/juan-orlando-hern%C3%A1ndez-former-president-
honduras-indicted-drug-trafficking.

Kalmbacher, Colin. "Rubio Posts Graphic Image of Gaddafi's Murder in Apparent
Threat to Maduro. Twitter Says It Didn't Violate Their Terms of Service." Law
and Crime, March 2, 2019. https://lawandcrime.com/high-profile/rubio-posts-
graphic-image-of-gaddafis-murder-in-apparent-threat-to-maduro-twitter-says-it-
didnt-violate-their-terms-of-service/.

Kilkenny, Allison. "Leaked Documents: Homeland Security Monitoring Occupy
Wall Street." *In These Times*, February 29, 2012. https://inthesetimes.com/article/
leaked-documents-homeland-security-monitoring-occupy-wall-street.

King, Rachael. "Venezuela Says It Will Drop US Dollar for Euros." Central
Banking, October 19, 2018. https://www.centralbanking.com/central-banks/
financial-stability/3805871/venezuela-says-it-will-drop-us-dollar-for-euros.

Koerner, Lucas. "Maduro Calls for Investigation of Blank Votes as Video Shows Opposition Mayor Handing out Cash." *Venezuelanalysis*, December 17, 2015. https://venezuelanalysis.com/news/11780.

Koerner, Lucas. "Venezuela Arrests 55 State Food Employees in Anti-Corruption Raid." *Venezuelanalysis*, February 17, 2016. https://venezuelanalysis.com/news/11858.

Koerner, Lucas. "Venezuelan National Assembly to Investigate Expropriated Land, Communes Threatened." *Venezuelanalysis*, January 28, 2016. https://venezuelanalysis.com/news/11841.

Koerner, Lucas. "Venezuelan Supreme Court Blocks Housing Privatization Law." *Venezuelanalysis*, May 9, 2016. https://venezuelanalysis.com/news/11965.

Koerner, Lucas. "Venezuelan's Maduro Creates Socialist Enterprise System to Kickstart Production." *Venezuelanalysis*, February 24, 2016. https://venezuelanalysis.com/news/11864.

Kovaleski, Serge F. "Venezuelan Vote Gives President New Powers." *Washington Post*, December 16, 1999. https://www.washingtonpost.com/wp-srv/WPcap/1999-12/16/111r-121699-idx.html.

Kourdi, Eyad, and Hande Atay Alam. "Saudi Arabia and Syria to Resume Diplomatic Missions after Decade-Long Freeze: State Media." CNN, May 10, 2023. https://edition.cnn.com/2023/05/09/middleeast/saudi-arabia-syria-diplomatic-ties-intl/index.html.

Kozloff, Nikolas. "The Coup and the U.S. Airbase in Honduras." CounterPunch, July 22, 2009. https://www.counterpunch.org/2009/07/22/the-coup-and-the-u-s-airbase-in-honduras/.

Kraul, Chris. "Venezuelan Voters Reject Bid by Chavez to Extend Powers." *LA Times*, December 3, 2007. https://www.latimes.com/archives/la-xpm-2007-dec-03-fg-venezuela3-story.html.

Krepp, Stella. "Cuba and the OAS: A Story of Dramatic Fallout and Reconciliation." Wilson Center, December 18, 2017. https://www.wilsoncenter.org/blog-post/cuba-and-the-oas-story-dramatic-fallout-and-reconciliation#:~:text=In%20early%201962%2C%20Fidel%20Castro,the%20peoples%20of%20Latin%20America.%E2%80%9D.

Krygier, Rachelle, and Anthony Faiola. "Venezuela's Last Democratic Institution Falls as Maduro Attempts De Facto Takeover of National Assembly." *Washington Post*, January 6, 2020. https://www.washingtonpost.com/world/the_americas/venezuelas-last-democratic-institution-falls-as-maduro-stages-de-facto-takeover-of-national-assembly/2020/01/05/8ba496fe-2d8f-11ea-bffe-020c88b3f120_story.html.

Kumar, Rishikesh. "Indian Government Urged to Set up Alternative to Swift Payment System over Us Misuse." Sputnik International, December 8, 2022.

https://sputniknews.com/20211217/indian-government-urged-to-set-up-alternative-to-swift-payment-system-over-us-misuse-1091575131.html.

Kurmanaev, Anatoly, and Andrew Rosati. "The $755 Condom Pack Is the Latest Indignity in Venezuela." *Bloomberg*, February 4, 2015. https://www.bloomberg.com/news/articles/2015-02-04/the-755-condom-is-the-latest-indignity-in-venezuela?leadSource=uverify+wall.

Kurmanaev, Anatoly, and María Silvia Trigo. "A Bitter Election. Accusations of Fraud. And Now Second Thoughts." *New York Times*, June 7, 2020. https://www.nytimes.com/2020/06/07/world/americas/bolivia-election-evo-morales.html.

Kurmanaev, Anatoly. "DolarToday, El Enemigo Más Temido De Nicolás Maduro." *Wall Street Journal*, November 20, 2016. https://www.wsj.com/articles/dolartoday-el-enemigo-mas-temido-de-nicolas-maduro-1479686594.

Kurmanaev, Anatoly. "U.S. Suspends Passenger and Cargo Flights to Venezuela." *New York Times*, May 15, 2019. https://www.nytimes.com/2019/05/15/world/americas/us-venezuela-flights.html.

Kurmanaev, Anatoly. "Venezuela's Leader Trades Old Guard for Slick Technocrats to Keep Power." *New York Times*, March 2, 2022. https://www.nytimes.com/2022/03/02/world/americas/venezuela-maduro-chavez.html.

Lahut, Luke. "Tucker Carlson, the Most Popular Cable News Host in US History, Claims He Has No Idea What His Ratings Are: 'I Don't Know How to Read a Ratings Chart'." Yahoo! News, July 7, 2022. https://news.yahoo.com/tucker-carlson-most-popular-cable-195601472.html?guccounter=1&-guce_referrer=aHR0cHM6Ly93d3cuZ29vZ2xlLmNvbS88&guce_refer-rer_sig=AQAAAN0Gv9xHbah74gQ5a-u7pzxtMdYCvPsno1CqcJJf4ghVlvY7fIHJpQCFD90lvtQ-_CHqevGk8CPOdOOUAuWKFmWfGD-g_OaEVPL94Jg9TCx4wirIIQlaHp-0JVhauNS6NYkSM5MbelMQNRR_sttqVBHdC-MzvjK1kLhF-f4w-owI.

Lalander, Rickard O. *Suicide of the Elephants?Venezuelan Decentralization between Partyarchy and Chavismo*. Helsinki: University of Helsinki, 2004.

Lamoreaux, Naomi R., and Ian Shapiro. *The Bretton Woods Agreements*. New Heaven: Yale University Press, 2019.

Lamy, Alexandre. "President Obama Signs Venezuela Defense of Human Rights and Civil Society Act of 2014 and Ukraine Freedom Support Act of 2014." Sanctions & Export Controls Update. Baker McKenzie, December 19, 2014. https://sanctionsnews.bakermckenzie.com/president-obama-signs-venezuela-defense-of-human-rights-and-civil-society-act-of-2014-and-ukraine-freedom-support-act-of-2014/.

Lang, Marissa J. "Venezuelan Embassy Goes Dark as Standoff Intensifies on Streets of Washington." *Washington Post*, May 9, 2019. https://www.washingtonpost.

com/local/venezuelan-embassy-goes-dark-as-standoff-intensifies-on-streets-of-washington/2019/05/09/e6263124-7272-11e9-9eb4-0828f5389013_story.html.

Latin America News. "Iran Negotiates with Cuba, Nicaragua and Venezuela to Build Power Plants." *Rio Times*, January 2, 2023. https://www.riotimesonline.com/brazil-news/rio-business/national-business/iran-negotiates-with-cuba-nicaragua-and-venezuela-to-build-power-plants/.

Laya, Patricia, and Anya Andrianova. "Weary of Sanctions, Venezuela Mulls Using Russian Payment System." *Bloomberg*, July 16, 2019. https://www.bloomberg.com/news/articles/2019-07-16/weary-of-sanctions-venezuela-mulls-using-russian-payment-system.

Laya, Patricia, and Jennifer Surane. "Citigroup Settles Venezuela Gold Swap Transaction." *Bloomberg*, March 20, 2019. https://www.bloomberg.com/news/articles/2019-03-20/citigroup-is-said-to-settle-venezuela-gold-swap-transaction#xj4y7vzkg.

The Lead. "That Time Tapper Asked Obama about Syria Inaction." CNN, September 2016. https://www.cnn.com/videos/tv/2017/04/04/jake-tapper-president-obama-town-hall-september-syria-civil-war-red-line.cnn.

Leetaru, Kalev. "Could Venezuela's Power Outage Really Be A Cyber Attack?" *Forbes*, March 9, 2019. https://www.forbes.com/sites/kalevleetaru/2019/03/09/could-venezuelas-power-outage-really-be-a-cyber-attack/?sh=5607cfc1607c.

Lennard, Jeremy. "Colombian Paramilitaries Arrested in Venezuela." *Guardian*, May 24, 2004. https://www.theguardian.com/world/2004/may/10/venezuela.jeremylennard.

Llamas, Tom. "Venezuelan President Nicolas Maduro's Defiant Interview with Tom Llamas: TRANSCRIPT." ABC News, February 27, 2019. https://abcnews.go.com/International/venezuelan-president-nicolas-maduros-defiant-interview-tom-llamas/story?id=61318540.

Llorente, Elizabeth. "Venezuela Turns the Lights Back on as Power Is Restored, but Access to Uncontaminated Water Is Critical." Fox News, March 14, 2019. https://www.foxnews.com/world/venezuela-turns-the-lights-back-on-as-power-is-restored-but-access-to-uncontaminated-water-is-critical.

Long, Guillaume, David Rosnick, Cavan Kharrazian, and Kevin Cashman. "What Happened in Bolivia's 2019 Vote Count?" Center for Economic and Policy Research, November 8, 2019. https://www.cepr.net/report/bolivia-elections-2019-11/.

Long, Guillaume. "Under Luis Almagro, the OAS Is Advancing the Trump Agenda in Latin America." Center for Economic and Policy Research, May 12, 2020. https://cepr.net/under-luis-almagro-the-oas-is-advancing-the-trump-agenda-in-latin-america/.

Lopez, German. "Marco Rubio's 'German Dam' Mistake, Explained." *Vox*, March 11, 2019. https://www.vox.com/policy-and-politics/2019/3/11/18259983/ marco-rubio-german-dam-venezuela-blackout.

Lopez, Ismael. "Nicaragua Says Anti-Government Protests Caused $1 Billion in Economic Damages." Reuters, November 12, 2018. https://www.reuters.com/ article/uk-nicaragua-protests-idAFKCN1NI08B.

"Los Países a Los Que Llegó La Plata Del Alex Saab." *El Espectador*, October 23, 2018. https://www.elespectador.com/investigacion/ los-paises-a-los-que-llego-la-plata-del-alex-saab-article-819613/.

Lugo, Luis Alonso. "President of Honduras Says He Faces No Us Criminal Charges." Yahoo! News, August 13, 2019. https://news.yahoo.com/president-honduras-visits-washington-163736709.html.

"Lukoil Dismissal." Court House News, March 8, 2019. https://www.courthouse-news.com/wp-content/uploads/2020/05/lukoil-dismissal.pdf.

López, Leopoldo (@leopoldolopez). Twitter post, November 30, 2020. https://twitter.com/leopoldolopez/status/1333537348123037698?s=20.

López, Virginia. "Venezuela: Police Helicopter Attacks Supreme Court with Grenades." *Guardian*, June 28, 2017. https://www.theguardian.com/world/2017/ jun/28/venezuela-supreme-court-grenade-police-helicopter.

MacAskill, Ewam, and Duncan Campbell. "Bush Bans Arms Sales to Chávez." *Guardian*, May 10, 2006. https://www.theguardian.com/world/2006/may/16/ usa.venezuela.

Machicao, Mónica, and Kirk Semple. "Bolivian Mayor Assaulted by Protesters in Postelection Mayhem." *New York Times*, November 7, 2019. https://www. nytimes.com/2019/11/07/world/americas/bolivia-mayor-protest-paint.html.

MacLeod, Alan. "Bolivia's New US-Backed Interim Gov't Wastes No Time Privatizing Economy." *MintPress News*, December 16, 2019. https://www.mint-pressnews.com/bolivia-interim-government-privatizing-economy/263529/.

MacLeod, Alan. "Mark Esper's Tell-Some Reveals US Plans for War and Terror against Venezuela." *MintPress News*, May 23, 2022. https://www.mintpressnews. com/mark-esper-reveals-us-plans-war-terror-against-venezuela/280930/.

MacLeod, Alan. "'Sexy Tricks': How 'Mercenary' Journalists Demonize Venezuela, in Their Own Words." *The Grayzone*, December 9, 2019. https://thegrayzone.com/2019/12/09/ sexy-tricks-journalists-demonize-venezuela-anatoly-kurmanaev/.

"Maduro Rejects Humanitarian Aid." Deutsche Welle. February 8, 2019. https://www.dw.com/en/ venezuela-maduro-rejects-humanitarian-aid-as-nation-starves/a-47435665.

Main, Alex. "A Blow to Brazilian Democracy: The Illegitimate Removal of Dilma Rousseff from Power." Center for Economic and Policy Research, January 17,

2017. https://cepr.net/a-blow-to-brazilian-democracy-the-illegitimate-removal-of-dilma-rousseff-from-power/.

Makuch, Ben. "Maga, the CIA, and Silvercorp: The Bizarre Backstory of the World's Most Disastrous Coup." *VICE*, October 26, 2021. https://www.vice.com/en/article/pkpex7/maga-the-cia-and-silvercorp-the-bizarre-backstory-of-the-worlds-most-disastrous-coup.

Makuch, Ben. "Mercenaries Behind Failed Venezuela Coup Claim to Have Done Trump Security." *VICE*, May 5, 2020. https://www.vice.com/en/article/v7g4d8/venezuela-mercenaries-silvercorp-gordon-goudreau-trump-rally.

Mallett-Outtrim, Ryan, and Tamara Pearson. "Venezuelan Guarimbas: 11 Things the Media Didn't Tell You." *Venezuelanalysis*, February 16, 2015. https://venezuelanalysis.com/analysis/11211.

Mallett-Outtrim, Ryan. "Inside Venezuela's 'Repressive' Regime." DISSENT! Sans Frontières, January 14, 2014. https://dissentsansfrontieres.com/2014/01/14/inside-venezuelas-repressive-regime/.

"Man Who Paid for Failed Invasion of Venezuela Resigns." Newsroom Panama, May 11, 2020. https://www.newsroompanama.com/news/man-who-paid-for-failed-invasion-of-venezuela-resigns.

Martin, Jorge. "Venezuela: Guaidó's Botched Coup – What Does It Mean and What's Next?" *Venezuelanalysis*, May 2, 2019. https://venezuelanalysis.com/analysis/14459.

Martínez, Mariana, and Anatoly Kurmanaev. "Venezuela's Opposition Splits over Taking Part in Coming Elections." *New York Times*, September 6, 2020. https://www.nytimes.com/2020/09/06/international-home/venezuela-elections-maduro.html.

María Cañizares, Ana. "Almagro Elogia La Respuesta Del Gobierno De Ecuador Ante Las Protestas Masivas En El País." CNN en Español, October 30, 2019. https://cnnespanol.cnn.com/2019/10/30/alerta-durante-inauguracion-del-vii-encuentro-de-ministros-de-seguridad-publica-almagro-habla-sobre-protestas-en-ecuador/.

"Masaya 2018 - an Interview with Comissioner General Ramón Avellán." Tortilla Con Sal, May 12, 2021. https://www.tortillaconsal.com/tortilla/node/13533.

Maté, Aaron. "Journalist Max Blumenthal Arrested on False Charge in DC." *The Grayzone*, November 3, 2019. https://thegrayzone.com/2019/11/03/journalist-max-blumenthal-arrested-on-false-charge-in-dc/.

McDonald, Brent. "A Bullet to the Eye Is the Price of Protesting in Chile." *The Independent*, November 21, 2019. https://www.independent.co.uk/news/world/americas/chile-protest-police-deaths-eye-injury-bullets-tear-gas-a9211946.html.

McEvoy, John. "Exclusive: Juan Guaidó Paid UK Legal Fees with Looted Venezuelan Money." *The Canary*, August 3,

2021. https://www.thecanary.co/exclusive/2021/08/03/exclusive-juan-guaido-paid-uk-legal-fees-with-looted-venezuelan-money/.

McEvoy, John. "Revealed: Secretive British Unit Planning for 'Reconstruction' of Venezuela." *The Canary*, May 13, 2020. https://www.thecanary.co/exclusive/2020/05/13/revealed-secretive-british-unit-planning-for-reconstruction-of-venezuela/.

McEvoy, John. "Two Weeks inside One of Venezuela's Notorious 'Colectivos'." *The Canary*, March 30, 2019. https://www.thecanary.co/feature/2019/03/30/two-weeks-inside-one-of-venezuelas-notorious-colectivos/.

McEvoy, John. "'I Was Outraged': Venezuelan Foreign Minister Responds to Secretive British 'Reconstruction' Plans." *The Canary*, May 19, 2020. https://www.thecanary.co/exclusive/2020/05/19/i-was-outraged-venezuelan-foreign-minister-responds-to-secretive-british-reconstruction-plans/.

McGonigal, Chris, and Jesselyn Cook. "Photos Of Empty Grocery Shelves Show Dire Situation In Venezuela." *Huffington Post*, January 10, 2018. https://www.huffpost.com/entry/venezuela-empty-grocery-shelves-photos_n_5a567751e4b08a1f624afcf6.

McLaughlin, Aidan. "Tucker Carlson Goes on Marathon Rant Questioning Whether Assad Is Behind Attack in Syria." Mediaite, April 9, 2018. https://www.mediaite.com/tv/tucker-carlson-goes-on-marathon-rant-questioning-whether-assad-is-behind-attack-in-syria/.

McLaughlin, Kelly. "Several Iowa Caucus Votes Ended in Coin Tosses When Delegate Counts Were Too Close to Call." *Business Insider*, February 4, 2020. https://www.businessinsider.com/iowa-caucus-coin-flips-helped-determine-tied-votes-2020-2.

McSherry, J. Patrice. "Chile's Struggle to Democratize the State." NACLA, February 24, 2020. https://nacla.org/news/2020/02/24/chile-struggle-democratize-state-plebescite.

"Medicina Legal De Colombia Confirma Que Diputado Superlano y Su Primo Fueron Drogados." *El Tiempo Ve*, October 10, 2020. https://eltiempove.com/medicina-legal-de-colombia-confirma-que-diputado-superlano-y-su-primo-fueron-drogados/.

Megerian, Chris, Vanessa Gera, and Aamer Madhani. "Biden Says Putin 'Cannot Remain in Power.'" PBS, March 26, 2022. https://www.pbs.org/newshour/world/biden-on-russias-putin-this-man-cannot-remain-in-power.

Merelli, Annalisa. "The WHO Has a Worrisome Reliance on the Bill & Melinda Gates Foundation." Quartz, December 16, 2021. https://qz.com/2102889/the-who-is-too-dependent-on-gates-foundation-donations.

"Message from OAS Secretary General on Elections in Venezuela." The
   Organization of American States, May 21, 2018. https://www.oas.org/en/
   media_center/press_release.asp?sCodigo=S-019/18.

Miller, Aaron David, and Richard Sokolsky. "Donald Trump in Helsinki
   Was Terrifying. Cancel the Washington Sequel." *USA Today*, July
   24, 2018. https://www.usatoday.com/story/opinion/2018/07/24/
   cancel-donald-trump-vladimir-putin-helsinki-sequel-column/816245002/.

"Ministerio De Relaciones Exteriores Deplora Ingreso Inaceptable De Diplomáticos
   a Sede De La Embajada De Venezuela En Costa Rica." Ministerio de Relaciones
   Exteriores y Culto, February 20, 2019. https://www.rree.go.cr/?sec=servicios&c
   at=prensa&cont=593&id=4479&fbclid=IwAR14uErZoXe9Spv7nQTd8aDri9Jh
   BOYeUSsexhudx--kTE0AChRFKFWk6tw.

Misión Verdad (@Mision_Verdad). Twitter post, March 26, 2020. https://twitter.
   com/Mision_Verdad/status/1243251030445494273?s=20.

Mitchell, Sam. "Larry Summers Is Not Your Friend." *Jacobin*, July 2, 2020. https://jacobin.
   com/2020/07/larry-summers-biden-campaign-economic-policy.

"MIXED REVIEWS OF LUGO AT THE ONE YEAR MARK." Cablegate,
   WikiLeaks. Accessed March 22, 2023. https://wikileaks.org/plusd/
   cables/09ASUNCION521_a.html.

"Model Rules Of Professional Conduct." American Bar Association.
   Accessed March 28, 2023. https://www.americanbar.org/groups/
   professional_responsibility/policy/ethics_2000_commission/e2k_redline/.

Moncada, Samuel (@SMoncada). Twitter post, April 15, 2019. https://twitter.com/
   SMoncada_VEN/status/1117643332975566848.

Moncada, Samuel (@SMoncada). Twitter post, April 15, 2019. https://twitter.com/
   SMoncada_VEN/status/1117975927089242113.

Moncada, Samuel (@SMoncada). Twitter post, May 2, 2019. https://twitter.com/
   SMoncada_VEN/status/1123805417241554946?s=20.

"Monroe Doctrine, 1823." United States Department of State Office
   of the Historian. Accessed April 4, 2023. https://history.state.gov/
   milestones/1801-1829/monroe.

Montoya-Galvez, Camilo, and Christina Ruffini. "Venezuelan Opposition Seizes
   Diplomatic Offices in U.S.; Maduro Official Warns of 'Reciprocal' Action."
   CBS News, March 18, 2019. https://www.cbsnews.com/news/venezuelan-
   opposition-juan-guaido-seizes-diplomatic-offices-ny-dc-maduro-official-warns-
   reciprocal-action/.

Motamayor, J C, A M Risterucci, P A Lopez, C F Ortiz, A Moreno, and C Lanaud.
   "Cacao Domestication I: The Origin of the Cacao Cultivated by the Mayas."
   Nature, October 28, 2002. https://www.nature.com/articles/6800156.

Murillo, Arturo (@ArturoMurilloS). Twitter post, October 15, 2020. https://twitter.com/ArturoMurilloS/status/1316700676903272448.

Murray, Mark. "Poll: 61% of Republicans Still Believe Biden Didn't Win Fair and Square in 2020." NBC, September 27, 2022. https://www.nbcnews.com/meet-the-press/meetthepressblog/poll-61-republicans-still-believe-biden-didnt-win-fair-square-2020-rcna49630.

MV English (@MV_Eng). Twitter post, October 18, 2021. https://twitter.com/MV_Eng/status/1450226433264078850.

Nadkarni, Rohan. "Marco Rubio May Never Live Down the Time He Wore Those Cool Chelsea Boots." *GQ*, January 22, 2016. https://www.gq.com/story/marco-rubio-may-never-live-down-the-time-he-wore-those-cool-chelsea-boots.

Nagel, Juan Cristobal. "El Gran Viraje, 25 Years On." *Caracas Chronicles*, February 16, 2014. https://www.caracaschronicles.com/2014/02/16/el-gran-viraje-25-years-on/.

"Nancy Pelosi Doesn't Remember Juan Guaido." Kawsachun News, June 15, 2022. https://www.youtube.com/watch?v=CageiGEPIsE.

"The National Endowment for Democracy Responds to Our Burma Nuclear Story — And Our Response." ProPublica. November 24, 2010. https://www.propublica.org/article/the-national-endowment-for-democracy-responds-to-our-burma-nuclear-story.

Nayak, Gayatri, and Saikat Das. "India Sold $11 Billion Worth US Treasury Securities since October." *Economic Times*, March 17, 2021. https://economictimes.indiatimes.com/markets/bonds/india-sold-11billion-worth-us-treasury-securities-since-october/articleshow/81555338.cms.

Neuman, William, and Patricia Torres. "Venezuela's Economy Suffers as Import Schemes Siphon Billions." *New York Times*, May 5, 2015. https://www.nytimes.com/2015/05/06/world/americas/venezuelas-econ.

Neuman, William. "Chávez Dies, Leaving Sharp Divisions in Venezuela." *New York Times*, March 5, 2013. https://www.nytimes.com/2013/03/06/world/americas/hugo-chavez-of-venezuela-dies.html.

"New Report Reviews Changes in Bolivia's Economy under Evo Morales's Presidency." Center for Economic and Policy Research, October 17, 2019. https://cepr.net/press-release/new-report-reviews-changes-in-bolivia-s-economy-under-evo-morales-s-presidency/.

Newman, Lily Hay. "Why It's So Hard to Restart Venezuela's Power Grid." *Wired*, March 12, 2019. https://www.wired.com/story/venezuela-power-outage-black-start/.

News Desk. "Iran Set to Repair Venezuela's Largest Oil Refinery Complex: Report." *The Cradle*, May 23, 2022. https://thecradle.co/article-view/10768/iran-set-to-repair-venezuelas-largest-oil-refinery-complex-report.

"Nicaragua Quits 'Diabolical' Regional Bloc OAS after Election Row." Al
    Jazeera, April 25, 2022. https://www.aljazeera.com/news/2022/4/25/
    nicaragua-says-early-oas-withdrawal-complete-after-election-row.

"Nicaraguan 'Political Prisoner' Freed under US Pressure Later
    Caught with Explosives Planning Terrorist Attack." *The Grayzone*,
    September 25, 2020. https://thegrayzone.com/2020/09/25/
    nicaragua-political-prisoner-us-pressure-terrorist/.

"Nicolás Maduro Moros - New Target." United States Department of State, March
    26, 2020. https://www.state.gov/nicolas-maduro-moros-new-target.

"Nicolás Maduro | Luke Denman, Confesión De Mercenario Estadounidense."
    Nicolás Maduro. YouTube, May 6, 2020. https://www.youtube.com/
    watch?v=8xS3onOoq4s.

"Nicolas Maduro Sworn in as New Venezuelan President." BBC, April 19, 2013.
    https://www.bbc.com/news/world-latin-america-22220526.

Nissenbaum, Dion, Stephen Kalin, and David S. Cloud. "Saudi, Emirati Leaders
    Decline Calls with Biden during Ukraine Crisis." *Wall Street Journal*, March 8,
    2022. https://www.wsj.com/articles/saudi-emirati-leaders-decline-calls-with-
    biden-during-ukraine-crisis-11646779430.

NTN24 Venezuela (@NTN24ve). Twitter post, February 23, 2019. https://twitter.
    com/NTN24ve/status/1099386437957574658?s=20.

OAS Adopts Resolution on Nicaragua. The Organization of American States, September
    12, 2018. https://usoas.usmission.gov/oas-adopts-resolution-on-nicaragua/.

Obiko Pearson, Natalie. "Leader of Strike to Oust Chavez Escapes."
    Associated Press, August 14, 2006. https://apnews.com/article/
    f29ac45cd990cb6c556508047769a450.

"Observing the Venezuela Presidential Recall Referendum." Carter Center, February
    2005. https://www.cartercenter.org/documents/2020.pdf.

O'Connor, Tom. "Venezuela Diplomat Reads Book during Trump's U.N. Speech
    Attacking Country." *Newsweek*, September 24, 2019. https://www.newsweek.
    com/venezuela-reads-book-trump-un-speech-attacking-country-1461053.

"Office of Transition Initiatives (OTI)." United States Agency for International
    Development. Accessed April 12, 2023. https://www.usaid.gov/about-us/
    organization/conflict-prevention-stabilization/office-transition-initiatives.

O'Grady, Siobhán. "The U.S. Says Maduro Is Blocking Aid to Starving People.
    The Venezuelan Says His People Aren't Beggars." *Washington Post*, February 19,
    2019. https://www.washingtonpost.com/world/2019/02/08/us-says-maduro-is-
    blocking-aid-starving-people-venezuelan-says-his-people-arent-beggars/.

"OI European's Complaint against Venezuela and Others (US Court Proceedings)."
    Italaw, February 11, 2019. https://www.italaw.com/cases/2979#:~:text=OI%20

European%27s%20Complaint%20against%20Venezuela%20and%20 Others%20(US%20Court%20Proceedings).

"O-I Prevails in International Arbitration against Venezuela." O-I, March 12, 2015. https://www.o-i.com/es/ news/o-i-prevails-in-international-arbitration-against-venezuela/.

"Oil Production." Our World in Data. Accessed March 31, 2023. https://our-worldindata.org/grapher/oil-production-by-country.

Omar, Abeer Abu, and Manus Cranny. "Saudi Arabia Says Open to Settling Trade in Other Currencies (2)." *Bloomberg Law*, January 17, 2023. https://news.bloomberglaw.com/international-trade/ saudi-arabia-says-open-to-settling-trade-in-other-currencies-2.

The Opinion Pages. "Hugo Chávez Departs." *New York Times*, April 13, 2002. https://www.nytimes.com/2002/04/13/opinion/hugo-chavez-departs.html.

Oré, Diego, and Andrew Cawthorne. "Venezuela's Maduro Decried as 'Dictator' after Congress Annulled." Reuters, March 30, 2017. https://www.reuters.com/ article/us-venezuela-politics-idUSKBN17122M.

Oropeza, Valentina. "El 'Delfín' Que Conducirá La Revolución Bolivariana." *El Tiempo*, April 15, 2013. www.eltiempo.com/archivo/documento/CMS-12742462.

Ortega Sanoja, Érika (@ErikaOSanoja). Twitter post, May 3, 2020. https://twitter. com/ErikaOSanoja/status/1257078346367762432.

Orr, James. "Venezuelans March against Chávez Reforms." *Guardian*, November 30, 2007. https://www.theguardian.com/world/2007/nov/30/venezuela.

"Our Donors." The Inter-American Dialogue. Accessed April 13, 2023. https:// www.thedialogue.org/support-us/our-donors/.

"Our Mission." Aid Live Foundation. Accessed March 11, 2023. https://aidlivefoun-dation.org/en/our-story/.

OV, Orlenys (@OrlenysOV). Twitter post, January 5, 2020. https://twitter.com/ OrlenysOV/status/1213955849535807490?s=20.

OV, Orlenys (@OrlenysOV). Twitter post [VIDEO], November 10, 2019. https:// twitter.com/OrlenysOV/status/1193713436871540737?s=20.

Pagliery, Jose. "Federal Judge Hands over Trump's Lawyer's Notes to DOJ." *Daily Beast*, March 18, 2023. https://www.thedailybeast.com/federal-judge-beryl-howell-hands-over-donald-trumps-lawyer-evan-corcorans-notes-to-doj.

Palencia, Gustavo. "Honduran President's Brother Arrested in Miami on Drug Charges." Reuters, November 23, 2018. https://www.reuters.com/article/ us-usa-honduras-drugs-idUSKCN1NT015.

Palencia, Gustavo. "OAS Says Honduran Presidential Election Should Be Redone." Reuters, December 17, 2017. https://www.reuters.com/article/ us-honduras-election-idUSKBN1EB0XH.

Parampil, Anya, and Diego Sequera. "From Exxon to 'Ambassador':
    How Carlos Vecchio Became Venezuela's Top Coup Lobbyist."
    The Grayzone, June 18, 2019. https://thegrayzone.com/2019/06/18/
    exxon-ambassador-carlos-vecchio-venezuela-coup-lobbyist/.

Parampil, Anya, and Max Blumenthal. "US 'Virtual Ambassador' to Venezuela
    Hosts Insurrectionist Summit Ahead of Biden's Guaidó Recognition."
    The Grayzone, March 3, 2021. https://thegrayzone.com/2021/03/03/
    virtual-ambassador-venezuela-hosts-insurrectionist-bidens-guaido/.

Parampil, Anya. "Alex Saab: Wife of Kidnapped Diplomat Describes His Torture
    & Illegal Arrest." *The Grayzone*, December 7, 2021. https://www.youtube.com/
    watch?v=iKNfvyKBDLw.

Parampil, Anya. "An Exclusive Look inside Iran's Supermarket in Venezuela."
    The Grayzone, December 30, 2020. https://thegrayzone.com/2020/12/30/
    inside-irans-supermarket-venezuela/.

Parampil, Anya. "Blockbuster Oil Bribery Scandal Exposes Corrupt Double-Dealing
    of Guaidó 'Attorney General'." *The Grayzone*, July 14, 2020. https://thegrayzone.
    com/2020/07/14/bribery-scandal-courts-corrupt-forces-guaidos-coup/.

Parampil, Anya. "Did Venezuelan Coup Leaders Pocket $70 Million from
    Citgo's Stolen US Assets?" *The Grayzone*, June 19, 2019. https://thegrayzone.
    com/2019/06/19/guaido-vecchio-citgo-theft-investigation/.

Parampil, Anya. "'Go to Hell': Venezuelan Coup Leader Ricardo Hausmann
    Stages WhatsApp Meltdown When Confronted with His Own Hypocrisy and
    Lack of Transparency." *The Grayzone*, September 6, 2019. https://thegrayzone.
    com/2019/09/06/go-to-hell-venezuelan-coup-leader-ricardo-hausmann-stages-
    whatsapp-meltdown-when-confronted-with-his-own-hypocrisy-and-lack-of-
    -transparency/.

Parampil, Anya. "Hausmann Hypocrisy: Guaido Coup Official Raked in Dollars
    from Dictators and Banking Behemoths While Promoting 'Democracy'
    for Venezuela." *The Grayzone*, August 31, 2019. https://thegrayzone.
    com/2019/08/31/hausmann-hypocrisy-guaido-dollars-dictators/.

Parampil, Anya. "How Bolivia Fights Fascism - It Takes More than the Ballot
    Box." *The Grayzone*, October 21, 2020. https://thegrayzone.com/2020/10/21/
    bolivia-fascism-coup-election/.

Parampil, Anya. "How Venezuela Defeated Washington's
    Coup Attempt at the United Nations." *The Grayzone*,
    October 2, 2019. https://thegrayzone.com/2019/10/02/
    how-venezuela-defeated-washingtons-coup-at-the-united-nations/#more-15174.

Parampil, Anya. "Meet Juan Guaido's First Ambassador, Fake Twitter Diplomat
    Slammed by Costa Rica for 'Unacceptable Entry.'" *The Grayzone*, February

21, 2019. https://thegrayzone.com/2019/02/21/meet-juan-guaidos-
first-ambassador-fake-twitter-diplomat-slammed-by-costa-rica-for-
unacceptable-entry/.

Parampil, Anya. "Ricardo Hausmann: The Neoliberal Brain behind Juan Guaido's
Agenda." *MintPress News*, March 15, 2019. https://www.mintpressnews.com/
ricardo-hausmann-morning-venezuela-neoliberal-brain-behind-juan-guaidos-
economic-agenda/256185/.

Parampil, Anya. "Silvercorp Co-Founder Speaks with The Grayzone:
What Did State Department Know about Failed Venezuela Invasion?"
The Grayzone, May 7, 2020. https://thegrayzone.com/2020/05/07/
silvercorp-founder-grayzone-state-department-venezuela-invasion/.

Parampil, Anya. "'Smoking Gun' Analysis Finds US Sanctions Produce 'War Time'
Economy in Venezuela." *The Grayzone*, January 14, 2022. https://www.youtube.
com/watch?v=I3_Od3T-FlI.

Parampil, Anya. "Survivors of Bolivia Coup Massacre Cry out for Justice –
A Grayzone Original Documentary." *The Grayzone*, November 2, 2020. https://
thegrayzone.com/2020/11/02/bolivia-coup-senkata-massacre-documentary/.

Parampil, Anya. "The Citgo Conspiracy: Opposition Figures Accuse Guaidó
Officials of 'Scam' to Liquidate Venezuela's Most Prized International Asset."
The Grayzone, September 3, 2019. https://thegrayzone.com/2019/09/03/
the-citgo-conspiracy-opposition-figures-accuse-guaido-officials-of-scam-to-
liquidate-venezuelas-most-prized-international-asset/.

Parampil, Anya. "'The Coup Turned Honduras into Hell': Interview with
President Manuel Zelaya on 10th Anniversary of Overthrow by US."
The Grayzone, July 1, 2019. https://thegrayzone.com/2019/07/01/
coup-honduras-interview-president-manuel-zelaya-10th-anniversary-us/.

Parampil, Anya. "Trump Admin. Behaves 'like Thugs in a Barrio':
Interview with Venezuelan Foreign Minister Jorge Arreaza." *The
Grayzone*, April 30, 2019. https://thegrayzone.com/2019/04/30/
interview-venezuelan-foreign-minister-jorge-arreaza/.

Parampil, Anya (@anyaparampil). Twitter post, April 10, 2019. https://twitter.com/
anyaparampil/status/1115840724182994944?s=20.

Parampil, Anya (@anyaparampil). Twitter post [VIDEO], April 16, 2020. https://
twitter.com/anyaparampil/status/1250953658772213760?s=20.

Parampil, Anya (@anyaparampil). Twitter post [VIDEO], April 23, 2019. https://
twitter.com/anyaparampil/status/1120806261518471168?s=20.

Parampil, Anya (@anyaparampil). Twitter post, May 1, 2019. https://twitter.com/
anyaparampil/status/1123706024672792576?s=20.

Parampil, Anya (@anyaparampil). Twitter post, May 1, 2019. https://twitter.com/
    anyaparampil/status/1123710389672398849?s=20.

Parampil, Anya (@anyaparampil). Twitter post, May 5, 2019. https://twitter.com/
    anyaparampil/status/1125113467676045312?s=20.

Parampil, Anya (@anyaparampil). Twitter post, May 8, 2019. https://twitter.com/
    anyaparampil/status/1126308077878370306?s=20.

Parampil, Anya (@anyaparampil). Twitter post, May 18, 2019. https://twitter.com/
    anyaparampil/status/1129795470488944640?s=20.

Parampil, Anya (@anyaparampil). Twitter post [VIDEO], October 19, 2020. https://
    twitter.com/anyaparampil/status/1318247885125857284?s=20.

Parampil, Anya. "US Kidnaps Venezuelan Diplomat: the Case of Alex Saab." *The
    Grayzone*, June 4, 2021. https://www.youtube.com/watch?v=Sz3AZcdSs88.

Parampil, Anya. "US State Department Publishes, Then Deletes Sadistic Venezuela
    Hit List Boasting of Economic Ruin." *The Grayzone*, May 6, 2019. https://
    thegrayzone.com/2019/05/06/us-state-department-publishes-then-deletes-
    sadistic-venezuela-hit-list-boasting-of-economic-ruin/.

Parampil, Anya. "US Trial of Venezuela's Alex Saab Exposes Diplomatic
    Espionage." *The Grayzone*, December 12, 2022. https://thegrayzone.
    com/2022/12/12/trial-venezuelan-alex-saab-diplomatic-espionage/.

Parampil, Anya. "Using Human Rights to Promote War:
    Debunking UN's New Venezuela Report." *The Grayzone*,
    October 1, 2020. https://thegrayzone.com/2020/10/01/
    using-human-rights-to-promote-war-debunking-uns-new-venezuela-report/.

Parampil, Anya. "Venezuela Coup Regime's OAS Rep Likens Situation to Nazi
    Invasion of USSR." *The Grayzone*, April 24, 2019. https://www.youtube.com/
    watch?v=yYy-lBV4cxI.

Parampil, Anya. "Venezuela UN Ambassador: US Gov. 'Psychologically
    Manipulating' Public to Support 'Colonial War.'" *The Grayzone*,
    April 29, 2019. https://thegrayzone.com/2019/04/29/
    venezuela-un-ambassador-samuel-moncada-interview/.

Parampil, Anya. "Venezuelan Embassy Protection Collective Wins Legal Victory in
    Face of Hostile Obama-Appointed Judge & Govt Prosecution." *The Grayzone*,
    June 3, 2020. https://thegrayzone.com/2020/06/03/venezuelan-embassy-
    protection-collective-wins-legal-victory-in-face-of-hostile-obama-appointed-
    judge-govt-prosecution/.

Parampil, Anya. "Venezuelan Voters Hit Back at US Election Hypocrisy."
    The Grayzone, December 9, 2020. https://www.youtube.com/
    watch?v=CPd3WU5JPO4&t=149s.

Parampil, Anya. "Venezuelans' Message to the US: Hands off Our Country." *The
    Grayzone*, February 11, 2019. https://www.youtube.com/watch?v=-LT_O7tI3DY.

Parampil, Anya. "Venezuela's Foreign Minister on 'Failed' Coup and Building New Non-Aligned Movement." *The Grayzone*, February 19, 2019. https://thegrayzone.com/2019/02/19/venezuelas-foreign-minister-on-the-failed-coup-and-building-a-new-non-aligned-movement/.

Parampil, Anya. "'We Are the Vaccine against Unilateralism': Non-Aligned Movement Gathers in Venezuela to Resist Dictatorship of Dollar." *The Grayzone*, July 28, 2019. https://thegrayzone.com/2019/07/28/we-are-the-vaccine-against-unilateralism-the-non-aligned-movement-gathers-in-venezuela-to-resist-the-dictatorship-of-the-dollar/.

Parampil, Anya. "'Weaponizing Human Rights': UN Chief Bachelet's Venezuela Report Follows US Regime Change Script." *The Grayzone*, July 6, 2019. https://thegrayzone.com/2019/07/06/weaponizing-human-rights-un-high-commissioner-bachelets-venezuela-report-follows-us-regime-change-script/.

Pardo, Daniel. "Maduro y Oposición En Venezuela Abren Una Puerta Al Diálogo." BBC, December 19, 2013. https://www.bbc.com/mundo/noticias/2013/12/131219_venezuela_maduro_oposicion_dialogo_dp.

Parraga, Marianna, and Mircely Guanipa. "Venezuela's Oil Exports in Sept Boosted by Sales to China, Swaps with Iran." Reuters, October 4, 2022. https://www.reuters.com/markets/commodities/venezuelas-oil-exports-sept-boosted-by-sales-china-swaps-with-iran-2022-10-04/.

Patton Walsh, Nick, Natalie Gallón, Evan Perez, Diana Castrillon, Barbara Arvanitidis, and Caitlin Hu. "Inside the August Plot to Kill Maduro with Drones." CNN, June 21, 2019. https://www.cnn.com/2019/03/14/americas/venezuela-drone-maduro-intl.

Penacca, Paula (@PaulaPenacca). Twitter post [VIDEO], October 16, 2020. https://twitter.com/PaulaPenacca/status/1317292221494906881?s=20.

Pence, Mike (@VP45). Twitter post, February 25, 2019. https://twitter.com/VP45/status/1100168044863721472?lang=en.

"Permanent Council Accepts Appointment of Designated Permanent Representative of Venezuela's National Assembly to the OAS". The Organization of American States, April 9, 2019. https://www.oas.org/en/media_center/press_release.asp?sCodigo=E-019/19.

"Peter Gabriel Will Not Perform at Venezuela Aid Live!" Genesis News, February 19, 2019. https://www.genesis-news.com/news-Peter-Gabriel-will-not-perform-at-Venezuela-Aid-Live-n560.html.

Picheta, Rob. "Bank of England Blocks Maduro's $1.2B Gold Withdrawal - Report." CNN, January 26, 2019. https://www.cnn.com/2019/01/26/uk/venezuela-maduro-bank-of-england-gold-withdrawal-gbr-intl/index.html.

Phillips, Tom. "Hugo Chávez Tells of Cancer Diagnosis." *Guardian*, June 30, 2011.

"Piden a Estados Unidos Investigar Actos Del Procurador
Especial." TalCual, August 8, 2019. https://talcualdigital.com/
piden-a-estados-unidos-investigar-actos-del-procurador-especial/.

"Pink Floyd's Roger Waters Says Richard Branson's Venezuela Concert Has
'Nothing to Do with Aid'." Global News, February 20, 2019. https://
globalnews.ca/video/4979779/pink-floyds-roger-waters-says-richard-bransons-
venezuela-concert-has-nothing-to-do-with-aid.

Planas, Roque. "Hillary Clinton's Response to Honduran Coup
Was Scrubbed from Her Paperback Memoirs." *Huffington
Post*, March 12, 2016. https://www.huffpost.com/entry/
hillary-clinton-honduras-coup-memoirs_n_56e34161e4b0b25c91820a08.

"Pobreza Monetaria y Pobreza Monetaria Extrema." Departamento Administrativo
Nacional de Estadística. Accessed April 11, 2023. https://www.dane.
gov.co/index.php/estadisticas-por-tema/pobreza-y-condiciones-de-vida/
pobreza-monetaria.

"Political Mastermind and Strategist JJ Rendon Once Again the Driving Force
Behind Juan Manuel Santos' Land-Slide Victory in Colombian Presidential
Election." Cision PR Newswire, June 22, 2010. https://www.prnewswire.com/
news-releases/political-mastermind-and-strategist-jj-rendon-once-again-the-
driving-force-behind-juan-manuel-santos-land-slide-victory-in-colombian-
presidential-election-96911889.html.

Politico Staff. "Full Text: Trump's 2018 UN Speech Transcript." *Politico*,
September 25, 2018. https://www.politico.com/story/2018/09/25/
trump-un-speech-2018-full-text-transcript-840043.

Pompeo, Mike. *Never Give an Inch: Fighting for the America I Love*. New York, NY:
Broadside Books, 2023.

Pompeo, Mike (@secpompeo). Twitter post, December 6, 2020. https://twitter.com/
SecPompeo/status/1335672345894268938?s=20.

Pompeo, Mike (@secpompeo). Twitter post, February 23, 2019. https://twitter.com/
secpompeo/status/1099472381838585856.

Pompeo, Mike (@secpompeo). Twitter post, June 18, 2020. https://twitter.com/
SecPompeo/status/1273712766340259841?s=20.

Pompeo, Mike (@secpomeo). Twitter post, March 7, 2019. https://twitter.com/
SecPompeo/status/1103872530450771968?s=20.

Pons, Corina. "Turkey's Erdogan Slams Venezuela Sanctions, Maduro Defends Gold
Exports." Reuters, December 3, 2018. https://www.reuters.com/article/us-
venezuela-turkey-erdogan/turkeys-erdogan-slams-venezuela-sanctions-maduro-
defends-gold-exports-idUSKBN1O22QM.

"'Por Ahora': 30 Años De La Rendición Que Catapultó a Chávez Tras UN
Golpe Fallido." France 24, February 3, 2022. https://www.france24.

com/es/minuto-a-minuto/20220203-por-ahora-30-a%C3%B1os-de-
la-rendici%C3%B3n-que-catapult%C3%B3-a-ch%C3%A1vez-tras-un-
golpe-fallido.

Porter, Gareth. "How the US Military Subverted the Afghan Peace Agreement to
Prolong an Unpopular War." *The Grayzone*, March 16, 2021. https://thegrayzone.
com/2021/03/16/trump-us-military-peace-agreement-war-afghanistan.

"President Delivers State of the Union Address." National Archives and Records
Administration, January 29, 2002. https://georgewbush-whitehouse.archives.
gov/news/releases/2002/01/20020129-11.html.

"President Donald J. Trump Announces Intent to Nominate and Appoint
Individuals to Key Administration Posts." National Archives and Records
Administration, May 6, 2020. https://trumpwhitehouse.archives.gov/
presidential-actions/president-donald-j-trump-announces-intent-nominate-
appoint-individuals-key-administration-posts-38/.

"President George W. Bush Welcomes Maria Corina Machado." National Archives
and Records Administration, May 31, 2005. https://georgewbush-whitehouse.
archives.gov/news/releases/2005/05/images/20050531_p44959-105jasjpg-
2-515h.html.

Price, Greg. "Watch: Mike Pompeo Faces 'No More War' Protest During First
Confirmation Hearing for Secretary of State." *Newsweek*, April 12, 2018. https://
www.newsweek.com/pompeo-protest-war-hearing-state-883602.

"Procurador Especial Designado Por Guaidó Desmiente Haber Participado
En Caso Crystallex." *La Patilla*, August 1, 2019. https://www.lapatilla.
com/2019/08/01/procurador-especial-designado-por-guaido-desmiente-haber-
participado-en-caso-crystallex/.

"Producto Interno Bruto (See: 'Producto Interno Bruto Por Sector Institucional
(Base 1997), Precios Constantes.'" Banco Central de Venezuela. Accessed April
4, 2023. https://www.bcv.org.ve/estadisticas/producto-interno-bruto.

"Projects - Las Cristinas." Crystallex International Corporation. Accessed March 28,
2023. http://www.crystallex.com/Projects/Projects/LasCristinas/.

"Rajoelina Stopped from Addressing UN General Assembly."
France 24, September 26, 2009. https://www.france24.com/
en/20090926-rajoelina-stopped-addressing-un-general-assembly-.

Ramos, Daniel. "Bolivia Election Delayed to October as Pandemic Bites,
Opposition Cries Foul." Reuters, July 23, 2020. https://www.reuters.com/
article/us-bolivia-politics-election-idUSKCN24O2PY.

Ramos, Jorge. "Complete Interview of Jorge Ramos to Nicolás Maduro." Univision
Noticias, June 2, 2019. https://www.youtube.com/watch?v=IOlSWdzx9z0.

"Rankings, Total Energy Production." United States Energy Information Administration. Accessed April 13, 2023. https://www.eia.gov/international/rankings/world.

Rapier, Robert. "Inside Venezuela's Contradictory Oil Industry." *Forbes*, February 22, 2023. https://www.forbes.com/sites/rrapier/2023/02/21/inside-venezuelas-contradictory-oil-industry/?sh=36149a1a7c13.

"Raw Footage: Police Raid Venezuelan Embassy in DC, Remove 'Embassy Protection Collective.'" NEWS2SHARE, May 16, 2019. https://www.youtube.com/watch?v=g8d_AXYRVsw.

"Re: and Now for Something Completelly Official." The Global Intelligence Files, WikiLeaks. February 19, 2013. https://wikileaks.org/gifiles/docs/10/104475_re-and-now-for-something-completelly-official-.html.

Re, Greg. "Bolton: 'No US Government Involvement' in Attempted Drone Assassination of Venezuelan President Maduro." Fox News, August 7, 2018. https://www.foxnews.com/politics/bolton-no-us-government-involvement-in-attempted-drone-assassination-of-venezuelan-president-maduro.

"Re: INSIGHT - VENEZUELA: CANVAS Analysis." The Global Intelligence Files, WikiLeaks. June 18, 2012. https://wikileaks.org/gifiles/docs/17/1713359_re-insight-venezuela-canvas-analysis-.html.

"Re: Question-Marija Stanisavljevic." The Global Intelligence Files, WikiLeaks. March 6, 2013. https://search.wikileaks.org/gifiles/?viewemailid=384127

"Record Turnout for Chavez Vote." CNN, August 16, 2004. https://www.cnn.com/2004/WORLD/americas/08/15/venezuela.recall/index.html.

Reed, Wyatt (@wyattreed13). Twitter post, May 1, 2019. https://twitter.com/wyattreed13/status/1123587231665487878?s=20.

"Regional Programs." Freedom House. Accessed March 8, 2023. https://freedom-house.org/programs/regional.

"Relatives of the Victims of Senkata and Sacaba Reach La Paz." Telesur English, October 21, 2021. https://www.telesurenglish.net/news/Relatives-of-the-Victims-of-Senkata-and-Sacaba-Reach-La-Paz-20211025-0008.html.

"Remarks at a UN Security Council Briefing on Venezuela." United States Mission to the United Nations, February 26, 2019. https://usun.usmission.gov/remarks-at-a-un-security-council-briefing-on-venezuela/.

"Remarks by President Biden on Gas Prices and Putin's Price Hike." The White House, June 22, 2022. https://www.white-house.gov/briefing-room/speeches-remarks/2022/06/22/remarks-by-president-biden-on-gas-prices-and-putins-price-hike/.

"Remarks by President Trump to the 73rd Session of the United Nations General Assembly." National Archives and Records Administration, September 25, 2018. https://trumpwhitehouse.archives.gov/briefings-statements/

remarks-president-trump-73rd-session-united-nations-general-assembly-new-york-ny/.

"Remarks by President Trump to the 74th Session of the United Nations General Assembly." National Archives and Records Administration, September 25, 2019. https://trumpwhitehouse.archives.gov/briefings-statements/remarks-president-trump-74th-session-united-nations-general-assembly/.

Rendon, Moises, and Claudia Fernandez. "The Fabulous Five: How Foreign Actors Prop up the Maduro Regime in Venezuela." Center for Strategic and International Studies, October 19, 2020. https://www.csis.org/analysis/fabulous-five-how-foreign-actors-prop-maduro-regime-venezuela.

Reuters. "Iran Signs 110 Million Euro Contract to Repair Venezuelan Refinery." Reuters, May 13, 2022. https://www.reuters.com/business/energy/iran-signs-110-mln-euro-contract-repair-venezuelan-refinery-2022-05-13/.

Reuters Staff. "Cape Verde Supreme Court Rules on Extradition of Maduro Envoy." Reuters, March 17, 2021. https://www.reuters.com/world/americas/cape-verde-supreme-court-rules-extradition-maduro-envoy-2021-03-17/.

Reuters Staff. "Court Grants House Arrest to Maduro Envoy Jailed in Cape Verde, Lawyers Say." Reuters, December 4, 2020. https://www.reuters.com/article/ozatp-us-venezuela-politics-capeverde-idAFKBN28E0SY-OZATP.

Reuters Staff. "Grupo Aeromexico Suspends Venezuela Operations, Cites Economy." Reuters, June 23, 2016. https://www.reuters.com/article/aeromexico-venezuela-idUSE1N18K021.

Reuters Staff. "Lufthansa Suspends Caracas Flights as Venezuelan Economy Struggles." Reuters, May 28, 2016. https://www.reuters.com/article/us-venezuela-airlines-idUSKCN0YJ0QS.

Reuters Staff. "Maduro Isolated as Latin American Nations Back Venezuela Opposition Leader." Reuters, January 23, 2019. https://www.reuters.com/article/us-venezuela-politics-latam-idUSKCN1PI01J.

Reuters Staff. "Maduro Says U.S. Seeks to Steal Citgo from Venezuela." Reuters, January 29, 2019. https://www.reuters.com/article/us-venezuela-politics-usa-citgo-idINKCN1PM2PL.

Reuters Staff. "Moody's Downgrades Venezuela Rating by Two Notches." Reuters, March 9, 2018. https://www.reuters.com/article/moodys-venezuela/moodys-downgrades-venezuela-rating-by-two-notches-idUSL4N1QR5NO.

Reuters Staff. "Portuguese Bank Halted $1.2 Billion Transfer of Venezuela Funds: Lawmaker." Reuters, February 5, 2019. https://www.reuters.com/article/us-venezuela-politics-portugal-idUSKCN1PU23S.

Reuters Staff. "Presidente De Venezuela Dice Que Hay Dos Estadounidenses En Grupo 'Mercenario.'" Reuters, May 4, 2020. https://www.reuters.com/article/venezuela-detenidos-idLTAKBN22G2NH.

Reuters Staff. "Timeline: Ousted President Zelaya to Leave Honduras." Reuters, December 9, 2009. https://www.reuters.com/article/us-honduras-zelaya-timeline-idUSTRE5B90BS20091210.

Reuters Staff. "Update 1-Turkey-Iran Central Banks Agree to Trade in Local Currencies - Turkish PM." Reuters, October 19, 2017. https://www.reuters.com/article/turkey-iran-currency-idUSL8N1MU4SQ.

Reuters Staff. "U.S. Will Act If Turkish Trade Violates Venezuela Sanctions, Official Says." Reuters, January 31, 2019. https://www.reuters.com/article/us-usa-venezuela-turkey/u-s-will-act-if-turkish-trade-violates-venezuela-sanctions-official-says-idUSKCN1PP2ET.

Reuters Staff. "Venezuela Restores Opposition Leader Lopez to House Arrest: Wife." Reuters, August 5, 2017. https://www.reuters.com/article/us-venezuela-politics-lopez-idUSKBN1AM02L.

Reuters Staff. "Venezuela to Withdraw from OAS, Denounces Campaign by Washington." Reuters, April 26, 2017. https://www.reuters.com/article/us-venezuela-oas-idUSKBN17S330.

Reuters Staff. "Venezuelan Opposition Politician Lopez Arrives in Madrid, Spain Says." Reuters, October 25, 2020. https://www.reuters.com/article/us-venezuela-politics-spain-lopez-idUSKBN27A0AE.

Reuters Staff. "Venezuela's Guaido Says Humanitarian Aid Will Arrive on Feb 23." Reuters, February 12, 2019. https://www.reuters.com/article/us-venezuela-politics-guaido-idUSKCN1Q1277.

Reuters Staff. "Venezuela's Major Opposition Parties Pledge to Boycott December Election." Reuters, August 2, 2020. https://www.reuters.com/article/us-venezuela-politics-idUSKBN24Y0ME.

Reuters Staff. "West African Court Orders Release of Maduro Envoy in Cape Verde." Reuters, March 15, 2021. https://www.reuters.com/article/venezuela-politics-saab-idAFL8N2LD50U.

Ricardo Hausmann public disclosure. Accessed March 22, 2023. https://apps.hks.harvard.edu/faculty/PublicDisclosure.aspx?id=20546255.

Rivas, Marcel (@Marcelrivasf). Twitter post, October 15, 2020. https://twitter.com/Marcelrivasf/status/1316710166293774336.

Rodrigues, Julio. "Opposition Candidate Neves Wins Cape Verde Election." Reuters, October 18, 2021. https://www.reuters.com/world/africa/opposition-candidate-neves-wins-cape-verde-election-2021-10-18/.

Rodríguez, Francisco. "Sanctions, Economic Statecraft, and Venezuela's Crisis." Sanctions and Security, January 2022. https://sanctionsandsecurity.org/wp-content/uploads/2022/01/January-2022-Venezuela-Case_Rodriguez.pdf.

Rodríguez, Delcy (@drodriven2). Twitter post, June 18, 2020. https://twitter.com/drodriven2/status/1273730550151421957?s=20.

Rodríguez, Francisco. "¿Cuál Es La Verdadera Relación De Fuerzas En La Asamblea Nacional De Venezuela?" January 11, 2020. https://franciscorodriguez.net/2020/01/11/cual-es-la-verdadera-relacion-de-fuerzas-en-la-asamblea-nacional-de-venezuela/.

Rodríguez, Francisco. The economic determinants of Venezuela's hunger crisis, June 23, 2022. https://papers.ssrn.com/sol3/papers.cfm?abstract_id=4138830.

Rodríguez, Jorge (@jorgerpsuv). Twitter post, February 25, 2019. https://x.com/jorgerpsuv/status/1100210145592774658?s=20.

Rohter, Larry. "Marcos Pérez Jiménez, 87, Venezuela Ruler." *New York Times*, September 22, 2001. www.nytimes.com/2001/09/22/world/marcos-perez-jimenez-87-venezuela-ruler.html.

Roig-Franzia, Manuel. "Marco Rubio's Compelling Family Story Embellishes Facts, Documents Show." *Washington Post*, October 20, 2011. https://www.washingtonpost.com/politics/marco-rubios-compelling-family-story-embellishes-facts-documents-show/2011/10/20/gIQAaVHD1L_story.html.

Rojas Jiménez, Andrés. "José Ignacio Hernández: He Sido Difamado y Sometido Al Escarnio Público." HispanoPost, August 9, 2019. https://hispanopost.com/jose-ignacio-hernandez-he-sido-difamado-y-sometido-al-escarnio-publico/.

Romero, Simon. "Gunmen Attack Opponents of Chávez's Bid to Extend Power." *New York Times*, November 8, 2007. https://www.nytimes.com/2007/11/08/world/americas/08venez.html.

"Ronald Maclean-Abaroa." Harvard Kennedy School. Accessed April 13, 2023. https://www.hks.harvard.edu/about/ronald-maclean-abaroa.

Rubinstein, Alex (@RealAlexRubi). Twitter post, May 8, 2019. https://twitter.com/RealAlexRubi/status/1126029731260981248?s=20.

Rubinstein, Alex (@RealAlexRubi). Twitter post, May 8, 2019. https://twitter.com/RealAlexRubi/status/1126219076731273218?s=20.

Rubinstein, Alex (@RealAlexRubi). Twitter post, May 8, 2019. https://twitter.com/RealAlexRubi/status/1126257716807262208?s=20.

Rubinstein, Alex (@RealAlexRubi). Twitter post, May 8, 2019. https://twitter.com/RealAlexRubi/status/1126289686916419584?s=20.

Rubinstein, Alex (@RealAlexRubi). Twitter post [VIDEO], May 13, 2019. https://twitter.com/RealAlexRubi/status/1128084822432284672?s=20.

Rubinstein, Alex. "Violent, Bigoted Supporters of Juan Guaidó Attempt to Invade Venezuela's D.C. Embassy." *MintPress News*, May 1, 2019. https://www.mintpressnews.com/guaido-supporters-attempt-invade-venezuelan-embassy/258062/.

"Rubio Comments on Venezuela's Future." United States Senator for Florida, Marco Rubio, March 6, 2013. https://www.rubio.senate.gov/public/index.cfm/mobile/press-releases?ID=0DE8D5F4-7E61-4B93-849A-48605593431D.

Rubio, Marco (@marcorubio). Twitter post, February 23, 2019. https://twitter.com/marcorubio/status/1099389541281132550.

Rubio, Marco (@marcorubio). Twitter post, February 23, 2019. https://twitter.com/marcorubio/status/1099512202799779841.

Rubio, Marco (@marcorubio). Twitter post, February 24, 2019. https://twitter.com/marcorubio/status/1099565854100992000?s=20.

Rubio, Marco (@marcorubio). Twitter post, February 24, 2019. https://twitter.com/marcorubio/status/1099726515292508162?s=20.

Rubio, Marco (@marcorubio). Twitter post, February 24, 2019. https://twitter.com/marcorubio/status/1099808766894190592?s=20.

Rubio, Marco (@marcorubio). Twitter post, March 7, 2019. https://twitter.com/marcorubio/status/1103782022537977857?s=20.

"Rubio Pide Que Régimen De Maduro y Colectivos Sean Designados Organizaciones Terroristas." Radio y Televisión Martí, April 5, 2019. https://www.radiotelevisionmarti.com/a/rubio-pide-regimen-maduro-colectivos-sean-designados-organizaciones-terroristas/235713.html.

Rueda, Jorge. "Univision Says It Recovered Contentious Maduro Interview." Associated Press, May 30, 2019. https://apnews.com/article/71ab99e73f6d46a69a44b8434211dec4.

Rugaber, Christopher. "U.S. Inflation at 9.1 Percent, a Record High." PBS, July 13, 2022. https://www.pbs.org/newshour/economy/u-s-inflation-at-9-1-percent-a-record-high.

Ruggiero, Gianfranco. "El Aissami: 'El Buque Fortune Se Convirtió En Símbolo De Hermandad Entre Irán y Venezuela.'" El Co-Operante, May 25, 2020. https://elcooperante.com/el-aissami-el-buque-fortune-se-convirtio-en-simbolo-de-hermandad-entre-iran-y-venezuela/.

Ruiz Leotaud, Valentina. "Maduro Exhorts Venezuelan Army to Combat Environmental Destruction ..." Mining, December 29, 2022. https://www.mining.com/maduro-exhorts-venezuelan-army-to-combat-environmental-destruction-caused-by-illegal-gold-mining/.

"Russia, Turkey to Create Joint Investment Fund for 900 MLN Euro." TASS, April 8, 2019. https://tass.com/economy/1052566.

"Russia-Ukraine Crisis Ignites Fertilizer Prices at Critical Time for World Crops." Gro Intelligence. Accessed August 22, 2023. https://www.gro-intelligence.com/insights/russia-ukraine-crisis-ignites-fertilizer-prices-at-critical-time-for-world-crops.

"SABIAS QUE LOS VENEZOLANOS ELEGIREMOS." International Foundation for Electoral Systems, November 8, 1998. https://web.archive.org/web/20171203195239/https://www.ifes.org/sites/default/files/ce02706_0.pdf.

Saito, Yuta, and Iori Kawate. "China's U.S. Treasury Holdings Hit 12-Year Low on Rate Hikes, Tensions." *Nikkei Asia*, February 17, 2023. https://asia.nikkei.com/Business/Markets/Bonds/China-s-U.S.-Treasury-holdings-hit-12-year-low-on-rate-hikes-tensions.

Sánchez, Karen. "Representantes De Guaidó Solicitan a Fiscalía Colombiana Investigar Mal Uso De Fondos." Voice of America, June 18, 2019. https://www.vozdeamerica.com/a/gobierno-encargado-de-venezuela-solicita-a-la-fiscalia-colombiana-investigar-presunto-desvio-de-fondos/4964131.html.

Sanders, Sir Ronald. "World View: Is the OAS Putting Its Credibility in Doubt?" *Tribune 242*, January 29, 2018. http://www.tribune242.com/news/2018/jan/29/world-view-is-the-oas-putting-its-credibility-in/.

Sanderson, Cosmo. "Air Canada Lands Win against Venezuela." *Global Arbitration Review*, September 14, 2021. https://globalarbitrationreview.com/article/air-canada-lands-win-against-venezuela.

Sanger, David E., and Nicole Perlroth. "U.S. Escalates Online Attacks on Russia's Power Grid." *New York Times*, June 15, 2019. https://www.nytimes.com/2019/06/15/us/politics/trump-cyber-russia-grid.html.

Scharfenberg, Ewald. "Duelo e Incertidumbre En Venezuela Tras La Muerte De Chávez." *El País*, March 5, 2013.

Scharfenberg, Ewald. "La Oposición Venezolana Convoca Una Gran Marcha Contra La Violencia." *El País*, February 16, 2014. https://elpais.com/internacional/2014/02/16/actualidad/1392578363_617270.html.

Scherer, Zachary. "Majority of Voters Used Nontraditional Methods to Cast Ballots in 2020." United States Census, April 8, 2021. https://www.census.gov/library/stories/2021/04/what-methods-did-people-use-to-vote-in-2020-election.html.

Schmitt, Eric, and Julie Turkewitz. "Navy Warship's Secret Mission Off West Africa Aims to Help Punish Venezuela." *New York Times*, December 22, 2020. https://www.nytimes.com/2020/12/22/us/politics/navy-cape-verde-venezuela.html.

Schwartz, Mattathias. "William Barr's State of Emergency." *New York Times*, June 1, 2020. https://www.nytimes.com/2020/06/01/magazine/william-barr-attorney-general.html.

Schwartz, Matthew S, and Amy Held. "Juan Guaidó Returns To Venezuela, Risking Arrest." NPR, March 4, 2019. https://www.npr.org/2019/03/04/699936880/guaid-plans-to-return-to-venezuela-risking-arrest.

Seddon, Mark. "British and US Intervention in the Venezuelan Oil Industry: A Case Study of Anglo-Us Relations, 1941-1948." PhD thesis, University of Sheffield, 2014. https://etheses.whiterose.ac.uk/6901/.

Selby-Green, Michael. "Russia Is Dumping US Debt and Buying Gold Instead." *Business Insider*, July 19, 2018. https://www.businessinsider.com/russia-sells-us-treasuries-debt-2018-7.

Sequera, Diego. "TAREK WILLIAM SAAB: 'EL MAYOR DESAFÍO ES LA REINVENCIÓN CONSTANTE.'" *Misión Verdad*, March 11, 2023. https://misionverdad.com/entrevistas/tarek-william-saab-el-mayor-desafio-es-la-reinvencion-constante.

Sequera, Vivian, Angus Berwick, and Luc Cohen. "Venezuela's Guaido Calls for Uprising but Military Loyal to Maduro for Now." Reuters, April 30, 2019. https://www.reuters.com/article/us-venezuela-politics/venezuelas-guaido-calls-for-uprising-but-military-loyal-to-maduro-for-now-idUSKCN1S60ZQ.

Shaikh, Salaar, and Azad Amanat. "Yale World Fellow in Hiding: Carlos Vecchio and the Situation in Venezuela." *Yale Globalist*, November 9, 2013. https://globalist.yale.edu/onlinecontent/blogs/yale-world-fellow-in-hiding-carlos-vecchio-and-the-situation-in-venezuela/.

Silvercorp USA (@silvercoupusa). Instagram post, March 21, 2018. https://www.instagram.com/p/BgmlCTsnf_V/?igshid=MDJmNzVkMjY%3D.

Simpson, Conner. "Hugo Chavez's Successor Is More or Less Decided." *The Atlantic*, March 5, 2013. https://www.theatlantic.com/international/archive/2013/03/hugo-chavez-successor/317706/.

Singman, Brooke. "Trump Targeted: A Look at Probes Involving the Former President; from Stormy Daniels to Russia to Mar-a-Lago." Fox News, March 31, 2023. https://www.foxnews.com/politics/trump-targeted-look-investigations-involving-former-president-from-russia-mar-a-lago.

Smartmatic. "Carter: 'The Electoral System in Venezuela Is the Best in the World.'" September 26, 2012. https://elections.smartmatic.com/carter-the-electoral-system-in-venezuela-is-the-best-in-the-world/.

Smith, Michael, and Monte Reel. "Venezuela's Trade Scheme With Turkey Is Enriching a Mysterious Maduro Crony." *Bloomberg Businessweek*, April 25, 2019. https://www.bloomberg.com/news/features/2019-04-25/venezuela-turkey-trading-scheme-enriches-mysterious-maduro-crony.

Smith, Scott, and Joshua Goodman. "Ex-Green Berets Sentenced to 20 Years for Venezuela Attack." Associated Press, August 8, 2020. https://apnews.com/article/ap-top-news-caracas-special-forces-latin-america-caribbean-48b805ba801bfa92495e24471751f1fe.

Smith, Scott, and Joshua Goodman. "Venezuela: 2 Us 'Mercenaries' among Those Nabbed after Raid." Associated Press, May 5, 2020. https://apnews.com/article/caribbean-ap-top-news-venezuela-international-news-television-fb3b0e84b1d58cb876fd38c7a9493fd5.

Smith, Scott. "Trump Sanctions Targeting Venezuela's Maduro Lead to Mexico." Associated Press, June 18, 2020. https://apnews.com/article/20cded816b7ca0fb6a7f8ce9635c8869.

Smith, Scott. "Venezuela Says It Foiled Attack by Armed Men on Boat, Blames Plot on Colombia, US." Associated Press. *Chicago Tribune*, May 3, 2020. https://www.chicagotribune.com/nation-world/ct-nw-venezuela-boat-attack-20200503-iwk3se6sfve5fpdovl365te3ru-story.html.

Smith, Scott. "Venezuela's Guaidó Leads Thousands in Anti-Maduro Protest." Associated Press, November 16, 2019. https://apnews.com/article/402a8d033e424dc185a0fa30b1367cab.

Soghom, Mardo. "Venezuela Boosting Oil Exports With Iranian Light Crude Supplies." *Iran International*, May 23, 2022. https://www.iranintl.com/en/202205233767.

"Somos Revolucionarios y Profundamente Patriotas." Prensa Presidencial, May 7, 2020. https://www.youtube.com/watch?v=DHY8Ap31ixA.

"Speech by Richard Nixon (15 August 1971)." Centre Virtuel de la Connaissance sur l'Europe. Accessed March 31, 2023. https://www.cvce.eu/content/publication/1999/1/1/168eed17-f28b-487b-9cd2-6d668e42e63a/publishable_en.pdf.

Spence, Eddie. "London Gold Dealer Runs out of Bullion as Truss Budget Shocks." *Bloomberg*, October 1, 2022. https://www.bloomberg.com/news/articles/2022-10-01/london-gold-dealer-runs-out-of-bars-as-truss-budget-shocks#xj4y7vzkg.

Spetalnick, Matt, and Humeyra Pamuk. "U.S. Will Use 'Every Tool' to Secure Release If Any Americans Held in Venezuela: Pompeo." Reuters, May 6, 2020. https://www.reuters.com/article/us-venezuela-security-usa/us-will-use-every-tool-to-secure-release-if-any-americans-held-in-venezuela-pompeo-idUSKBN22I2DM.

Srivastava, Shruti, and Vrishti Beniwal. "Russia Offers Swift Payment System Alternative to India for Buying Oil in Rubles." *Bloomberg*, March 30, 2022. https://www.bloomberg.com/news/articles/2022-03-30/russia-proposes-swift-alternative-to-india-for-ruble-payments.

The Staff of the Board of Governors of the Federal Reserve System. "CURRENT ECONOMIC AND FINANCIAL CONDITIONS." The United States Federal Reserve, July 21, 1971. https://www.federalreserve.gov/monetarypolicy/files/FOMC19710727greenbook19710721.pdf.

State Department Spokesperson (@StateDeptSpox). Twitter post, July 5, 2019. https://twitter.com/StateDeptSpox/status/1147293203055312897?s=20.

"Statement of President Obama on the Death of Venezuelan President Hugo Chavez." National Archives and Records Administration, March 5, 2013. https://

obamawhitehouse.archives.gov/realitycheck/the-press-office/2013/03/05/
statement-president-obama-death-venezuelan-president-hugo-chavez.

"Statement of the Group of Auditors Electoral Process in Bolivia." Organization of
American States, November 10, 2019. https://www.oas.org/en/media_center/
press_release.asp?sCodigo=E-099/19.

Stratfor. "Venezuela: The Marigold Revolution?" October 5, 2007. https://world-
view.stratfor.com/article/venezuela-marigold-revolution.

"The Struggle Against Sanctions: The Case of Venezuela." The
People's Forum NYC, June 25, 2019. https://www.youtube.com/
watch?v=HTA93dI3l1k&t=6768s.

Suggett, James. "Venezuela to Nationalize Country's Largest Gold Mine Las
Cristinas." *Venezuelanalysis*, November 6, 2008. https://venezuelanalysis.com/
news/3932.

Swift. "Discover Swift." Accessed March 24, 2023. https://www.swift.com/es/
about-us/discover-swift.

"SWIFT Unlinks Iran's Central Bank." *Financial Tribune*, November 13, 2018.
https://financialtribune.com/articles/business-and-markets/95063/
swift-unlinks-irans-central-bank.

"Switzerland Not To Investigate Venezuelan Diplomatic Envoy." Telesur English,
March 26, 2021. https://www.telesurenglish.net/news/Switzerland-Not-To-
Investigate-Venezuelan-Diplomatic-Envoy-20210326-0010.html.

Tamayo Gomez, Camilo. "Return of Mass Killings Threaten
Colombia's Fragile Peace Deal." UPI, February 16, 2021.
https://www.upi.com/Top_News/Voices/2021/02/16/
Return-of-mass-killings-threaten-Colombias-fragile-peace-deal/7011613479722/.

"Tareck Zaidan El Aissami Maddah- New Target." United States
Department of State, March 26, 2020. https://www.state.gov/
tareck-zaidan-el-aissami-maddah-new-target/.

"Tasty Name but No Big Mac: Russia Opens Rebranded McDonald's Restaurants."
Reuters, June 13, 2022. https://www.reuters.com/world/europe/mcdonalds-
russia-reopens-under-new-ownership-renamed-vkusno-tochka-2022-06-12/.

Taylor, Adam. "Venezuela's Maduro: How Long Can an Isolated
Strongman Last?" *Washington Post*, February 5, 2019.
https://www.washingtonpost.com/world/2019/02/05/
despite-protests-isolation-strongmen-like-venezuelas-maduro-can-cling-power/.

Taylor, Matthew. "Evo Morales Hails 'New Bolivia' as Constitution Is Approved."
Guardian, January 26, 2009. https://www.theguardian.com/world/2009/
jan/26/bolivia.

"'They Attacked Civilians, They Are Not Heroes': Journalist Recounts Trampling by Venezuela Defectors." RT, February 24, 2019. https://www.rt.com/news/452317-journalist-hurt-defectors-venezuela/.

"Thousands Protest against Chavez's Education Reforms in Venezuela." Associated Press, January 19, 2001. https://www.latinamericanstudies.org/venezuela/education.htm.

"Timeline: Oil Dependence and U.S. Foreign Policy." Council on Foreign Relations. Accessed March 24, 2023. https://tinyurl.com/b9w9h559.

Torres, Adry, and the Associated Press. "'You Are Going to Swallow Your Provocations with a Coca-Cola': Univision Recovers the Footage of Its Tense Interview with Venezuelan President Nicolás Maduro That Was Cut Short and Led to the Detention and Deportation of Journalist Jorge Ramos." *Daily Mail*, May 30, 2019. https://www.dailymail.co.uk/news/article-7089409/Univision-says-recovered-contentious-Maduro-interview.html.

Torres, Patricia, and Nicholas Casey. "Venezuela Muzzles Legislature, Moving Closer to One-Man Rule." *New York Times*, March 30, 2017. /www.nytimes.com/2017/03/30/world/americas/venezuelas-supreme-court-takes-power-from-legislature.html. "Torture and Nicaragua's Fascist Opposition." Tortilla Con Sal, March 19, 2019. https://www.tortillaconsal.com/tortilla/node/5889.

"Torture Survivor Bachelet Takes Human Rights Lead at UN – DW – 09/01/2018." Deutsche Welle, September 1, 2018. https://www.dw.com/en/michelle-bachelet-from-torture-survivor-to-un-human-rights-head/a-45319900.

"Treasury Disrupts Corruption Network Stealing from Venezuela's Food Distribution Program, CLAP." United States Department of the Treasury, July 25, 2019. https://home.treasury.gov/news/press-releases/sm741.

"Treasury Removes Sanctions Imposed on Former High-Ranking Venezuelan Intelligence Official after Public Break with Maduro and Dismissal." United States Department of the Treasury, May 7, 2019. shorturl.at/mvQY4.

"Treasury Sanctions Maduro Regime Officials for Undermining Democratic Order in Venezuela." United States Department of the Treasury, September 4, 2020. https://home.treasury.gov/news/press-releases/sm1115.

"Treasury Sanctions Venezuelan Minister of Foreign Affairs." United States Department of the Treasury, April 26, 2019. https://home.treasury.gov/news/press-releases/sm670.

Trish Regan: Primetime. "John Bolton: I Don't Think Maduro Has the Military on His Side." Fox Business, January 25, 2019. https://video.foxbusiness.com/v/5993599263001#sp=show-clips.

"Trump Sides with Russia against FBI at Helsinki Summit." BBC, July 16, 2018. https://www.bbc.com/news/world-europe-44852812.

"Tucker vs Critic Who Calls Him Cheerleader for Russia." Fox News, July 12, 2017.
https://www.youtube.com/watch?v=4HjVipLZYns.

"Tucker: US Came within Minutes of War with Iran." Fox News, June 21, 2019.
https://www.youtube.com/watch?v=-c0jMsspE7Y.

"Turkey (Tur) and Venezuela (VEN) Trade." The Observatory of Economic
Complexity. Accessed April 6, 2023. https://oec.world/en/profile/
bilateral-country/tur/partner/ven.

"Turkish Central Bank Sells off Half of US Government Bonds in 6 Months." Daily
Sabah, August 15, 2018. https://www.dailysabah.com/economy/2018/08/15/
turkish-central-bank-sells-off-half-of-us-government-bonds-in-6-months.

TVV Noticias (@TVVnoticias). Twitter post, July 31, 2019. https://twitter.com/
TVVnoticias/status/1156735765239324672.

"Two Colombian Businessmen Charged with Money Laundering in Connection
with Venezuela Bribery Scheme." United States Attorney's Office, The
Southern District of Florida, July 25, 2019. https://www.justice.gov/usao-sdfl/
pr/two-colombian-businessmen-charged-money-laundering-connection-
venezuela-bribery-scheme#:~:text=Alex%20Nain%20Saab%20Moran%20
(Saab,seven%20counts%20of%20money%20laundering.

"UK Recognises Juan Guaido as Interim President of Venezuela." Government of
the United Kingdom, February 4, 2019. https://www.gov.uk/government/news/
uk-recognises-juan-guaido-as-interim-president-of-venezuela.

"U.N. Chief Must Condemn Own Expert's 'Fake Investigation' of Venezuela
Rights Record." UN Watch, November 29, 2017. https://unwatch.
org/u-n-experts-venezuela-visit-fake-investigation-swiss-rights-group/.

"Un Hotel, La Vivienda De Los Militares De Guaidó." El Colombiano,
April 24, 2019. https://www.elcolombiano.com/internacional/
un-hotel-la-vivienda-de-los-militares-de-guaido-MM10586208.

"UN Human Rights Report on Venezuela Urges Immediate Measures
to Halt and Remedy Grave Rights Violations." OHCHR, July
4, 2019. https://www.ohchr.org/en/press-releases/2019/07/
un-human-rights-report-venezuela-urges-immediate-measures-halt-and-remedy.

"UN Watch." Militarist Monitor, December 1, 2011. https://militarist-monitor.org/
profile/un_watch/.

"The United States Sanctions Additional Individuals Involved in the Illegitimate
Maduro Regime's Attempts to Corrupt Democratic Elections in Venezuela."
United States Embassy in Georgia, September 22, 2020. https://ge.usembassy.
gov/the-united-states-sanctions-additional-individuals-involved-in-the-
illegitimate-maduro-regimes-attempts-to-corrupt-democratic-elections-in-
venezuela/.

USA Gold. "De Gaulle Criterion Speech." Accessed March 30, 2023. https://www.
    usagold.com/cpmforum/favorite-web-pages-degaulle/.
"USA: Multiple Arrests as pro and Anti-Guaido Activists Face off at Embassy in
    DC." Ruptly, May 4, 2019. https://www.ruptly.tv/en/videos/20190505-007-
    USA--Multiple-arrests-as-pro-and-anti-Guaido-activists-face-off-at-embassy-in-
    DC?search_key=346299f2-5e80-43c5-8dea-b2f59a4077fa.
"US and OAS Lobby for Nicaraguan 'Political Prisoners' Who Butcher Their
    Pregnant Girlfriends." *The Grayzone*, February 28, 2020. https://thegrayzone.
    com/2020/02/28/us-oas-nicaragua-political-prisoners-murder/.
"U.S. Coast Guard Cutter Bear Underway." Defense Visual Information
    Distribution Center, October 28, 2020. https://www.dvidshub.net/
    image/6405420/us-coast-guard-cutter-bear-underway.
"U.S.-Colombia Anti-Drug Plan Pushes Failed Policy of Aerial Fumigation."
    Washington Office on Latin America, March 6, 2020. https://www.wola.
    org/2020/03/usa-colombia-anti-drug-plan-failed-aerial-fumigation/.
"U.S. Congressman Introduces Gold Standard Bill as Inflation Spirals out of
    Control." Yahoo! Finance, October 9, 2022. https://finance.yahoo.com/news/u--
    congressman-introduces-gold-standard-000000486.html.
"US Government Drops Case against Max Blumenthal after Jailing Journalist
    on False Charges." *The Grayzone*, December 7, 2019. https://thegrayzone.
    com/2019/12/07/us-government-dropped-charges-max-blumenthal-arrest/.
"U.S. Imports from Venezuela of Crude Oil (Thousand Barrels per Day)." U.S.
    Energy Information Administration. Accessed August 22, 2023. https://www.
    eia.gov/dnav/pet/hist/LeafHandler.ashx?n=PET&s=MCRIMUSVE2&f=M.
"US Indicts Venezuela's Maduro for 'Narco-Terrorism', Offer $15 Million for
    Arrest." France 24, March 26, 2020. https://www.france24.com/en/20200326-
    us-indicts-venezuela-s-maduro-for-narco-terrorism-offer-15-million-for-arrest.
U.S. Mission Italy. "Secretary Michael R. Pompeo At a Press Availability, April 29,
    2020." U.S. Embassy & Consulates in Italy, April 29, 2020. https://it.usembassy.
    gov/secretary-michael-r-pompeo-at-a-press-availability-april-29-2020/.
U.S. Mission to the UN (@USUN). Twitter post, May 20, 2018. https://twitter.com/
    USUN/status/998304169982349313.
U.S. Mission to the UN (@USUN). Twitter post, September 27, 2019. https://twit-
    ter.com/USUN/status/1177686281112801280?s=20.
"US Sanctions 'Have Taken Thousands of Venezuelan Lives' Says Arreaza to
    UN." Telesur English, April 25, 2019. https://www.telesurenglish.net/news/
    US-Sanctions-Have-Taken-Thousands-of-Venezuelan-Lives-Says-Arreaza-to-
    UN--20190425-0023.html.

"US Sends Warships to Caribbean to Stop Illegal Drugs." BBC, April 2, 2020. https://www.bbc.com/news/world-latin-america-52133500.

"US to Inject $100m into Cape Verdean Economy; Begins Construction of New Embassy." *Business and Financial Times Online*, July 6, 2021. https://thebftonline. com/2021/07/06/us-to-inject-100m-into-cape-verdean-economy-begins-construction-of-new-embassy/.

Urdaneta, Daniela (@DianelaUrdaneta). Twitter post, May 3, 2019. https://twitter. com/DianelaUrdaneta/status/1124439142602039296?s=20.

Utrera, Yesman. "Pets on the Menu as Venezuelans Starve." *Daily Beast*, November 4, 2017. https://www.thedailybeast.com/ zoo-animals-on-the-menu-as-venezuelans-starve.

Valencia, Nick. "U.S. Aid Blocked by President Maduro." CNN, February 17, 2019. http://www.cnn.com/TRANSCRIPTS/1902/17/cnr.04.html.

Valero, Marlene. "¿Quién Es J.J. Rendón y Para Quién Trabaja?" La Silla Rota, January 15, 2018. https://lasillarota.com/nacion/2018/1/15/quien-es-jj-rendon-para-quien-trabaja-149717.html.

Valverde, Rita (@ritvv). Twitter post, February 20, 2019. https://twitter.com/ritvv/ status/1098328982095835136?s=08.

Vanek Smith, Stacey. "The New Global Gold Rush." NPR, February 3, 2023. https://www.npr.org/2023/02/03/1154104672/gold-investment-hot-inflation.

Vaz, Ricardo. "Venezuelan Armed Forces: Paramilitary Incursion Neutralized." *Venezuelanalysis*, May 3, 2020. https://venezuelanalysis.com/news/14861.

Vecchio, Carlos. *Libres: El Nacimiento De Una Nueva Venezuela*. Venezuela: Dahbar, 2018.

Vecchio, Carlos (@carlosvecchio). Twitter post, August 3, 2019. https://twitter.com/ carlosvecchio/status/1157652745274449921?s=20.

Vecchio, Carlos (@carlosvecchio). Twitter post, May 8, 2019. https://twitter.com/ carlosvecchio/status/1126285926668414976?s=20.

"Venezuela Aid Live: A Music Event Spurs Confrontations at the Border." *Rolling Stone*, February 23, 2019. https://www.rollingstone.com/music/music-news/ venezuelan-live-aid-border-music-concert-humanitarian-maduro-799348/.

"Venezuela (Bolivarian Republic of) 1999 (Rev. 2009)." Constitute Project. Accessed April 4, 2023. https://www.constituteproject.org/constitution/ Venezuela_2009?lang=en.

"Venezuela: Helicopter Pilot Appears in Video, Vows to Keep Fighting." NBC, July 5, 2017. https://www.nbcnews.com/news/latino/ venezuela-helicopter-pilot-appears-video-vows-keep-fighting-n779641.

"Venezuela Man Set Alight at Anti-Government Protest Dies." BBC, June 5, 2017. https://www.bbc.com/news/world-latin-america-40157729.

"Venezuela: New UN Report Details Responsibilities for Crimes against Humanity to Repress Dissent and Highlights Situation in Remotes Mining Areas." OHCHR, September 20, 2022. https://www.ohchr.org/en/press-releases/2022/09/venezuela-new-un-report-details-responsibilities-crimes-against-humanity.

"Venezuela President Maduro Survives 'Drone Assassination Attempt'." BBC, August 5, 2018. https://www.bbc.com/news/world-latin-america-45073385.

"Venezuela Presidential Election 2012: Everything You Need To Know in One Post." ABC, October 7, 2012. https://abcnews.go.com/ABC_Univision/News/page/venezuela-presidential-election-2012-17413482.

"Venezuela: The Rise and Fall of a Petrostate." Council on Foreign Relations, March 10, 2023. https://www.cfr.org/backgrounder/venezuela-crisis.

"Venezuela Rivals Seek to Capitalise on Bolivia Crisis." TRTWorld, November 16, 2019. https://www.trtworld.com/americas/venezuela-rivals-seek-to-capitalise-on-bolivia-crisis-31425.

"Venezuela Sells Additional $570mln in Gold, Skirts US Sanctions – Report." Sputnik International, May 18, 2019. https://sputniknews.com/20190518/us-sanctions-gold-venezuela-1075123415.html.

"Venezuela: Stabilization and Transitions." United States Agency for International Development. Accessed April 12, 2023. https://www.usaid.gov/stabilization-and-transitions/closed-programs/venezuela.

"Venezuela: UN Creates Independent Investigative Body." Human Rights Watch, September 27, 2019. https://www.hrw.org/news/2019/09/27/venezuela-un-creates-independent-investigative-body.

"Venezuela - Vice-President Addresses General Debate, 74th Session." United Nations, September 27, 2019. https://www.youtube.com/watch?v=L_5-voGau0I.

Venezuelan Economic and Social Performance Under Hugo Chávez, in Graphs (blog). Center for Economic and Policy Research, March 7, 2013. https://cepr.net/venezuelan-economic-and-social-performance-under-hugo-chavez-in-graphs/.

"Venezuelan Foreign Minister Announces Group to Protect UN Charter's Principles." Telesur English, February 14, 2019. https://www.telesurenglish.net/news/Venezuelan-Foreign-Minister-Announces-Group-to-Protect-UN-Charters-Principles-20190214-0015.html.

"Venezuelan Government Has Built 4.2 Million Homes So Far." Telesur, October 28, 2022. https://www.telesurenglish.net/news/Venezuelan-Government-Has-Built-4.2-Million-Homes-So-Far-20221028-0002.html.

"Venezuelan Profiles and Personalities." Brown University Library. Accessed
    April 4, 2023. https://library.brown.edu/create/modernlatinamerica/chapters/
    chapter-8-venezuela/figures-in-venezuelan-history/.
"Venezuela's Guaido Blocked from Congress as Rival Lawmaker Claims Speaker
    Post." Voice of America, January 6, 2020. https://www.voanews.com/a/
    americas_venezuelas-guaido-blocked-congress-rival-lawmaker-claims-speaker-
    post/6182154.html.
"Venezuela's Guaido Vows to Challenge Maduro's Congress Win." Al
    Jazeera, December 7, 2020. https://www.aljazeera.com/news/2020/12/7/
    venezuelan-president-maduro-claims-sweep-of-boycotted-election.
"Venezuela's National Assembly Passes Amnesty Bill." BBC, March 30, 2016.
    https://www.bbc.com/news/world-latin-america-35924647.
Viana, Natalia. "USAID's Dubious Allies in Paraguay." The Nation, April 10, 2013.
    https://www.thenation.com/article/archive/usaids-dubious-allies-paraguay/.
"Vienna Convention on Diplomatic Relations, 1961." United Nations Office of
    Legal Affairs, 1961. https://legal.un.org/ilc/texts/instruments/english/conven-
    tions/9_1_1961.pdf.
Villafañe, Veronica. "Univision Recovers And Will Air Confiscated Jorge
    Ramos Interview With Nicolás Maduro." Forbes, May 30, 2019. https://www.
    forbes.com/sites/veronicavillafane/2019/05/30/univision-recuperates-
    and-will-air-confiscated-jorge-ramos-interview-with-president-nicolas-
    maduro/?sh=289c2ea73475.
The Visual Journalism team. "Venezuela: All You Need to Know about the
    Crisis in Nine Charts." BBC, February 4, 2019. https://www.bbc.com/news/
    world-latin-america-46999668.
VIVOplay (@vivoplaynet). Twitter post, January 5, 2020. https://twitter.com/
    vivoplaynet/status/1213877037187944452?s=20.
VTV Canal 8 (@VTVcanal8). Twitter post, June 18, 2020. https://twitter.com/
    VTVcanal8/status/1273678037662474245.
Vulliamy, Ed. "Venezuela Coup Linked to Bush Team." Observer Worldview, April 21,
    2002. https://www.theguardian.com/world/2002/apr/21/usa.venezuela.
"VZ Elections." The Global Intelligence Files, WikiLeaks. October 18, 2012.
    https://search.wikileaks.org/gifiles/?viewemailid=218642.
Wamsley, Lauren. "Humanitarian Aid Arrives For Venezuela — But Maduro Blocks
    It." NPR, February 8, 2019. https://www.npr.org/2019/02/08/692698637/
    humanitarian-aid-arrives-for-venezuela-but-maduro-blocks-it.
"War in Ukraine Drives Global Food Crisis." UN World Food Programme, June 24,
    2022. https://www.wfp.org/publications/war-ukraine-drives-global-food-crisis.

Wallace, Joe, and Anna Hirtenstein. "Russia Confounds the West by Recapturing Its Oil Riches." *Wall Street Journal*, August 30, 2022. https://www.wsj.com/articles/russia-confounds-the-west-by-recapturing-its-oil-riches-11661781928.

"Watch: Tapper and Bolton Debate Trump's Ability to Plan a Coup | CNN Politics." CNN, July 13, 2022. https://www.cnn.com/videos/politics/2022/07/12/jake-tapper-john-bolton-debate-january-6-coup-attempt-sot-lead-vpx.cnn.

Watson, Kathryn, and Andres Triay. "U.S. Arrests and Indicts Former Honduran President Juan Orlando Hernández." CBS News, April 21, 2022. https://www.cbsnews.com/live-updates/us-arrests-indicts-former-honduran-president-juan-orlando-hernandez/.

"'We Lied, Cheated and Stole': Pompeo Comes Clean About CIA." Telesur English, April 24, 2019. https://www.telesurenglish.net/news/We-Lied-Cheated-and-Stole-Pompeo-Comes-Clean-About-CIA-20190424-0033.html.

Weinstein, Adam. "How Venezuela Became a 'Warzone.'" *Gawker*, February 20, 2014. https://www.gawker.com/how-venezuela-became-a-warzone-1526857816.

Weisbrot, Mark, David Rosnick, and Todd Tucker. "Black Swans, Conspiracy Theories, and the Quixotic Search for Fraud: A Look at Hausmann and Rigobón's 1 Analysis of Venezuela's Referendum Vote." Center for Economic and Policy Research, September 20, 2004. https://cepr.net/press-release/study-finds-economists-allegations-of-fraud-in-venezuelan-referendum-to-be-groundless/.

Weisbrot, Mark, and Jeffrey Sachs. "Economic Sanctions as Collective Punishment: The Case of Venezuela." Center for Economic and Policy Research, April 2019. https://cepr.net/report/economic-sanctions-as-collective-punishment-the-case-of-venezuela/.

Weisbrot, Mark. "Behind the Scenes in Venezuela." *U.S. News*, March 3, 2018. https://www.usnews.com/opinion/world-report/articles/2018-03-03/new-evidence-the-trump-administration-is-meddling-in-venezuelas-elections.

Weisbrot, Mark. "Trump's Other 'National Emergency': Sanctions That Kill Venezuelans." *The Nation*, February 28, 2019. https://www.thenation.com/article/archive/venezuela-sanctions-emergency/.

Weisenthal, Joe. "A Hedge Fund Has Physically Taken Control of a Ship Belonging to Argentina's Navy." *Business Insider*, October 4, 2012. https://www.businessinsider.com/hedge-fund-elliott-capital-management-seizes-ara-libertad-ship-owned-by-argentina-2012-10.

Wemer, David A. "John Bolton Takes Latin American 'Troika of Tyranny' to Task." *New Atlanticist*. November 1, 2018. https://www.atlanticcouncil.org/blogs/new-atlanticist/john-bolton-takes-latin-american-troika-of-tyranny-to-task/.

"Western Countries Imposed Some 11,000 Sanctions on Russia - Diplomat." TASS, September 8, 2022. https://tass.com/politics/1505157.

"What Killed Bolivar?" *Johns Hopkins Magazine*, September 10, 2010. https://magazine.jhu.edu/2010/09/03/what-killed-bolivar/.

"What's Behind US-Backed Electricity Blackout in Venezuela." Telesur English, March 9, 2019. https://www.telesurenglish.net/news/What-Is-Behind-US-Backed-Electricity-Blackout-in-Venezuela--20190309-0015.html.

Whitaker, Trevor John. "The Economic and Military Impact of Privateers and Pirates on Britain's Rise as a World Power." Arizona State University Library, April 2020. https://keep.lib.asu.edu/items/158272.

"Who We Are." Canvas. Accessed March 8, 2023. https://canvasopedia.org/who-we-are/.

"Why Jorge Ramos Took on Trump." *CBS News: The National*, October 18, 2016. https://www.youtube.com/watch?v=yC1vhzm-itg.

"Why People Flee Honduras." *Politico*, June 7, 2019. https://www.politico.com/magazine/story/2019/06/07/honduras-why-people-flee-photos-227087/.

Wilkins, Brett. "Peace Activist Interrupts General Dynamics Shareholder Meeting to Blast the Business of War." Common Dreams, May 6, 2021. https://www.commondreams.org/news/2021/05/06/peace-activist-interrupts-general-dynamics-shareholder-meeting-blast-business-war.

Wintour, Patrick. "Iran and Saudi Arabia Agree to Restore Ties after China-Brokered Talks." *Guardian*, March 10, 2023. https://www.theguardian.com/world/2023/mar/10/iran-saudi-arabia-agree-restore-ties-china-talks.

Wong, Edward, and Nicholas Casey. "U.S. Targets Venezuela With Tough Oil Sanctions During Crisis of Power." *New York Times*, January 28, 2019. https://www.nytimes.com/2019/01/28/us/politics/venezuela-sanctions-trump-oil.html.

Woodrow Cox, John, and Steven Rich. "Billions Are Now Spent to Protect Kids from School Shootings. Has It Made Them Safer?" *Washington Post*, November 13, 2018. https://www.washingtonpost.com/classic-apps/billions-are-now-spent-to-protect-kids-from-school-shootings-has-it-made-them-safer/2018/10/29/6fdfd5f4-ccac-11e8-a3e6-44daa3d35ede_story.html.

Woods, Alan. "Venezuela: The Referendum Defeat - What Does It Mean?" *Venezuelanalysis*, December 4, 2007. https://venezuelanalysis.com/analysis/2955.

World Affairs Council of Greater Houston. "Ricardo Hausmann on the Venezuela Crisis and The Road Ahead (11/01/18)." YouTube, November 7, 2018. https://www.youtube.com/watch?t=3222&v=Ic4V6mXDxoM&feature=youtu.be.

Wright, Turner. "US Printed More Money in One Month than in Two Centuries." Cointelegraph, July 31, 2020. https://cointelegraph.com/news/us-printed-more-money-in-one-month-than-in-two-centuries.

Wroughton, Lesley. "Kerry, Saudi King Discuss Oil Supply, U.S. Official Says." Reuters, June 27, 2014. https://www.reuters.com/article/us-usa-saudi-oil/kerry-saudi-king-discuss-oil-supply-u-s-official-says-idUSKBN0F300P20140628.

Yagova, Olga, Chen Aizhu, and Marianna Parraga. "Rosneft Becomes Top Venezuelan Oil Trader, Helping Offset U.S. Pressure." Reuters, August 22, 2019. https://www.reuters.com/article/us-russia-venezuela-oil-idUSKCN1VC1PF.

Yang, Joy Y. "Donald Trump Says Anchor Jorge Ramos Was 'Totally, Absolutely Out of Line'." NBC News, August 25, 2021. https://www.nbcnews.com/news/latino/donald-trump-says-anchor-jorge-ramos-was-totally-absolutely-out-n416011.

Ying Shan, Lee. "Gold Prices Could Notch an All-Time High Soon - and Stay There." CNBC, March 23, 2023. https://www.cnbc.com/2023/03/22/gold-price-could-hit-high-amid-svb-credit-suisse-bank-problems.html.

Yonekura, Kaoru. "The Miracle of Producing the World's Best Cocoa." *Caracas Chronicles*, August 2, 2022. https://www.caracaschronicles.com/2022/08/02/the-miracle-of-producing-the-worlds-best-cocoa/.

Zapata, Carlos. "Venezuela: ¿'Ayuda Humanitaria' También Incluye Alcohol y Prostitutas?" Aleteia, June 17, 2019. https://es.aleteia.org/2019/06/17/venezuela-ayuda-humanitaria-tambien-incluye-alcohol-y-prostitutas/.

Zarroli, Jim. "Trump Favors Returning to the Gold Standard, Few Economists Agree." NPR, June 16, 2016. https://www.npr.org/2016/06/16/482279689/trump-favors-returning-to-the-gold-standard-few-economists-agree.

Zerpa, Fabiola, and Alex Vasquez. "Venezuela's Guaido Names PDVSA Board in Haste to Seize Assets." *Bloomberg*, February 12, 2019. https://www.bloomberg.com/news/articles/2019-02-13/venezuela-s-guaido-is-said-to-announce-pdvsa-board-this-week#xj4y7vzkg.

Zerpa, Fabiola, and Ezra Fieser. "Creditors Close in on Citgo, the Last Asset Guaido Has Left." *Bloomberg*, August 5, 2021. https://www.bloomberg.com/news/articles/2021-08-05/creditors-close-in-on-citgo-the-last-asset-guaido-.

Zeveloff, Naomi. "U.N. Official Answers Questions about Fierce Criticism of Israel." The Forward, July 21, 2011. https://forward.com/news/140075/un-official-answers-questions-about-fierce-critici/.

Zivanovic, Maja. "Serbian Activist Denies 'Training' Venezuela's Guaido in Rebellion." *Balkan Insight*, February 13, 2019. https://balkaninsight.com/2019/02/13/serbian-activist-denies-training-venezuelas-guaido-in-rebellion/.

ANYA PARAMPIL is a journalist for the independent news site *The Grayzone*, based in Washington, D.C. She has produced and reported several documentaries, including on-the-ground dispatches from the Korean peninsula, Palestine, Venezuela, and Honduras.

Printed in the USA
CPSIA information can be obtained
at www.ICGtesting.com
JSHW020229270924
70480JS00002B/2